VOL. 11
Action Edition

Story and Art by
RUMIKO TAKAHASHI

English Adaptation by Gerard Jones

Translation/Mari Morimoto
Touch-Up Art & Lettering/Wayne Truman
Cover and Interior Graphics & Design/Yuki Ameda
Editor (1st Edition)/Julie Davis
Editor (Action Edition)/Avery Gotoh
Supervising Editor (Action Edition)/Michelle Pangilinan

Managing Editor/Annette Roman
Editorial Director/Alvin Lu
Director of Production/Noboru Watanabe
Sr. Dir. of Licensing and Acquisitions/Rika Inouye
VP of Sales & Marketing/Liza Coppola
Executive VP/Hyoe Narita
Publisher/Seiji Horibuchi

INUYASHA is rated "T+" for Older Teens. This volume con-
tains violence, language, and suggestive situations.

Published by VIZ, LLC
P.O. Box 77010
San Francisco, CA 94107

1st Edition Published 2002

Action Edition
10 9 8 7 6 5 4 3 2
First printing, June 2004
Second printing, October 2004

store.viz.com

www.viz.com

InuYasha

VOL. 11   Action Edition

STORY AND ART BY
RUMIKO TAKAHASHI

CONTENTS

THE STORY THUS FAR

Long ago, in the "Warring States" era of Japan's Muromachi period (*Sengoku-jidai*, approximately 1467-1568 CE), a legendary doglike half-demon called "Inu-Yasha" attempted to steal the Shikon Jewel—or "Jewel of Four Souls"—from a village, but was stopped by the enchanted arrow of the village priestess, Kikyo. Inu-Yasha fell into a deep sleep, pinned to a tree by Kikyo's arrow, while the mortally wounded Kikyo took the Shikon Jewel with her into the fires of her funeral pyre. Years passed.

Fast-forward to the present day, Kagome, a Japanese high-school girl, is pulled into a well one day by a mysterious centipede monster, and finds herself transported into the past, only to come face to face with the trapped Inu-Yasha. She frees him, and Inu-Yasha easily defeats the centipede monster.

The residents of the village, now 50 years older, readily accept Kagome as the reincarnation of their deceased priestess Kikyo, a claim supported by the fact that the Shikon Jewel emerges from a cut on Kagome's body. Unfortunately, the jewel's rediscovery means that the village is soon under attack by a variety of demons in search of this treasure. Then, the jewel is accidentally shattered into many shards, each of which may have the fearsome power of the entire jewel.

Although Inu-Yasha says he hates Kagome because of her resemblance to Kikyo—the woman who "killed" him—he is forced to team up with her when Kaede, the village leader, binds him to Kagome with a powerful spell. Now the two grudging companions must fight to reclaim and reassemble the shattered shards of the Shikon Jewel before they fall into the wrong hands...

THIS VOLUME Cursed from birth to die an early death by that which gives him most power—the "Wind Tunnel" in his palm—the possible hastening of his end leads lecherous monk Miroku to his mentor, a monk who may be even more dissolute than he...

CHARACTERS

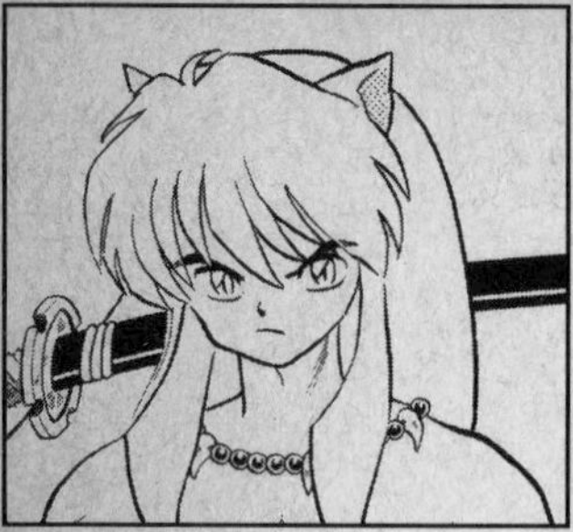

INU-YASHA
Half-demon hybrid, son of a human mother and demon father. His necklace is enchanted, allowing Kagome to control him with a word.

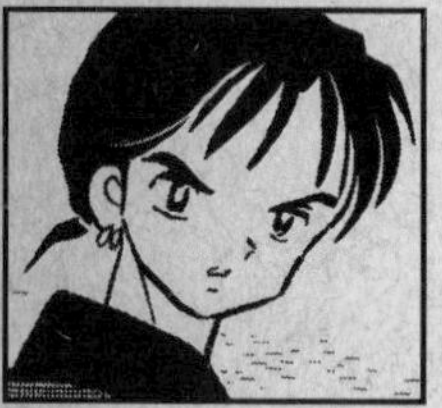

MIROKU
Lecherous Buddhist priest cursed with a mystical "hellhole" in his hand that's slowly killing him.

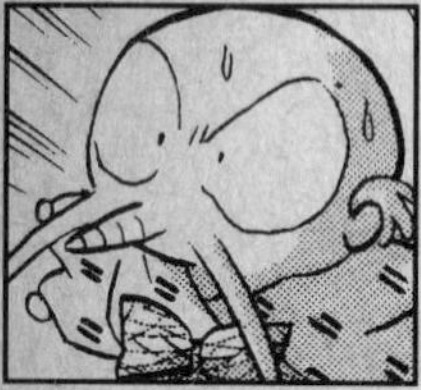

MYOGA
Tiny flea-demon and servant to Inu-Yasha. A pain in his master's side...and not just because of the bloodsucking.

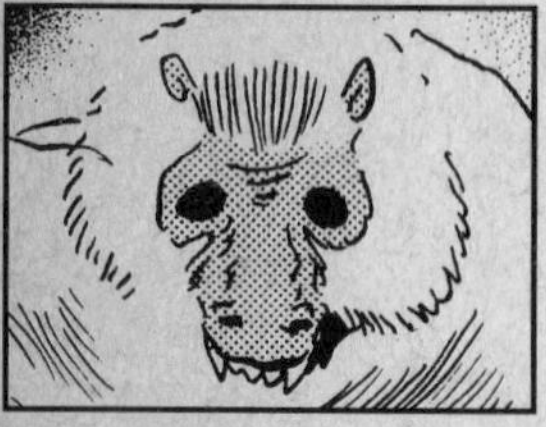

NARAKU
Enigmatic demon-mastermind behind the miseries of nearly everyone in the story.

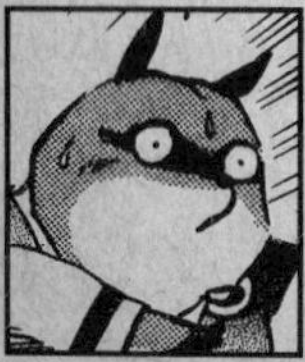

HACHIEMON ("HACHI")
Skilled shape-shifter (like Shippo). Usually found in the company of Miroku.

KAGOME
Modern-day Japanese schoolgirl who can travel back and forth between the past and present through an enchanted well.

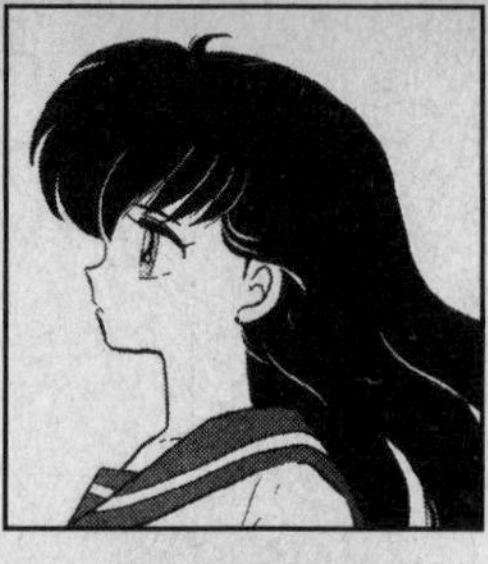

KIKYO
Powerful priestess who died protecting the Shikon Jewel, now resurrected to a kind of "life" by equally powerful magic.

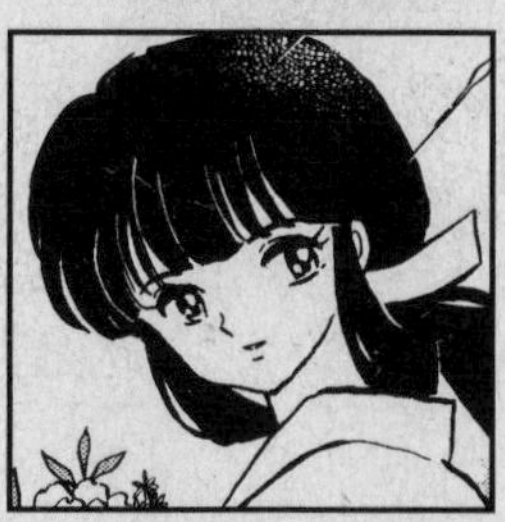

KAEDE
Kikyo's "little sister," now 50-plus years old. It was her spell that bound Inu-Yasha to Kagome with the spoken word, "Sit!"

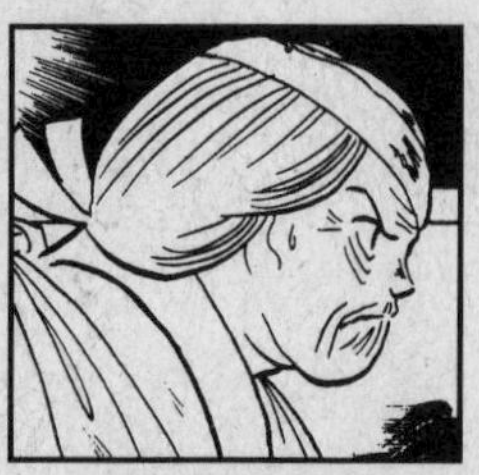

SHIPPO
Orphaned young fox-demon who likes to play shape-changing tricks.

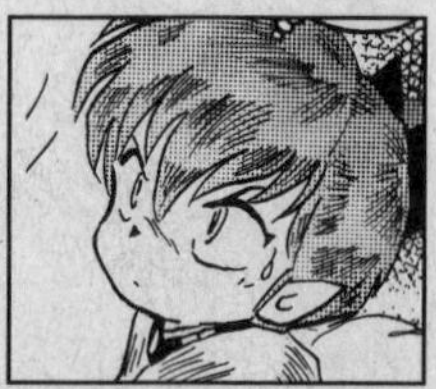

SANGO
"Demon Exterminator" or slayer from the village where the Shikon Jewel was first born.

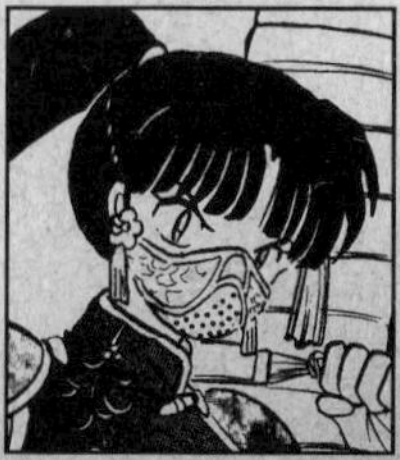

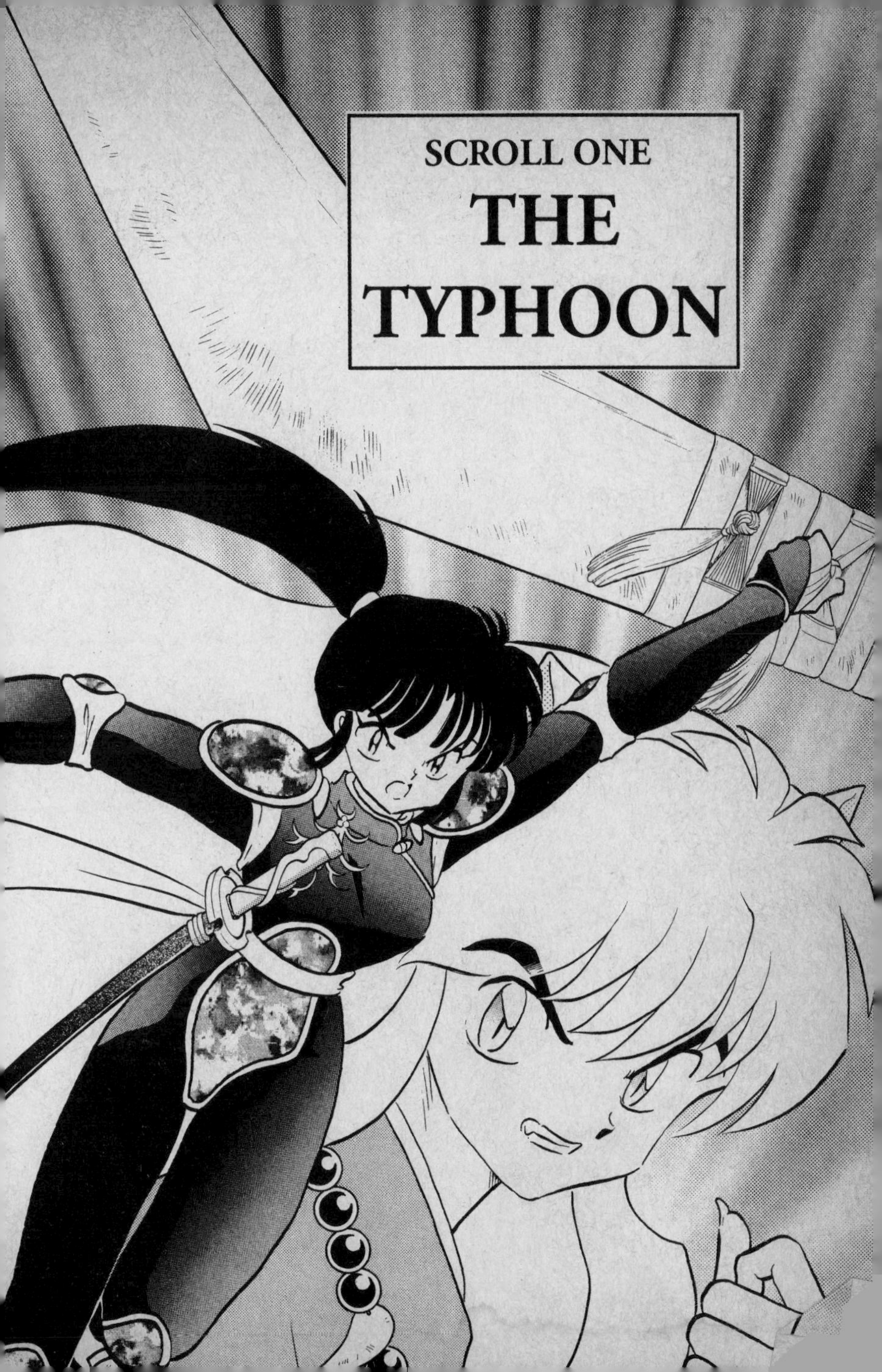
SCROLL ONE
THE TYPHOON

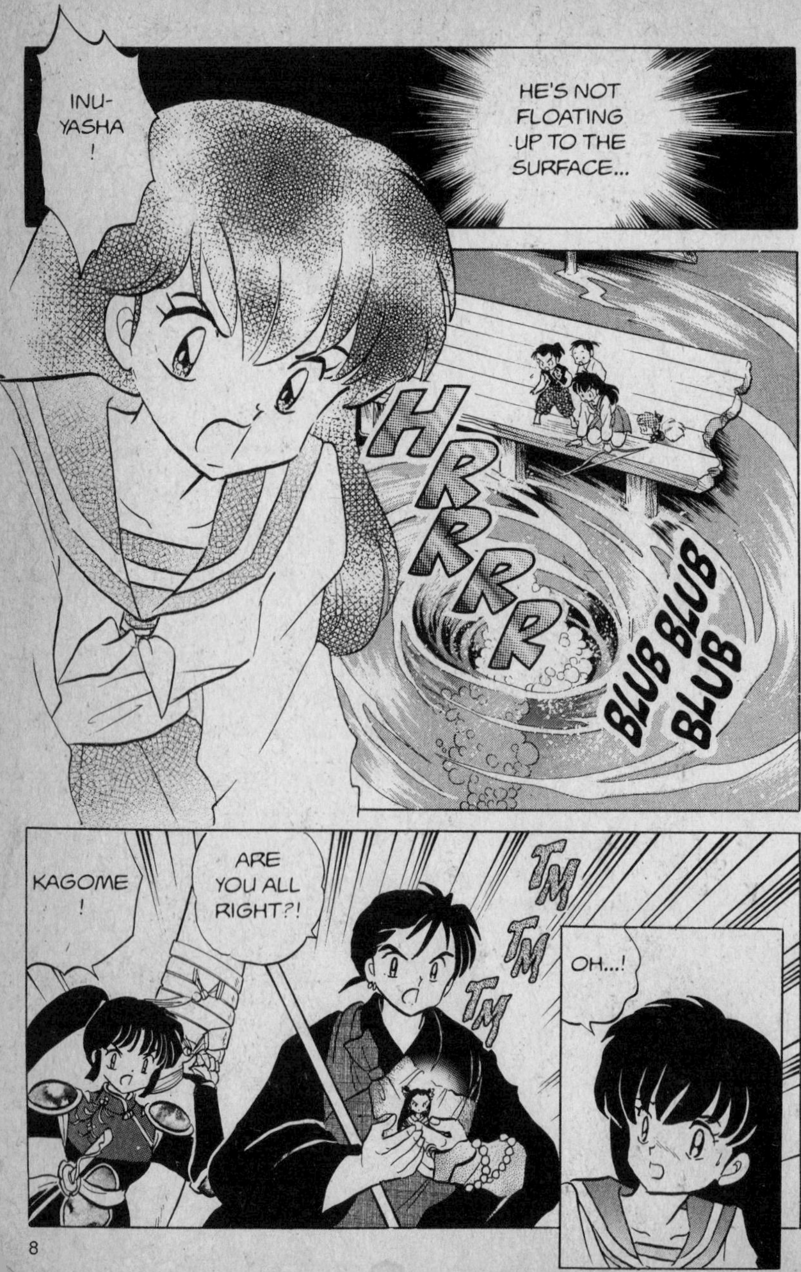
INU-YASHA!
HE'S NOT FLOATING UP TO THE SURFACE...
HRRRR
BLUB BLUB BLUB
KAGOME!
ARE YOU ALL RIGHT?!
TM TM TM
OH...!

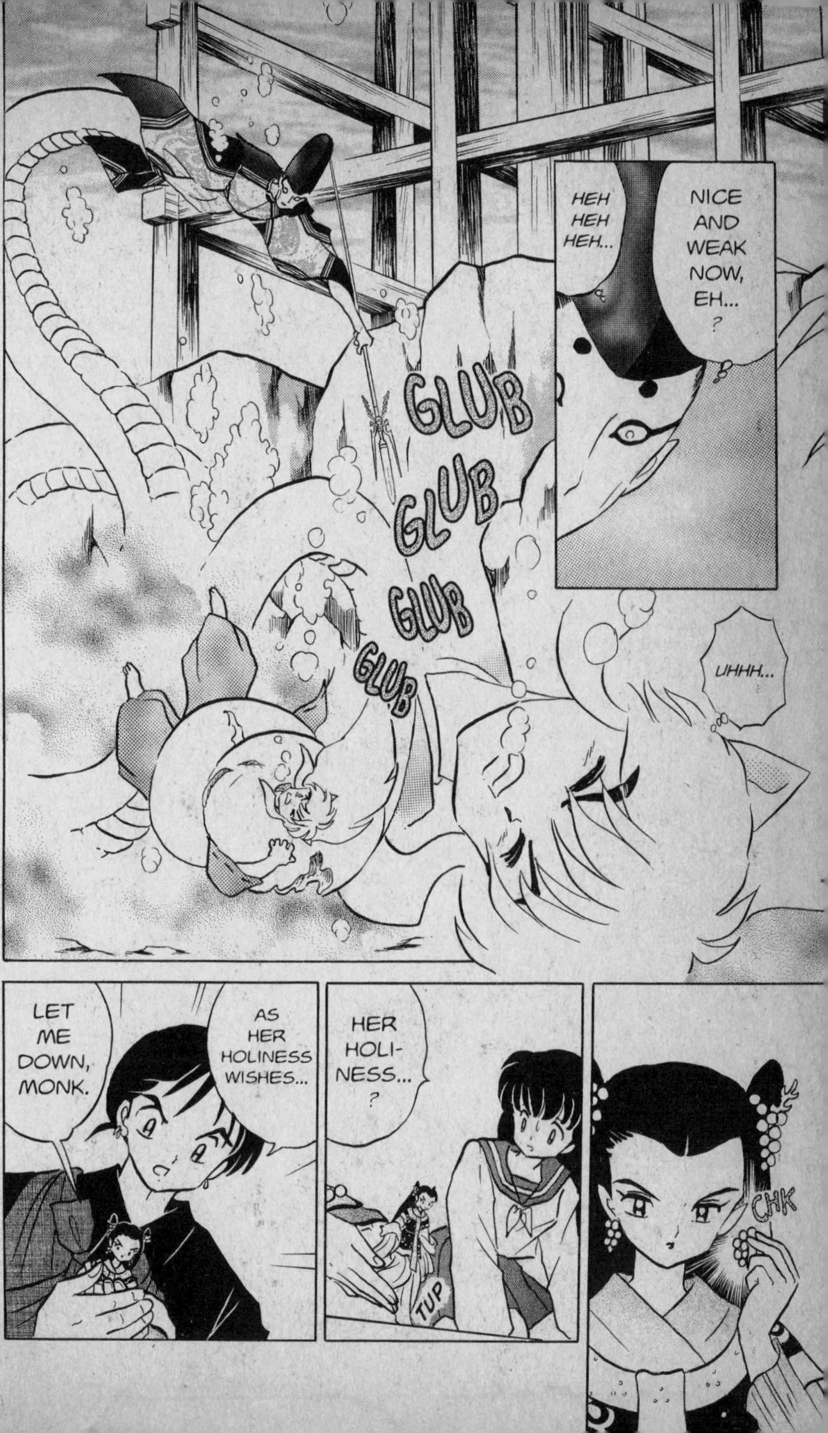
GLUB
GLUB
GLUB
GLUB
UHHH...
HEH HEH HEH...
NICE AND WEAK NOW, EH...?
LET ME DOWN, MONK.
AS HER HOLINESS WISHES...
HER HOLI-NESS...?
TUP
CHK

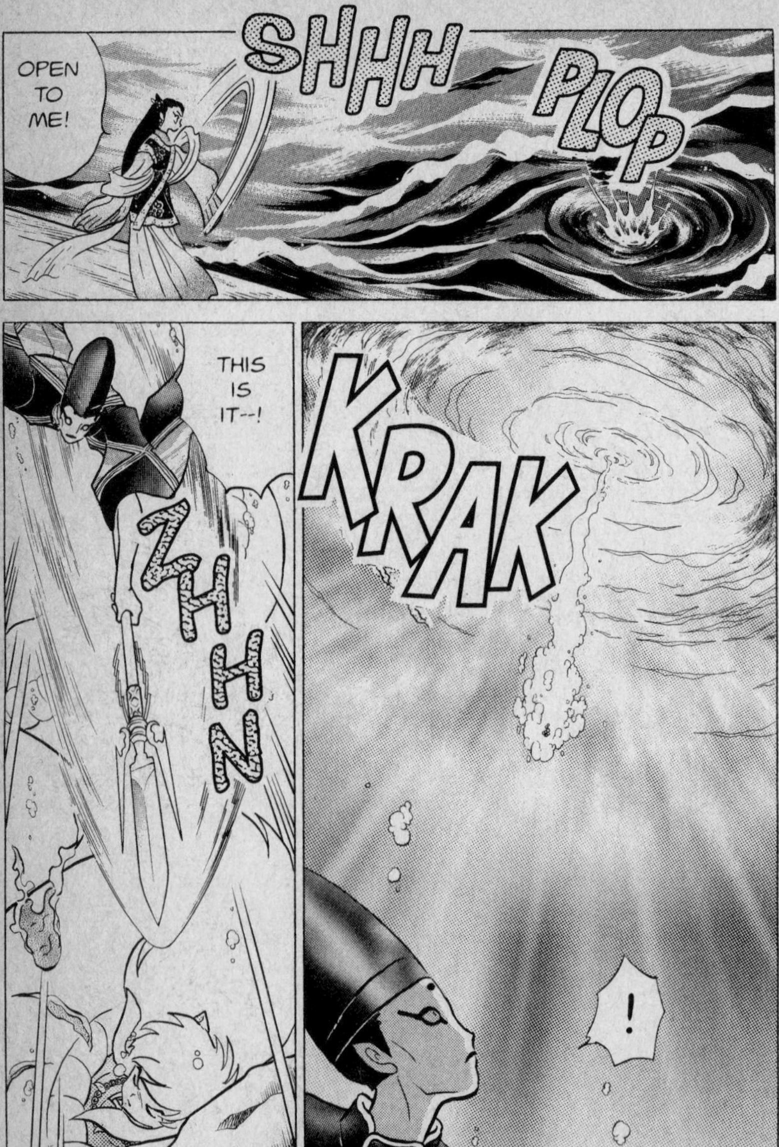
OPEN TO ME!
SHHH
PLOP
THIS IS IT--!
ZHHN
KRAK
!

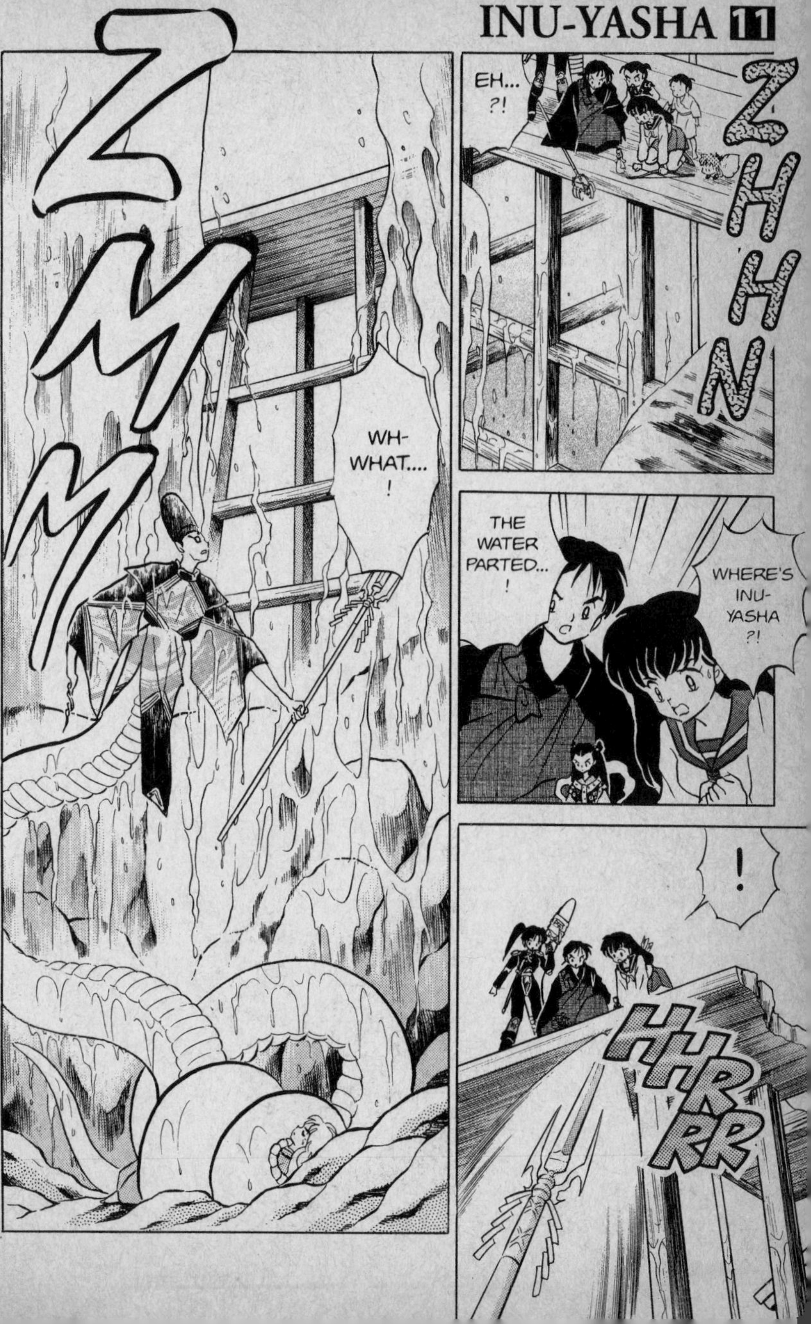
ZMMM
WH- WHAT.... !
EH... ?!
ZHHHN
THE WATER PARTED... !
WHERE'S INU-YASHA ?!
!
HHRRR

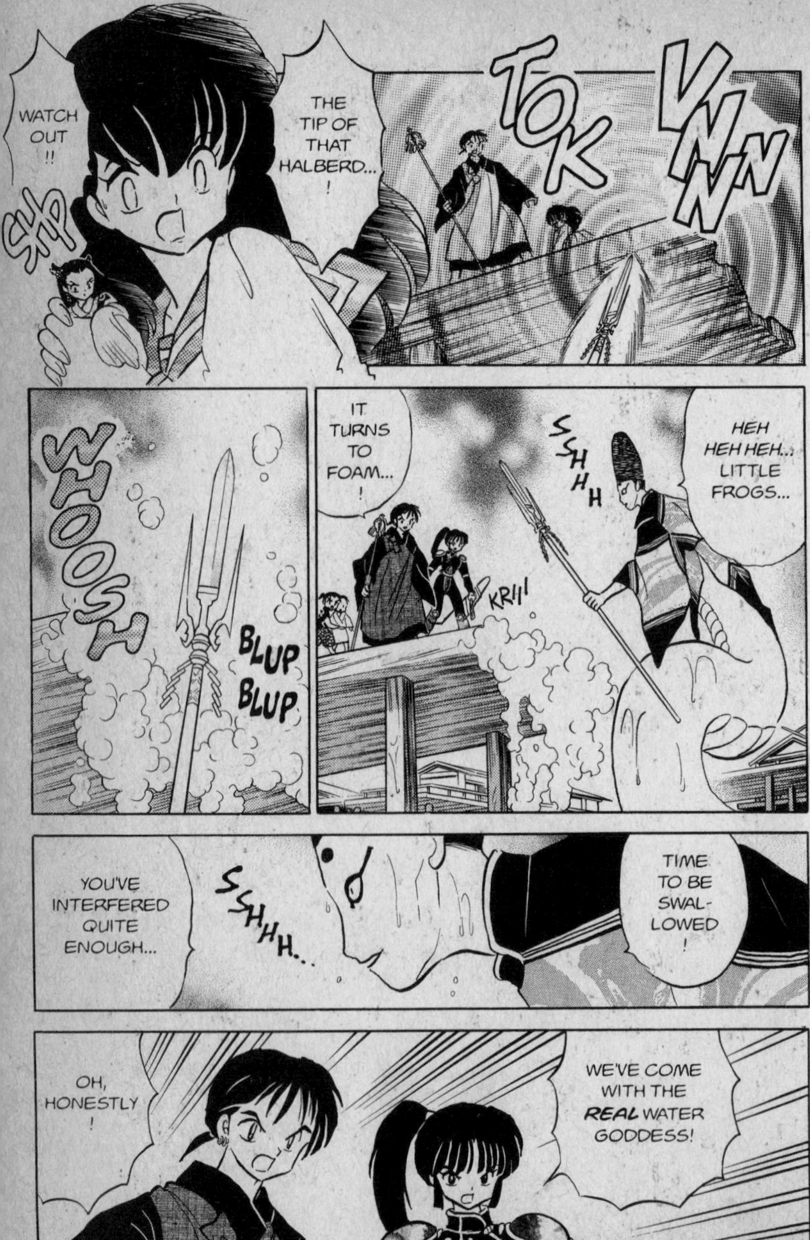
WATCH OUT !!
THE TIP OF THAT HALBERD... !
TOK
VNNN
WHOOSH
BLUP BLUP
IT TURNS TO FOAM... !
SSHHH
KRIII
HEH HEH HEH... LITTLE FROGS...
YOU'VE INTERFERED QUITE ENOUGH...
SSHHH...
TIME TO BE SWAL-LOWED !
OH, HONESTLY !
WE'VE COME WITH THE **REAL** WATER GODDESS!

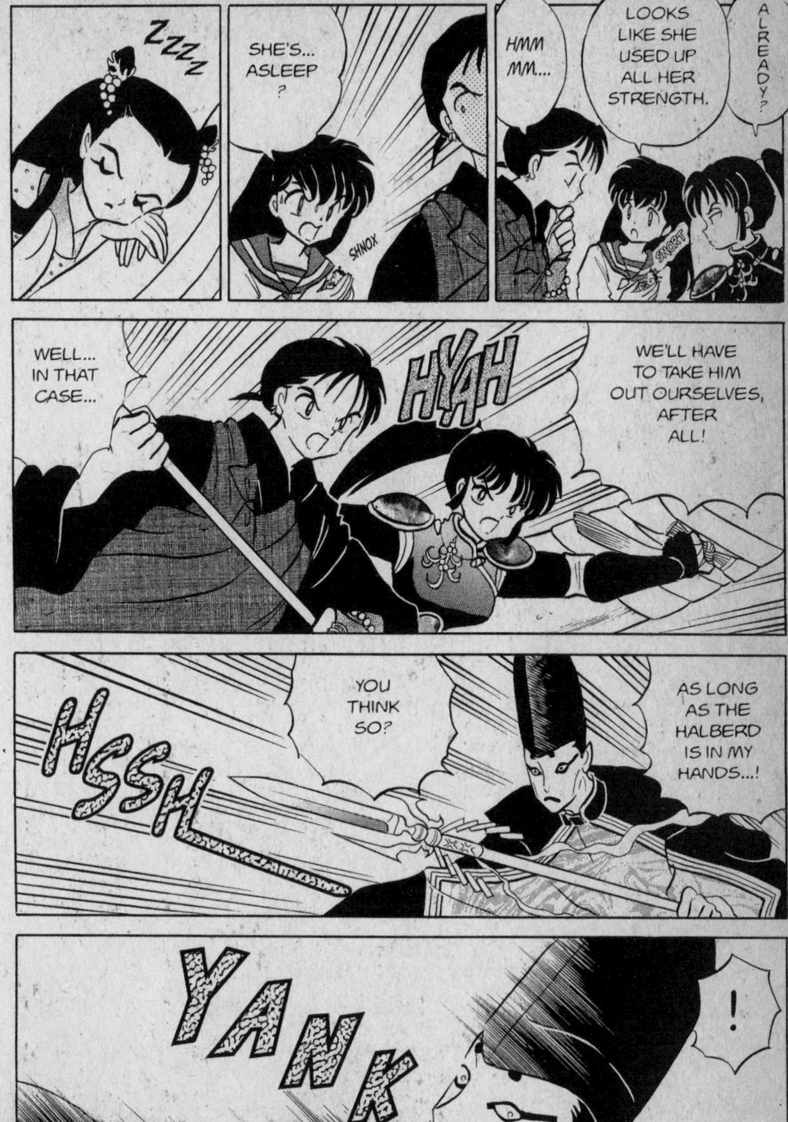
ZZZZ
SHE'S... ASLEEP?
SHNOX
HMM MM....
LOOKS LIKE SHE USED UP ALL HER STRENGTH.
ALREADY?
SNORT
WELL... IN THAT CASE...
HYAH
WE'LL HAVE TO TAKE HIM OUT OURSELVES, AFTER ALL!
HSSH
YOU THINK SO?
AS LONG AS THE HALBERD IS IN MY HANDS...!
YANK
!

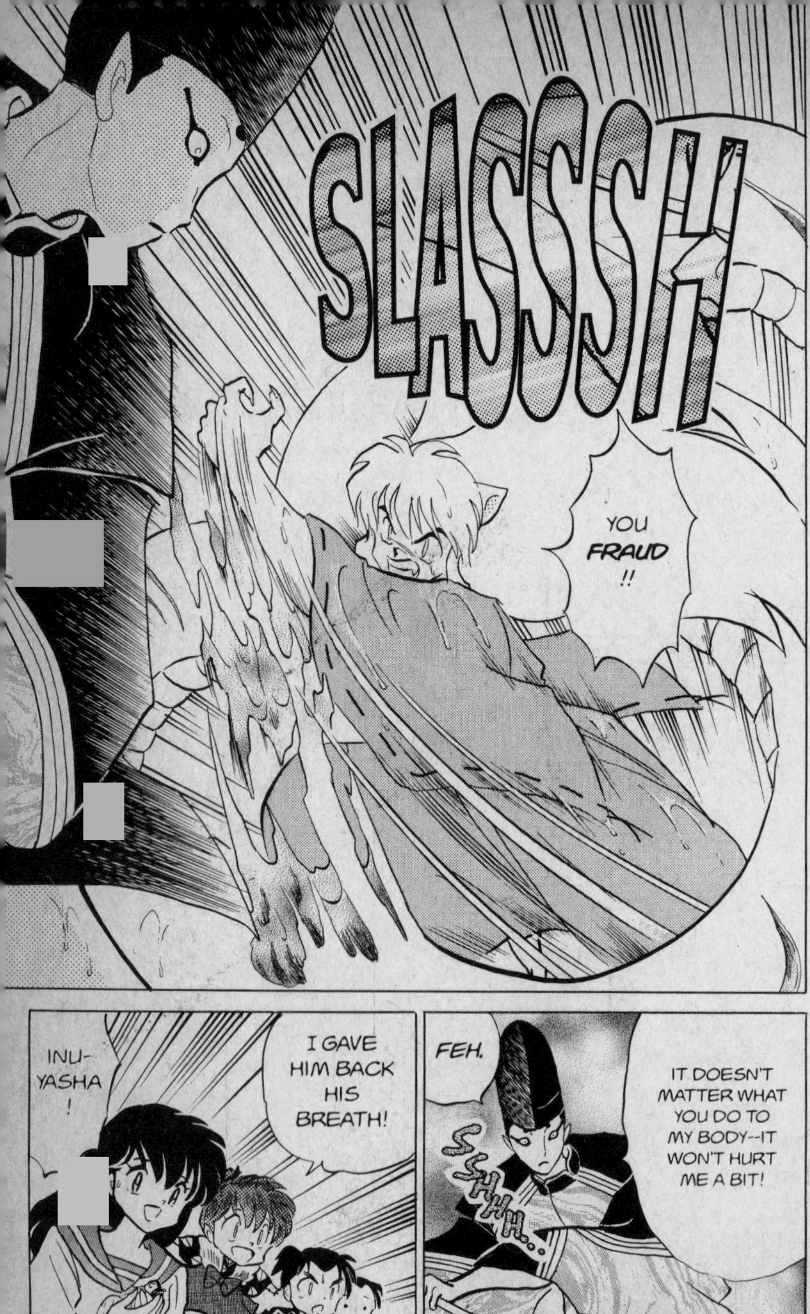
SLASSSH
YOU FRAUD !!
INU-YASHA !
I GAVE HIM BACK HIS BREATH!
FEH.
SSHHH...
IT DOESN'T MATTER WHAT YOU DO TO MY BODY--IT WON'T HURT ME A BIT!

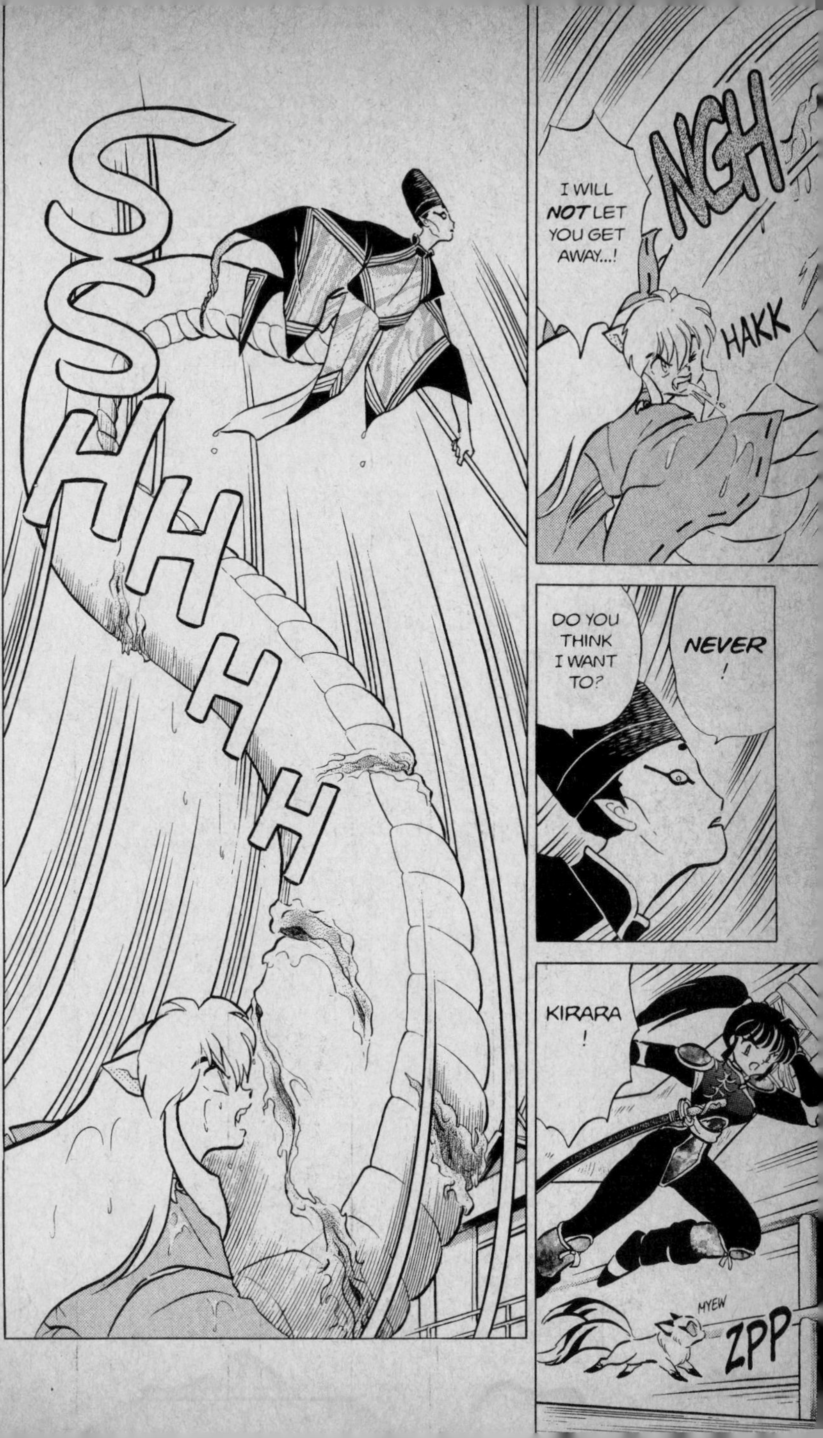
SHHHH
I WILL NOT LET YOU GET AWAY...!
NGH
HAKK
DO YOU THINK I WANT TO?
NEVER!
KIRARA!
MYEW
ZPP

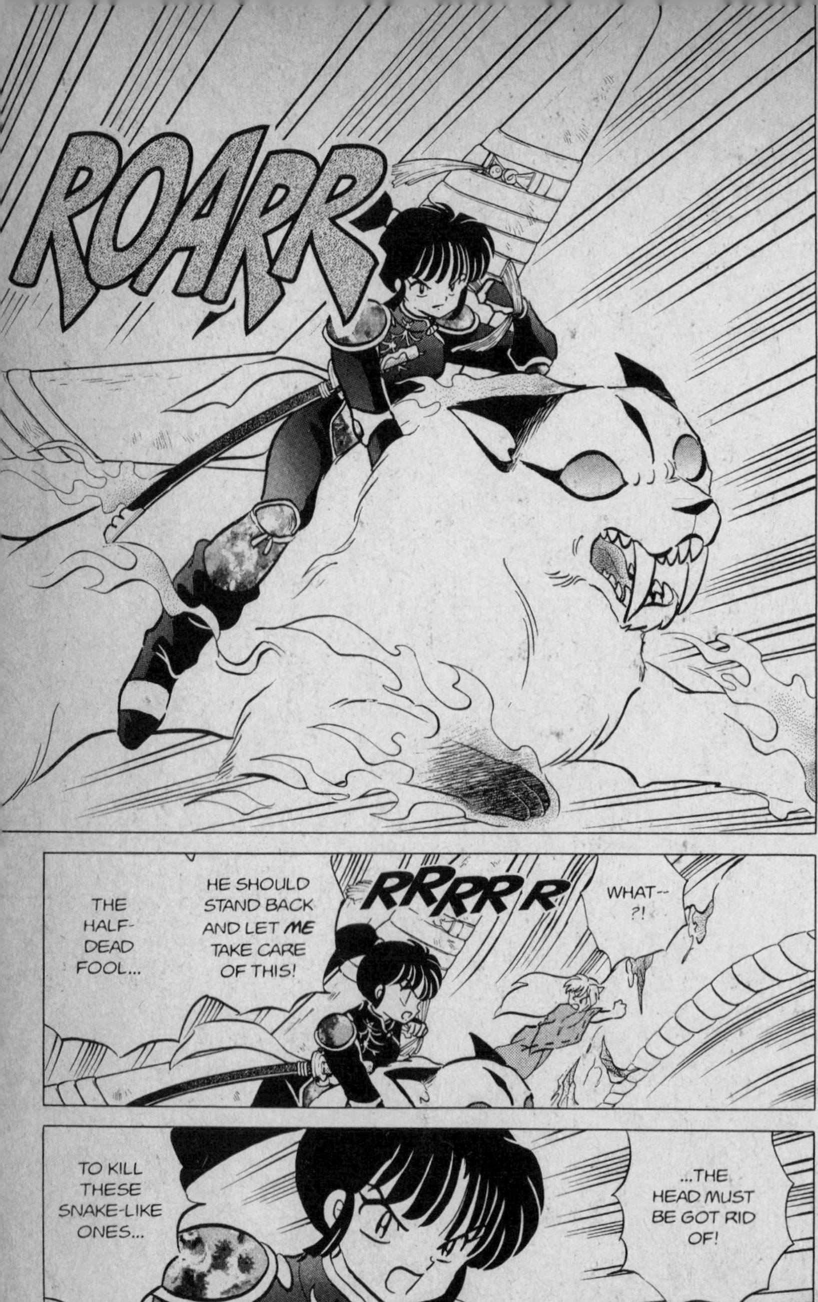
ROARR
THE HALF-DEAD FOOL...
HE SHOULD STAND BACK AND LET ME TAKE CARE OF THIS!
RRRRR
WHAT--?!
TO KILL THESE SNAKE-LIKE ONES...
...THE HEAD MUST BE GOT RID OF!

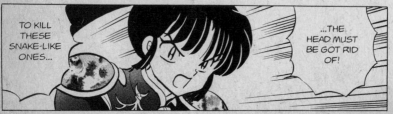

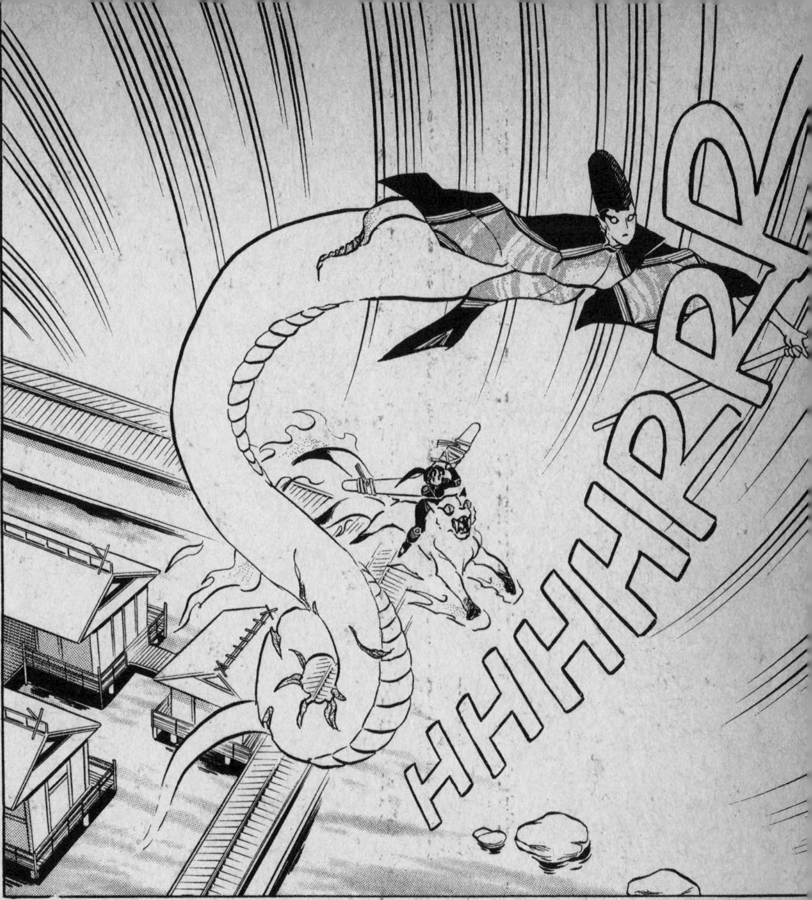
HHHHHRRR

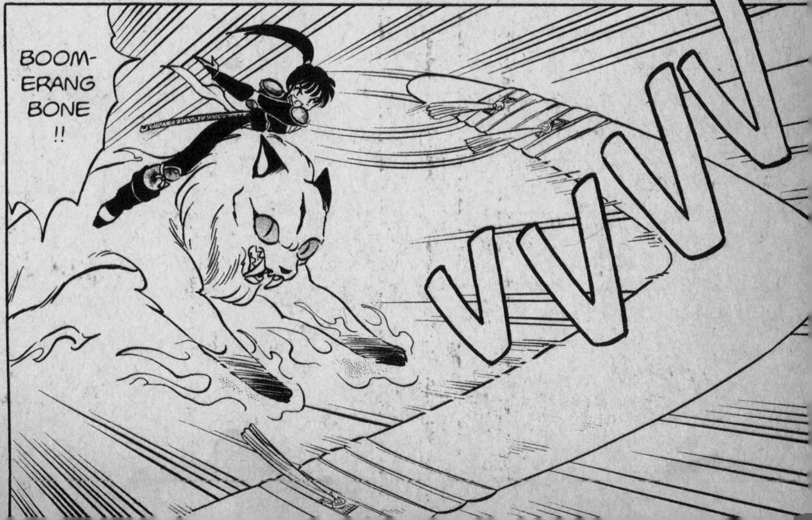
BOOM-
ERANG
BONE
!!
VVVVV

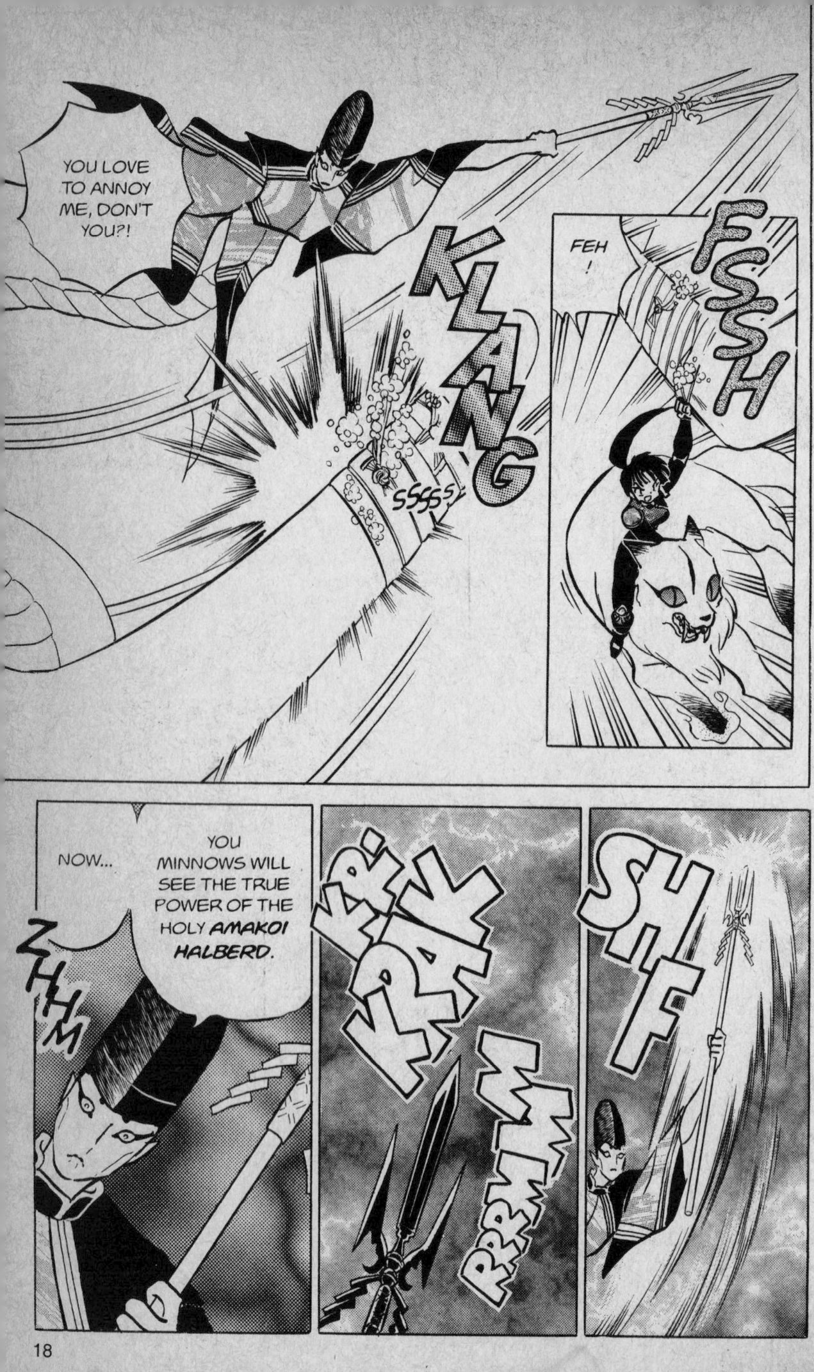
YOU LOVE TO ANNOY ME, DON'T YOU?!
KLANG
SSSSS
FEH!
FSSSH
NOW...
YOU MINNOWS WILL SEE THE TRUE POWER OF THE HOLY **AMAKOI HALBERD**.
ZHHM
KRI KRAK
RRRMMM
SHF

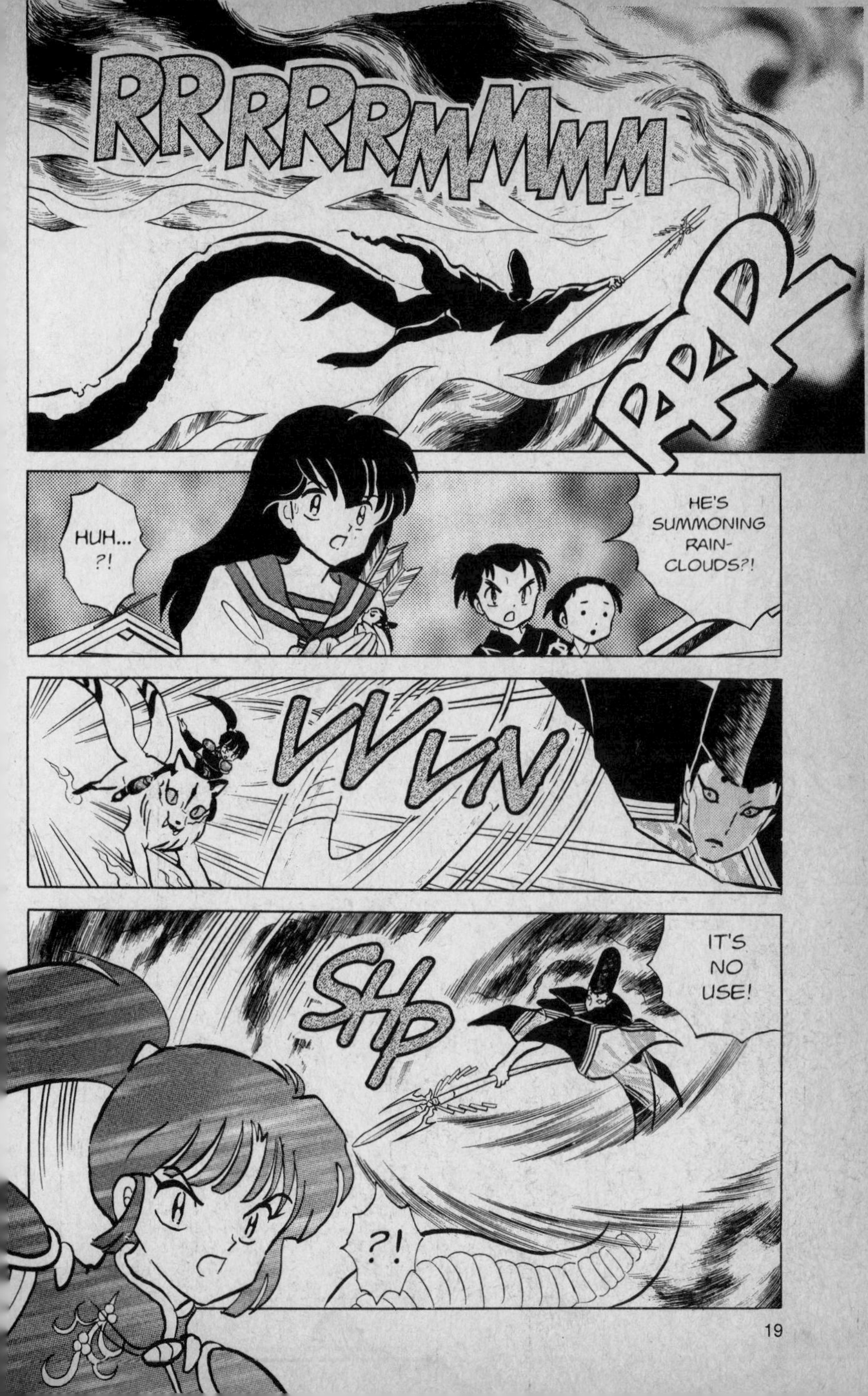
RRRRRRMMMMMM
RRRP
HUH... ?!
HE'S SUMMONING RAIN-CLOUDS?!
VVVN
SHP
IT'S NO USE!
?!

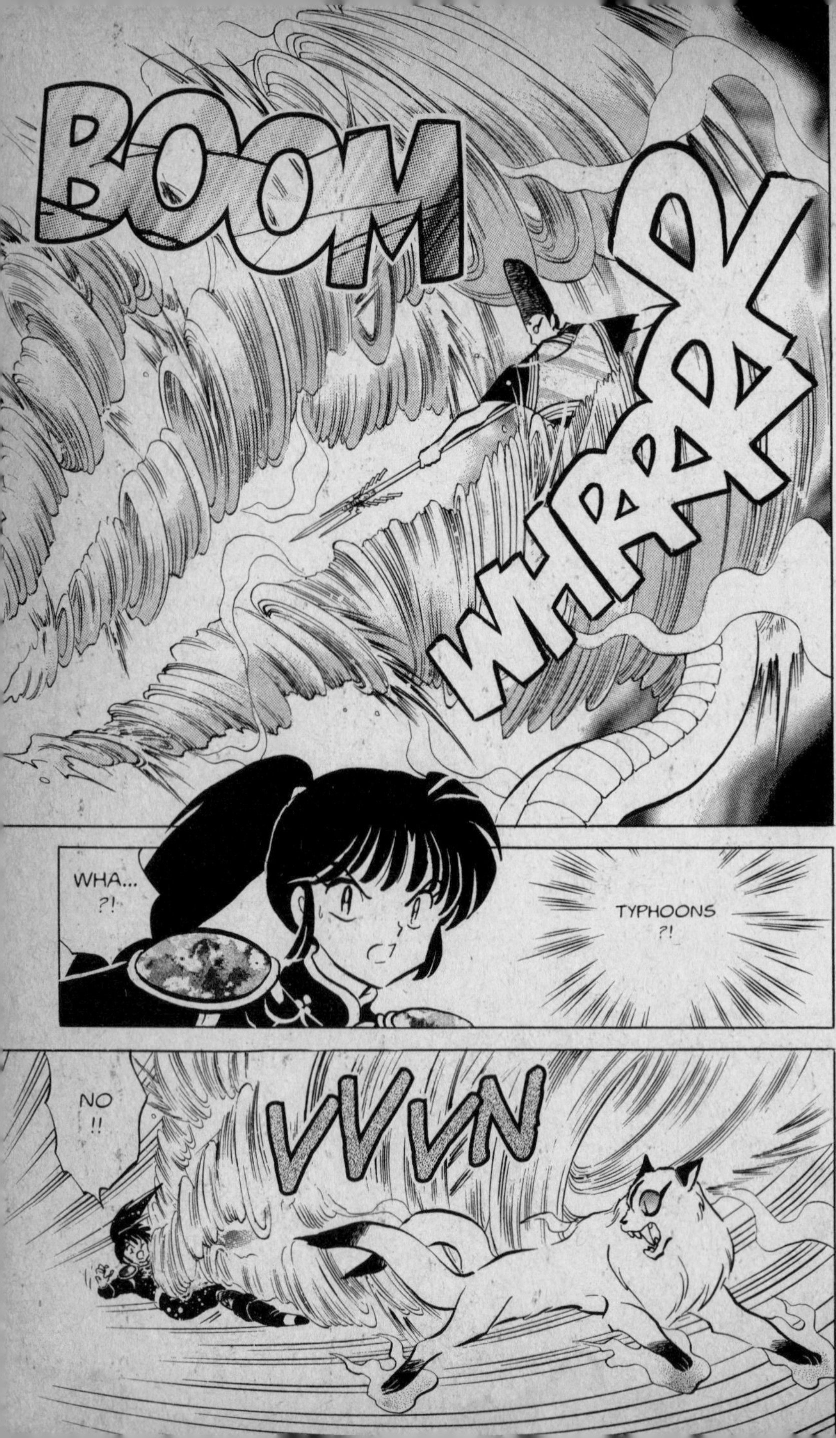
BOOM
WHRRR
WHA... ?!
TYPHOONS ?!
NO !!
VVVN

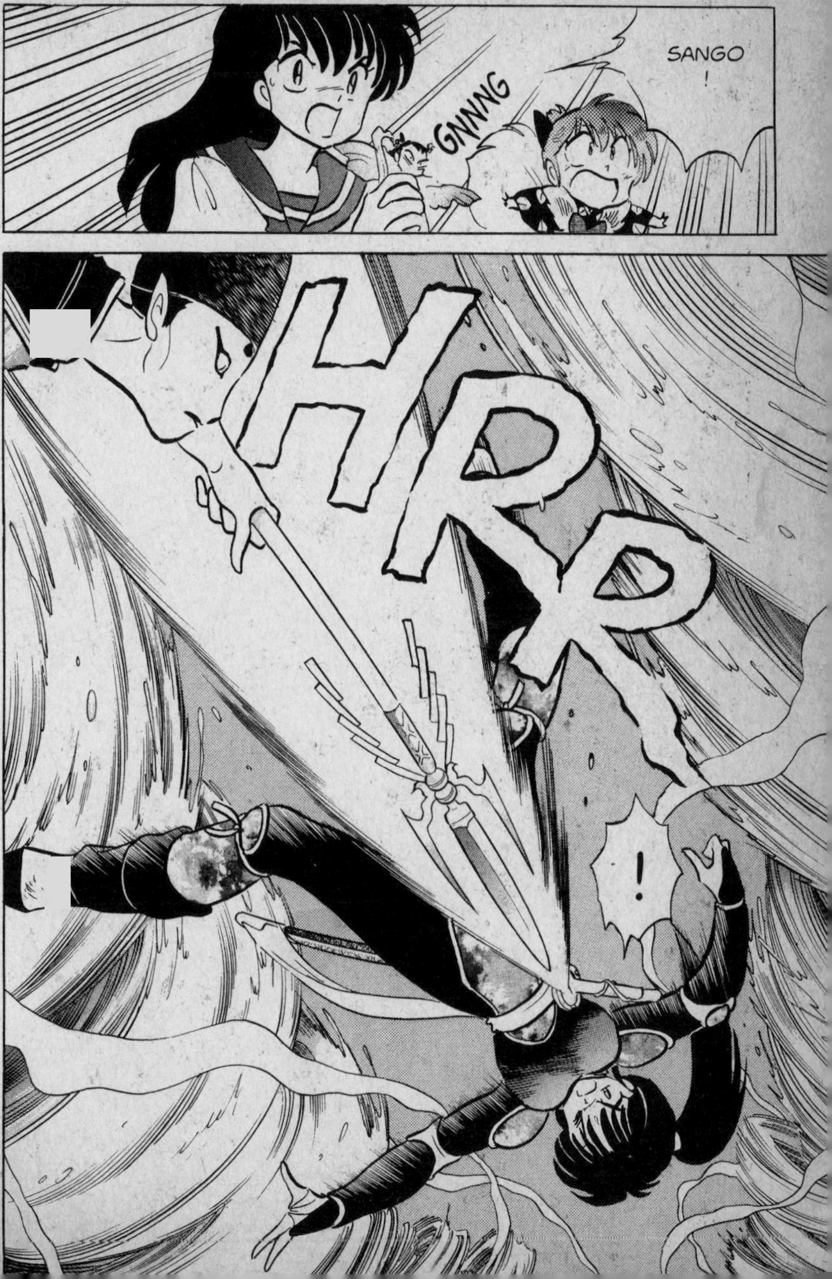
GNNNG
SANGO!
HRR
!

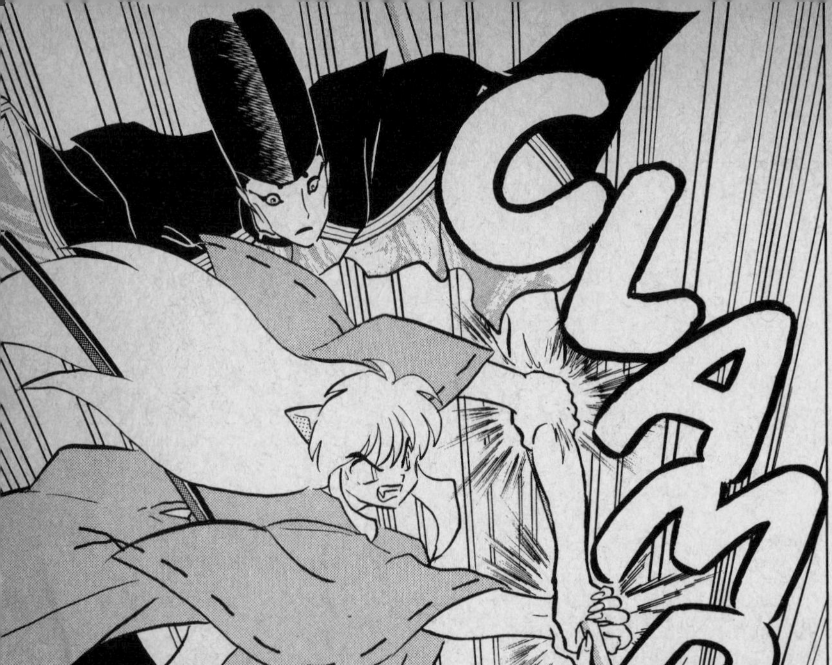
CLAMP
EH ?!

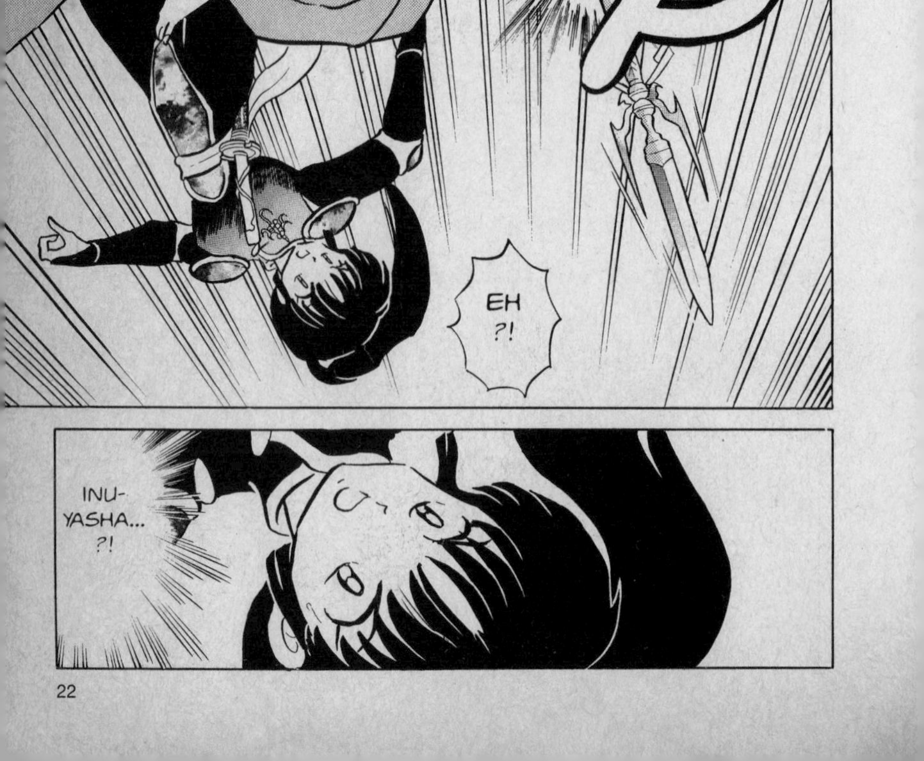
INU-YASHA... ?!

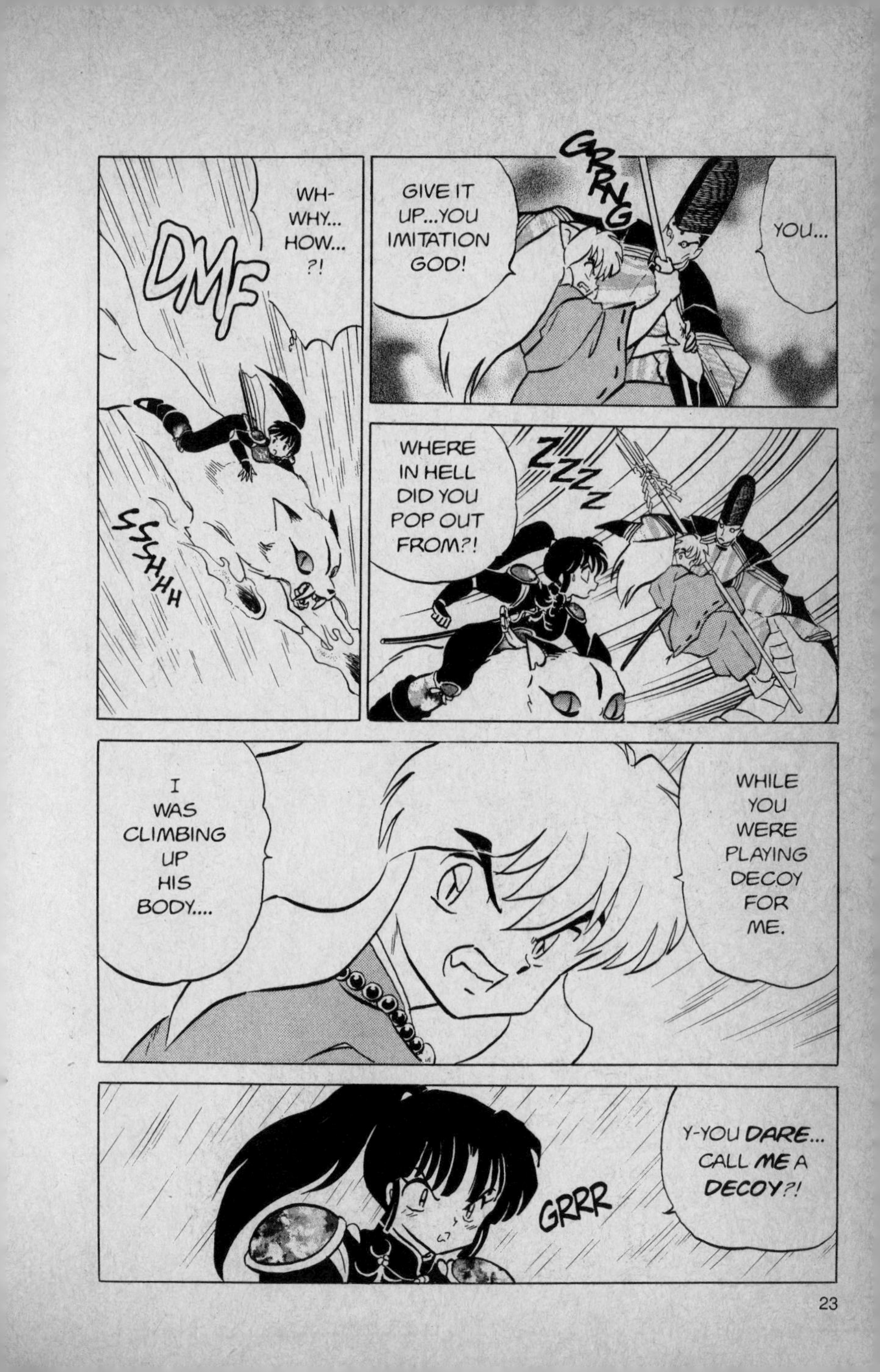
DMF
WH- WHY... HOW... ?!
SSSHHH
GIVE IT UP...YOU IMITATION GOD!
GRRNG
YOU...
WHERE IN HELL DID YOU POP OUT FROM?!
ZZZZ
I WAS CLIMBING UP HIS BODY....
WHILE YOU WERE PLAYING DECOY FOR ME.
GRRR
Y-YOU **DARE**... CALL **ME** A **DECOY**?!

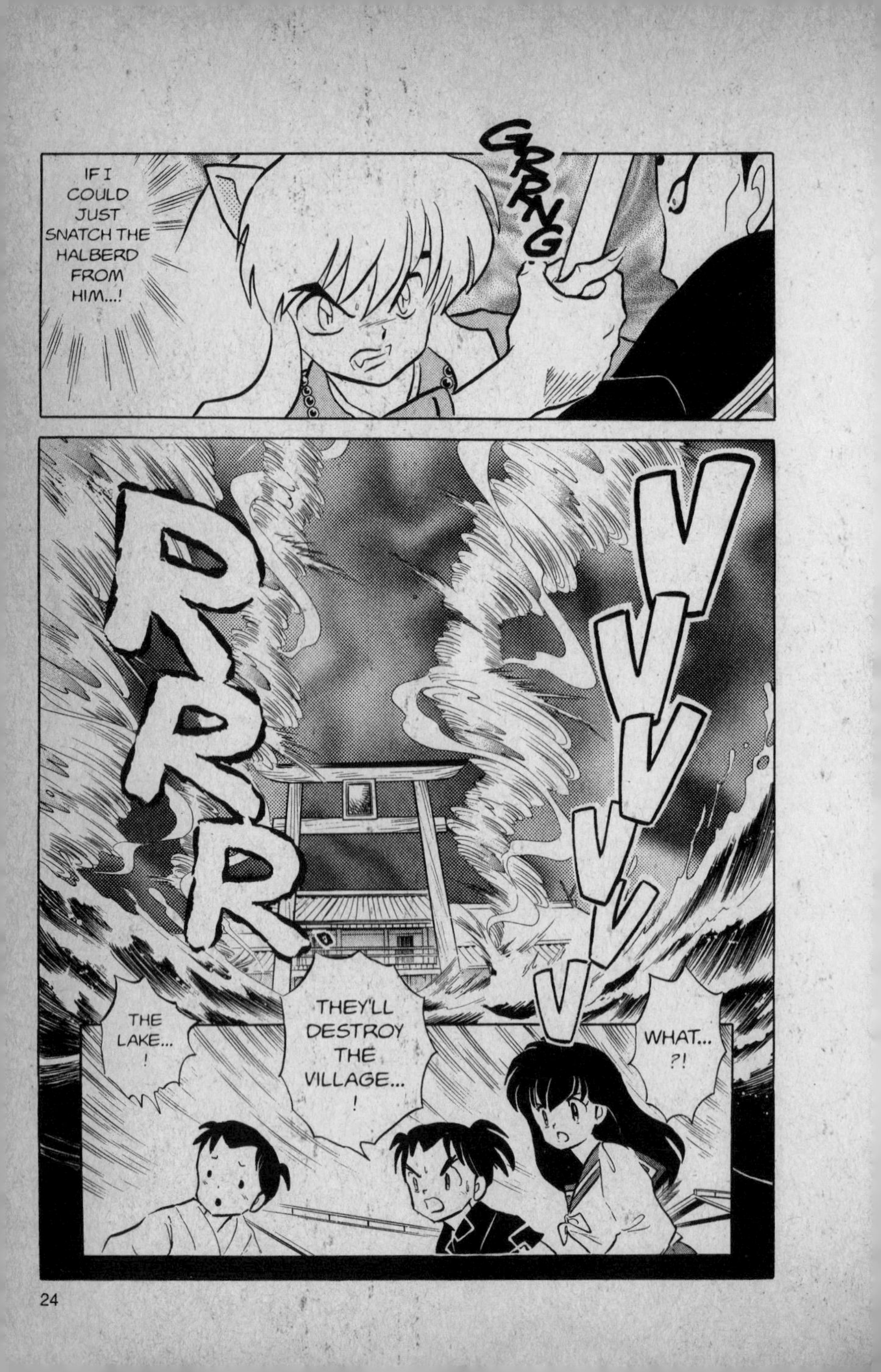
IF I COULD JUST SNATCH THE HALBERD FROM HIM...!
GRRNG
RRR
VVVVVVVV
THE LAKE...!
THEY'LL DESTROY THE VILLAGE...!
WHAT...?!

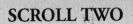

SCROLL TWO
THE SLAYING OF
THE SNAKE

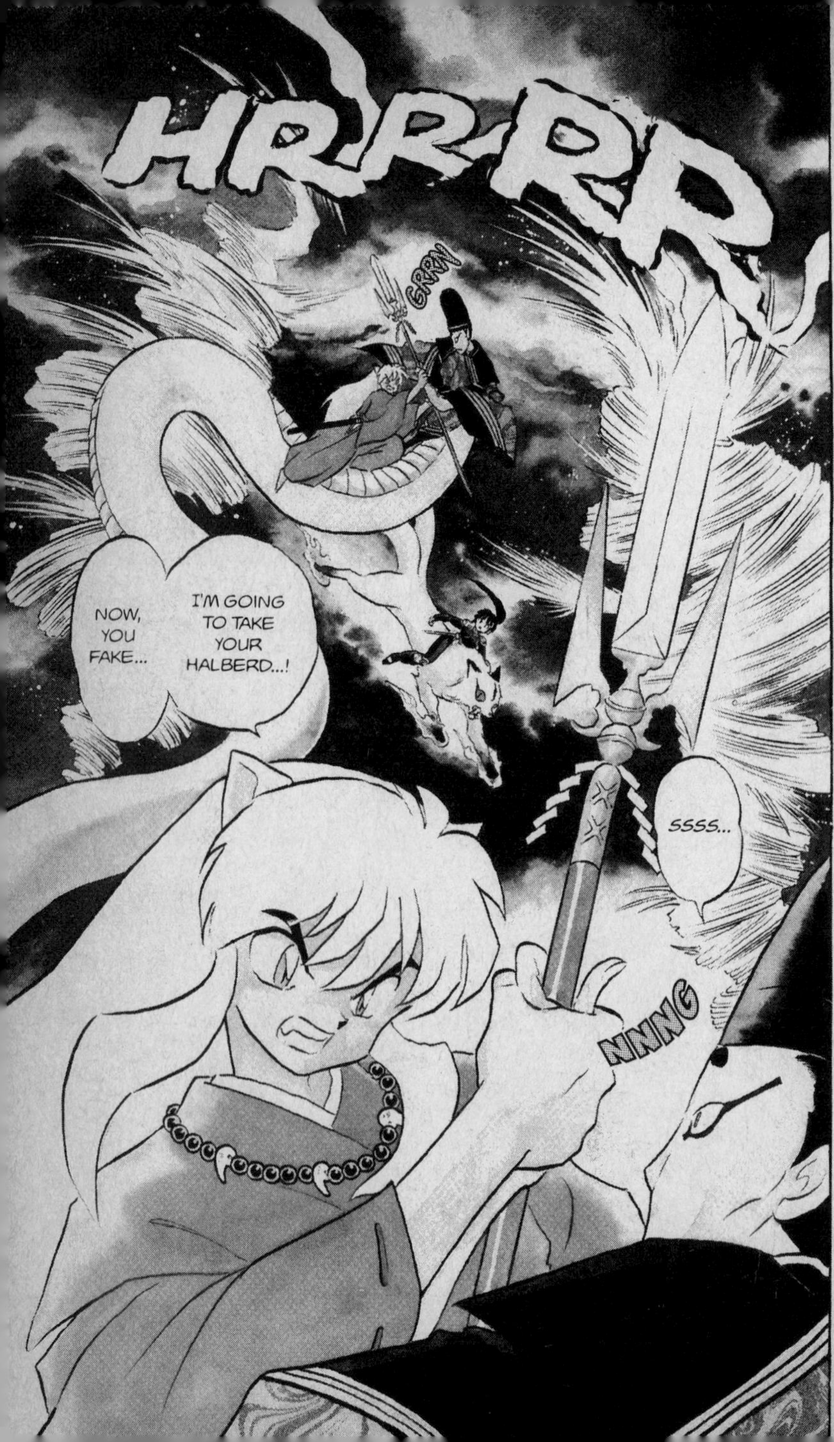
HRRRR
GRRN
NOW, YOU FAKE...
I'M GOING TO TAKE YOUR HALBERD...!
SSSS...
NNNG

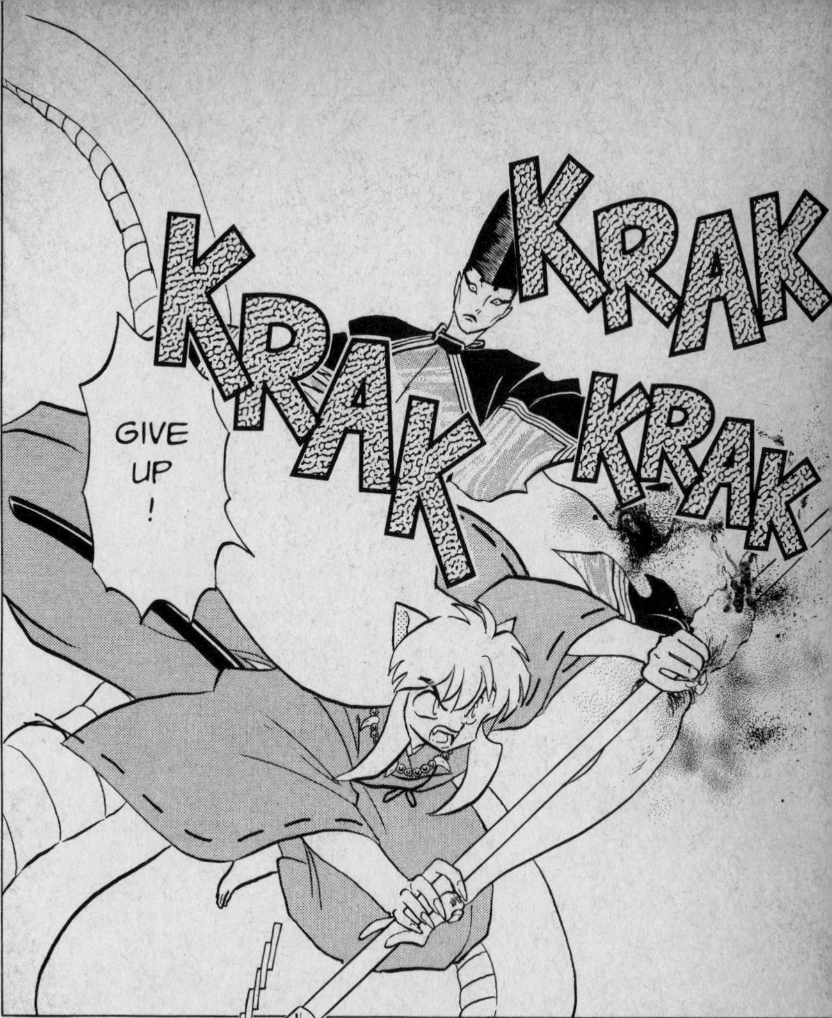
KRAK
KRAK
KRAK
KRAK
GIVE UP !
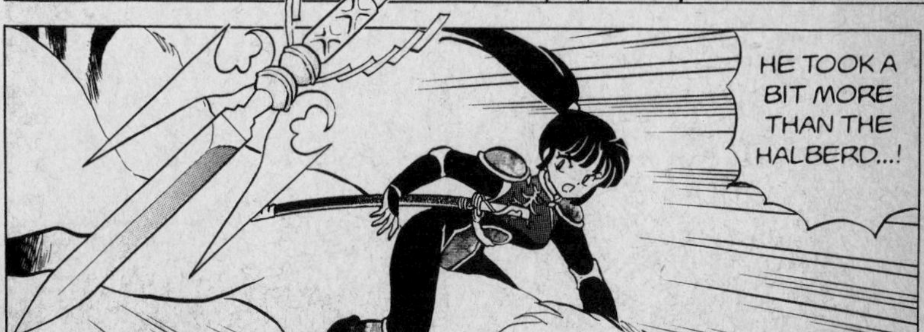
HE TOOK A BIT MORE THAN THE HALBERD...!

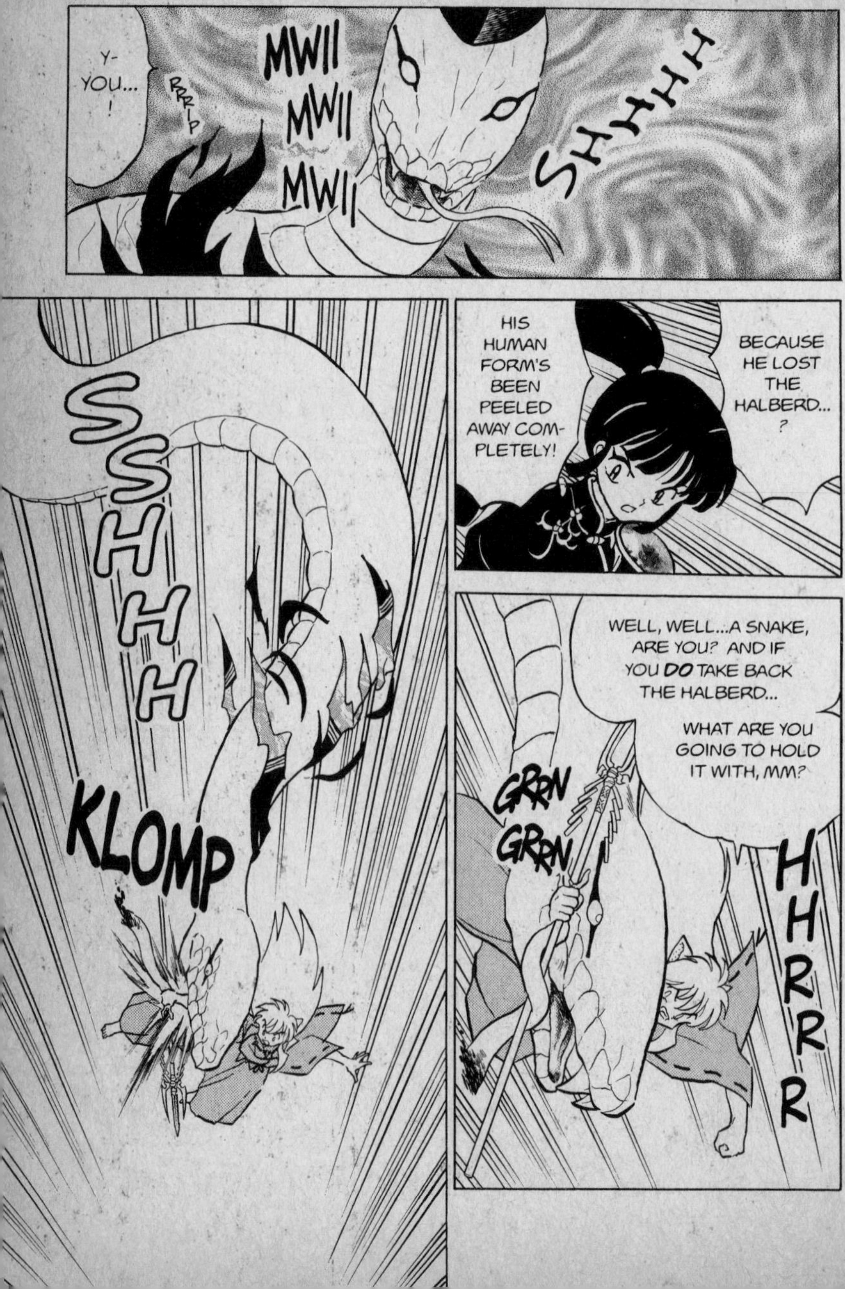

Y-
YOU...
!
RRRIP
MWII
MWII
MWII
SHHHH
SSHHHH
KLOMP
HIS HUMAN FORM'S BEEN PEELED AWAY COMPLETELY!
BECAUSE HE LOST THE HALBERD...?
WELL, WELL...A SNAKE, ARE YOU? AND IF YOU **DO** TAKE BACK THE HALBERD...
WHAT ARE YOU GOING TO HOLD IT WITH, MM?
GRRN
GRRN
HHRRR

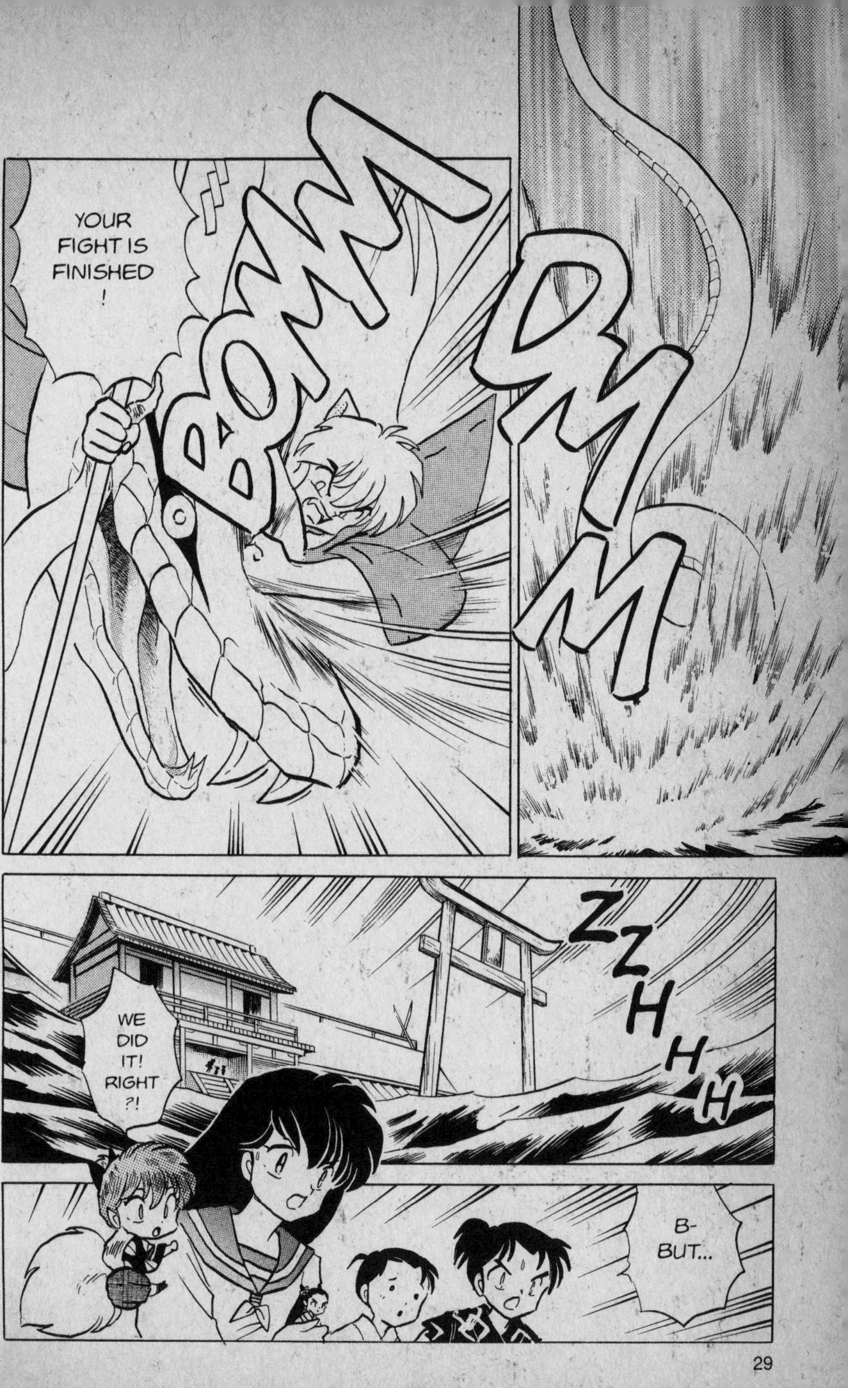
YOUR FIGHT IS FINISHED!
BOOM
DMMM
WE DID IT! RIGHT?!
ZZHHHH
B-BUT...

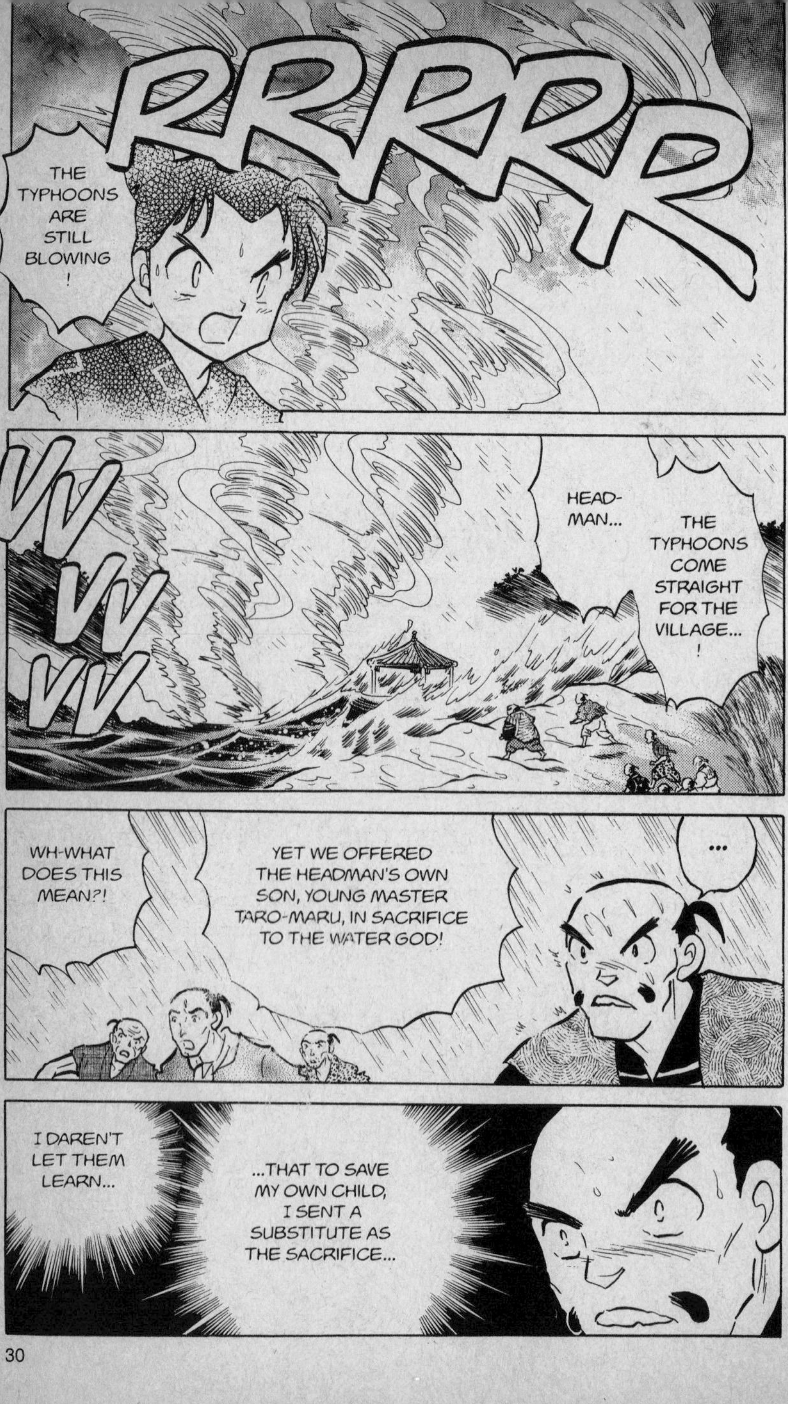
RRRRR
THE TYPHOONS ARE STILL BLOWING!
VVVVVV
HEAD-MAN...
THE TYPHOONS COME STRAIGHT FOR THE VILLAGE...!
WH-WHAT DOES THIS MEAN?!
YET WE OFFERED THE HEADMAN'S OWN SON, YOUNG MASTER TARO-MARU, IN SACRIFICE TO THE WATER GOD!
...
I DAREN'T LET THEM LEARN...
...THAT TO SAVE MY OWN CHILD, I SENT A SUBSTITUTE AS THE SACRIFICE...

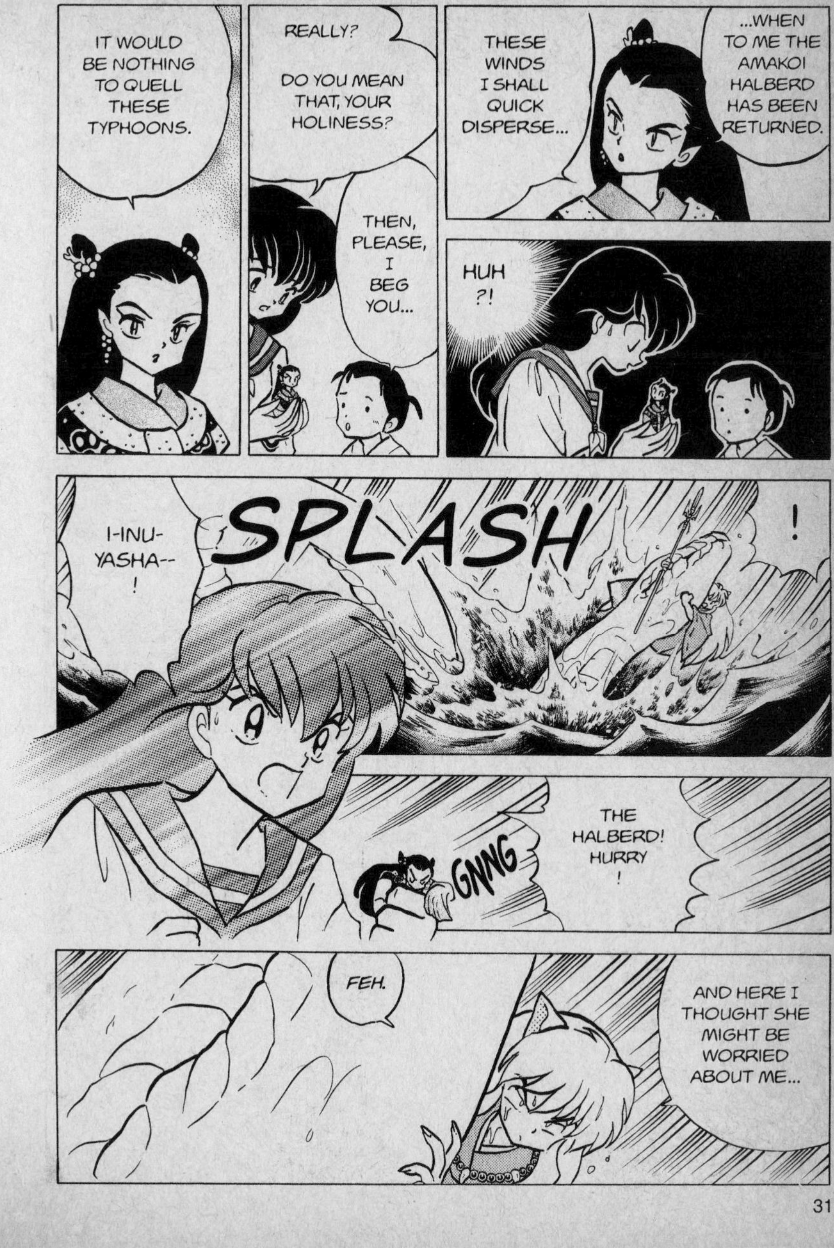
IT WOULD BE NOTHING TO QUELL THESE TYPHOONS.
REALLY?
DO YOU MEAN THAT, YOUR HOLINESS?
THEN, PLEASE, I BEG YOU...
THESE WINDS I SHALL QUICK DISPERSE...
...WHEN TO ME THE AMAKOI HALBERD HAS BEEN RETURNED.
HUH ?!
I-INU-YASHA-- !
SPLASH
!
THE HALBERD! HURRY !
GNNG
FEH.
AND HERE I THOUGHT SHE MIGHT BE WORRIED ABOUT ME...

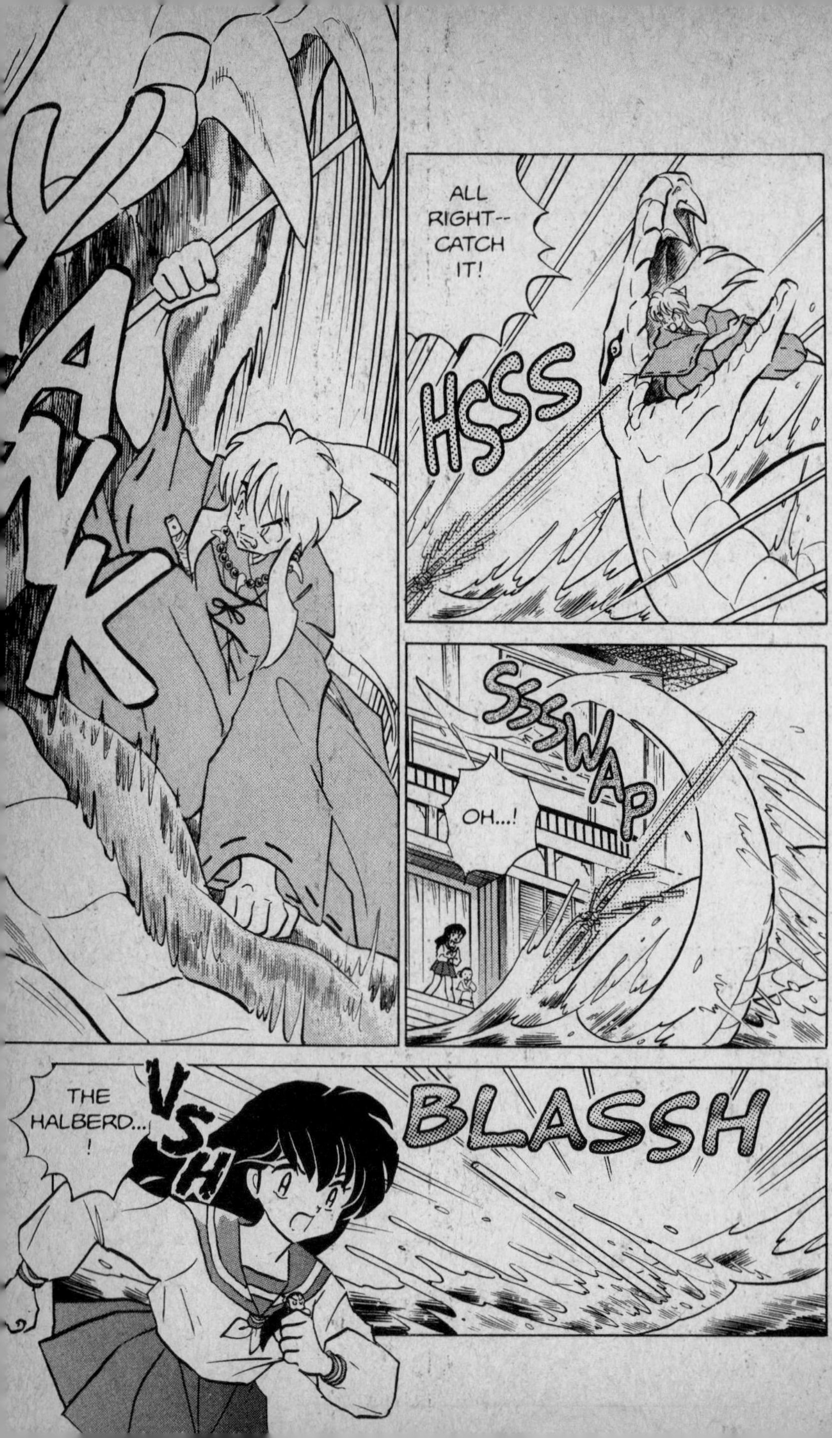
ALL RIGHT-- CATCH IT!
HSSS
SSSWAP
OH...!
THE HALBERD...!
VSH
BLASSH

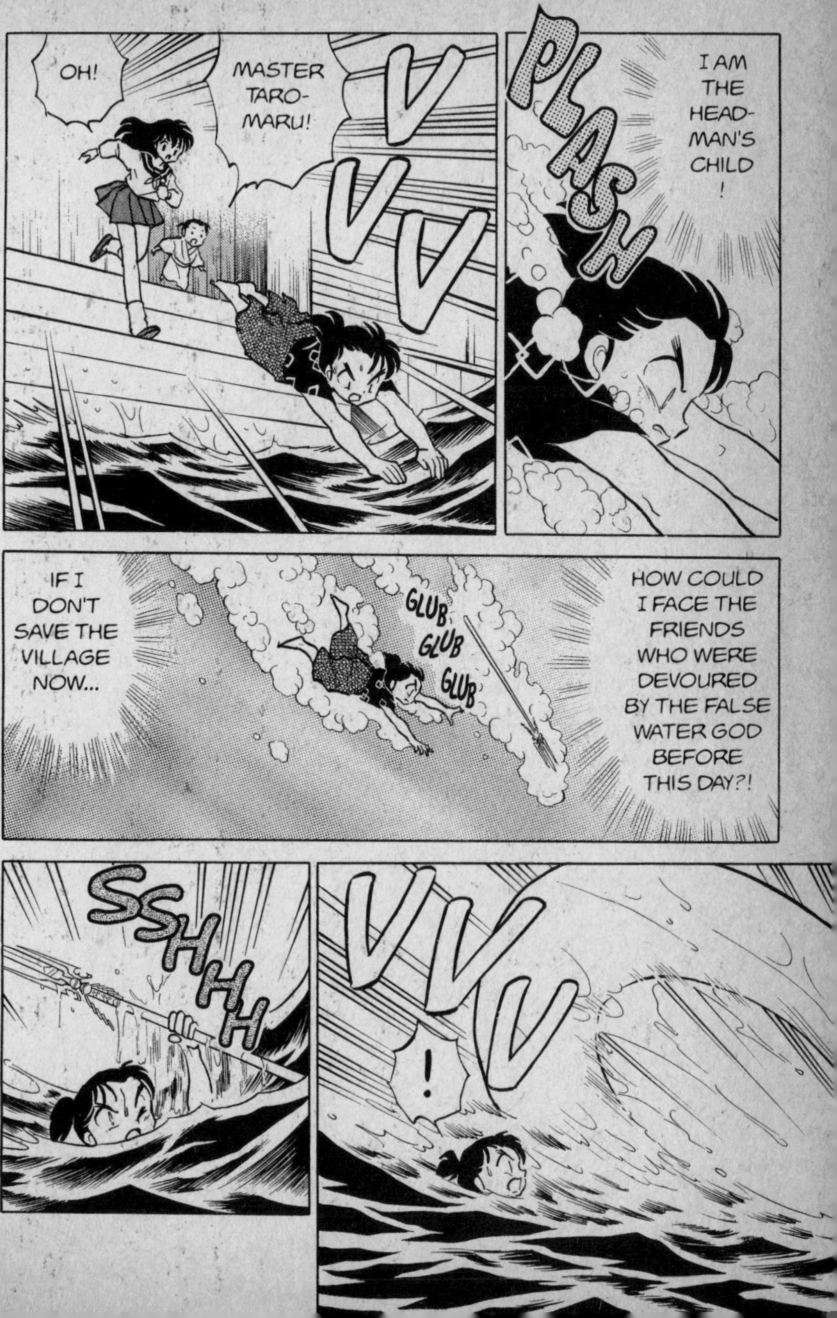
OH!
MASTER TARO-MARU!
VVV
PLASH
I AM THE HEAD-MAN'S CHILD!
IF I DON'T SAVE THE VILLAGE NOW...
GLUB GLUB GLUB
HOW COULD I FACE THE FRIENDS WHO WERE DEVOURED BY THE FALSE WATER GOD BEFORE THIS DAY?!
SSHHHH
VVVV
!

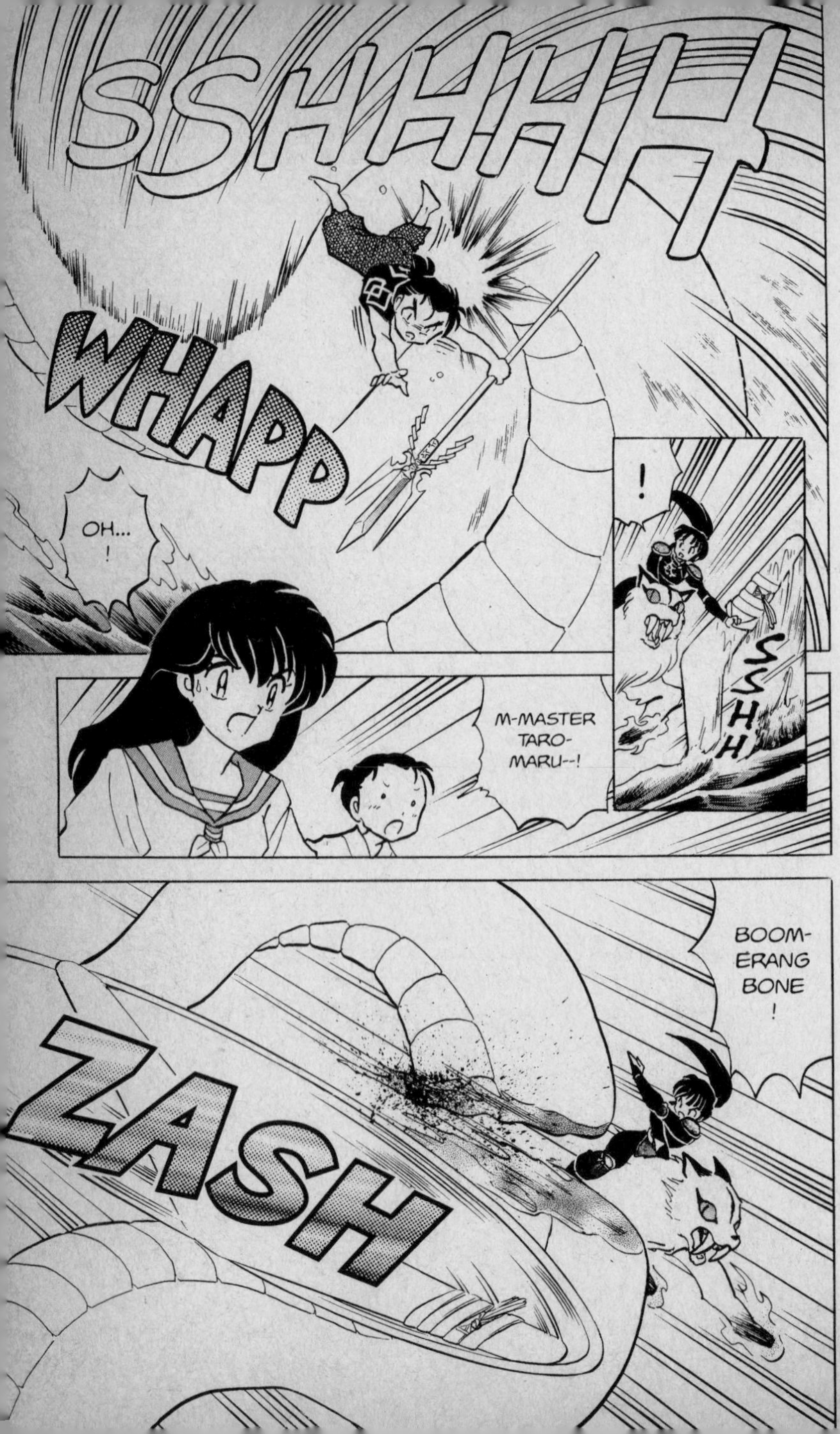

SSHHHHH
WHAPP
OH... !
M-MASTER TARO-MARU--!
!
SSHH
BOOM-ERANG BONE !
ZASH

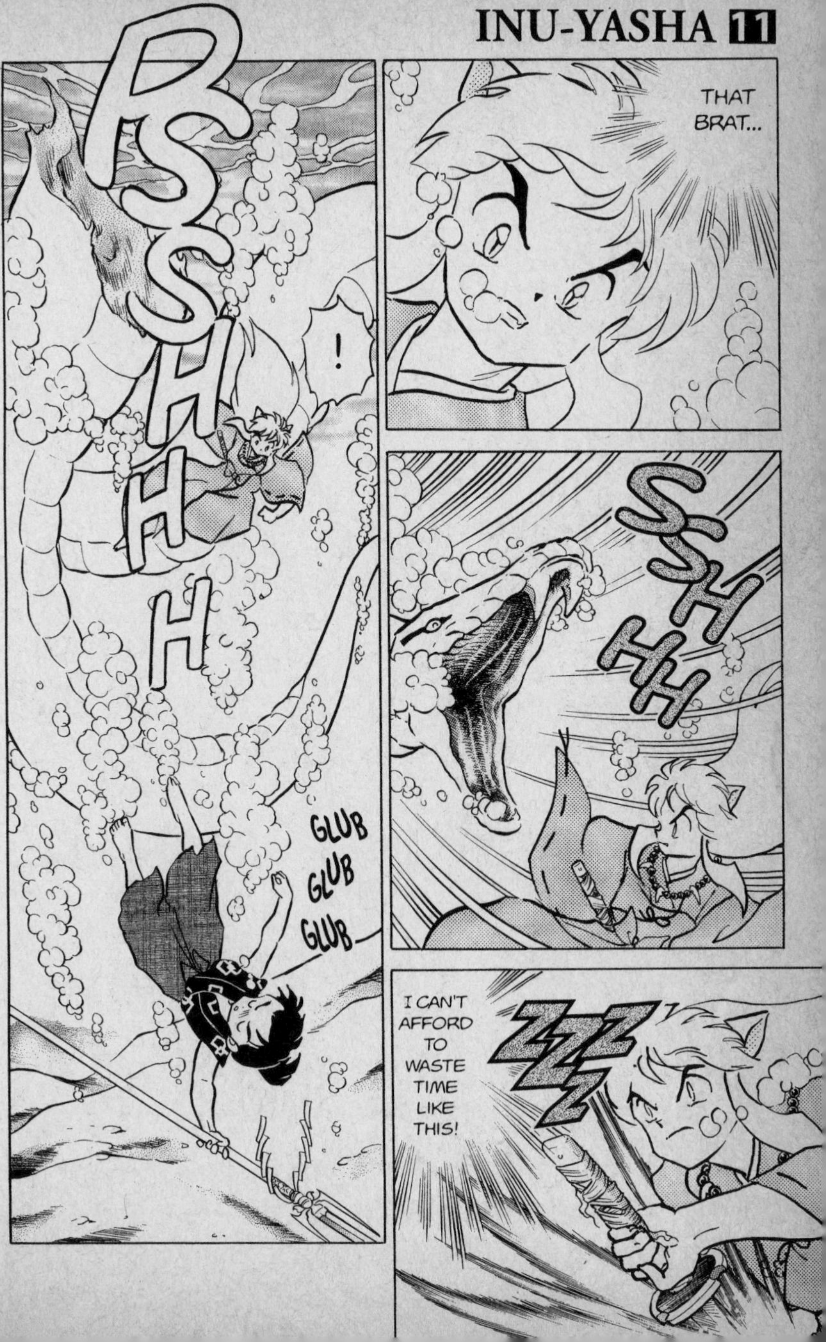
PSSHHH
!
GLUB
GLUB
GLUB
THAT BRAT...
SHHHH
I CAN'T AFFORD TO WASTE TIME LIKE THIS!
ZZZ

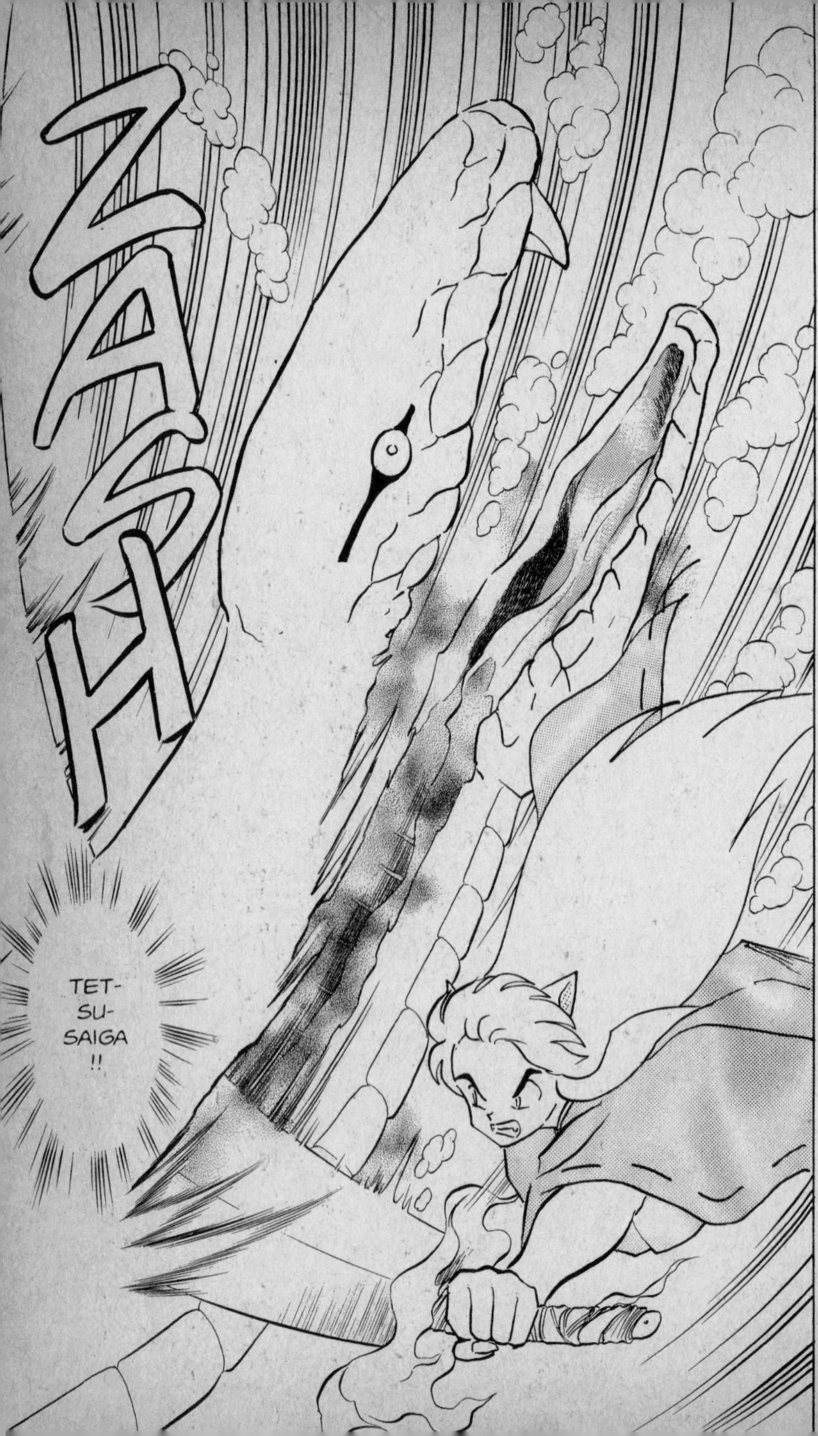
ZASH
TET-SU-SAIGA!!

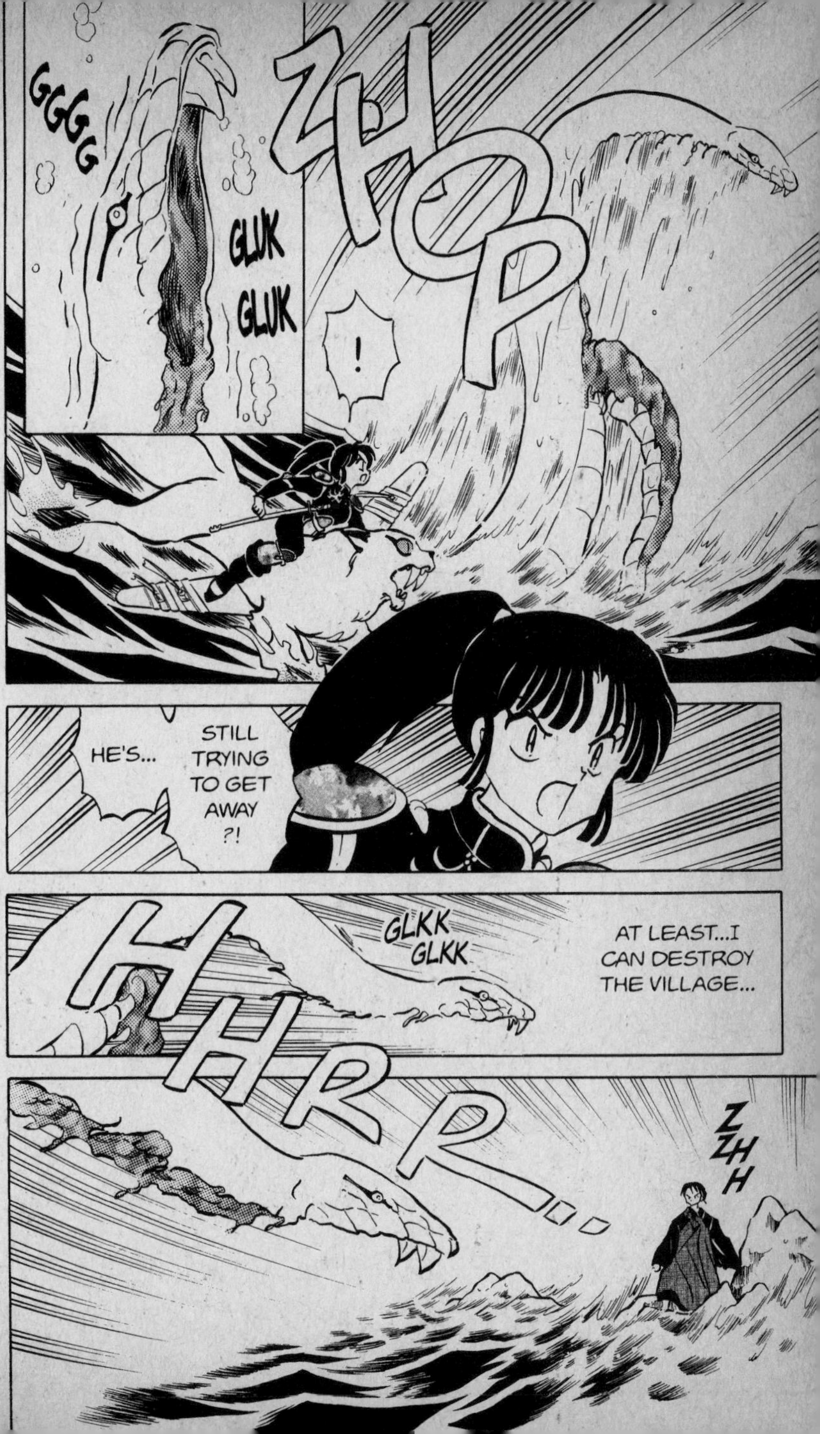
GGGG
GLUK
GLUK
ZHOP
!
HE'S...
STILL TRYING TO GET AWAY ?!
HHRR...
GLKK
GLKK
AT LEAST...I CAN DESTROY THE VILLAGE...
ZHH

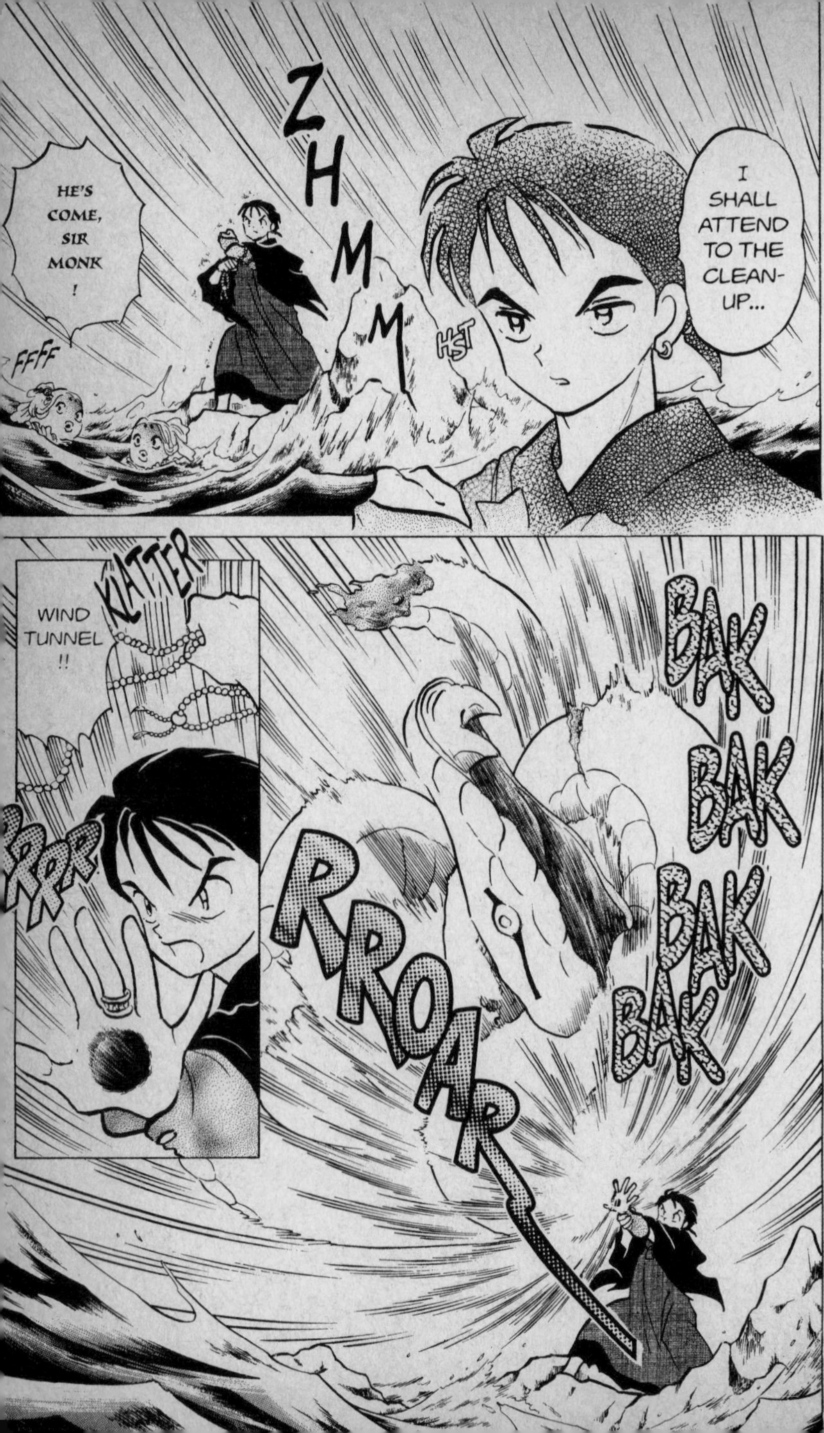
HE'S COME, SIR MONK!
FFFF
ZHMMM
HST
I SHALL ATTEND TO THE CLEAN-UP...
WIND TUNNEL!!
KLATTER
RROAR
BAK
BAK
BAK
BAK

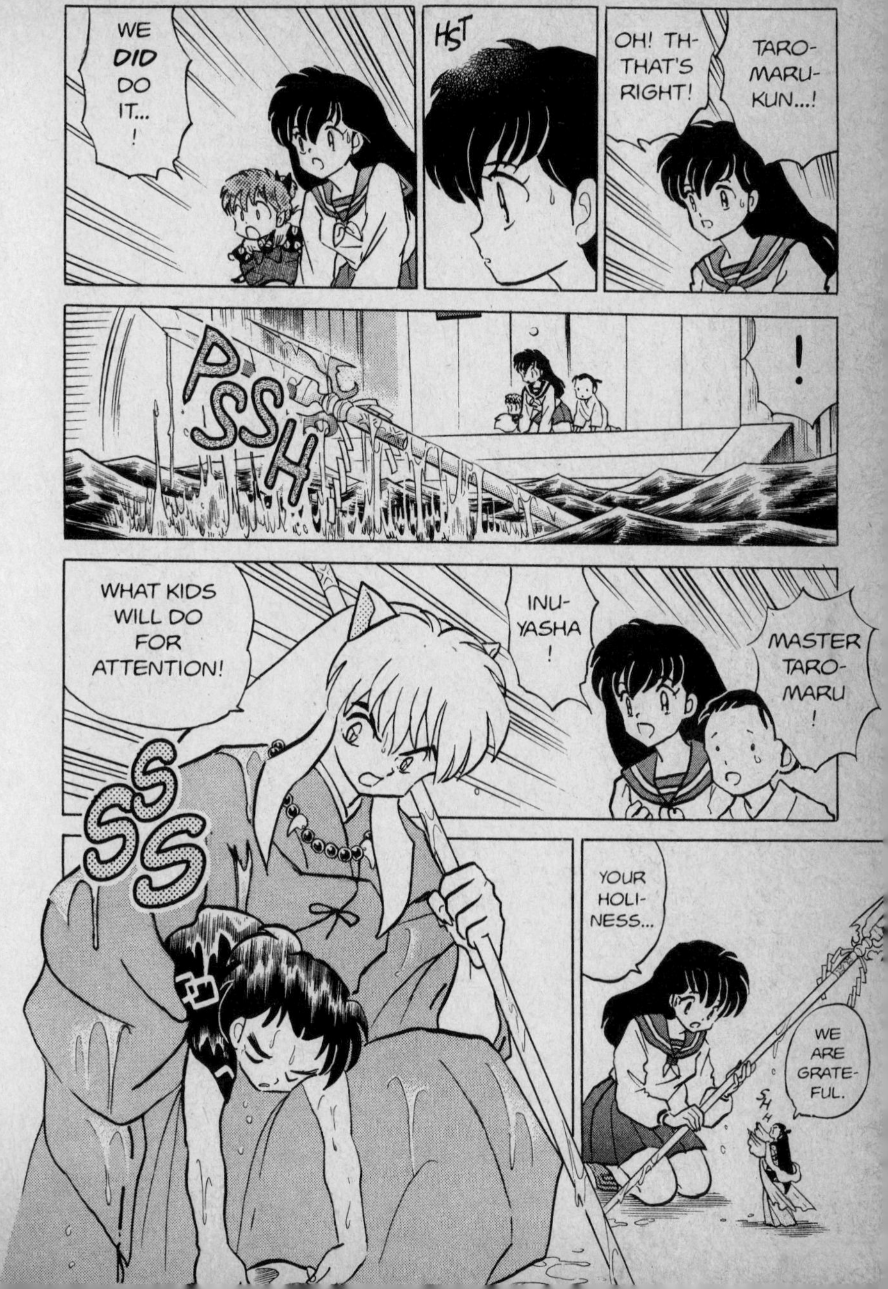
WE DID DO IT... !
HST
OH! TH-THAT'S RIGHT!
TARO-MARU-KUN...!
PSSH
!
WHAT KIDS WILL DO FOR ATTENTION!
INU-YASHA !
MASTER TARO-MARU !
SSS
YOUR HOLI-NESS...
WE ARE GRATE-FUL.
SHH

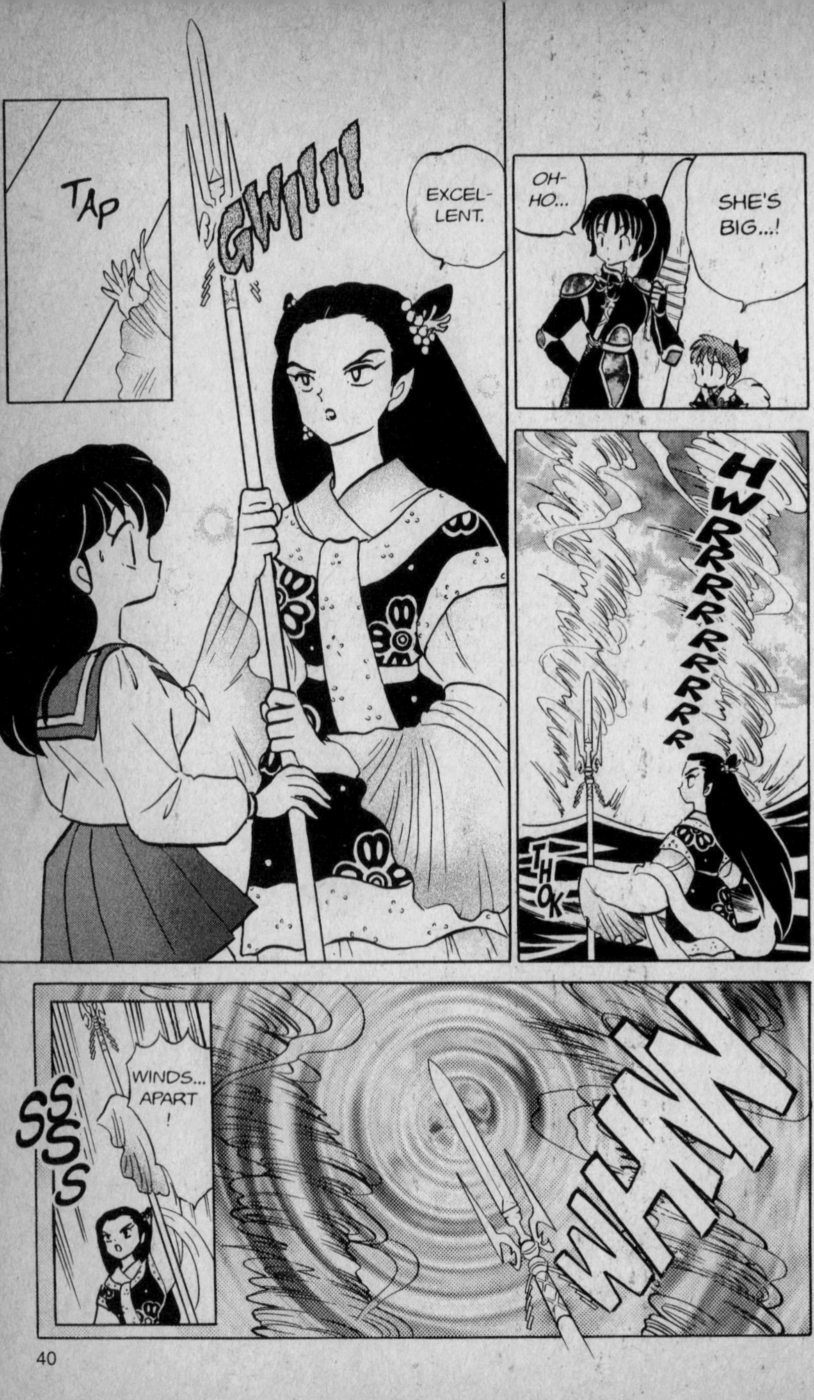
TAP
GWIIII
EXCEL-
LENT.
OH-
HO...
SHE'S
BIG...!
HWRRRRRRRRRR
THOK
SSSS
WINDS...
APART
!
WHN

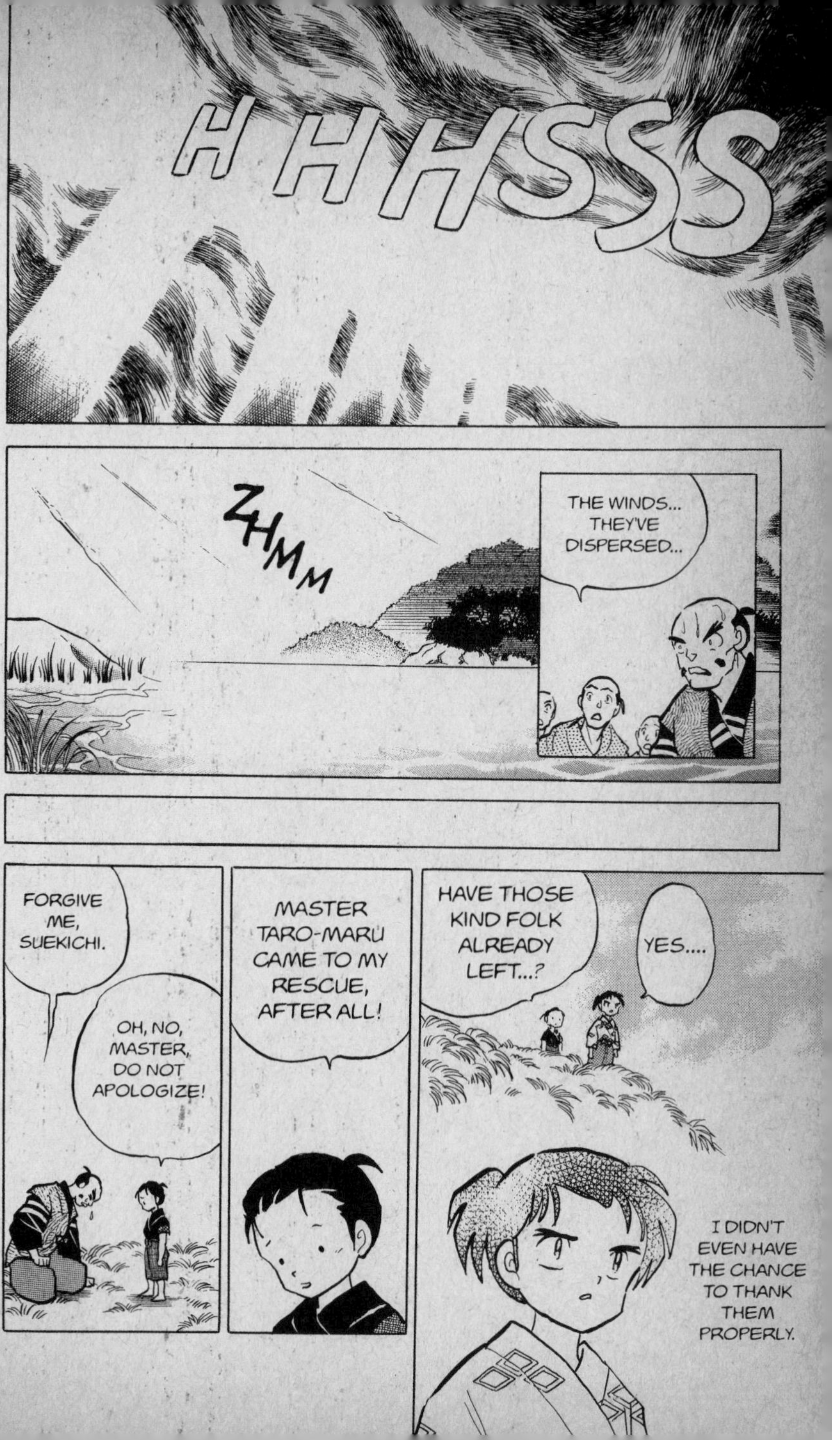
HHHSSS
ZHMM
THE WINDS... THEY'VE DISPERSED...
FORGIVE ME, SUEKICHI.
OH, NO, MASTER, DO NOT APOLOGIZE!
MASTER TARO-MARU CAME TO MY RESCUE, AFTER ALL!
HAVE THOSE KIND FOLK ALREADY LEFT...?
YES....
I DIDN'T EVEN HAVE THE CHANCE TO THANK THEM PROPERLY.

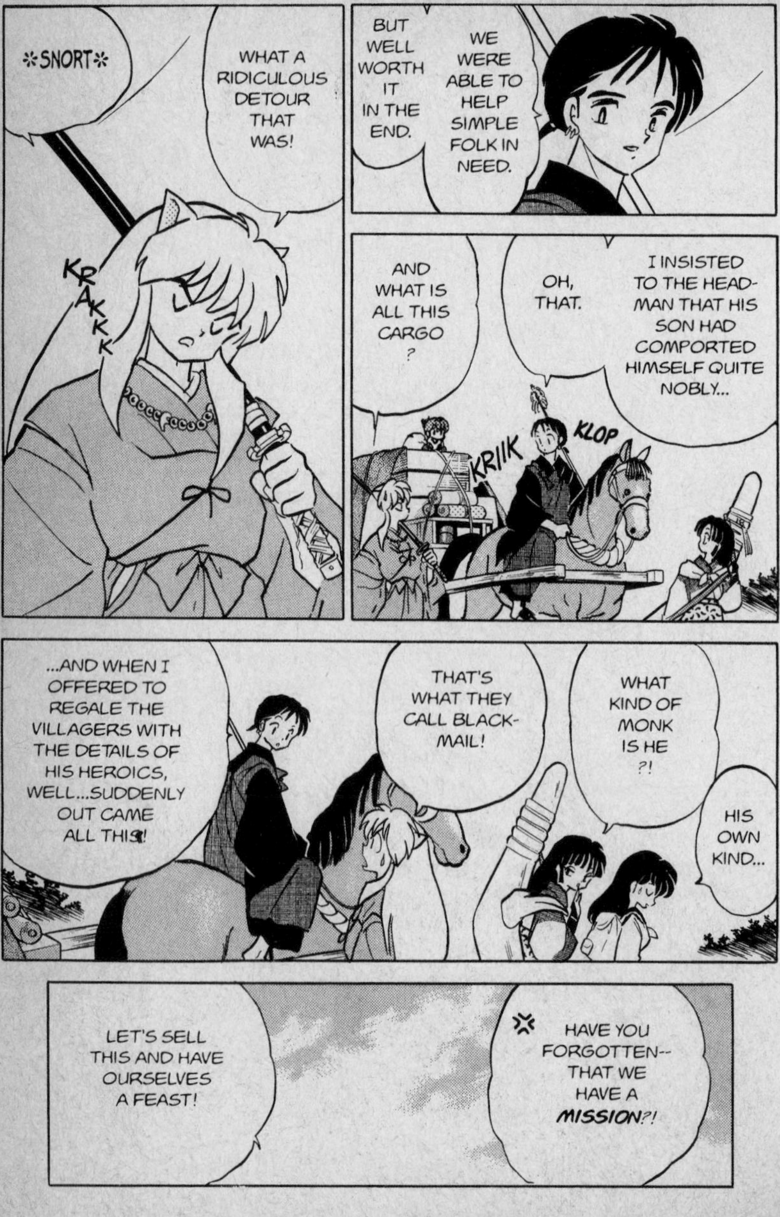

SNORT
WHAT A RIDICULOUS DETOUR THAT WAS!
KRAKKK
BUT WELL WORTH IT IN THE END.
WE WERE ABLE TO HELP SIMPLE FOLK IN NEED.
AND WHAT IS ALL THIS CARGO?
OH, THAT.
I INSISTED TO THE HEAD-MAN THAT HIS SON HAD COMPORTED HIMSELF QUITE NOBLY...
KLOP
KRIIK
...AND WHEN I OFFERED TO REGALE THE VILLAGERS WITH THE DETAILS OF HIS HEROICS, WELL...SUDDENLY OUT CAME ALL THIS!
THAT'S WHAT THEY CALL BLACK-MAIL!
WHAT KIND OF MONK IS HE?!
HIS OWN KIND...
LET'S SELL THIS AND HAVE OURSELVES A FEAST!
HAVE YOU FORGOTTEN-- THAT WE HAVE A MISSION?!

SCROLL THREE

THE WOUND AND THE WIND

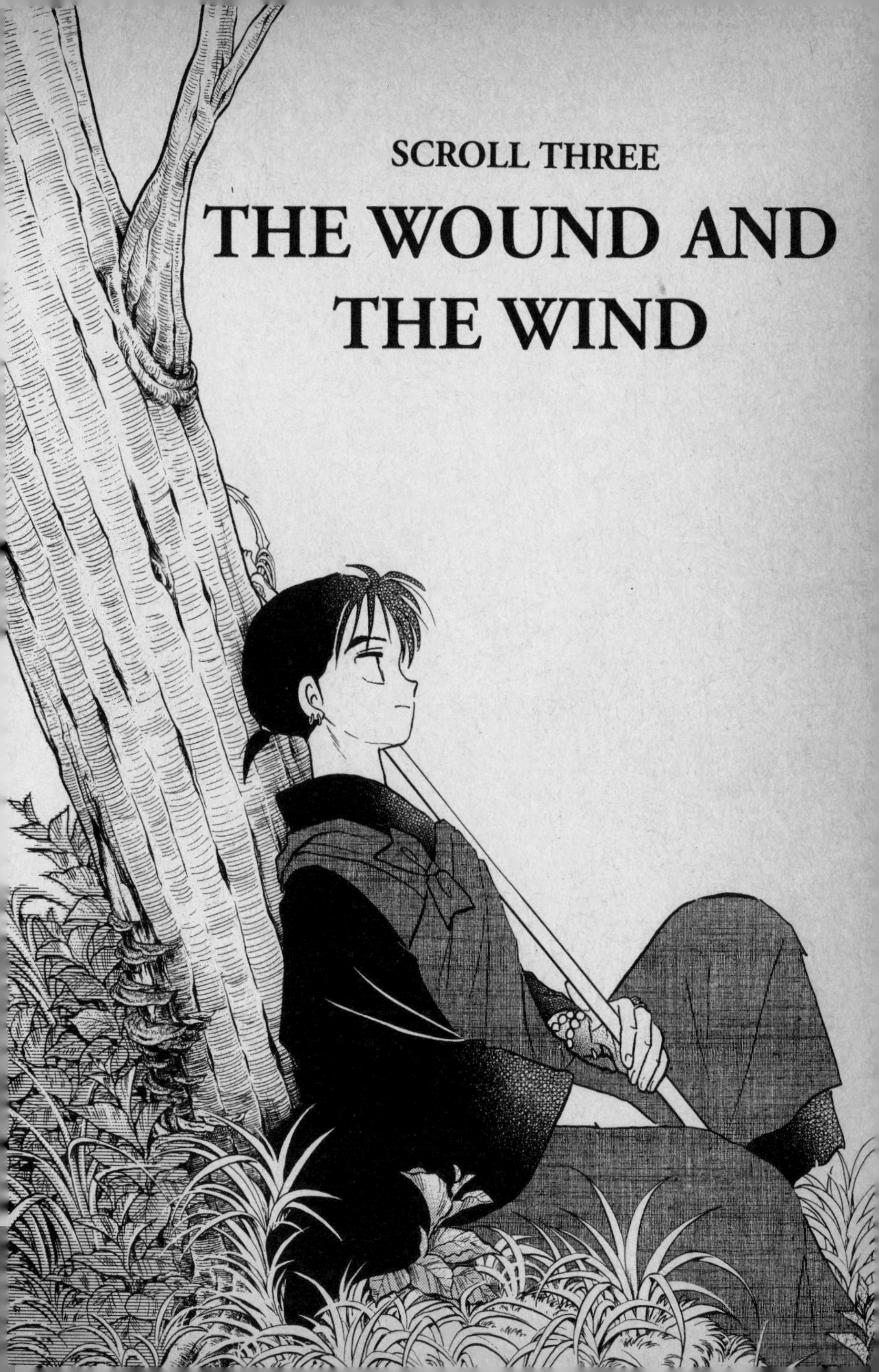

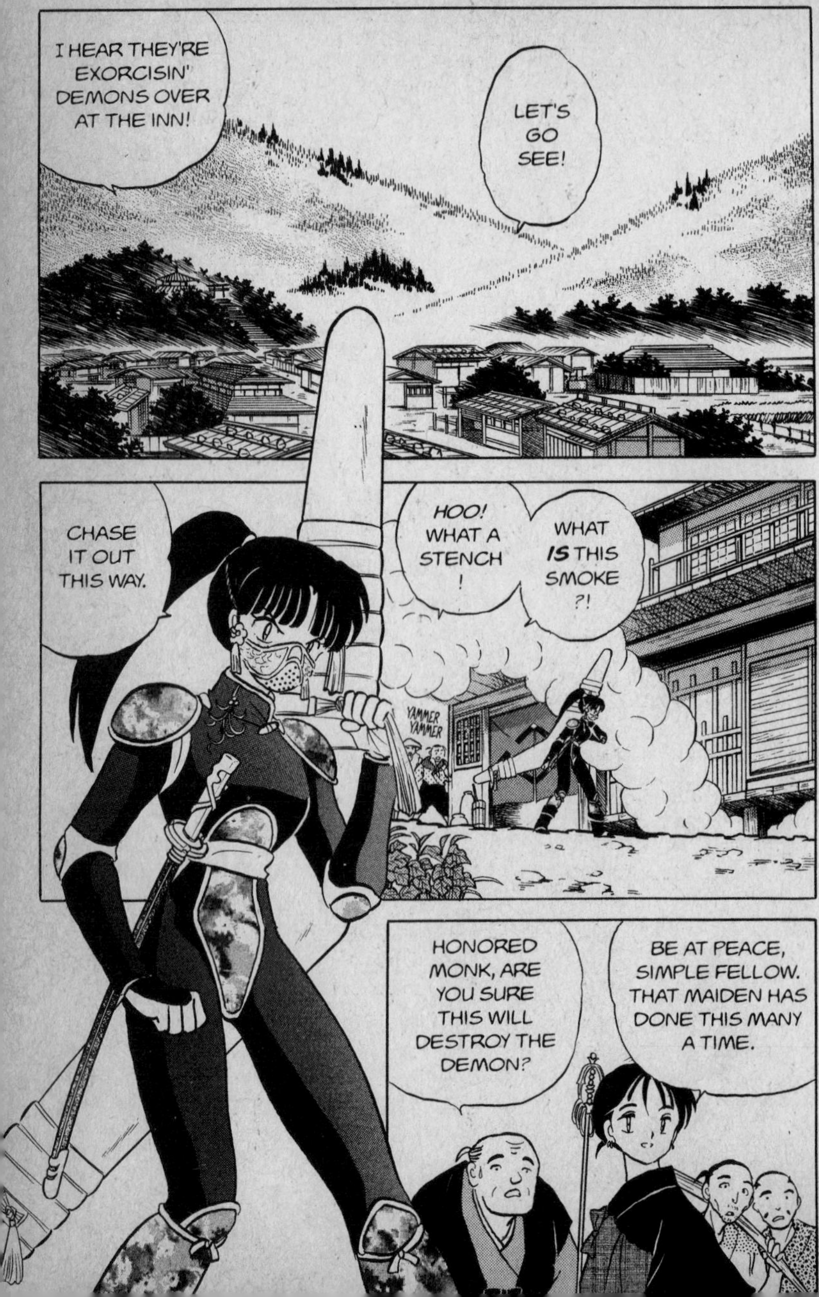
I HEAR THEY'RE EXORCISIN' DEMONS OVER AT THE INN!
LET'S GO SEE!
CHASE IT OUT THIS WAY.
HOO! WHAT A STENCH!
WHAT IS THIS SMOKE?!
YAMMER YAMMER
HONORED MONK, ARE YOU SURE THIS WILL DESTROY THE DEMON?
BE AT PEACE, SIMPLE FELLOW. THAT MAIDEN HAS DONE THIS MANY A TIME.

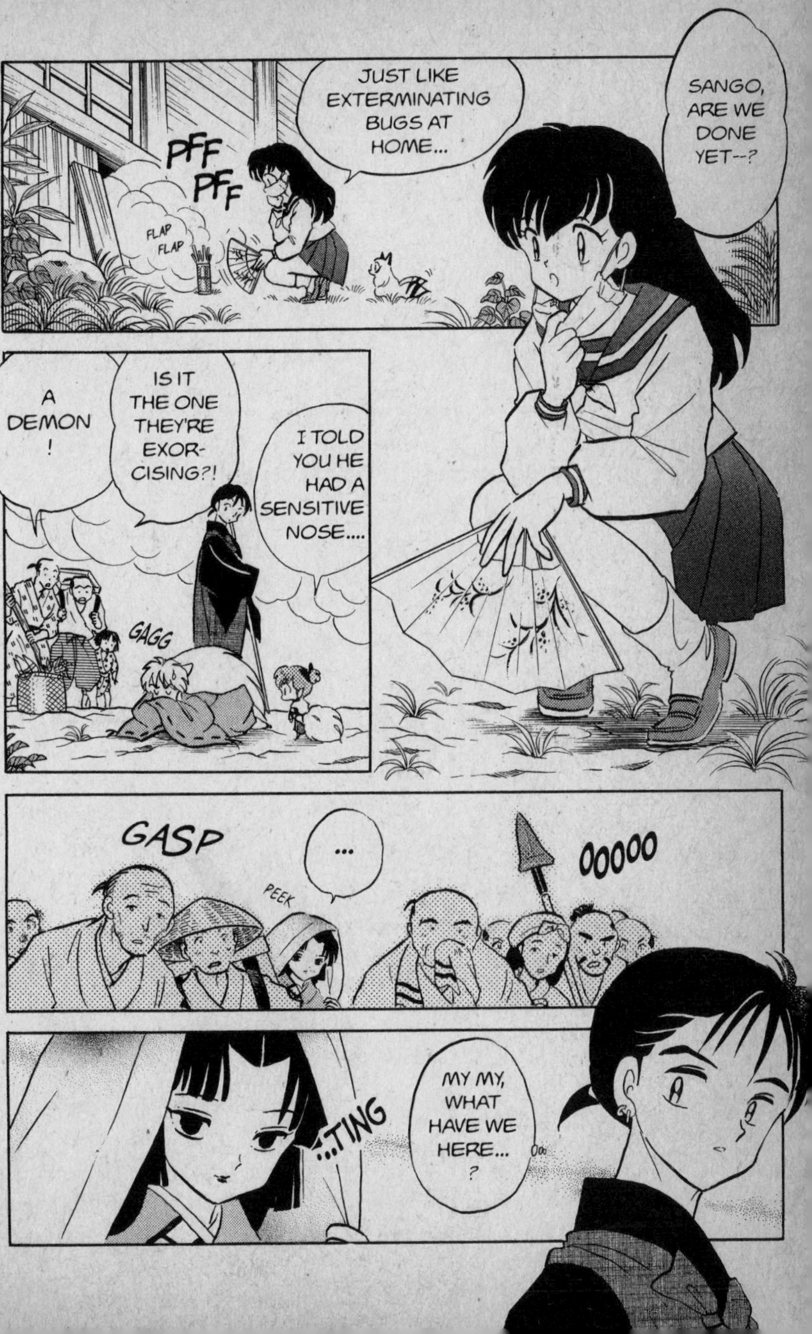
PFF
PFF
FLAP
FLAP
JUST LIKE EXTERMINATING BUGS AT HOME...
SANGO, ARE WE DONE YET--?
A DEMON!
IS IT THE ONE THEY'RE EXOR-CISING?!
I TOLD YOU HE HAD A SENSITIVE NOSE....
GAGG
GASP
...
PEEK
OOOOO
...TING
MY MY, WHAT HAVE WE HERE...?

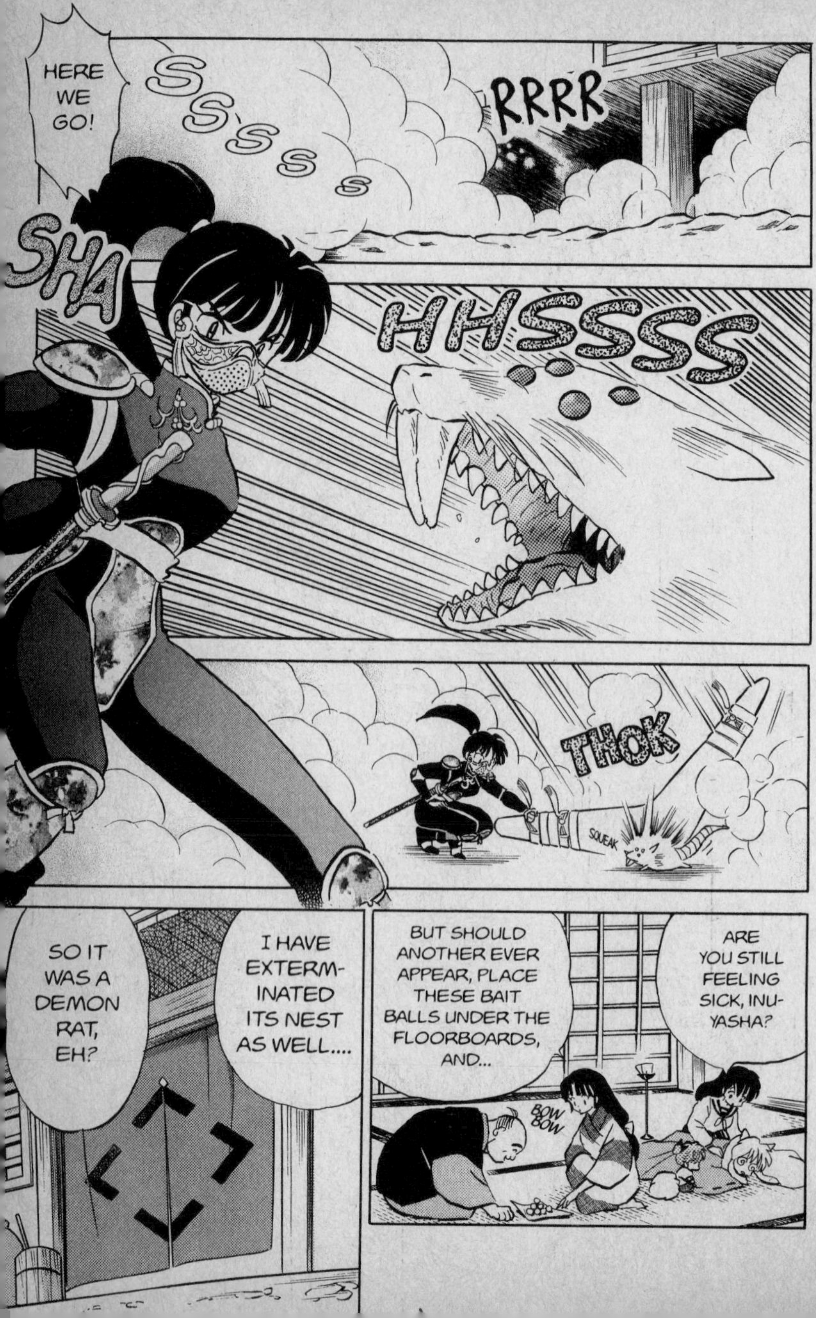
HERE WE GO!
SSSSSS
RRRR
SHA
HHSSSSS
THOK
SQUEAK
SO IT WAS A DEMON RAT, EH?
I HAVE EXTERMINATED ITS NEST AS WELL....
BUT SHOULD ANOTHER EVER APPEAR, PLACE THESE BAIT BALLS UNDER THE FLOORBOARDS, AND...
ARE YOU STILL FEELING SICK, INU-YASHA?
BOW BOW

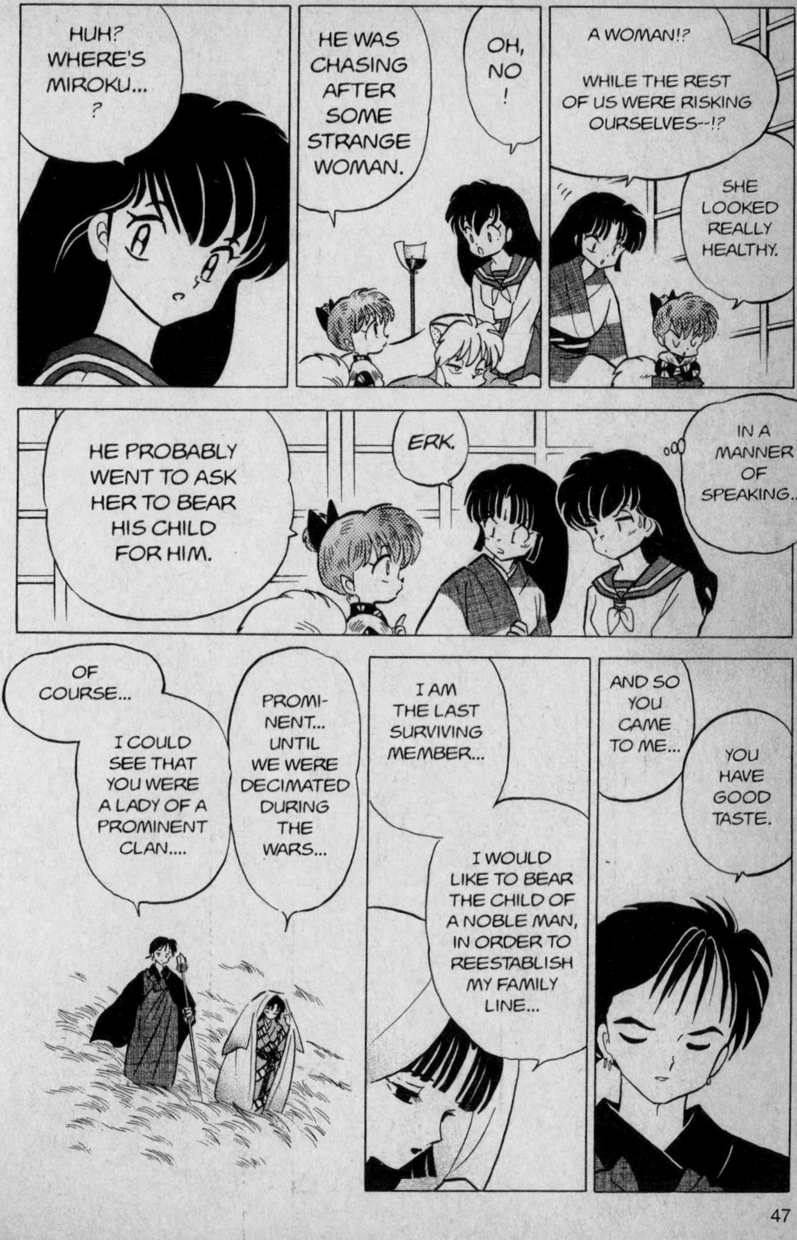
HUH? WHERE'S MIROKU... ?
HE WAS CHASING AFTER SOME STRANGE WOMAN.
OH, NO !
A WOMAN!?
WHILE THE REST OF US WERE RISKING OURSELVES--!?
SHE LOOKED REALLY HEALTHY.
HE PROBABLY WENT TO ASK HER TO BEAR HIS CHILD FOR HIM.
ERK.
IN A MANNER OF SPEAKING....
OF COURSE...
I COULD SEE THAT YOU WERE A LADY OF A PROMINENT CLAN....
PROMI-NENT... UNTIL WE WERE DECIMATED DURING THE WARS...
I AM THE LAST SURVIVING MEMBER...
I WOULD LIKE TO BEAR THE CHILD OF A NOBLE MAN, IN ORDER TO REESTABLISH MY FAMILY LINE...
AND SO YOU CAME TO ME...
YOU HAVE GOOD TASTE.

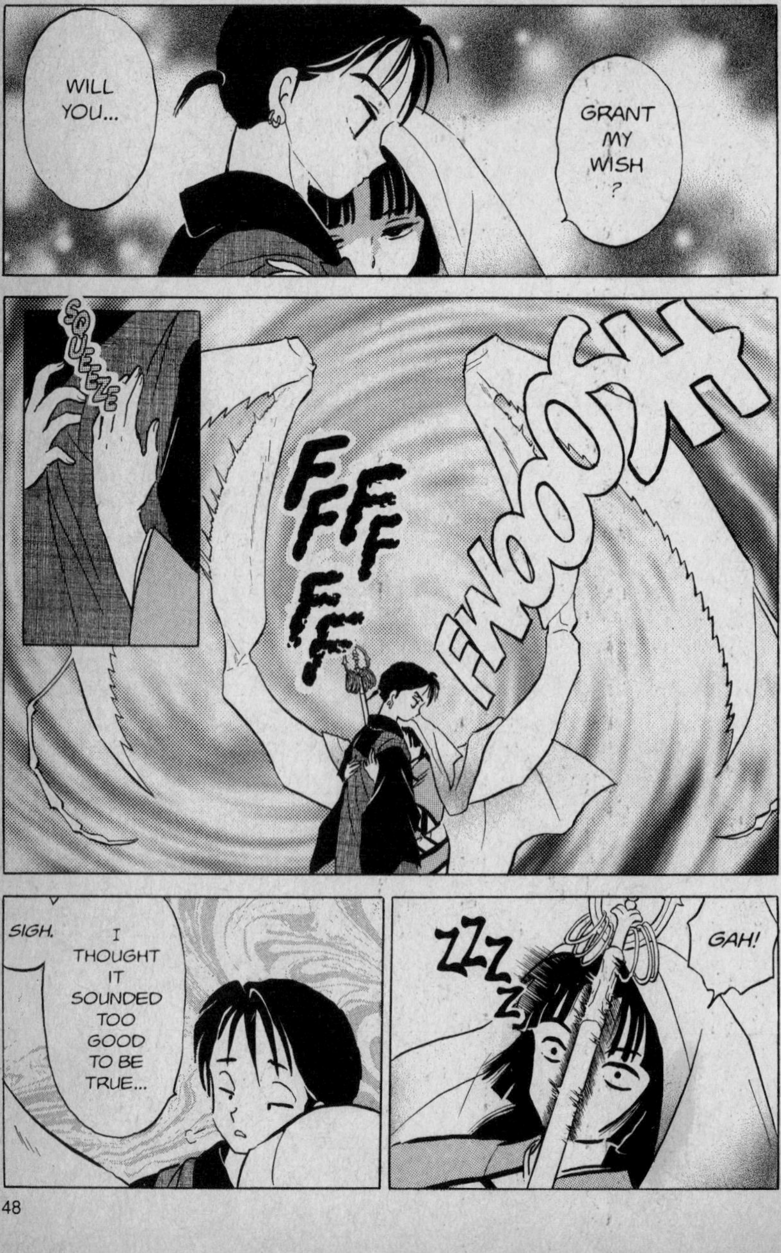
WILL YOU...
GRANT MY WISH ?
SQUEEZE
FFFFFF
FWOOSH
SIGH.
I THOUGHT IT SOUNDED TOO GOOD TO BE TRUE...
ZZZZ
GAH!

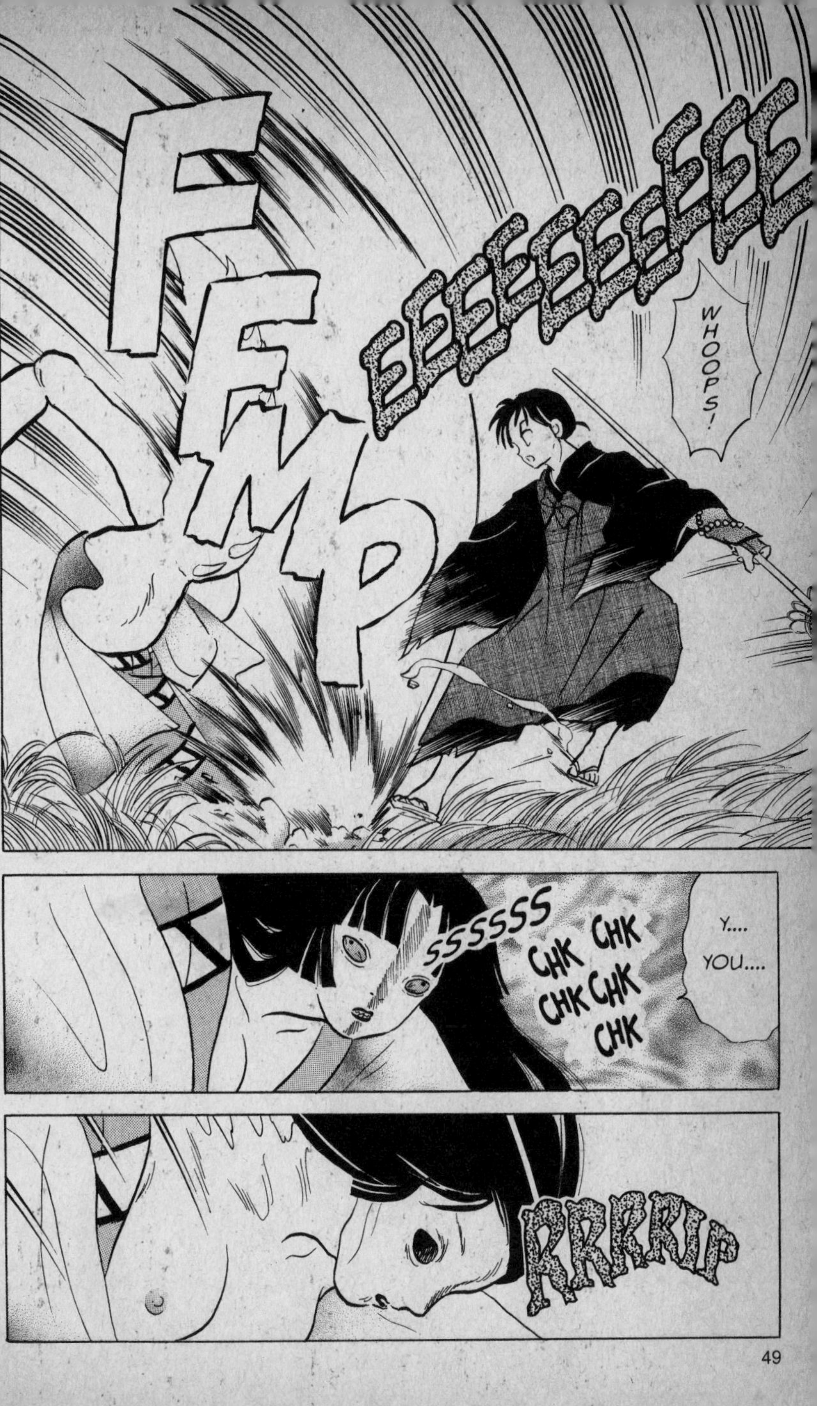
FFMP
EEEEEEEEEEE
WHOOPS!
SSSSSS
CHK CHK
CHK CHK
CHK
Y....
YOU....
RRRRIP

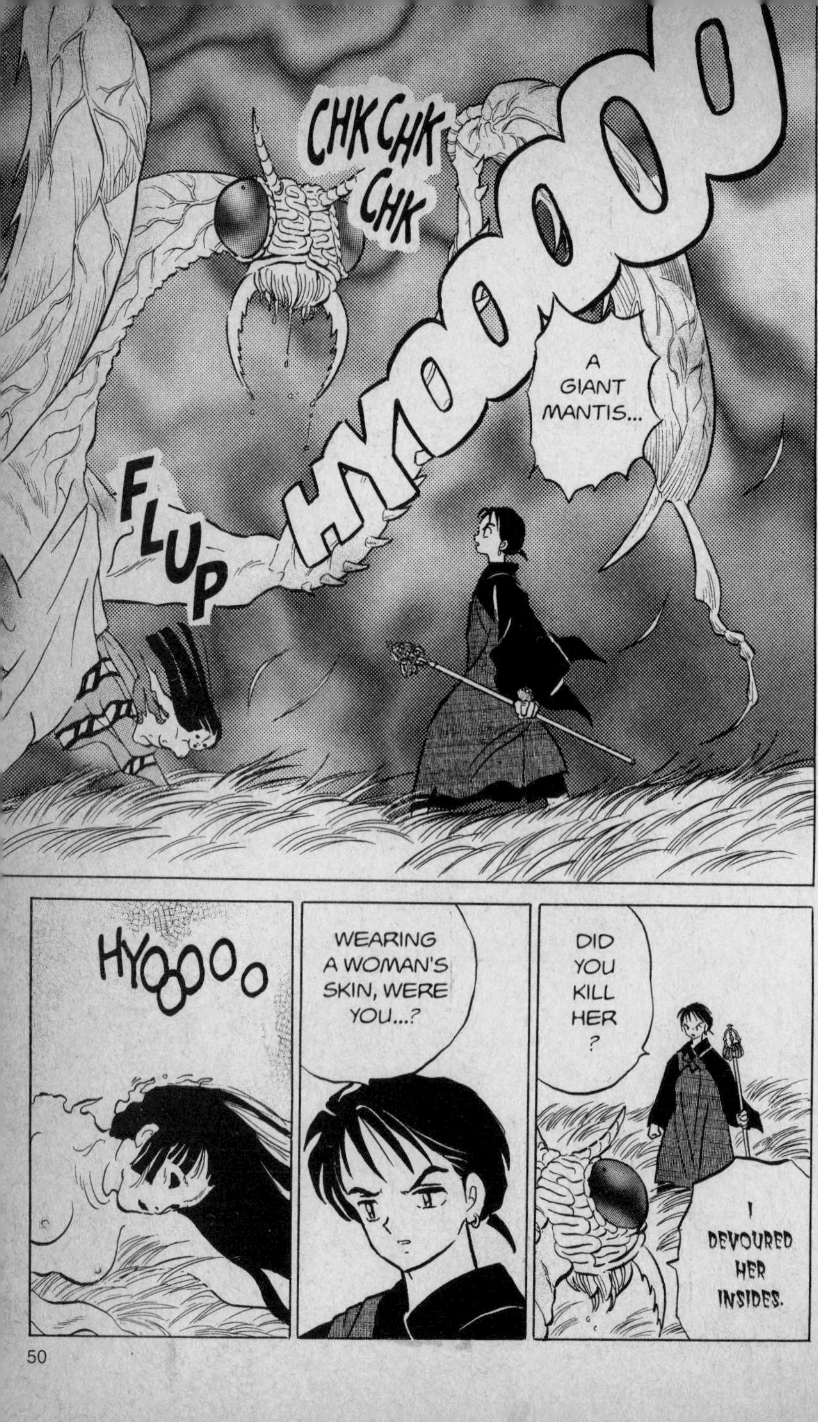
CHK CHK CHK
HYOOOOOO
A GIANT MANTIS...
FLUP
HYOOOOO
WEARING A WOMAN'S SKIN, WERE YOU...?
DID YOU KILL HER?
I DEVOURED HER INSIDES.

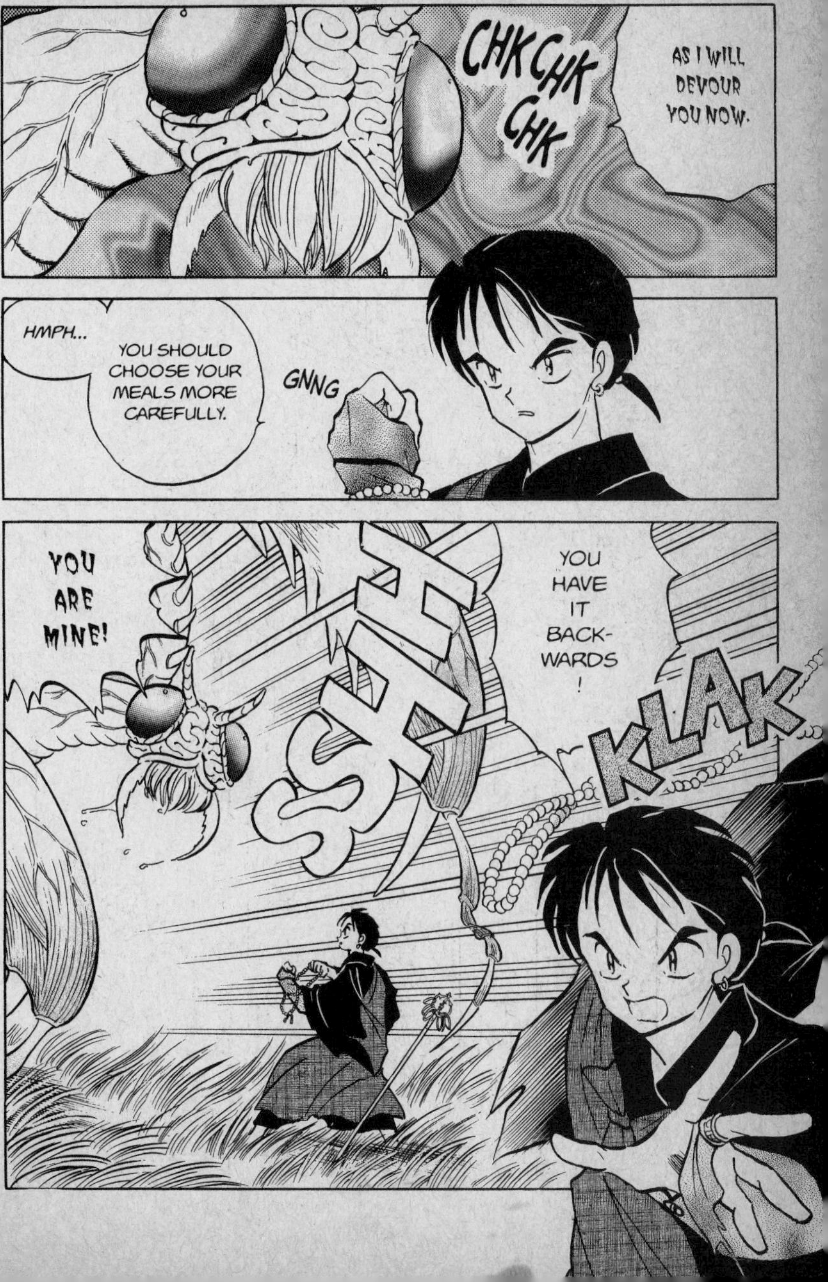
CHK CHK CHK
AS I WILL DEVOUR YOU NOW.
HMPH...
YOU SHOULD CHOOSE YOUR MEALS MORE CAREFULLY.
GNNG
YOU ARE MINE!
SHH
YOU HAVE IT BACK-WARDS!
KLAK

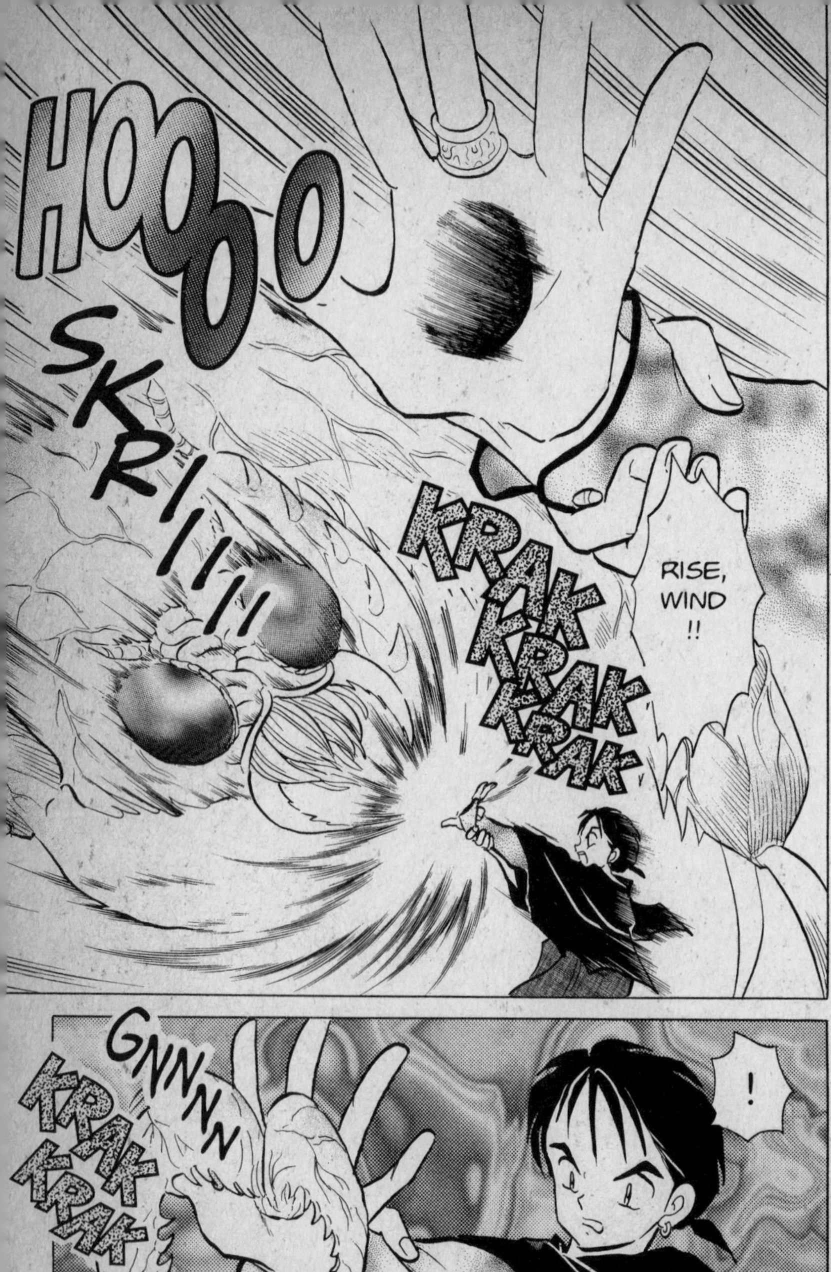
HOOOOO
SKRIIIIII
KRAK KRAK KRAK KRAK
RISE, WIND !!
GNNNNN
KRAK KRAK KRAK
!

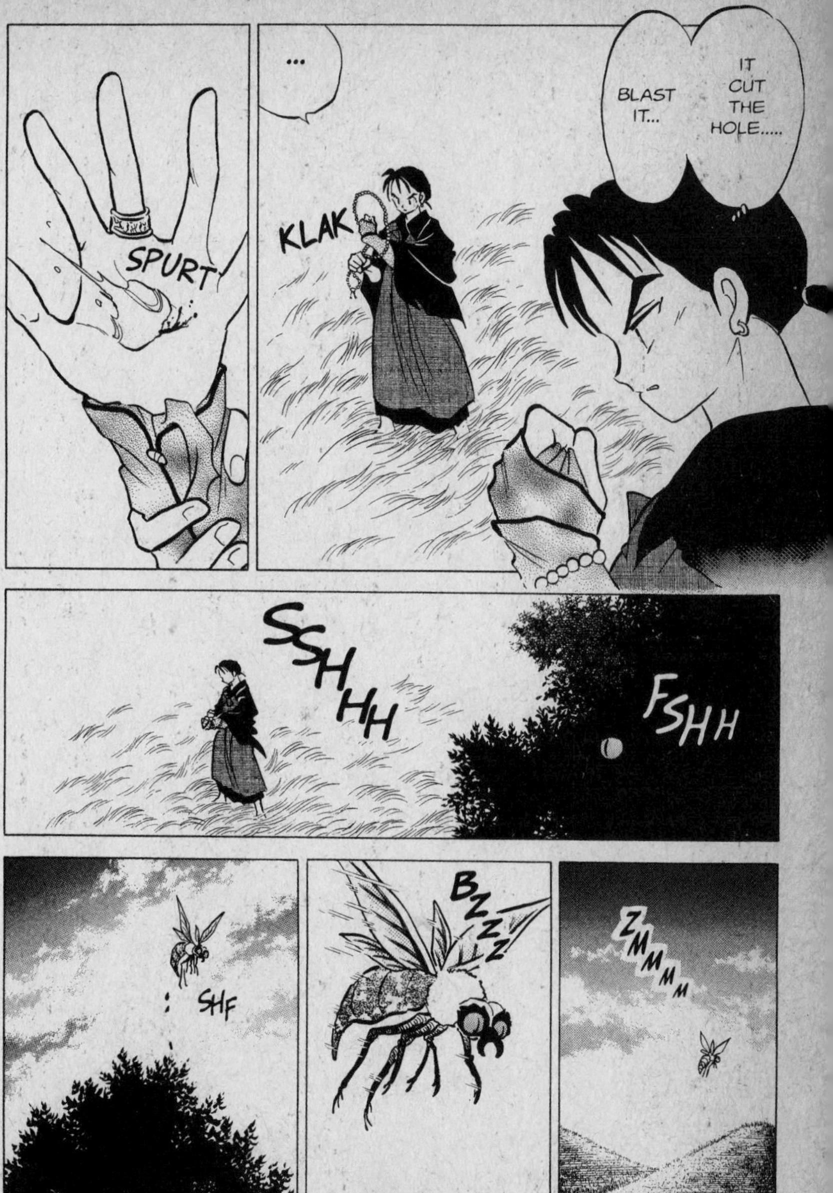
SPURT
...
KLAK
BLAST IT...
IT CUT THE HOLE.....
SSHHHH
FSHH
SHF
BZZZ
ZMMMM

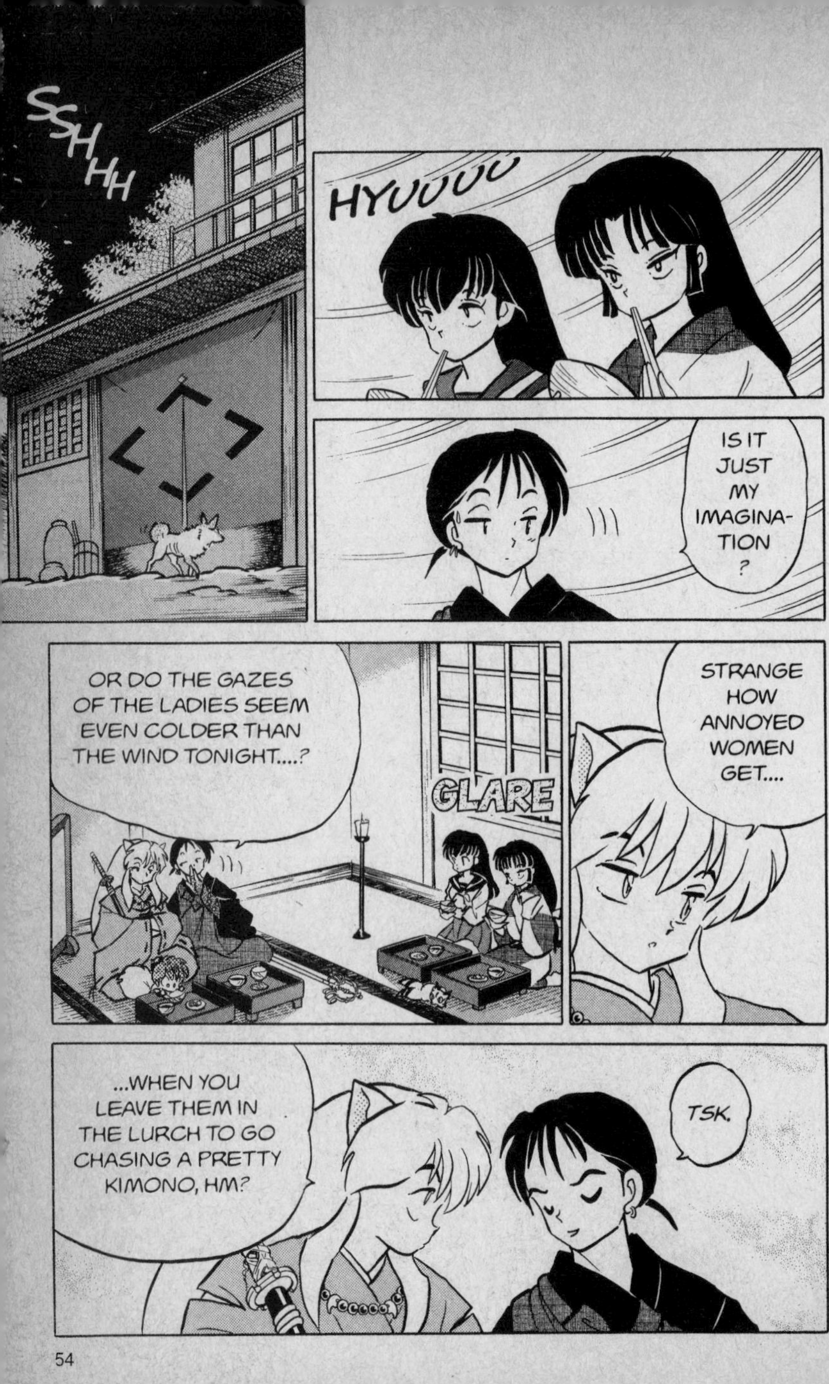
SSHHH
HYUUUU
IS IT JUST MY IMAGINATION-TION ?
OR DO THE GAZES OF THE LADIES SEEM EVEN COLDER THAN THE WIND TONIGHT....?
GLARE
STRANGE HOW ANNOYED WOMEN GET....
...WHEN YOU LEAVE THEM IN THE LURCH TO GO CHASING A PRETTY KIMONO, HM?
TSK.

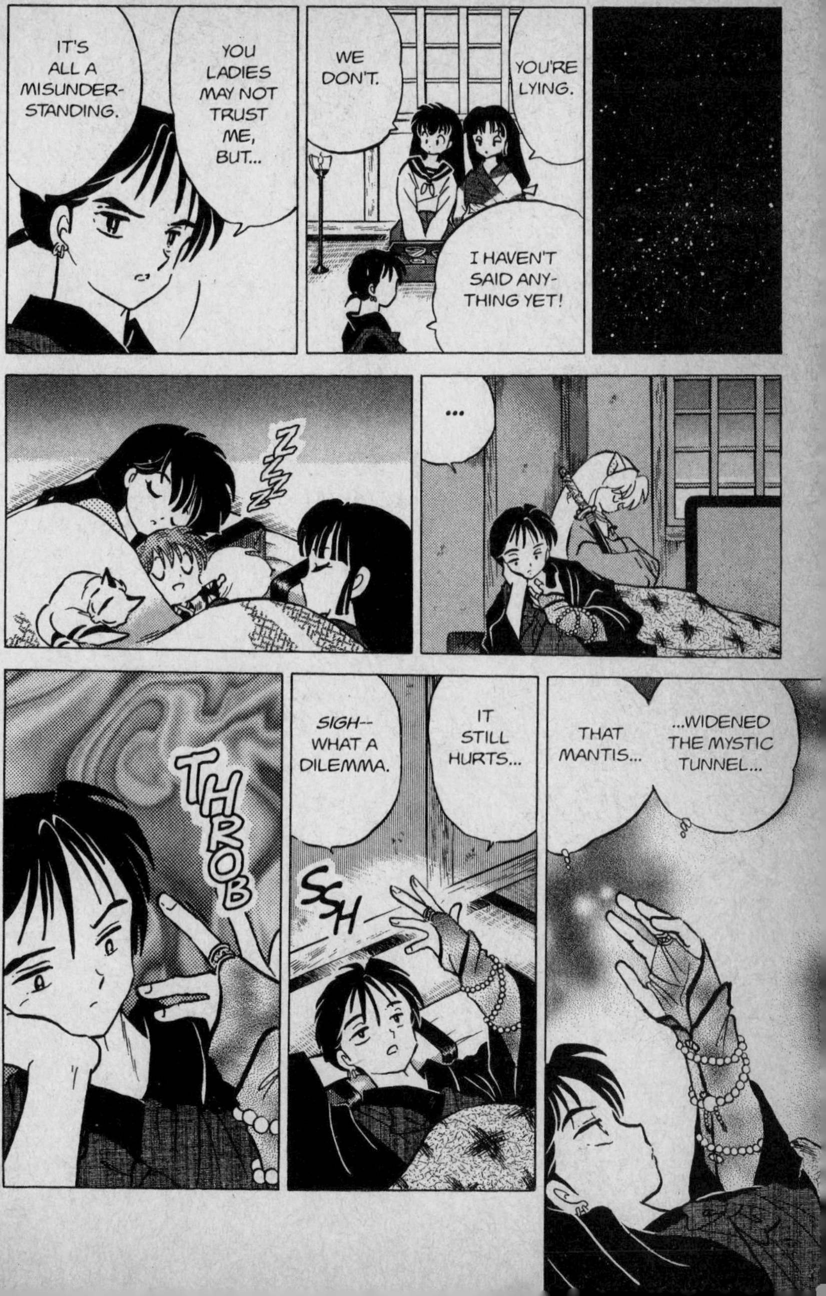
IT'S ALL A MISUNDER-STANDING.
YOU LADIES MAY NOT TRUST ME, BUT...
WE DON'T.
YOU'RE LYING.
I HAVEN'T SAID ANY-THING YET!
ZZZ
...
THROB
SIGH-- WHAT A DILEMMA.
SSH
IT STILL HURTS...
THAT MANTIS...
...WIDENED THE MYSTIC TUNNEL...

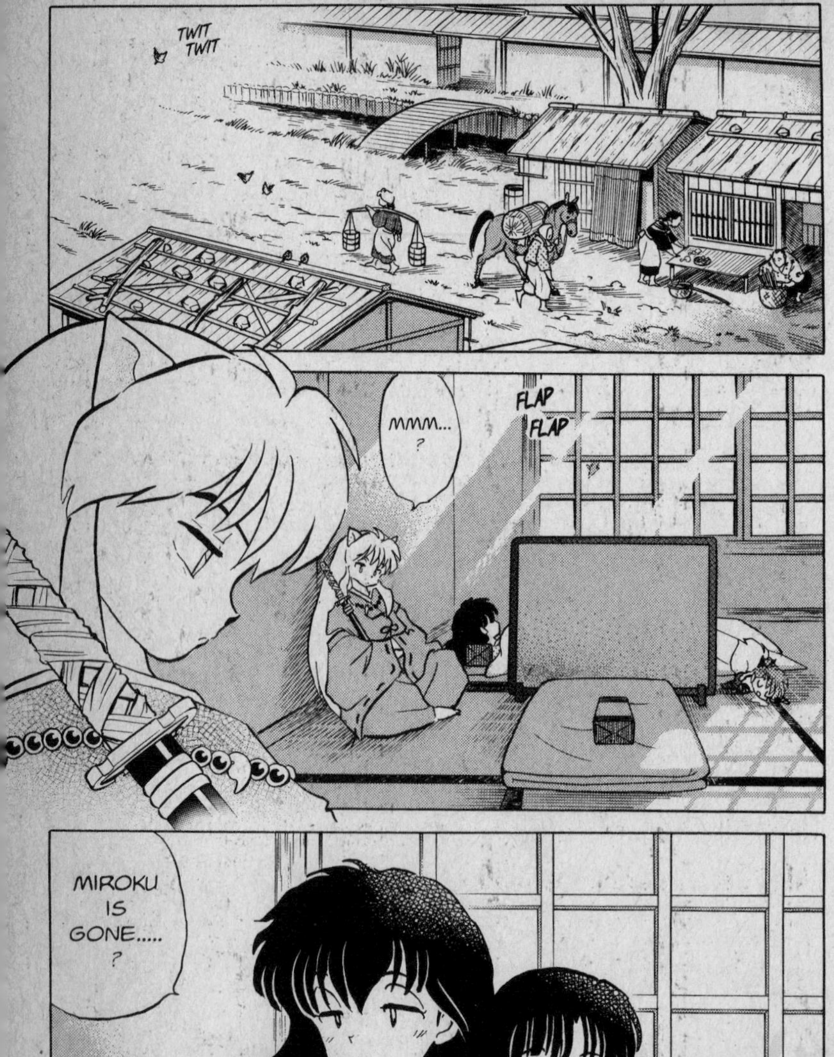
TWIT TWIT
MMM... ?
FLAP FLAP
MIROKU IS GONE..... ?

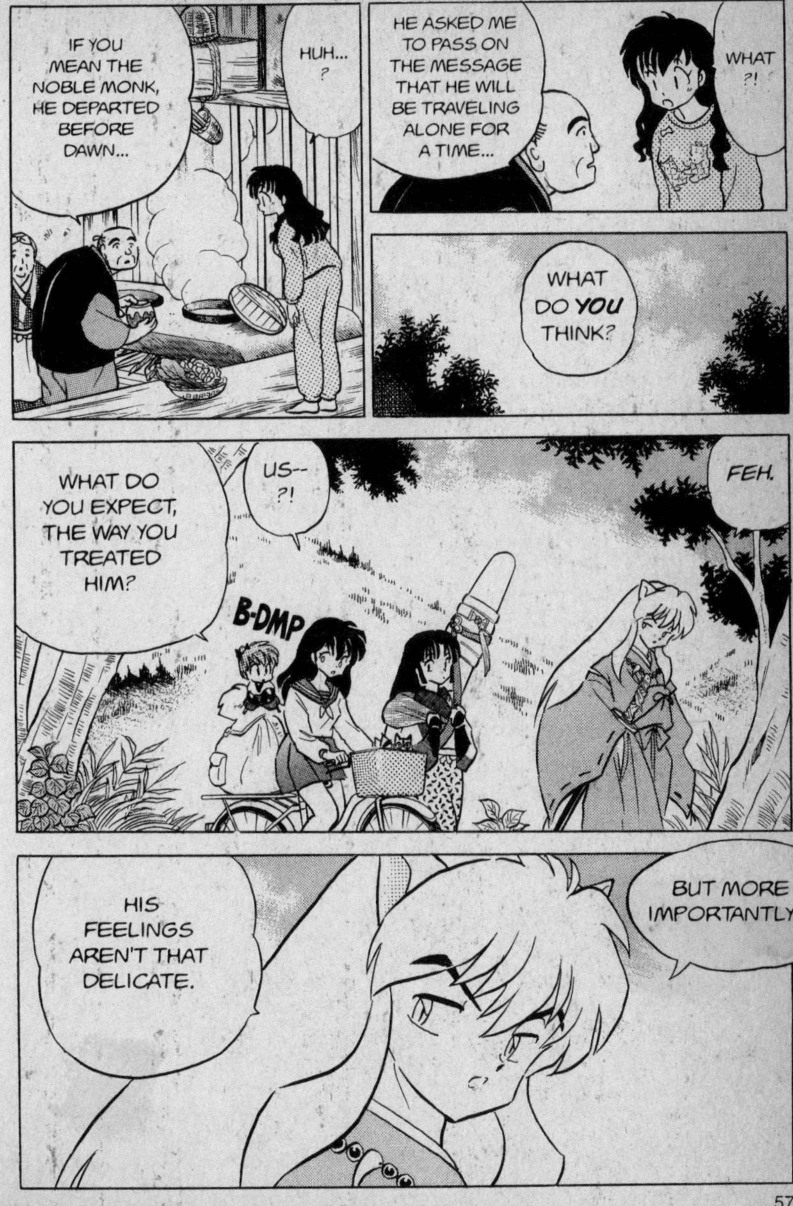
IF YOU MEAN THE NOBLE MONK, HE DEPARTED BEFORE DAWN...
HUH...?
HE ASKED ME TO PASS ON THE MESSAGE THAT HE WILL BE TRAVELING ALONE FOR A TIME...
WHAT?!
WHAT DO **YOU** THINK?
WHAT DO YOU EXPECT, THE WAY YOU TREATED HIM?
US--?!
B-DMP
FEH.
HIS FEELINGS AREN'T THAT DELICATE.
BUT MORE IMPORTANTLY....

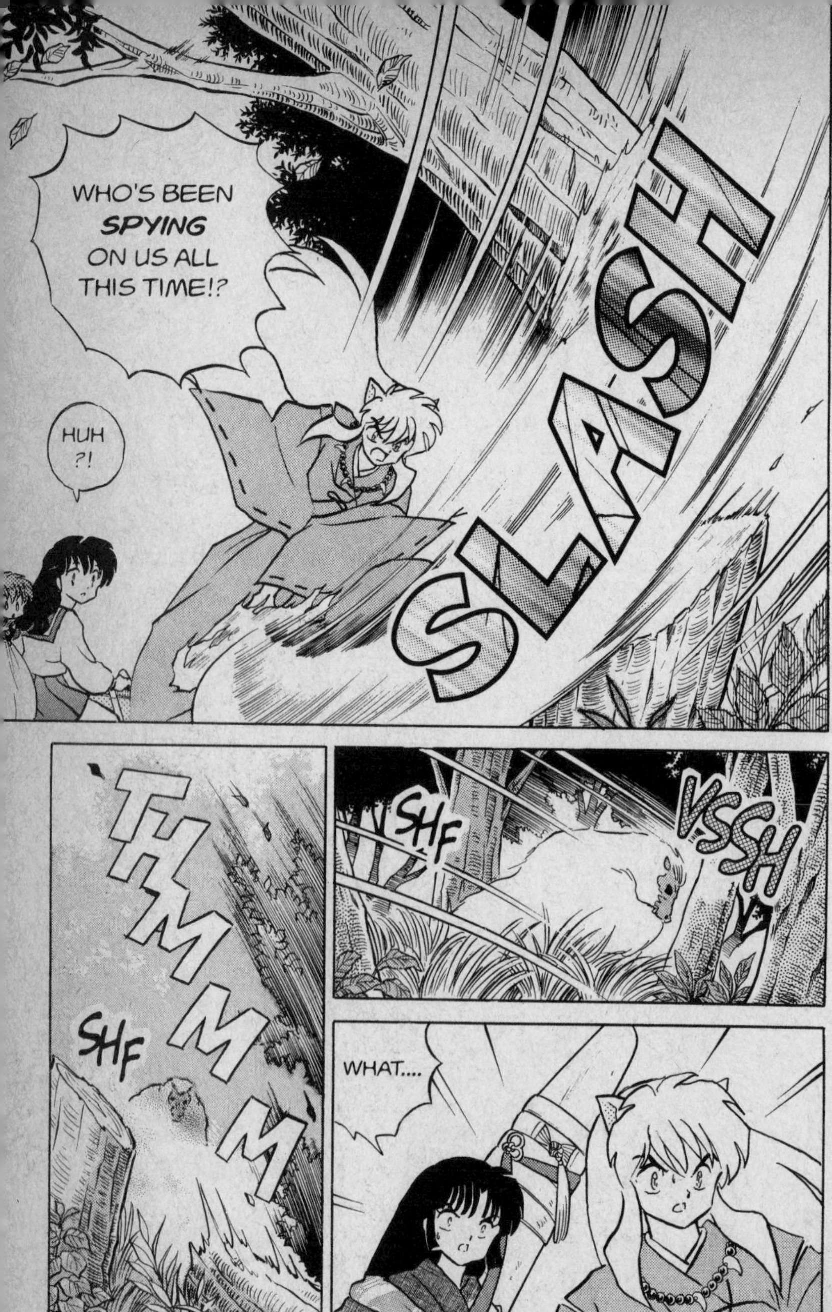
WHO'S BEEN **SPYING** ON US ALL THIS TIME!?
HUH ?!
SLASH
THMMMM
SHF
SHF
VSSH
WHAT....

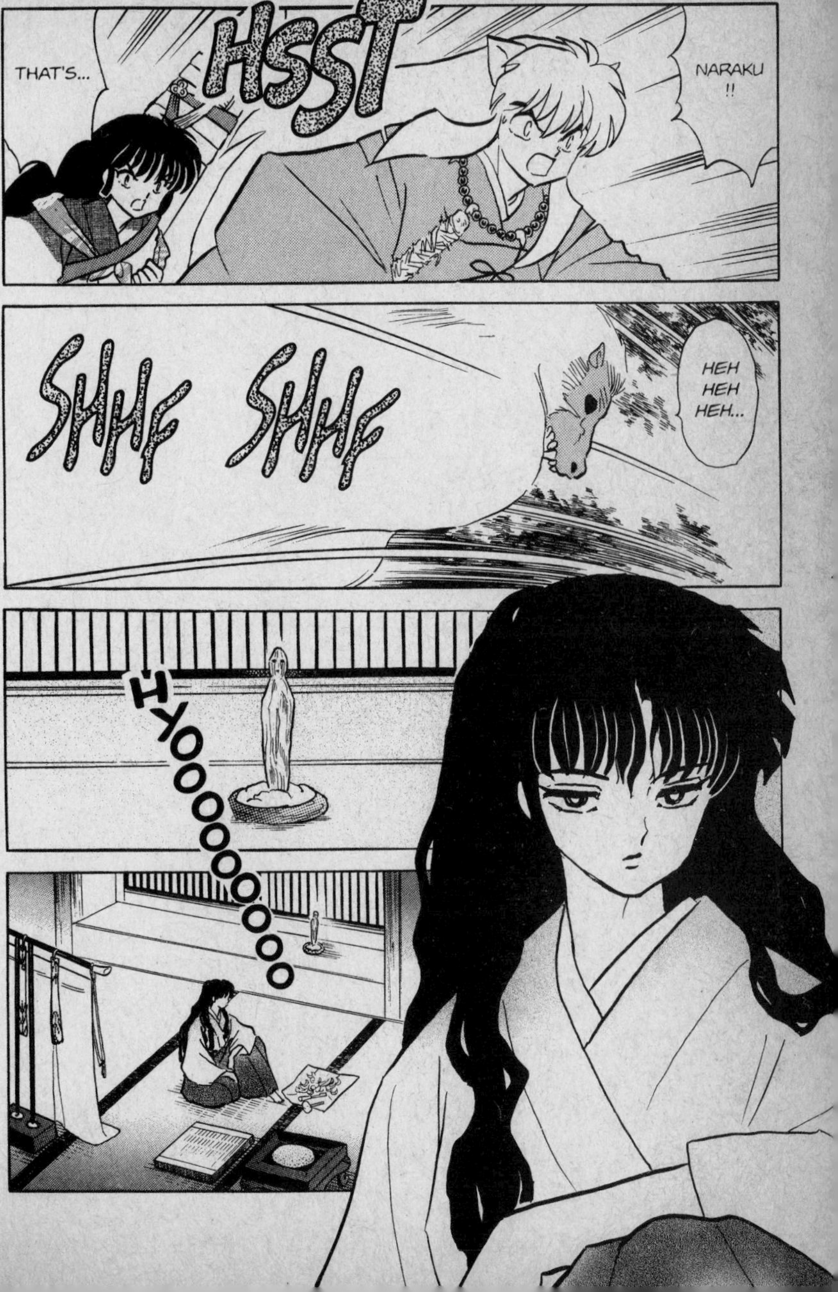
NARAKU !!
HSST
THAT'S...
HEH HEH HEH...
SHHF SHHF
HYOOOOOOOOOOOO

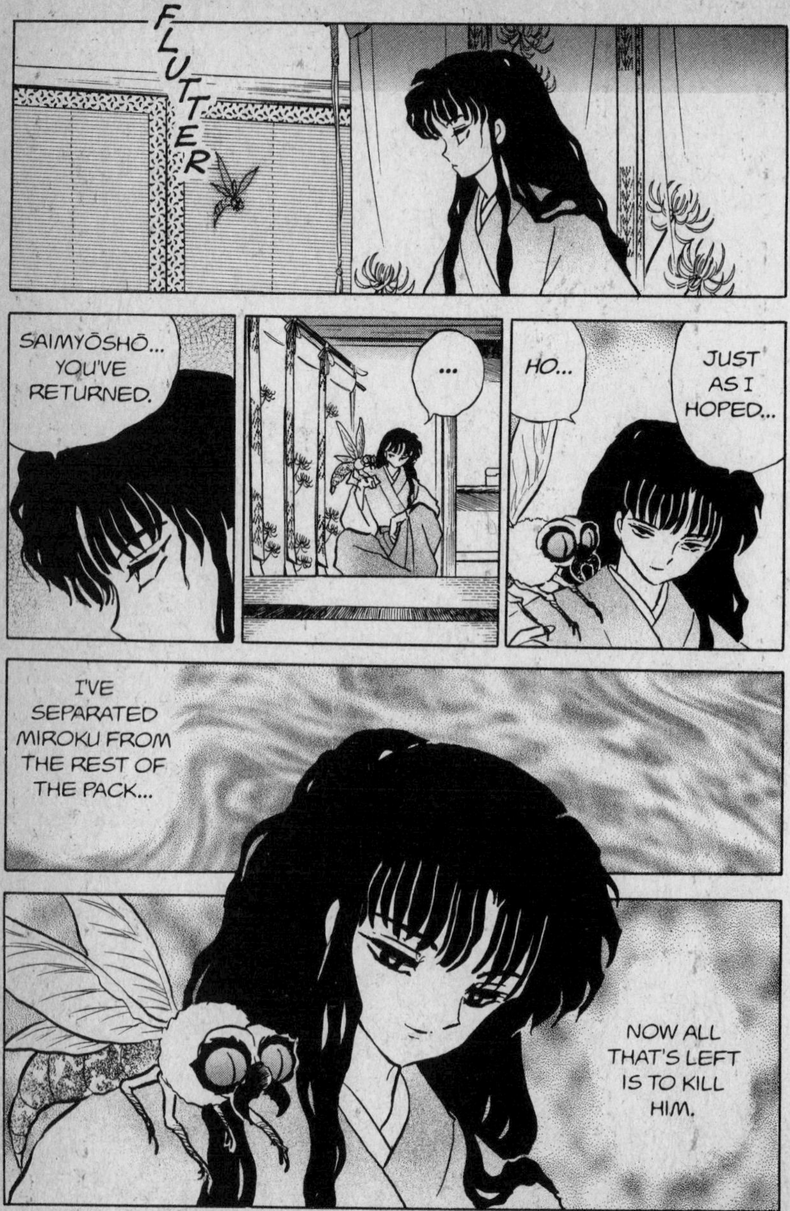
FLUTTER
SAIMYŌSHŌ... YOU'VE RETURNED.
...
HO...
JUST AS I HOPED...
I'VE SEPARATED MIROKU FROM THE REST OF THE PACK...
NOW ALL THAT'S LEFT IS TO KILL HIM.

SCROLL FOUR

THE TEMPLE OF INNOCENCE

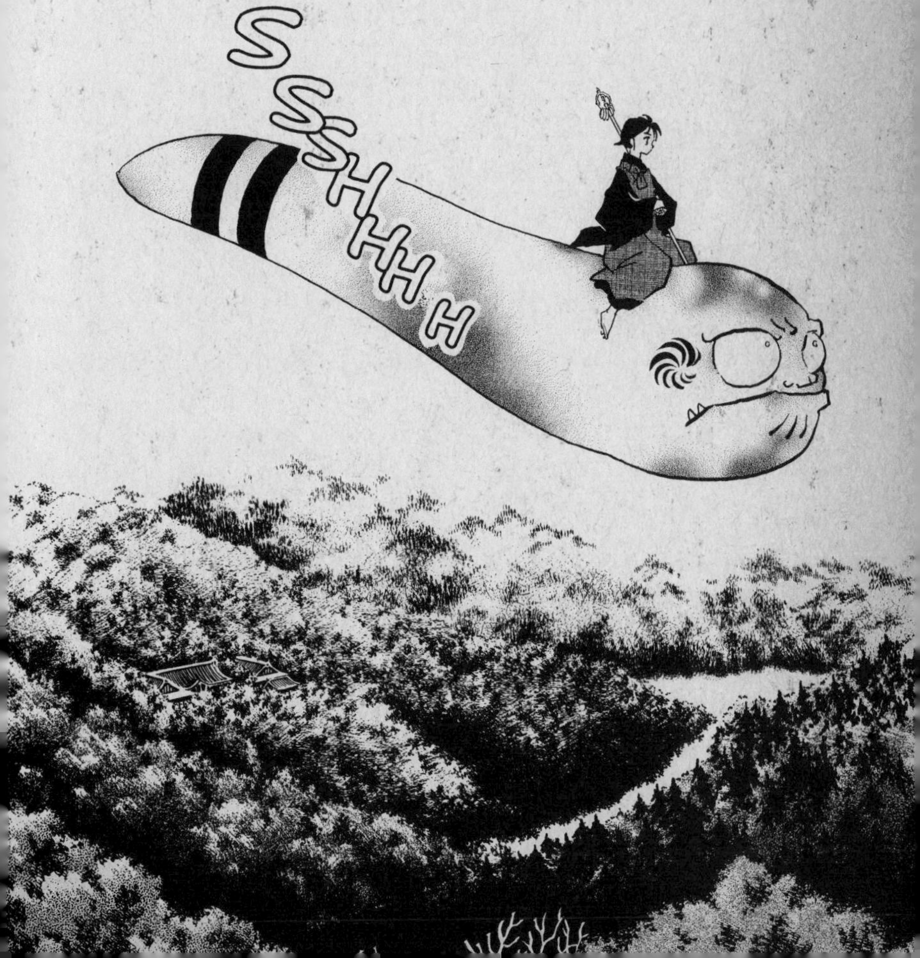
SSSHHHH

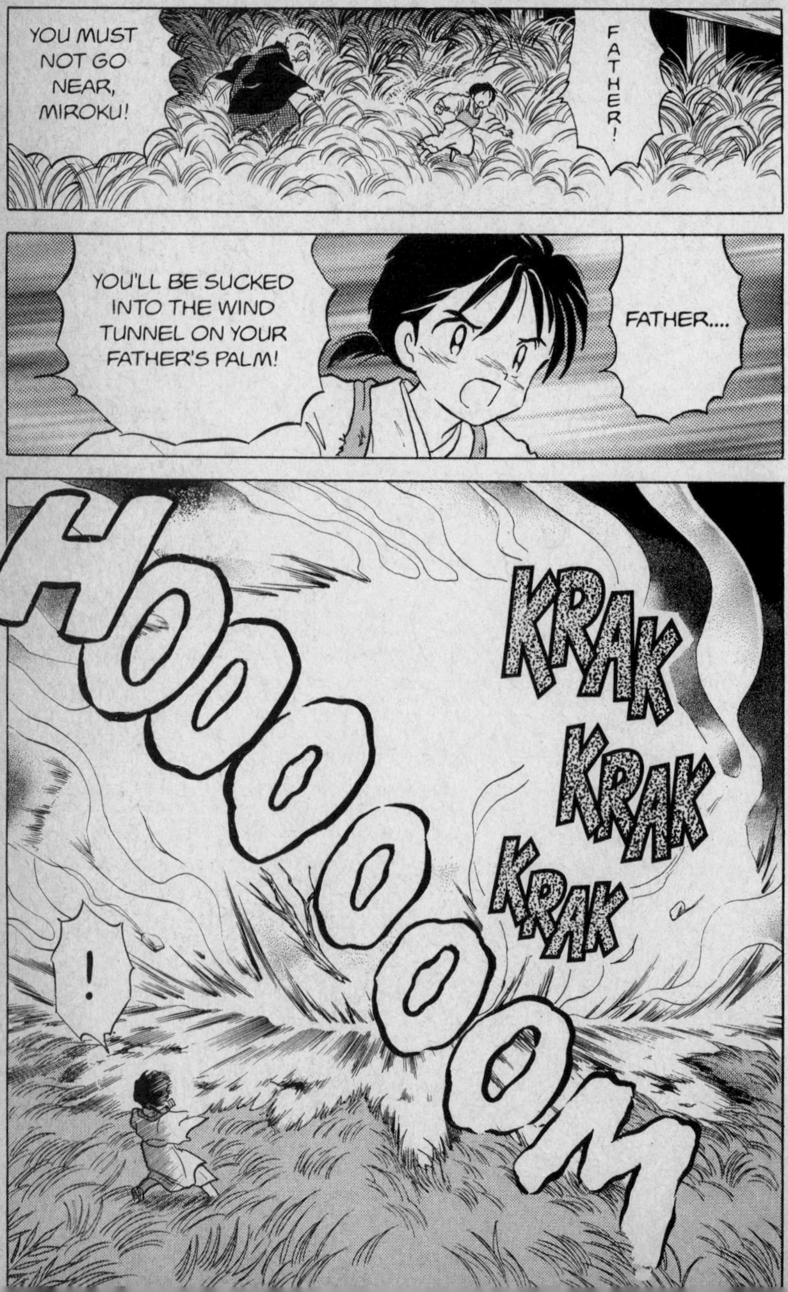
YOU MUST NOT GO NEAR, MIROKU!
FATHER!
YOU'LL BE SUCKED INTO THE WIND TUNNEL ON YOUR FATHER'S PALM!
FATHER....
HOOOOOOOM
KRAK KRAK KRAK
!

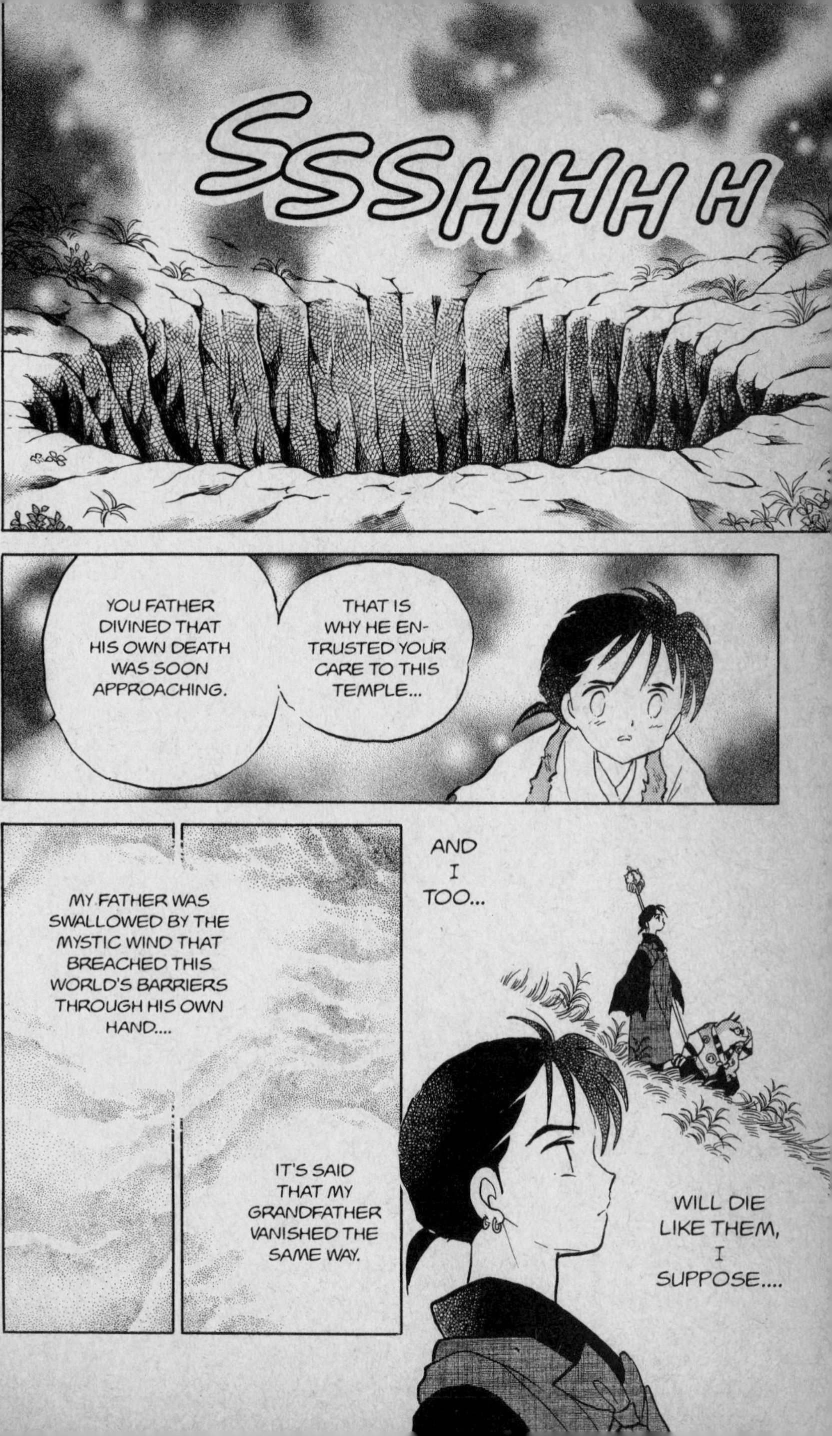
SSSHHH H
YOU FATHER DIVINED THAT HIS OWN DEATH WAS SOON APPROACHING.
THAT IS WHY HE EN-TRUSTED YOUR CARE TO THIS TEMPLE...
MY FATHER WAS SWALLOWED BY THE MYSTIC WIND THAT BREACHED THIS WORLD'S BARRIERS THROUGH HIS OWN HAND....
IT'S SAID THAT MY GRANDFATHER VANISHED THE SAME WAY.
AND I TOO...
WILL DIE LIKE THEM, I SUPPOSE....

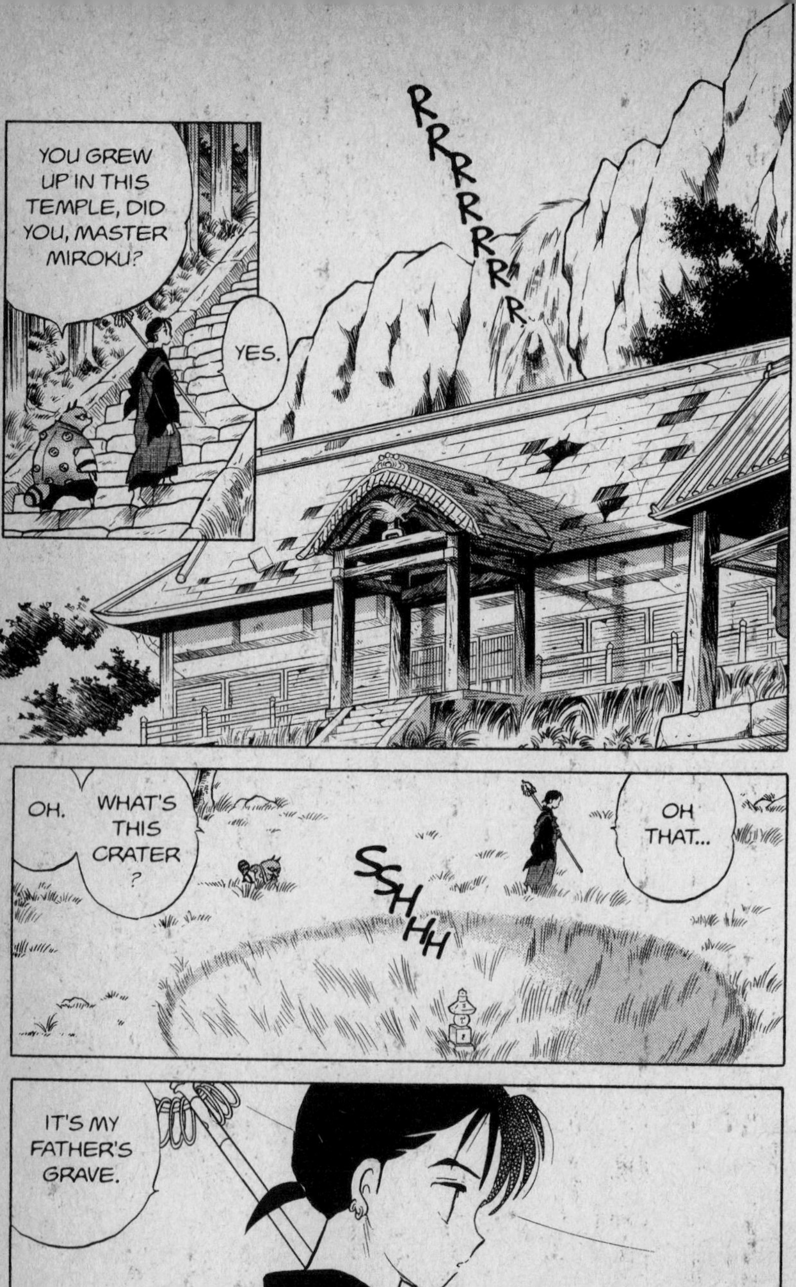
YOU GREW UP IN THIS TEMPLE, DID YOU, MASTER MIROKU?
YES.
RRRRRRRR.
OH.
WHAT'S THIS CRATER?
SSHHH
OH THAT...
IT'S MY FATHER'S GRAVE.

MASTER MUSHIN, ARE YOU IN?

MASTER MUSHIN--

IT IS I, MIROKU.

TP...

SHNORR

SCRATCH SCRATCH

Z Z Z

SIGH.

YOU'VE DRUNK YOURSELF INTO A STUPOR, AGAIN.

WAKE UP, YOU DEPRAVED OLD MONK!

BOOT

KLANG

SNORT.

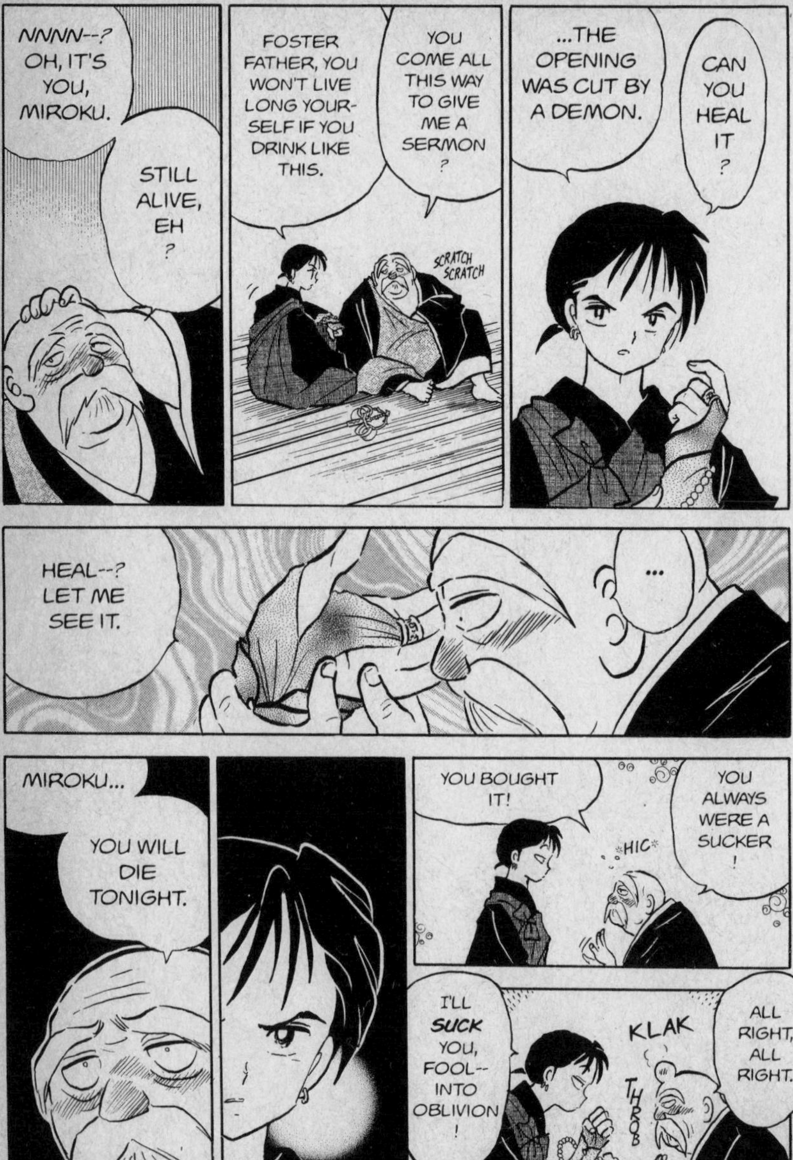
NNNN--? OH, IT'S YOU, MIROKU.
STILL ALIVE, EH?
FOSTER FATHER, YOU WON'T LIVE LONG YOURSELF IF YOU DRINK LIKE THIS.
YOU COME ALL THIS WAY TO GIVE ME A SERMON?
SCRATCH SCRATCH
...THE OPENING WAS CUT BY A DEMON.
CAN YOU HEAL IT?
HEAL--? LET ME SEE IT.
...
MIROKU...
YOU WILL DIE TONIGHT.
YOU BOUGHT IT!
YOU ALWAYS WERE A SUCKER!
HIC
I'LL **SUCK** YOU, FOOL-- INTO OBLIVION!
KLAK
THROB
ALL RIGHT, ALL RIGHT.

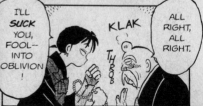

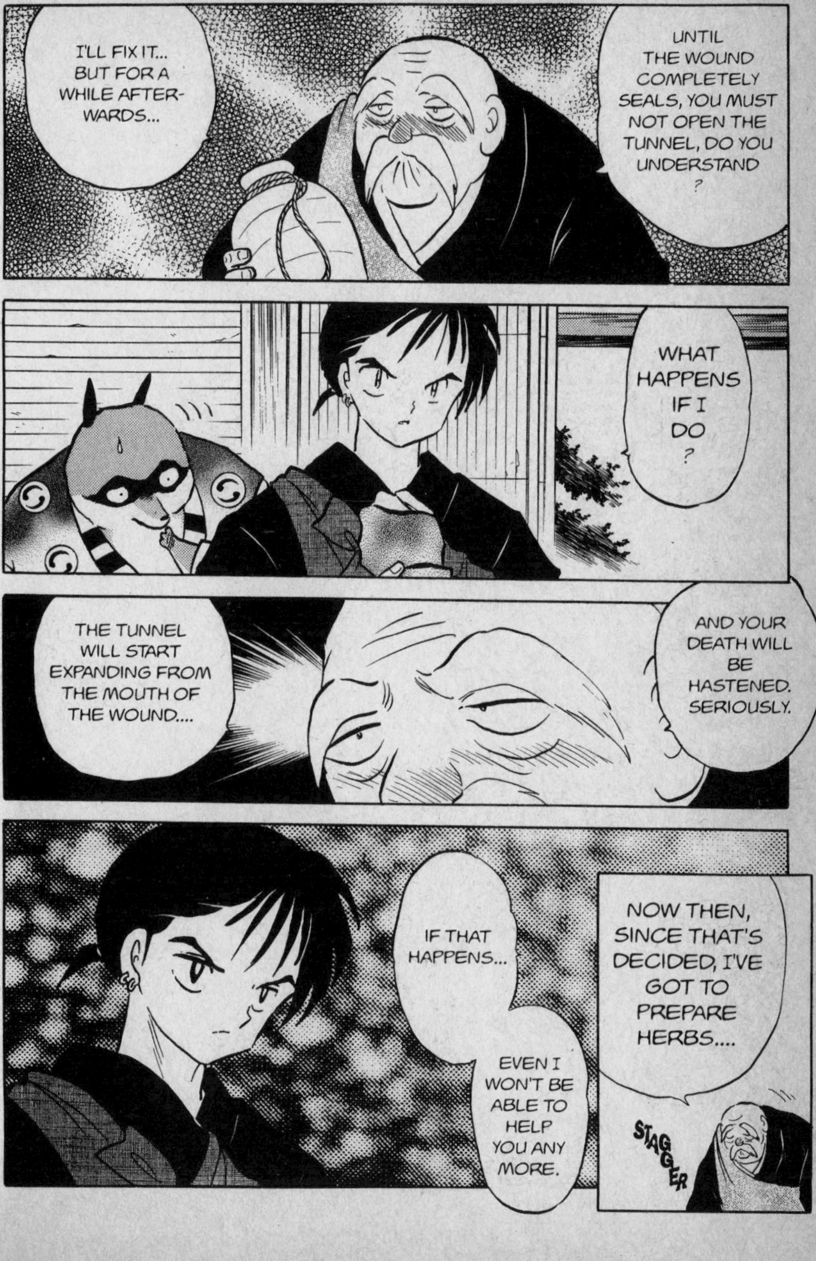
I'LL FIX IT... BUT FOR A WHILE AFTER-WARDS...
UNTIL THE WOUND COMPLETELY SEALS, YOU MUST NOT OPEN THE TUNNEL, DO YOU UNDERSTAND?
WHAT HAPPENS IF I DO?
THE TUNNEL WILL START EXPANDING FROM THE MOUTH OF THE WOUND....
AND YOUR DEATH WILL BE HASTENED. SERIOUSLY.
IF THAT HAPPENS...
EVEN I WON'T BE ABLE TO HELP YOU ANY MORE.
NOW THEN, SINCE THAT'S DECIDED, I'VE GOT TO PREPARE HERBS....
STAGGER

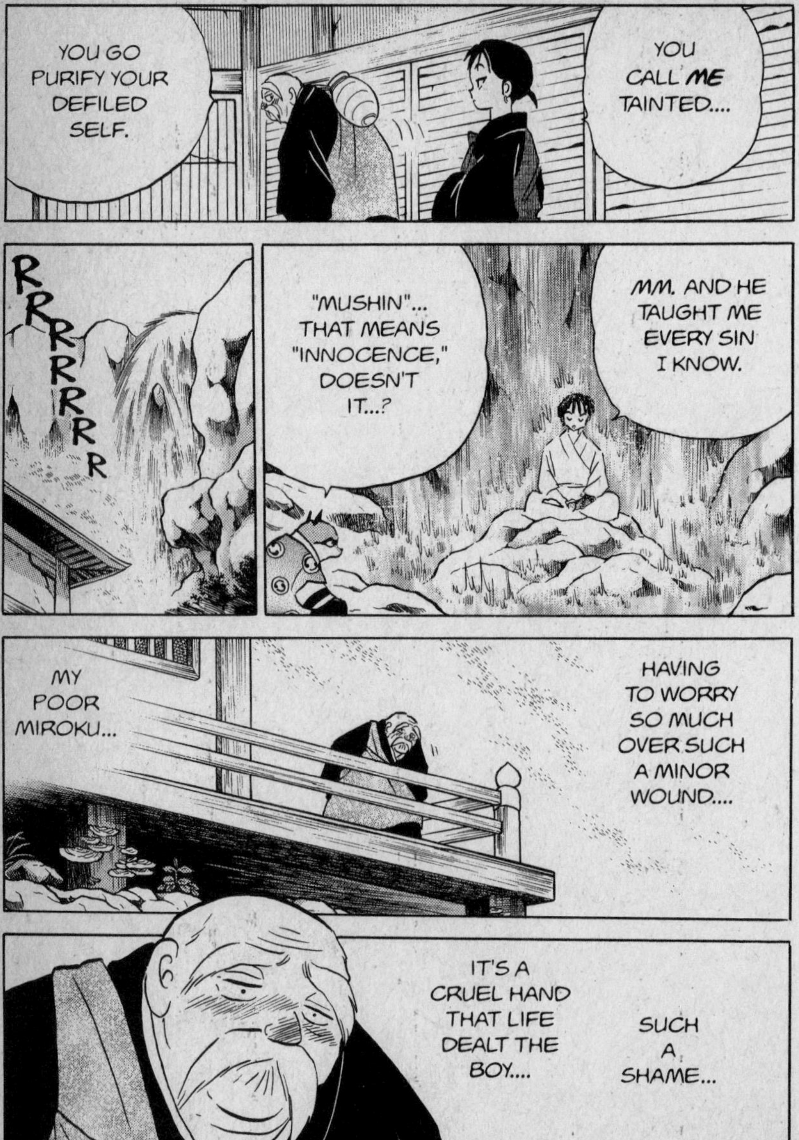
YOU GO PURIFY YOUR DEFILED SELF.
YOU CALL *ME* TAINTED....
RRRRRRRR
"MUSHIN"... THAT MEANS "INNOCENCE," DOESN'T IT...?
MM. AND HE TAUGHT ME EVERY SIN I KNOW.
MY POOR MIROKU...
HAVING TO WORRY SO MUCH OVER SUCH A MINOR WOUND....
IT'S A CRUEL HAND THAT LIFE DEALT THE BOY....
SUCH A SHAME...

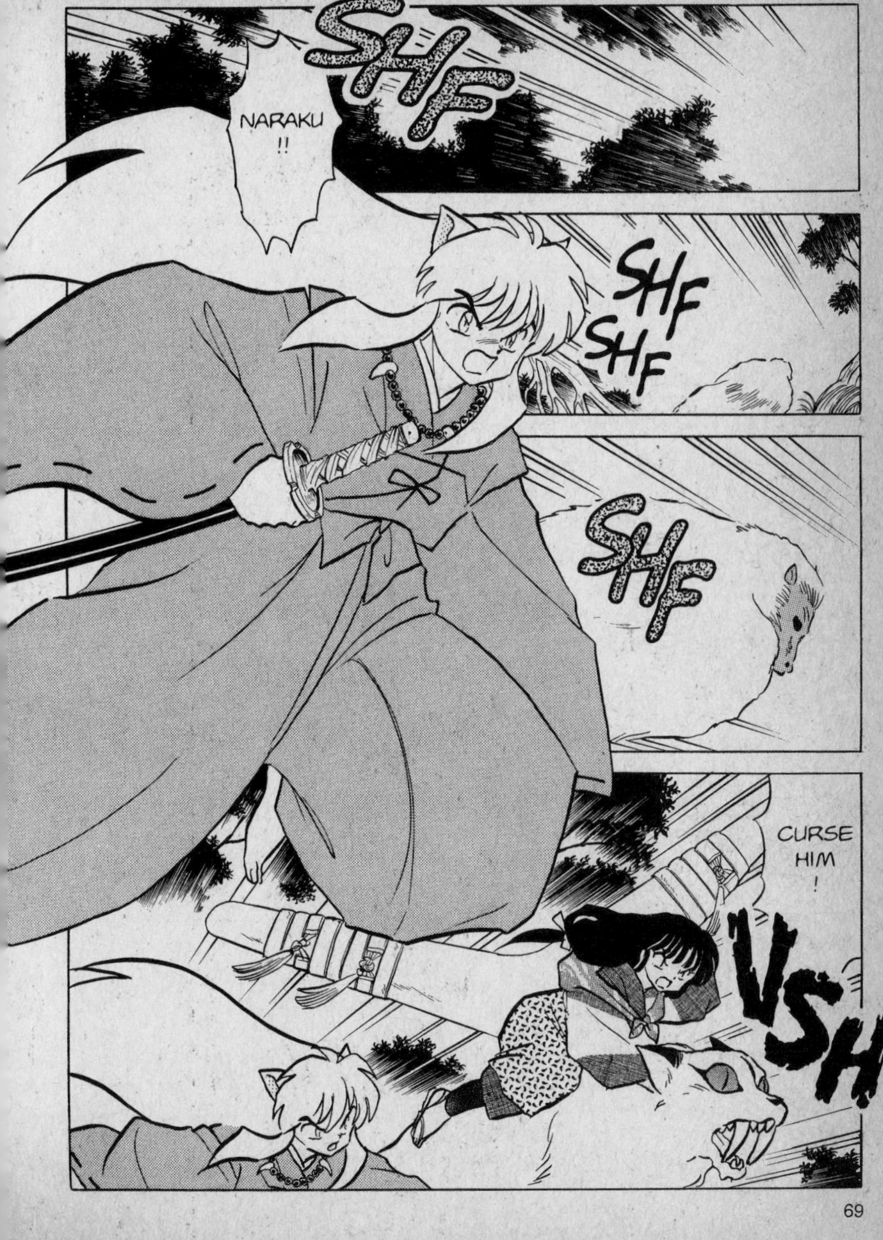
SHF
NARAKU !!
SHF SHF SHF
SHF
CURSE HIM !
VSH

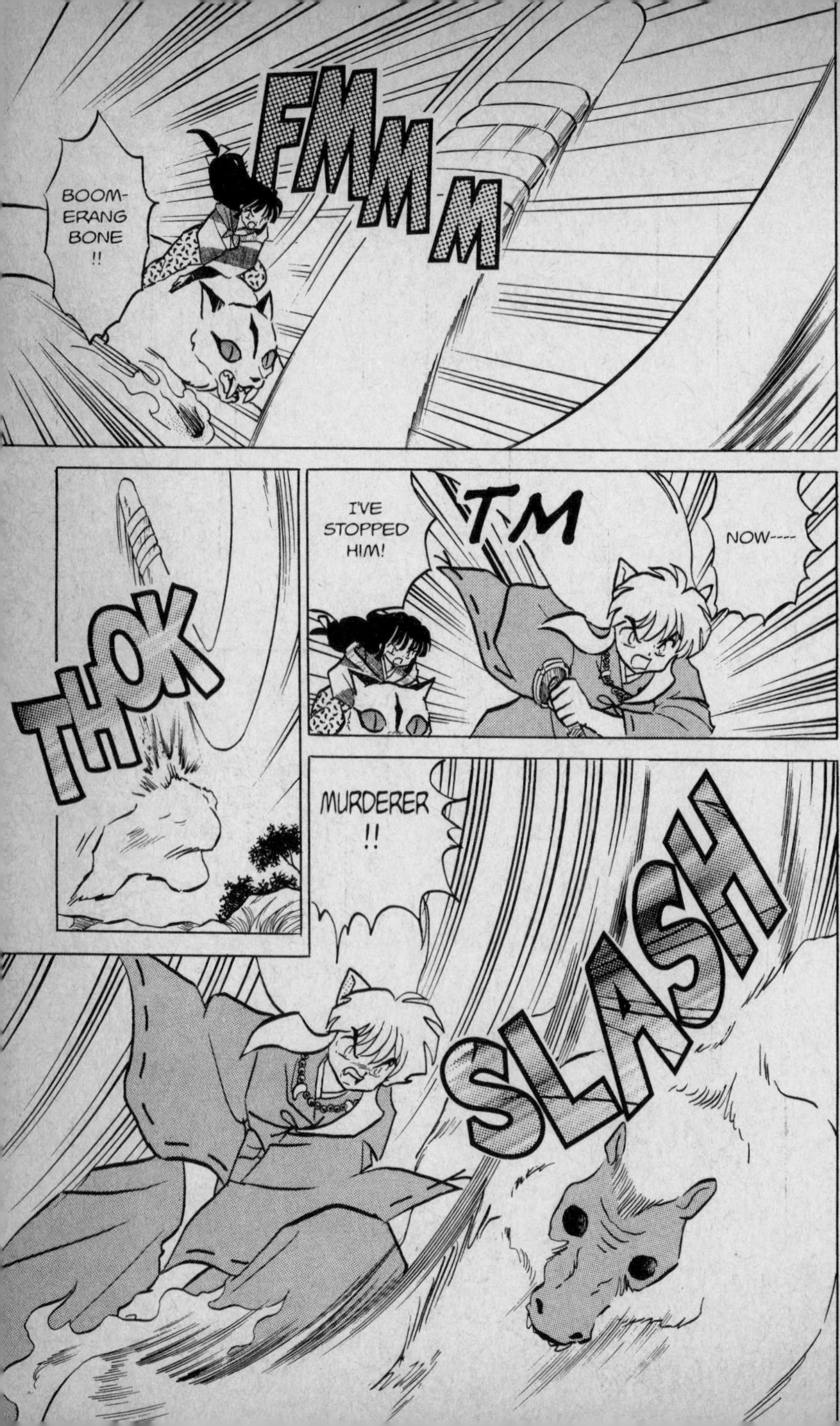
BOOM-
ERANG
BONE
!!
FMMMM
THOK
I'VE STOPPED HIM!
TM
NOW----
MURDERER !!
SLASH

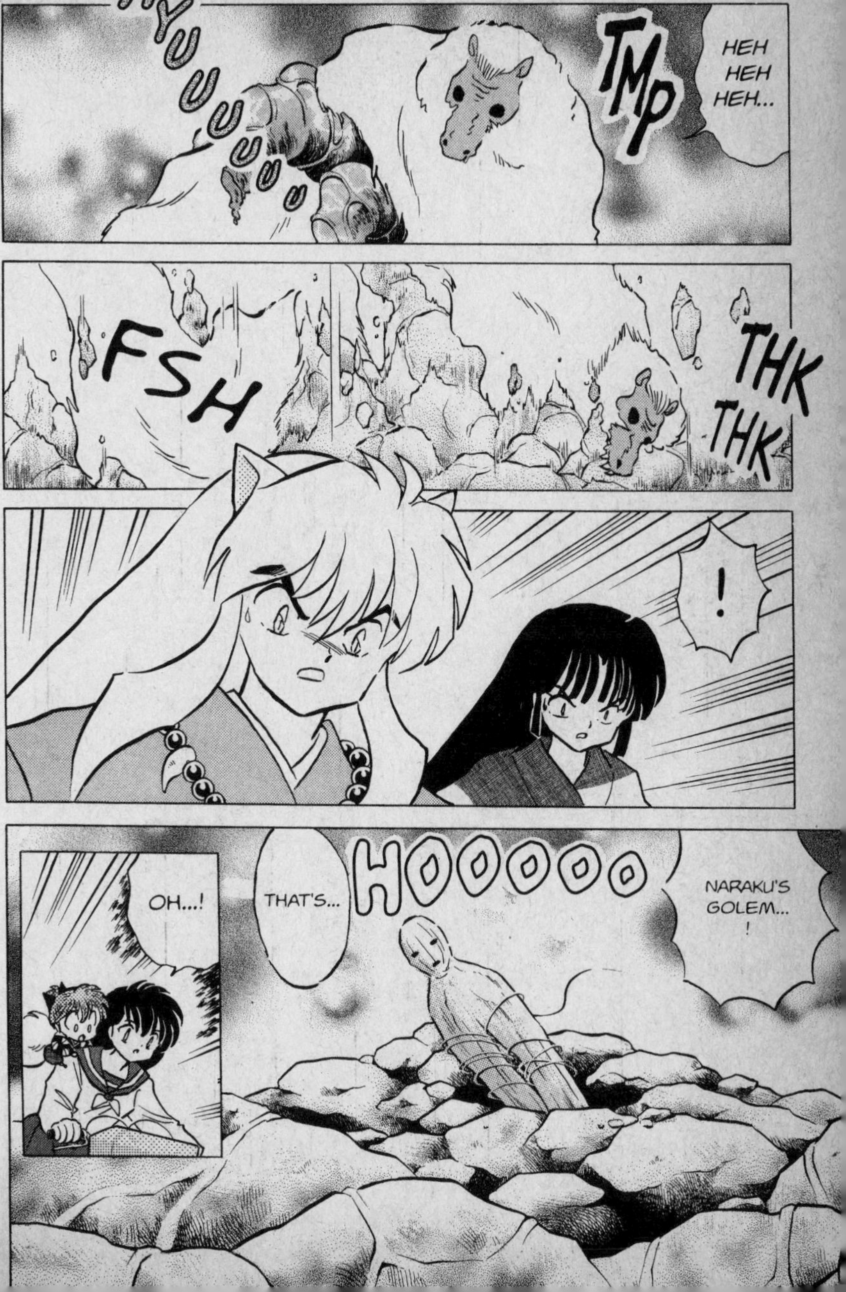
HYUUUUUUU
TMP
HEH HEH HEH...
FSH
THK THK
!
OH...!
THAT'S...
HOOOOO
NARAKU'S GOLEM... !

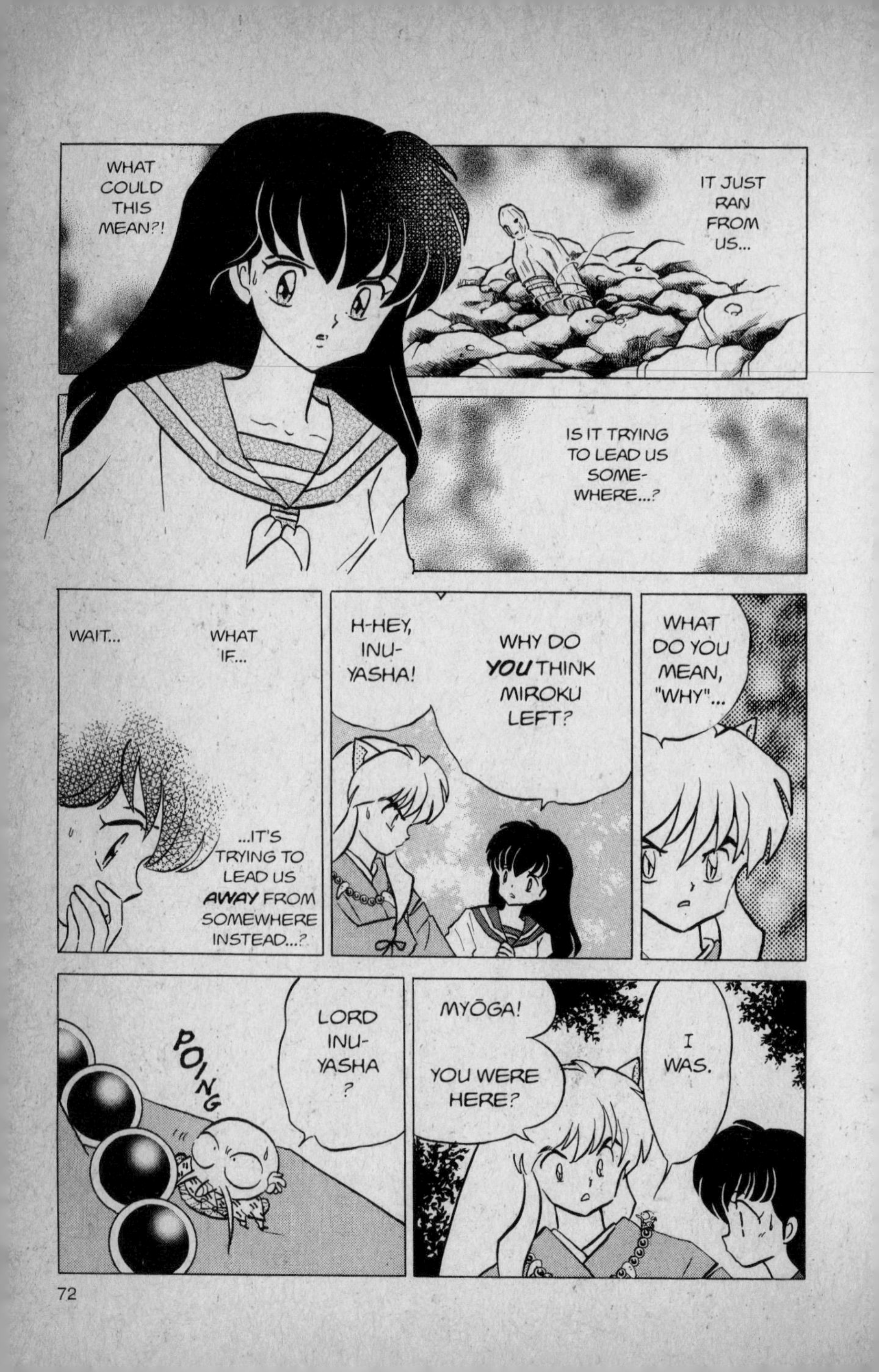
WHAT COULD THIS MEAN?!
IT JUST RAN FROM US...
IS IT TRYING TO LEAD US SOME-WHERE...?
WAIT...
WHAT IF...
...IT'S TRYING TO LEAD US AWAY FROM SOMEWHERE INSTEAD...?
H-HEY, INU-YASHA!
WHY DO YOU THINK MIROKU LEFT?
WHAT DO YOU MEAN, "WHY"...
POING
LORD INU-YASHA?
MYŌGA!
YOU WERE HERE?
I WAS.

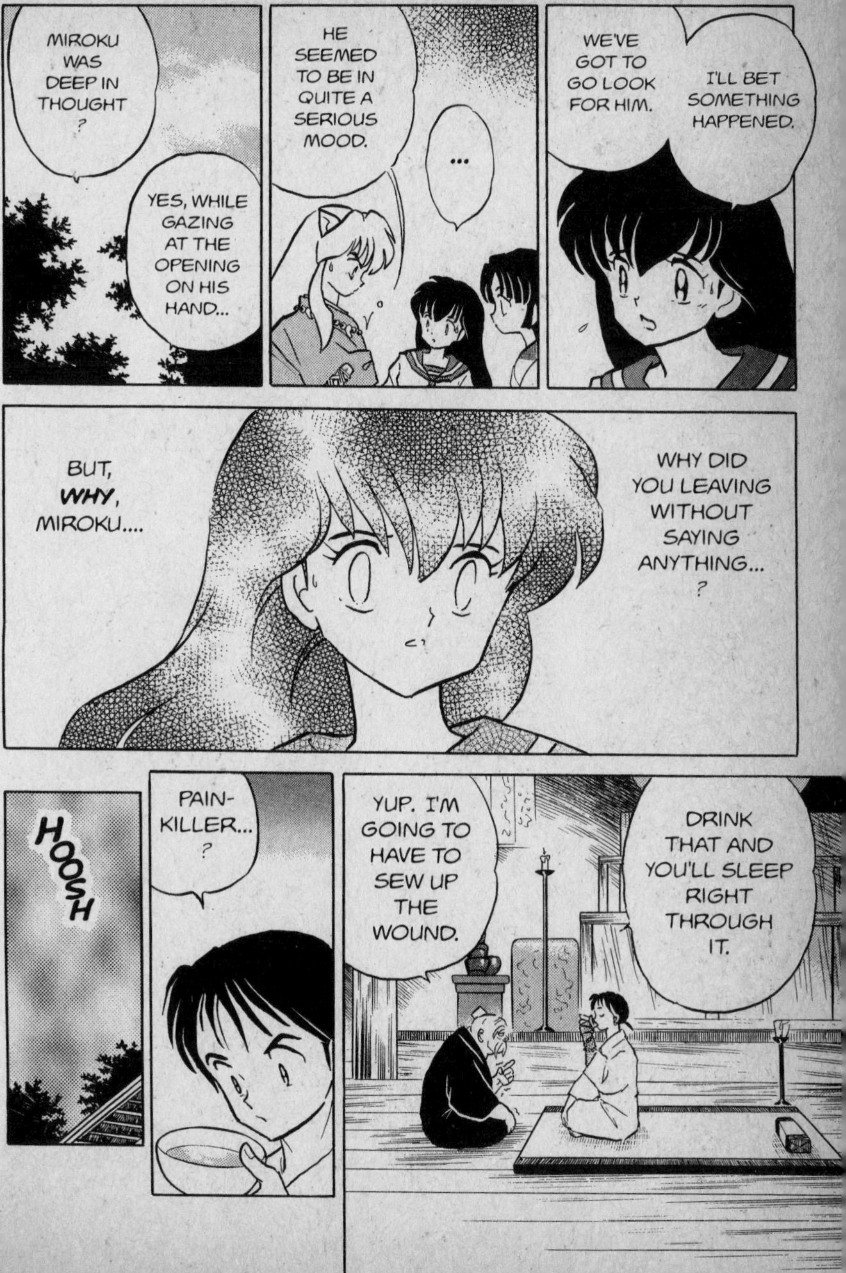
MIROKU WAS DEEP IN THOUGHT ?
YES, WHILE GAZING AT THE OPENING ON HIS HAND...
HE SEEMED TO BE IN QUITE A SERIOUS MOOD.
...
WE'VE GOT TO GO LOOK FOR HIM.
I'LL BET SOMETHING HAPPENED.
BUT, **WHY**, MIROKU....
WHY DID YOU LEAVING WITHOUT SAYING ANYTHING... ?
HOOSH
PAIN-KILLER... ?
YUP. I'M GOING TO HAVE TO SEW UP THE WOUND.
DRINK THAT AND YOU'LL SLEEP RIGHT THROUGH IT.

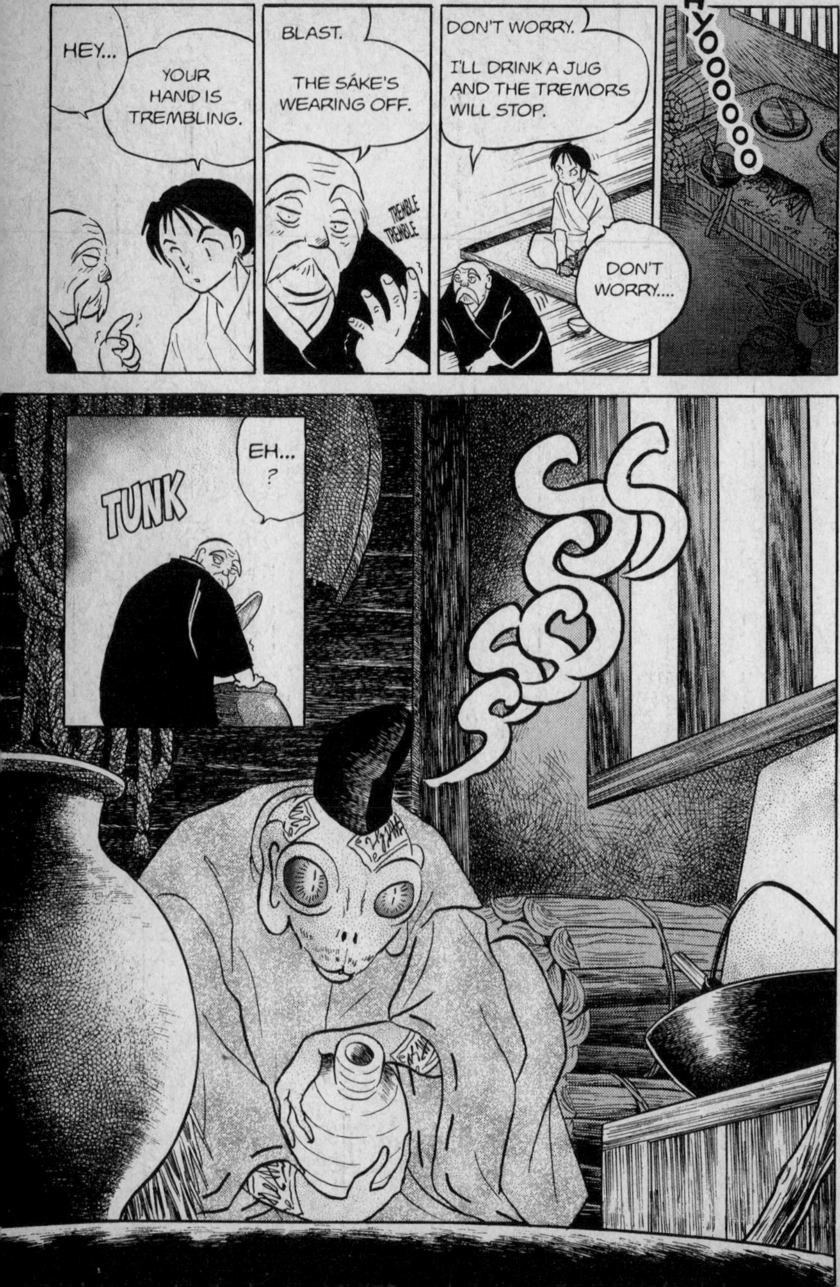
HEY...
YOUR HAND IS TREMBLING.
BLAST.
THE SÁKE'S WEARING OFF.
TREMBLE TREMBLE
DON'T WORRY.
I'LL DRINK A JUG AND THE TREMORS WILL STOP.
DON'T WORRY....
HYOOOOOO
TUNK
EH...?

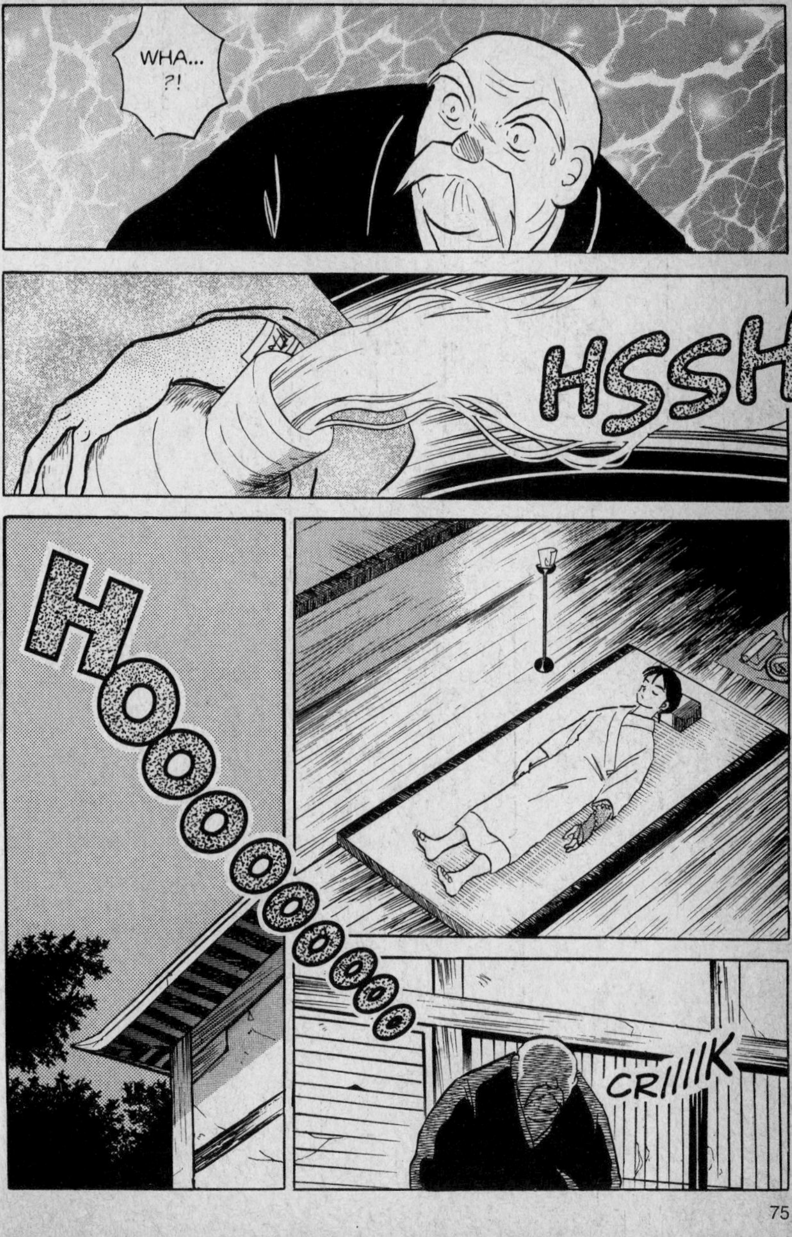
WHA... ?!
HSSH
HOOOOOOOOOO
CRIIIIK

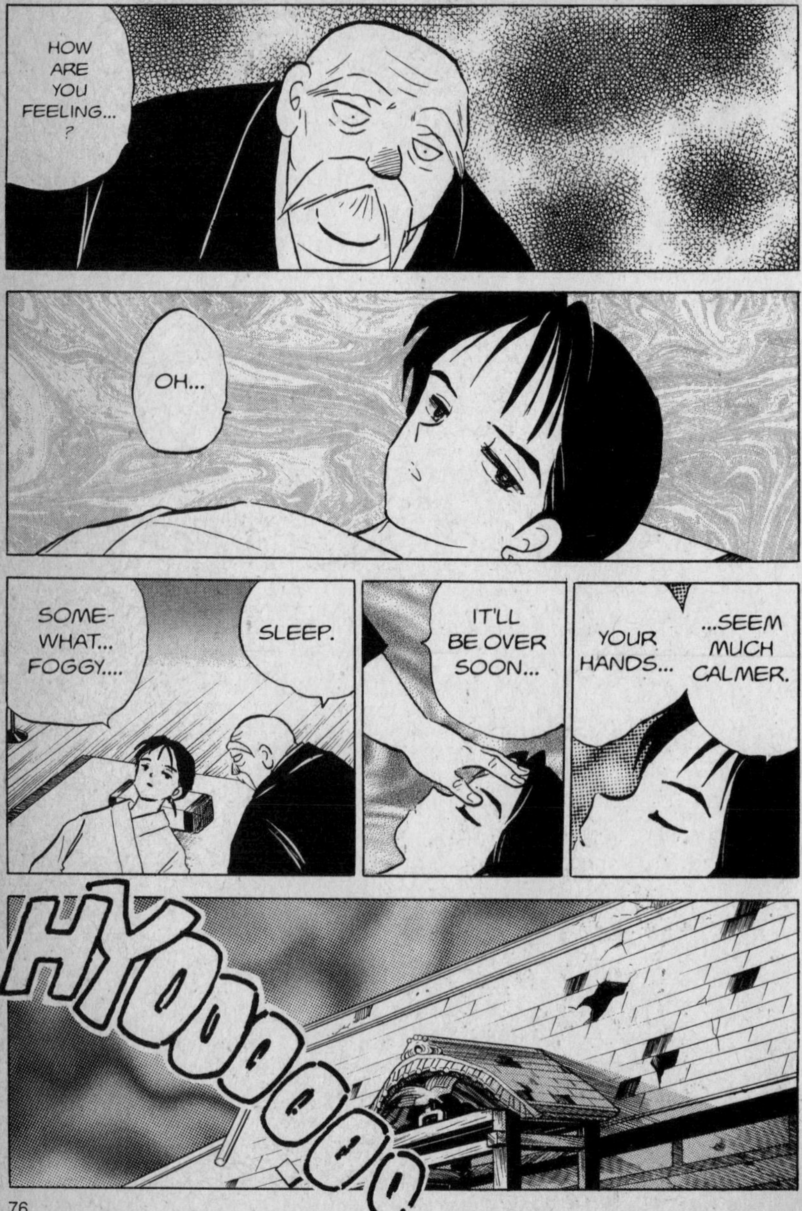
HOW ARE YOU FEELING... ?
OH...
SOME-WHAT... FOGGY....
SLEEP.
IT'LL BE OVER SOON...
YOUR HANDS...
...SEEM MUCH CALMER.
HYOOOOOO

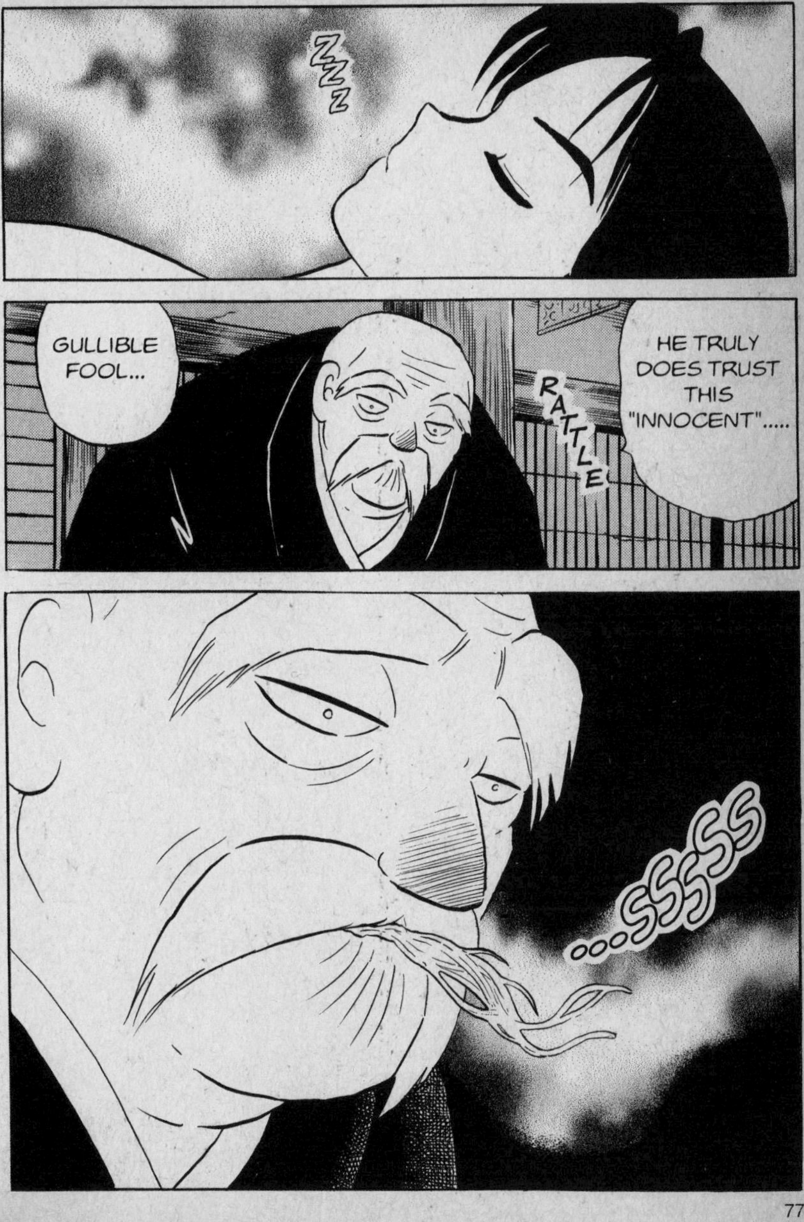
ZZZ
GULLIBLE FOOL...
RATTLE
HE TRULY DOES TRUST THIS "INNOCENT".....
...OOOSSSSS

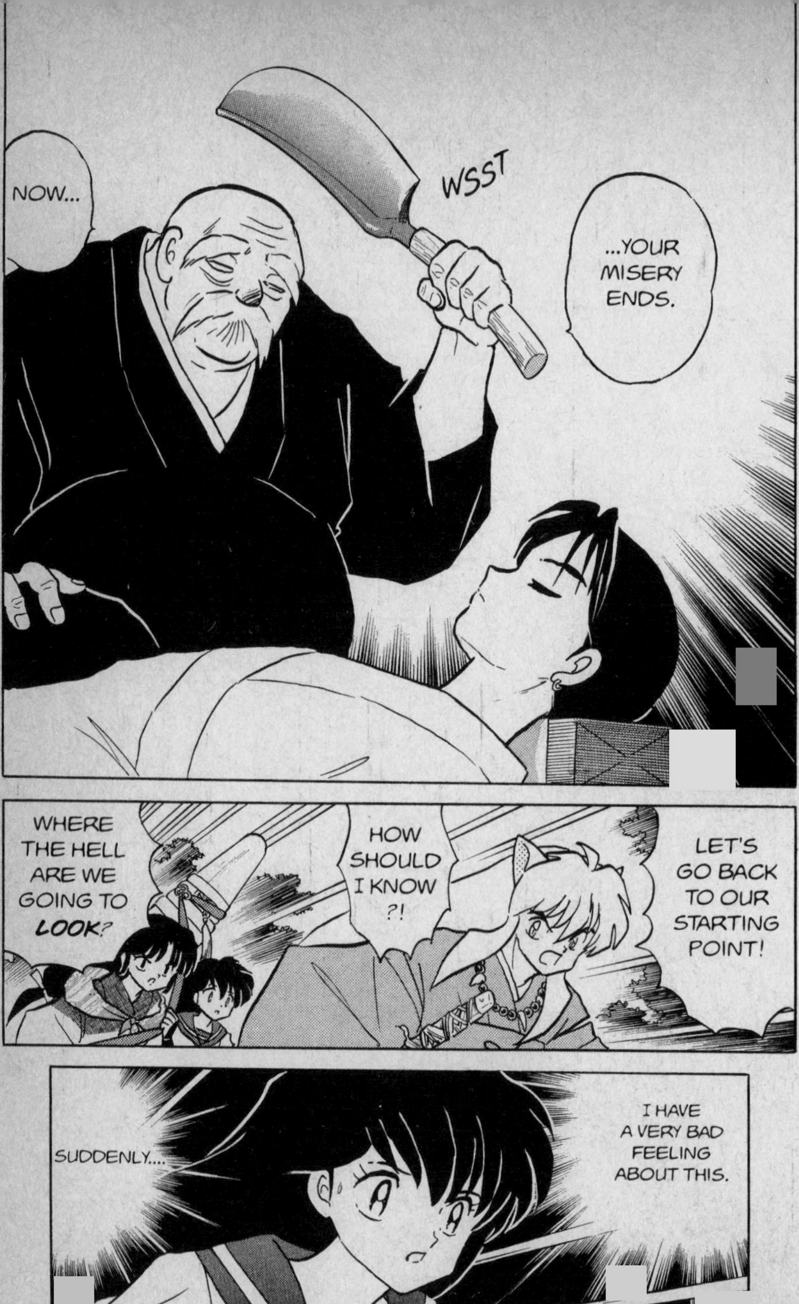
NOW...
WSST
...YOUR MISERY ENDS.
WHERE THE HELL ARE WE GOING TO LOOK?
HOW SHOULD I KNOW ?!
LET'S GO BACK TO OUR STARTING POINT!
SUDDENLY....
I HAVE A VERY BAD FEELING ABOUT THIS.

SCROLL FIVE

TO THE RESCUE

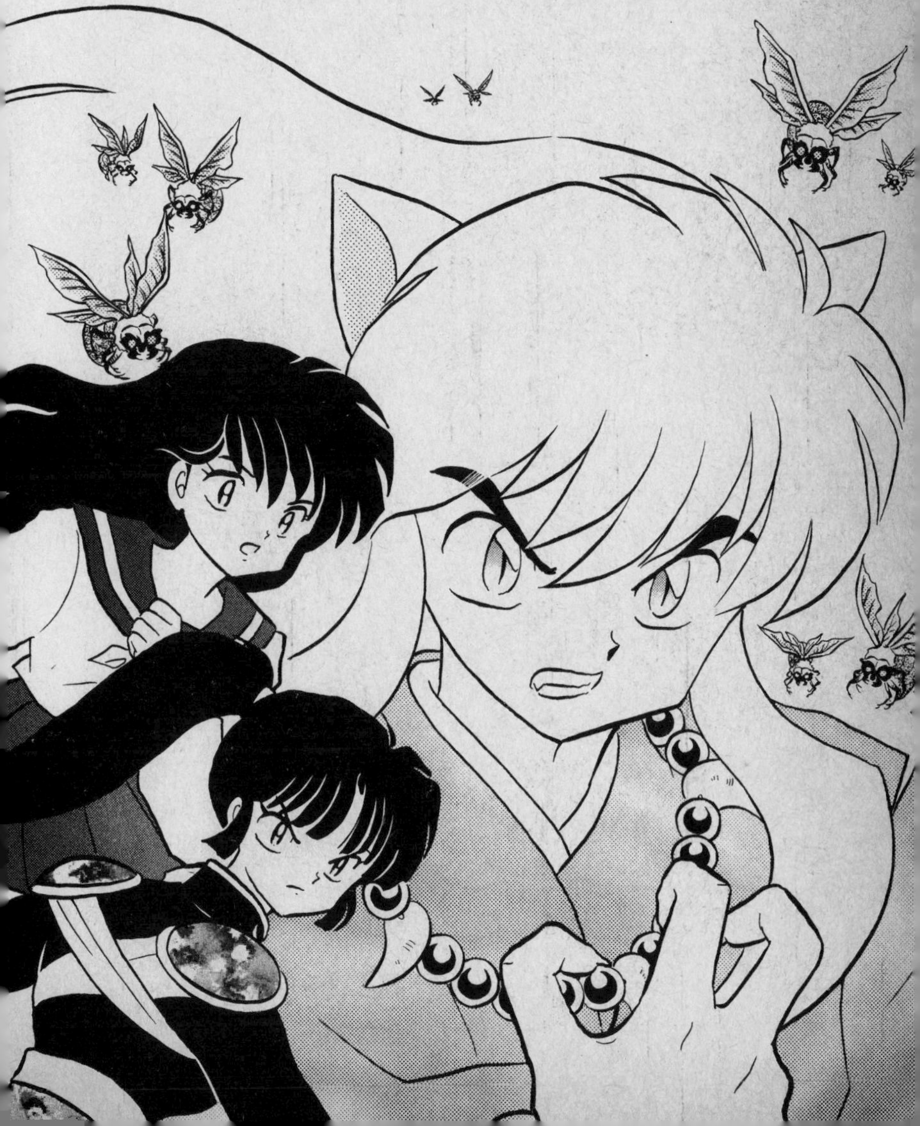

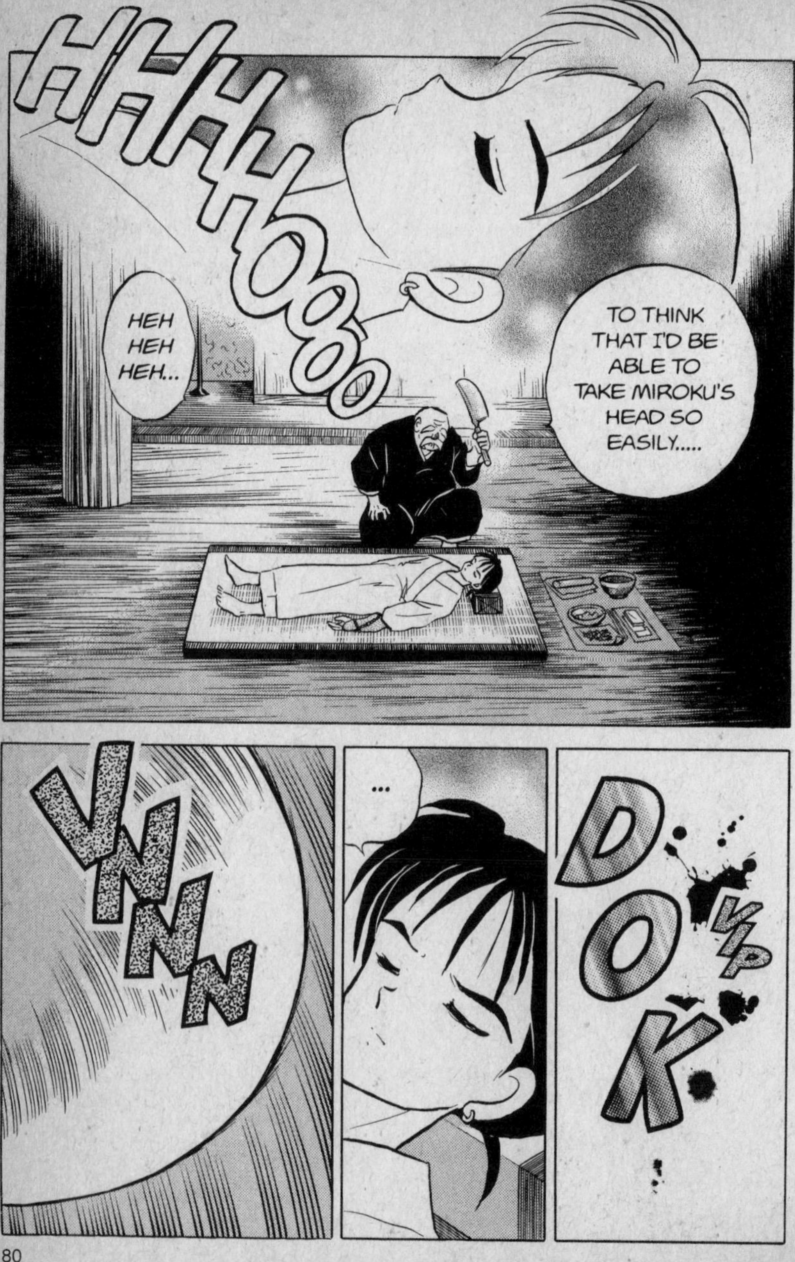
HHHHHOOOOO
HEH HEH HEH...
TO THINK THAT I'D BE ABLE TO TAKE MIROKU'S HEAD SO EASILY.....
VNNNN
...
DOK
DRIP

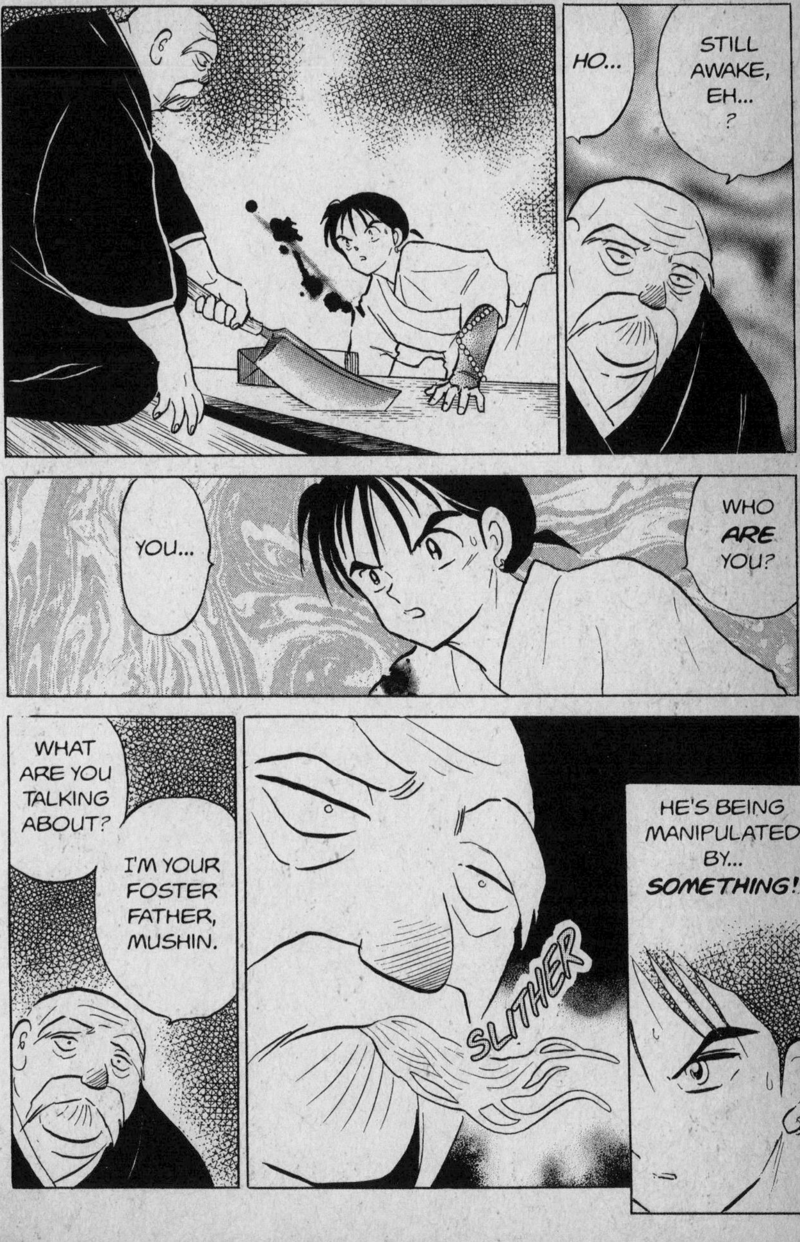
HO...
STILL AWAKE, EH... ?
YOU...
WHO ARE YOU?
WHAT ARE YOU TALKING ABOUT?
I'M YOUR FOSTER FATHER, MUSHIN.
SLITHER
HE'S BEING MANIPULATED BY... SOMETHING!

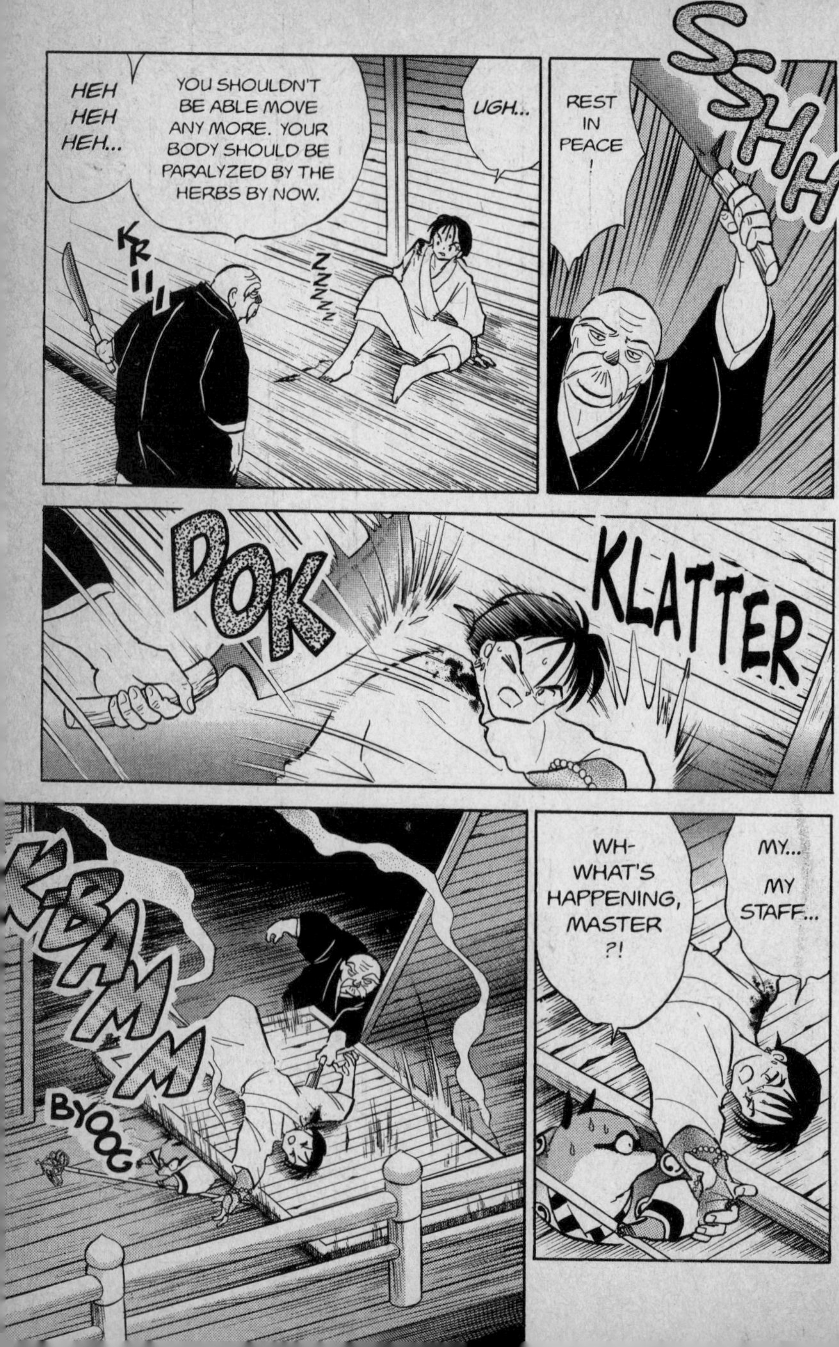
HEH HEH HEH...
YOU SHOULDN'T BE ABLE MOVE ANY MORE. YOUR BODY SHOULD BE PARALYZED BY THE HERBS BY NOW.
KRII
ZZZZZ
UGH...
REST IN PEACE!
SSHHH
DOK
KLATTER
KBAMMM
BYOOG
WH- WHAT'S HAPPENING, MASTER?!
MY... MY STAFF...

KLAK

EH ?!

SSSHHHH

Y... Y...

GLLP GLLP

YAAA !

BOM

HYUUUUU

...

I WON'T LET YOU ESCAPE...

YOU SHOULD... GET YOURSELF AWAY FROM HERE...

ZINCH ZINCH

I-I CAN'T DO *THAT*... !

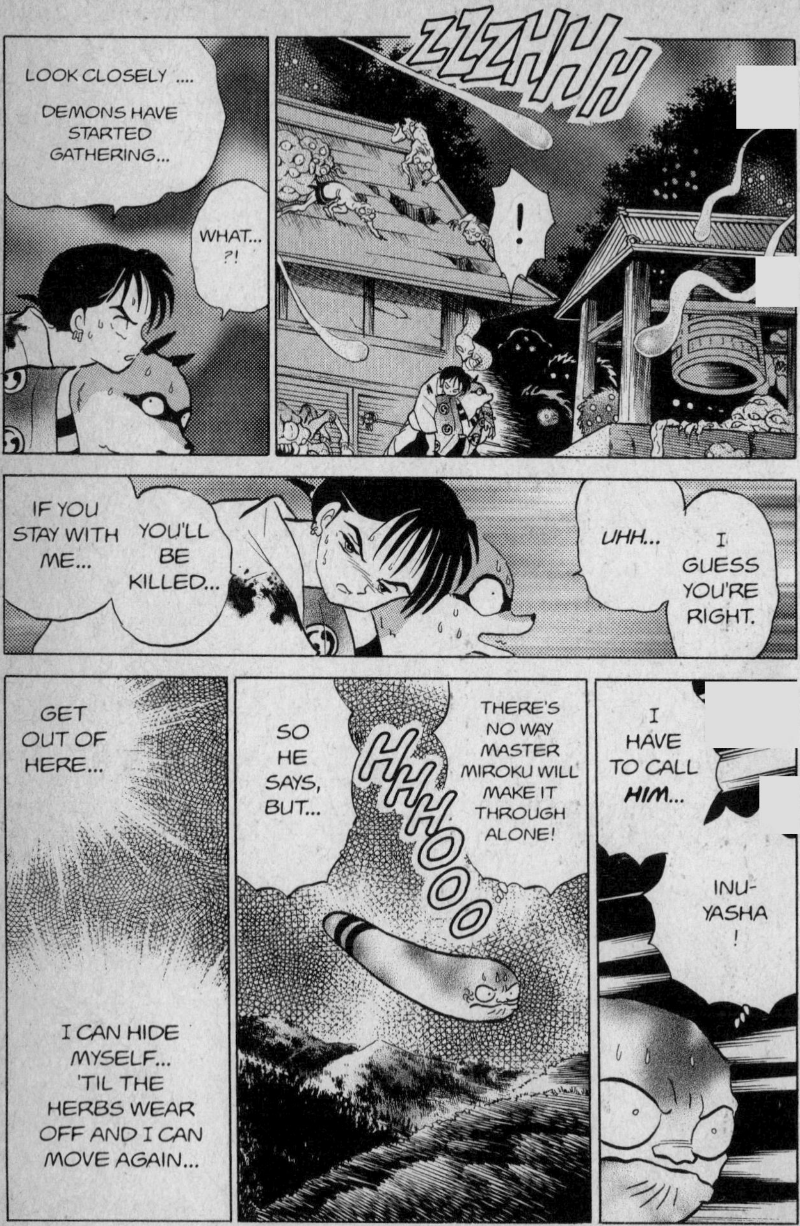
LOOK CLOSELY ....
DEMONS HAVE STARTED GATHERING...
WHAT... ?!
ZZZHHHH
!
IF YOU STAY WITH ME...
YOU'LL BE KILLED...
UHH...
I GUESS YOU'RE RIGHT.
GET OUT OF HERE...
I CAN HIDE MYSELF... 'TIL THE HERBS WEAR OFF AND I CAN MOVE AGAIN...
SO HE SAYS, BUT...
HHHOOOO
THERE'S NO WAY MASTER MIROKU WILL MAKE IT THROUGH ALONE!
I HAVE TO CALL ***HIM***...
INU-YASHA!

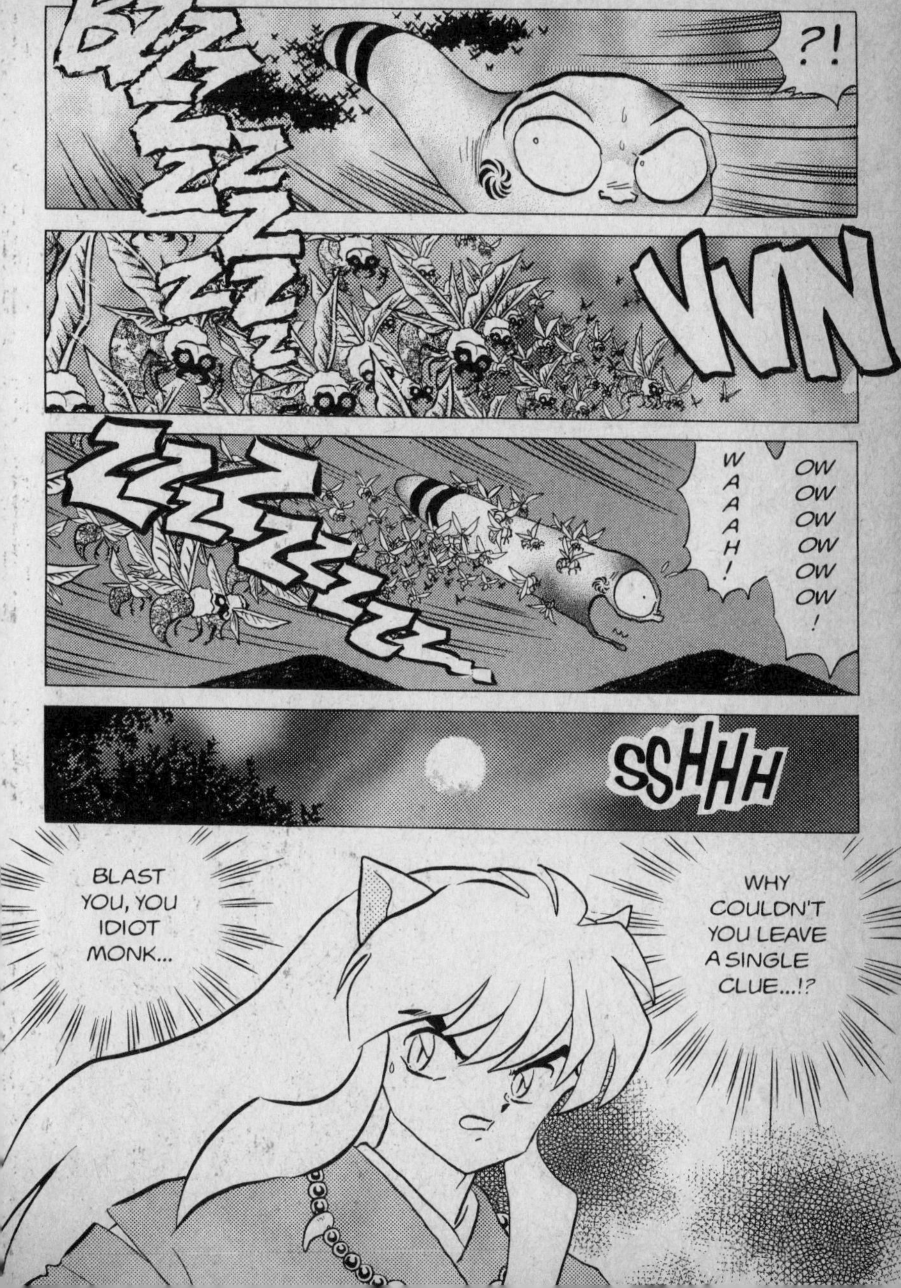
BZZZZZZZZ
?!
VVVN
ZZZZZZZZ...
WAAAAH!
OW OW OW OW OW OW!
SSHHH
BLAST YOU, YOU IDIOT MONK...
WHY COULDN'T YOU LEAVE A SINGLE CLUE...!?

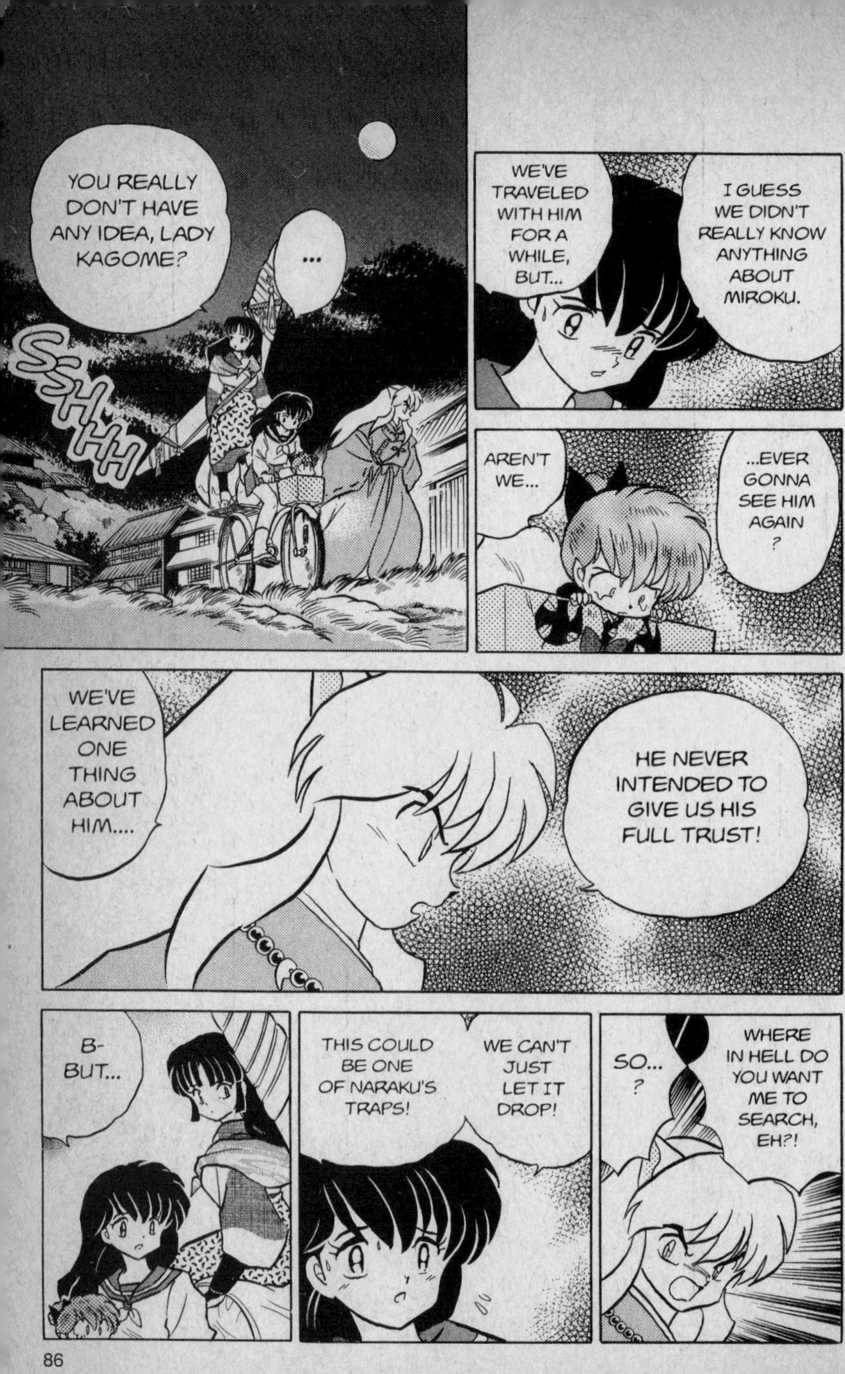
YOU REALLY DON'T HAVE ANY IDEA, LADY KAGOME?
...
S-SHHH
WE'VE TRAVELED WITH HIM FOR A WHILE, BUT...
I GUESS WE DIDN'T REALLY KNOW ANYTHING ABOUT MIROKU.
AREN'T WE...
...EVER GONNA SEE HIM AGAIN ?
WE'VE LEARNED ONE THING ABOUT HIM....
HE NEVER INTENDED TO GIVE US HIS FULL TRUST!
B-BUT...
THIS COULD BE ONE OF NARAKU'S TRAPS!
WE CAN'T JUST LET IT DROP!
SO... ?
WHERE IN HELL DO YOU WANT ME TO SEARCH, EH?!

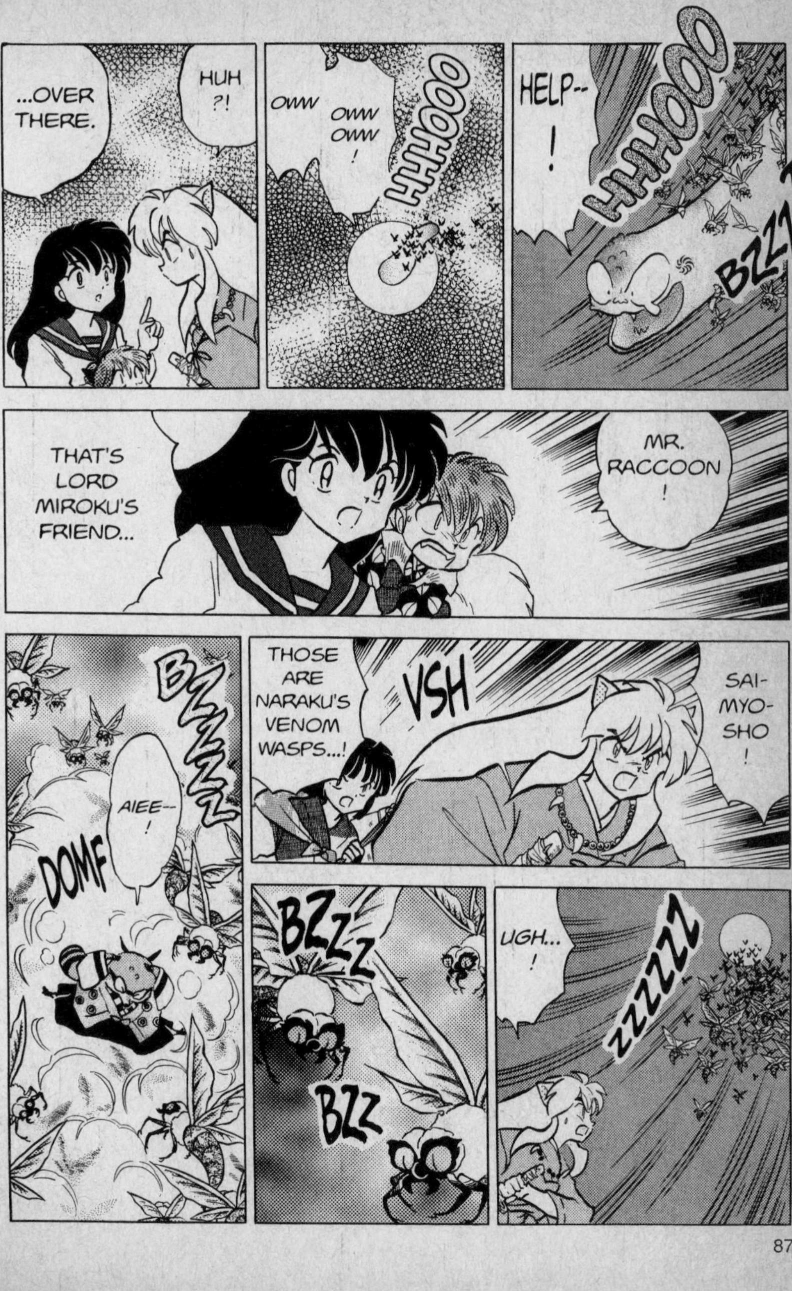

...OVER THERE.
HUH ?!
OWW
OWW OWW !
OOOOHHH
HELP-- !
OOOOHHH
BZZZZ
THAT'S LORD MIROKU'S FRIEND...
MR. RACCOON !
BZZZZZ
AIEE-- !
DOMF
THOSE ARE NARAKU'S VENOM WASPS...!
VSH
SAI-MYO-SHO !
BZZZ
BZZ
UGH... !
ZZZZZZ

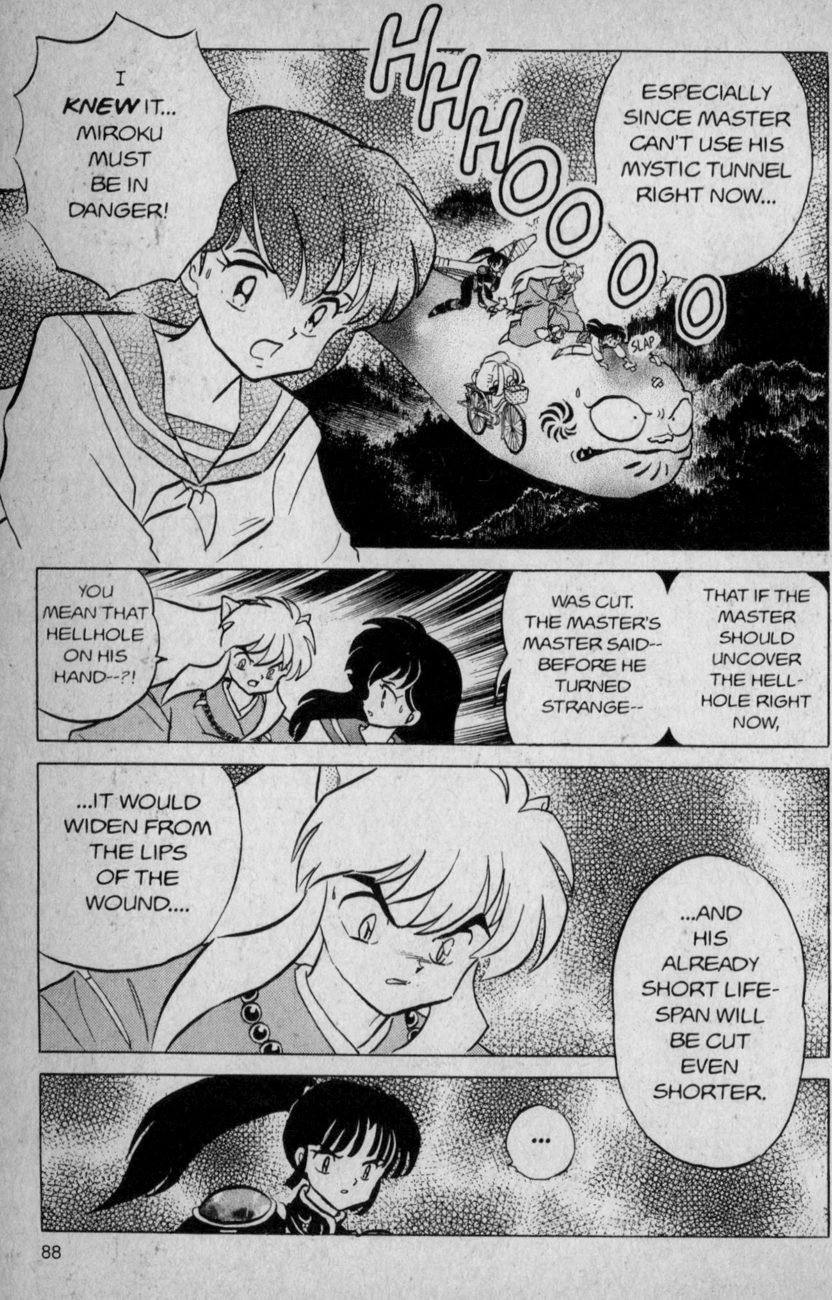
I KNEW IT... MIROKU MUST BE IN DANGER!
HHHOOOOO
ESPECIALLY SINCE MASTER CAN'T USE HIS MYSTIC TUNNEL RIGHT NOW...
SLAP
YOU MEAN THAT HELLHOLE ON HIS HAND--?!
WAS CUT. THE MASTER'S MASTER SAID-- BEFORE HE TURNED STRANGE--
THAT IF THE MASTER SHOULD UNCOVER THE HELL-HOLE RIGHT NOW,
...IT WOULD WIDEN FROM THE LIPS OF THE WOUND....
...AND HIS ALREADY SHORT LIFE-SPAN WILL BE CUT EVEN SHORTER.
...

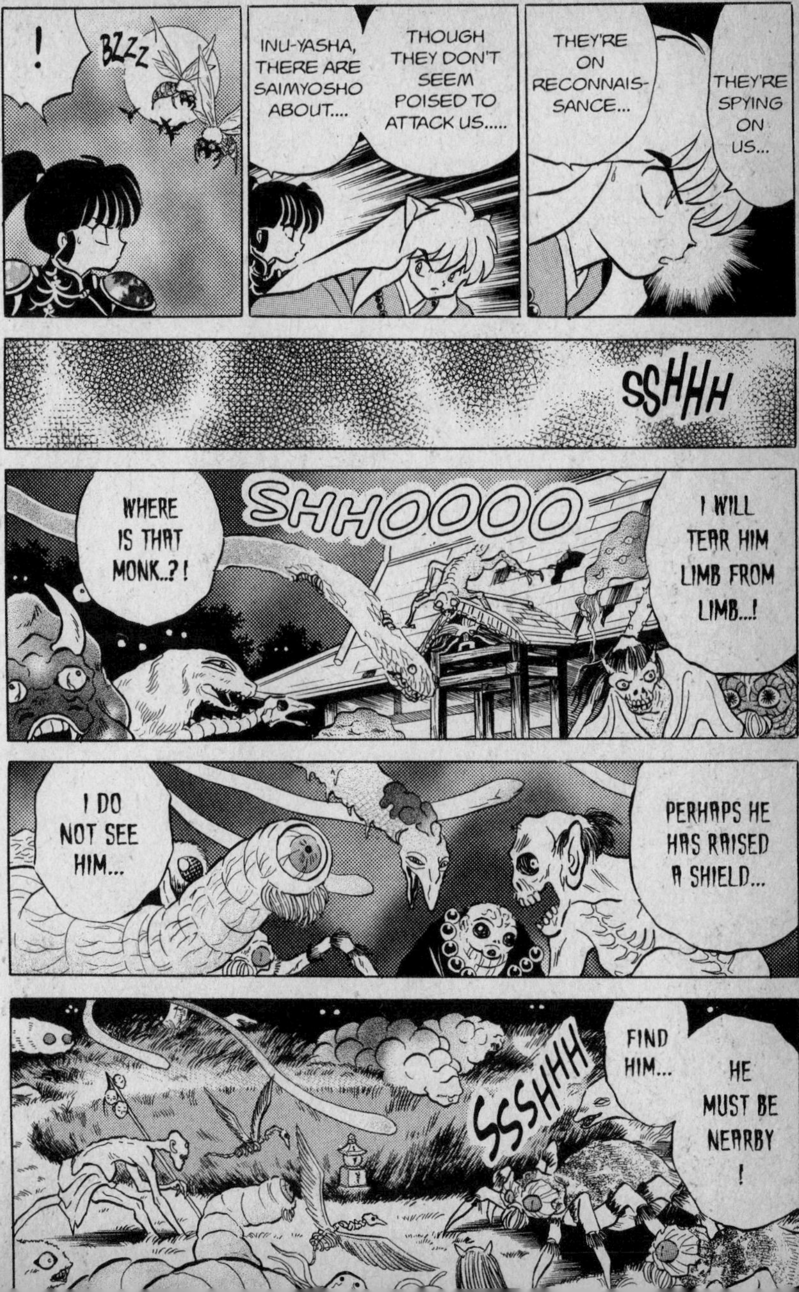
!
BZZz
INU-YASHA, THERE ARE SAIMYOSHO ABOUT....
THOUGH THEY DON'T SEEM POISED TO ATTACK US.....
THEY'RE ON RECONNAIS-SANCE...
THEY'RE SPYING ON US...
SSHHH
WHERE IS THAT MONK..?!
SHHOOOO
I WILL TEAR HIM LIMB FROM LIMB...!
I DO NOT SEE HIM...
PERHAPS HE HAS RAISED A SHIELD...
SSSHHH
FIND HIM...
HE MUST BE NEARBY!

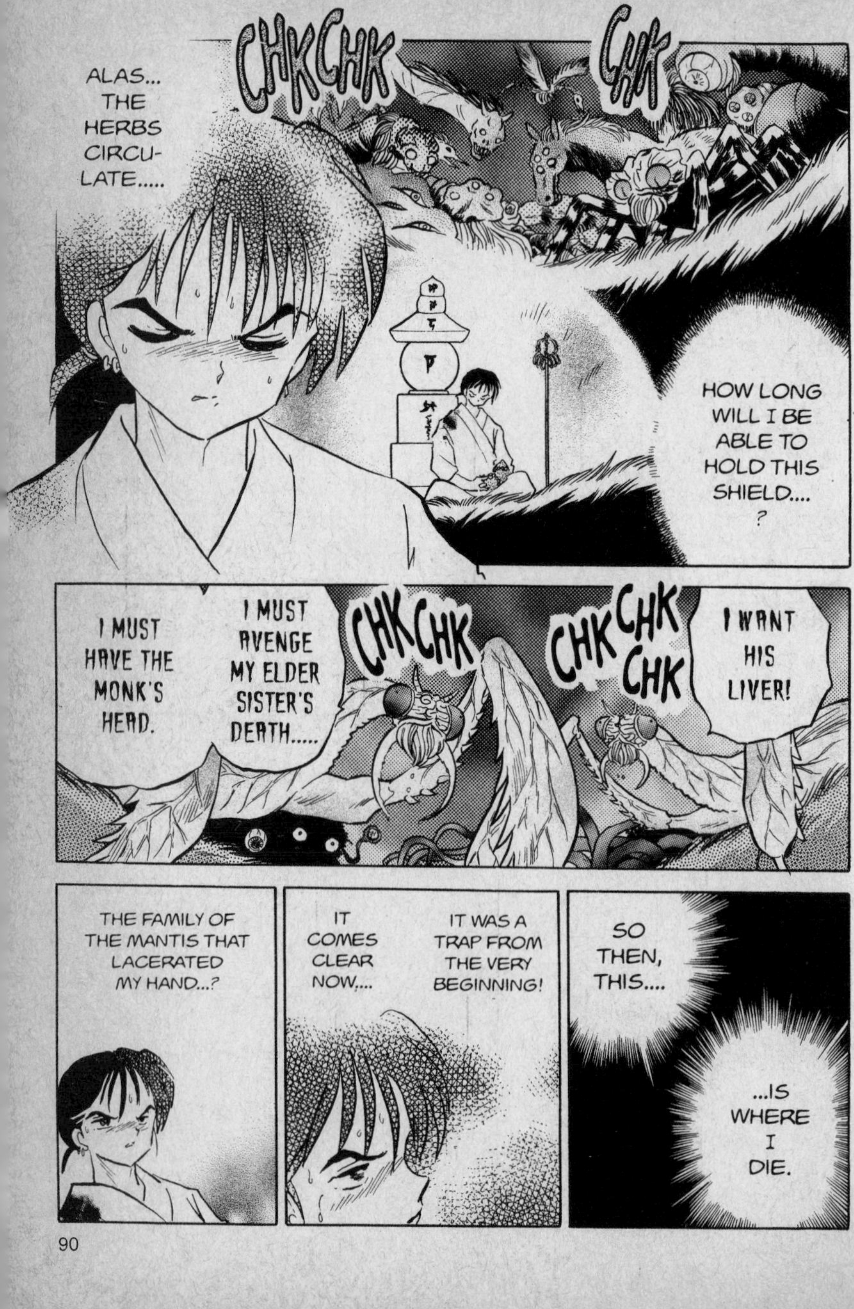
ALAS... THE HERBS CIRCULATE.....
CHKCHK
CHK
HOW LONG WILL I BE ABLE TO HOLD THIS SHIELD....?
I MUST HAVE THE MONK'S HEAD.
I MUST AVENGE MY ELDER SISTER'S DEATH.....
CHKCHK
CHKCHK CHK
I WANT HIS LIVER!
THE FAMILY OF THE MANTIS THAT LACERATED MY HAND...?
IT COMES CLEAR NOW....
IT WAS A TRAP FROM THE VERY BEGINNING!
SO THEN, THIS....
...IS WHERE I DIE.

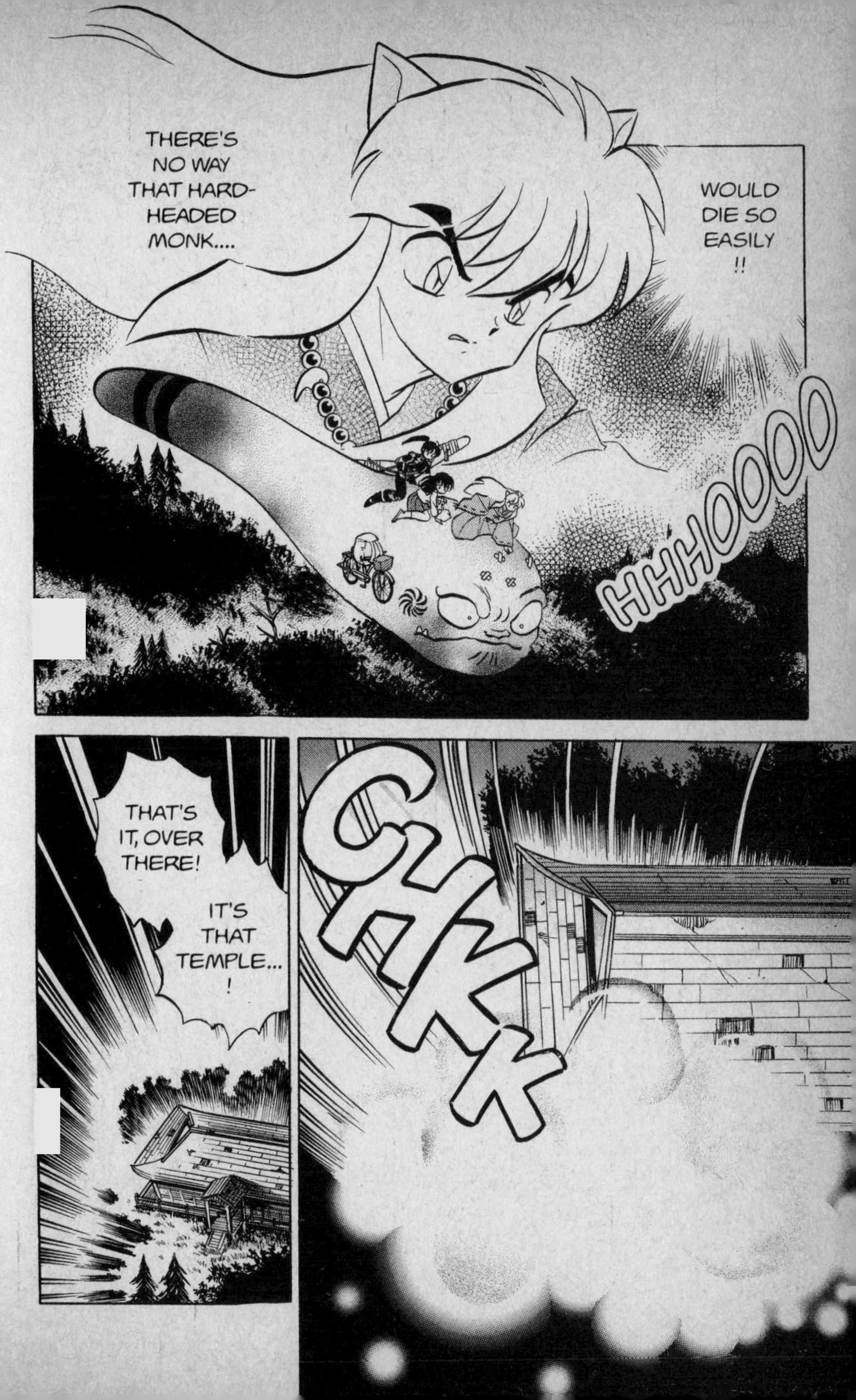
THERE'S NO WAY THAT HARD-HEADED MONK....
WOULD DIE SO EASILY !!
HHHOOOO
THAT'S IT, OVER THERE!
IT'S THAT TEMPLE... !
CHKK

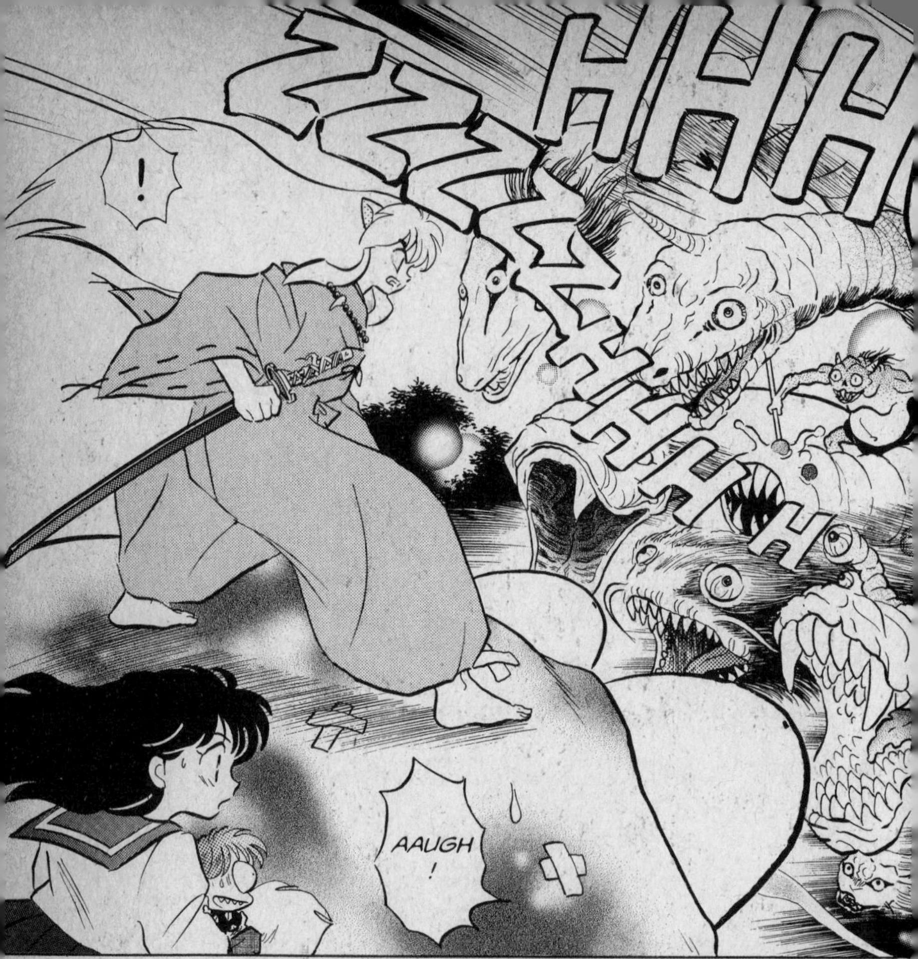
ZZZZHHHH
HHHH
!
AAUGH!
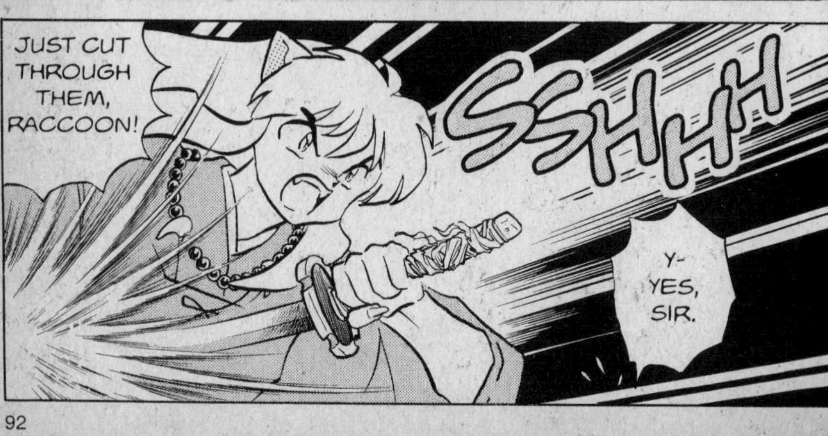
JUST CUT THROUGH THEM, RACCOON!
SSHHH
Y-YES, SIR.

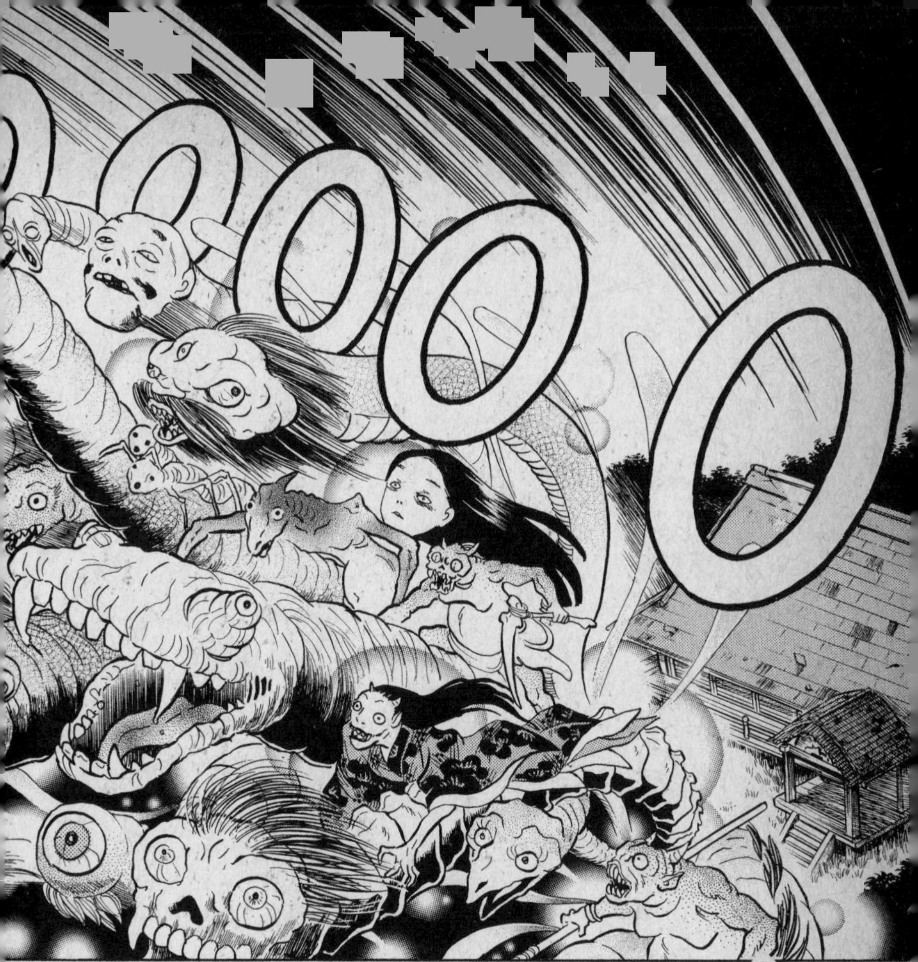

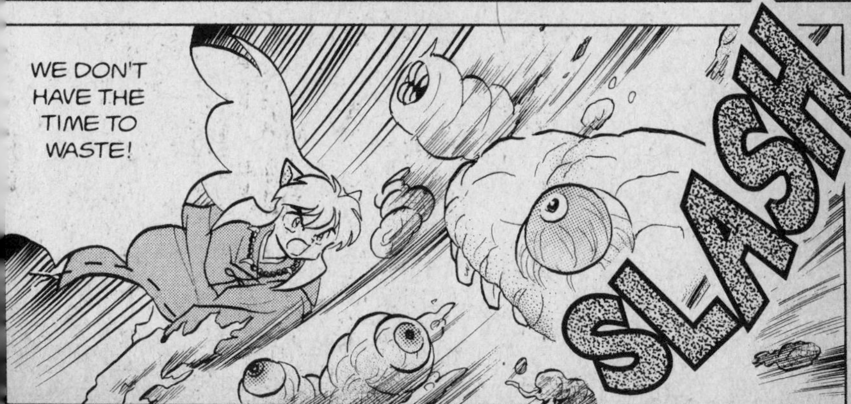
WE DON'T HAVE THE TIME TO WASTE!
SLASH

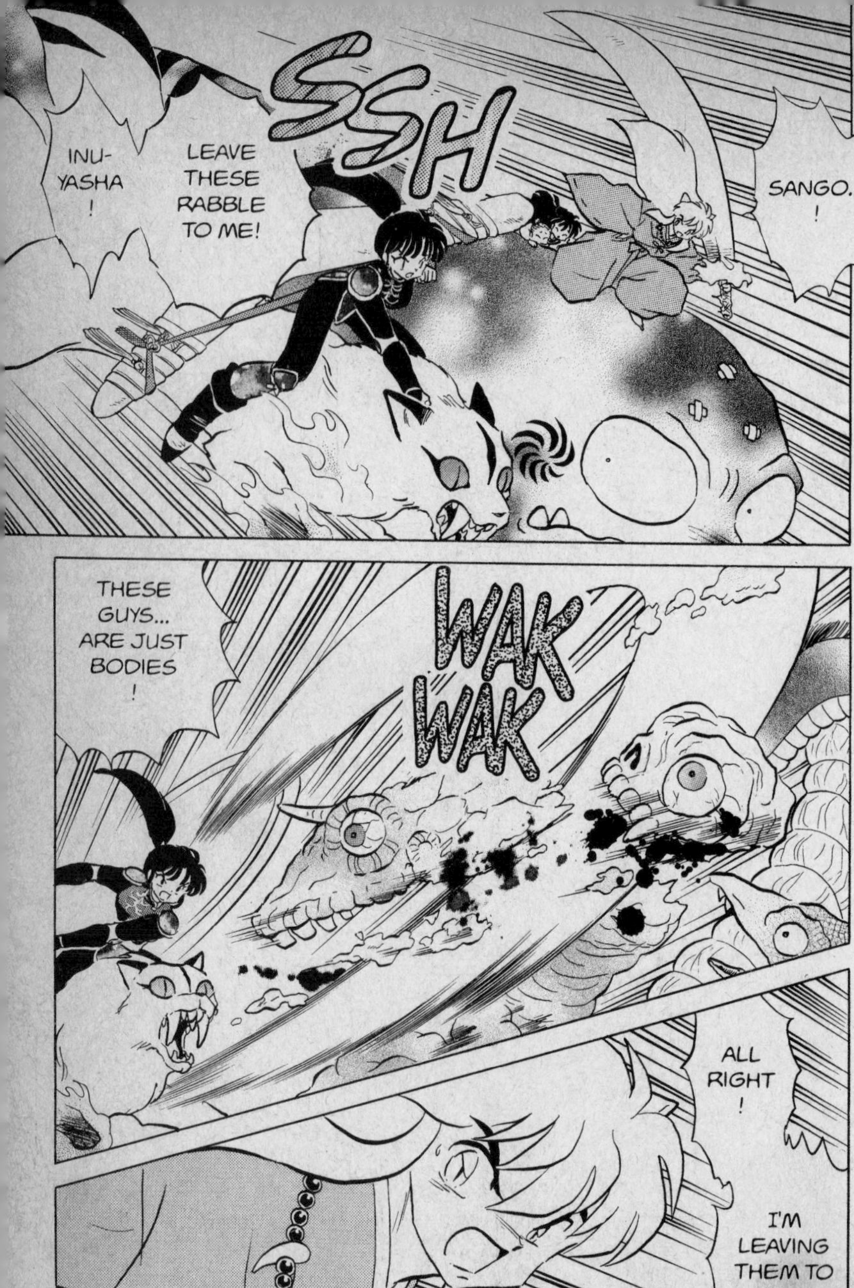
INU-YASHA!
LEAVE THESE RABBLE TO ME!
SSH
SANGO...!
THESE GUYS... ARE JUST BODIES!
WAK WAK
ALL RIGHT!
I'M LEAVING THEM TO YOU!!

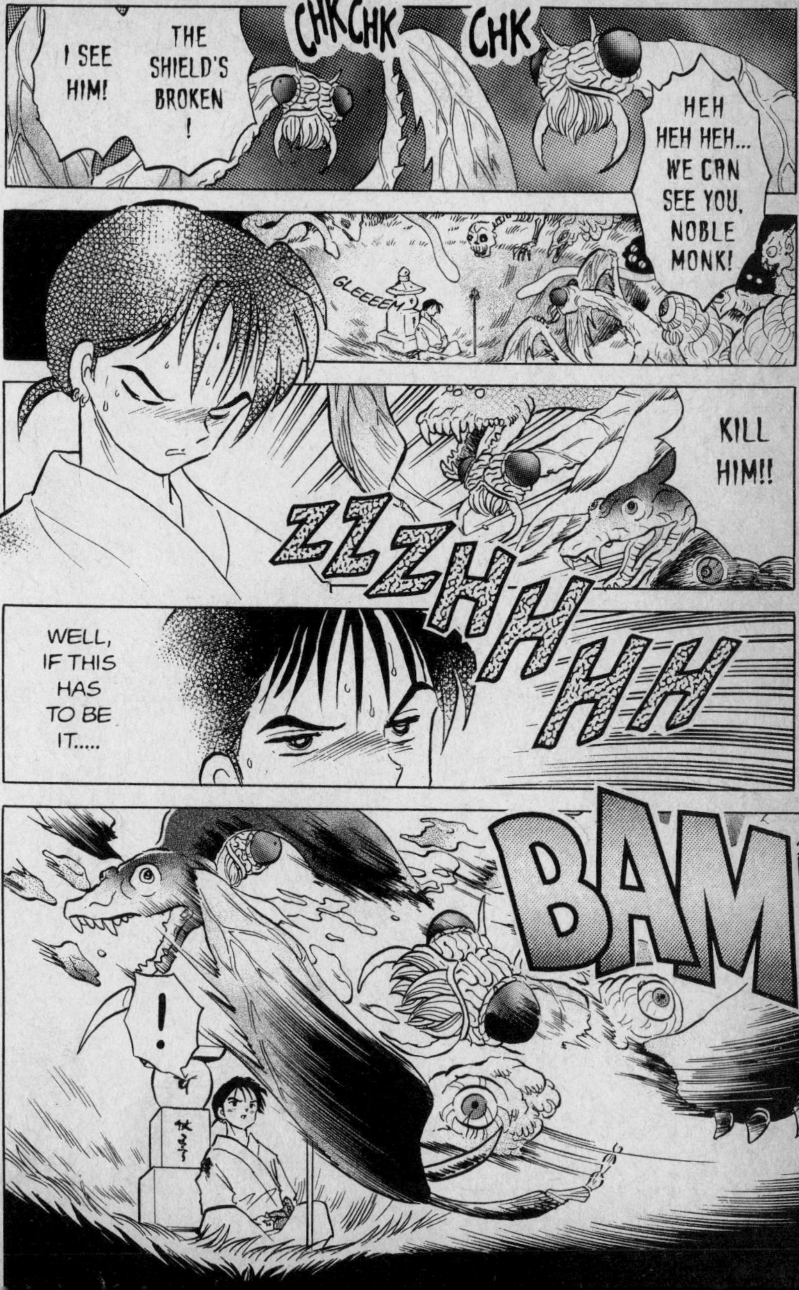
I SEE HIM!
THE SHIELD'S BROKEN!
CHKCHK
CHK
HEH HEH HEH... WE CAN SEE YOU, NOBLE MONK!
GLEEEEM
KILL HIM!!
ZZZHHHHH
WELL, IF THIS HAS TO BE IT.....
BAM
!

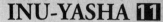

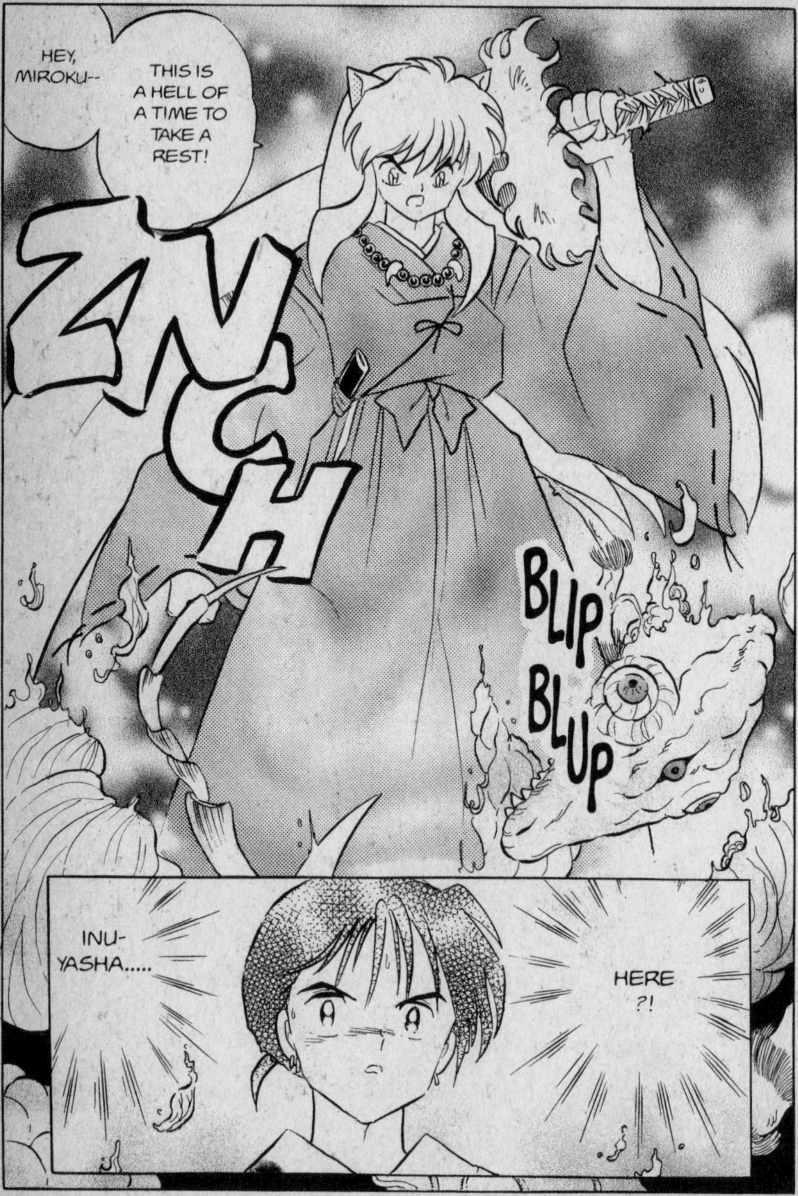
HEY, MIROKU--
THIS IS A HELL OF A TIME TO TAKE A REST!
ZNCH
BLIP BLUP
INU-YASHA.....
HERE ?!

SCROLL SIX

URN GRUBS

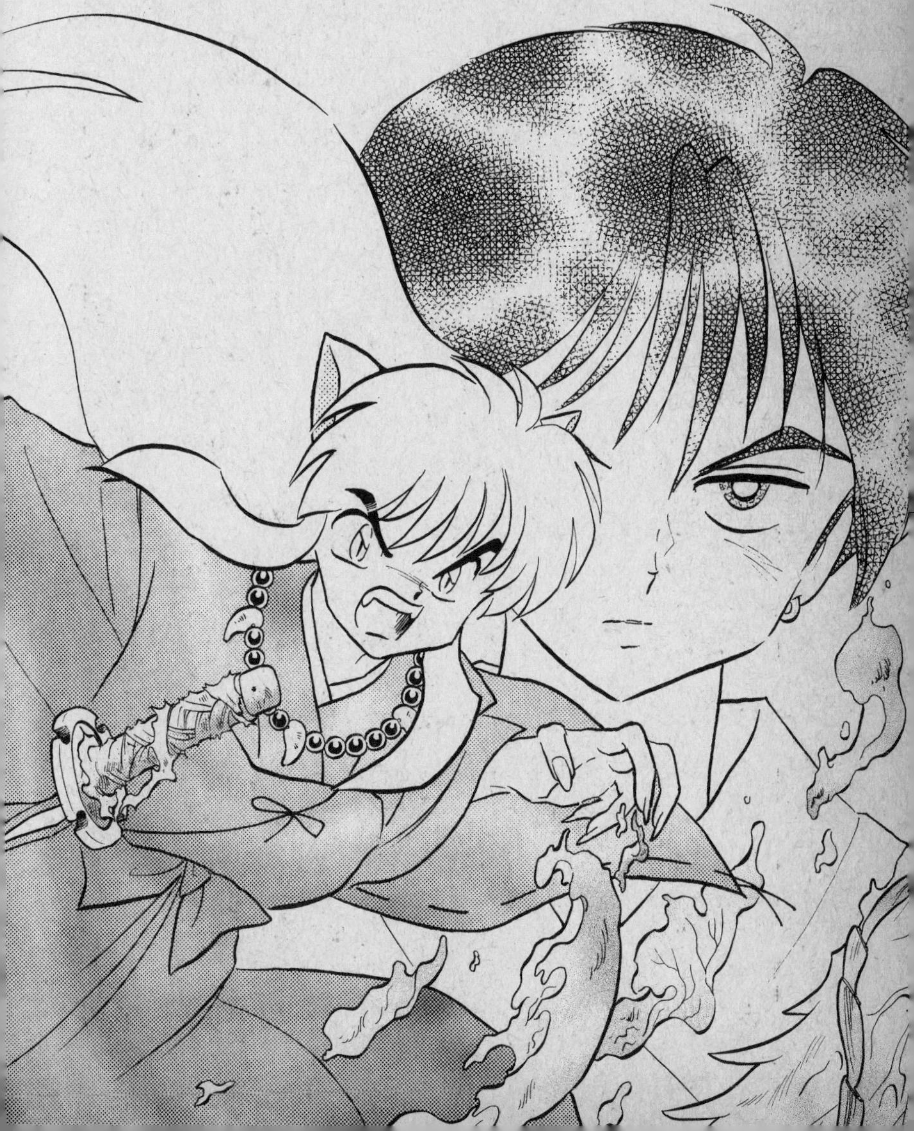

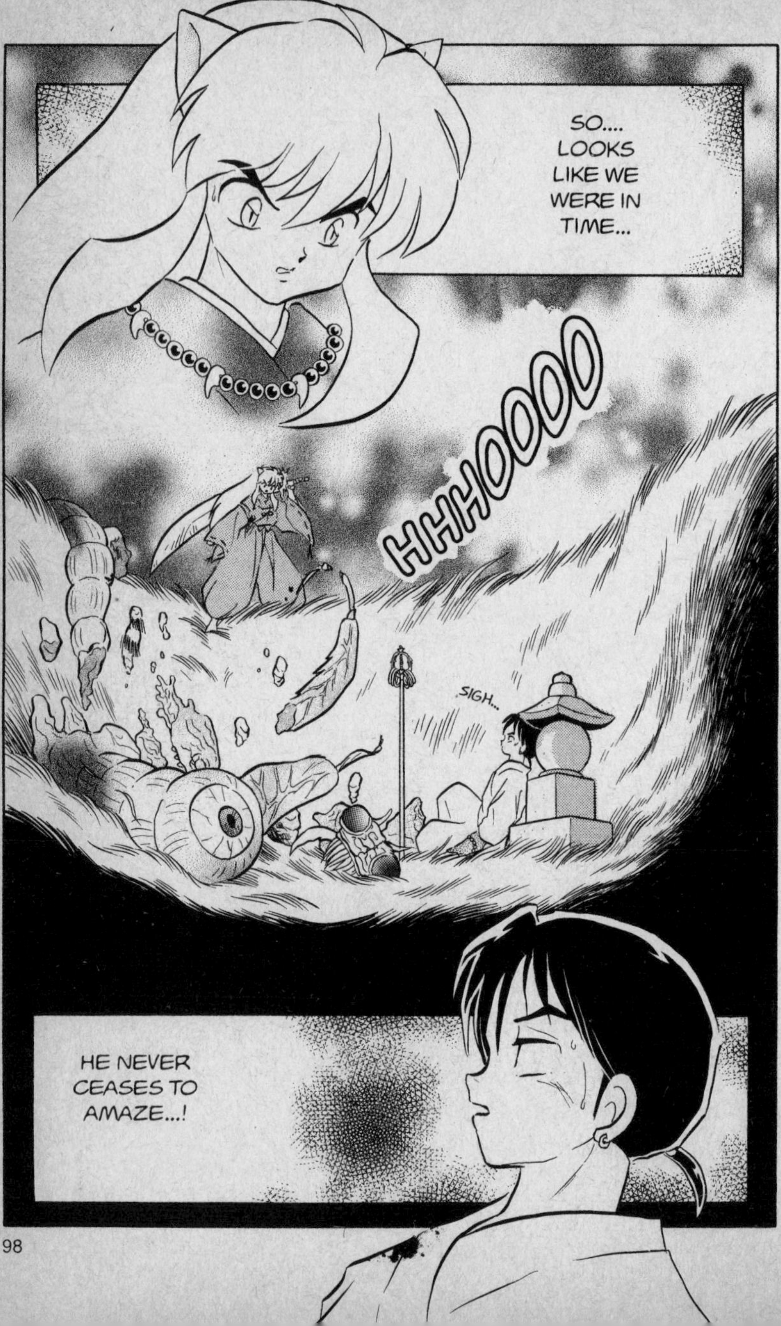
SO.... LOOKS LIKE WE WERE IN TIME...
HHHOOOO
SIGH...
HE NEVER CEASES TO AMAZE...!

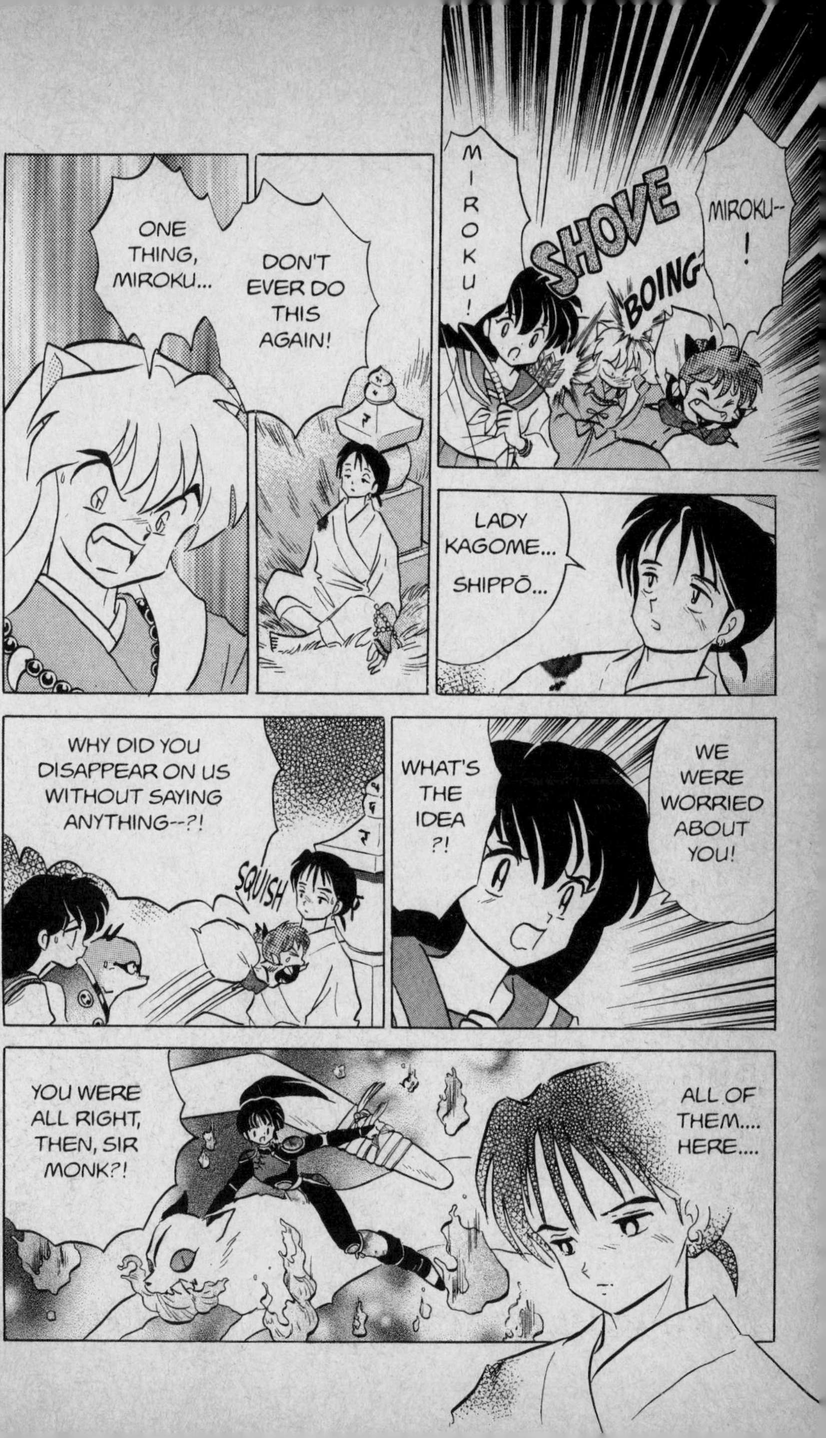
ONE THING, MIROKU...
DON'T EVER DO THIS AGAIN!
MIROKU!
SHOVE
BOING
MIROKU--!
LADY KAGOME... SHIPPŌ...
WHY DID YOU DISAPPEAR ON US WITHOUT SAYING ANYTHING--?!
SQUISH
WHAT'S THE IDEA?!
WE WERE WORRIED ABOUT YOU!
YOU WERE ALL RIGHT, THEN, SIR MONK?!
ALL OF THEM.... HERE....

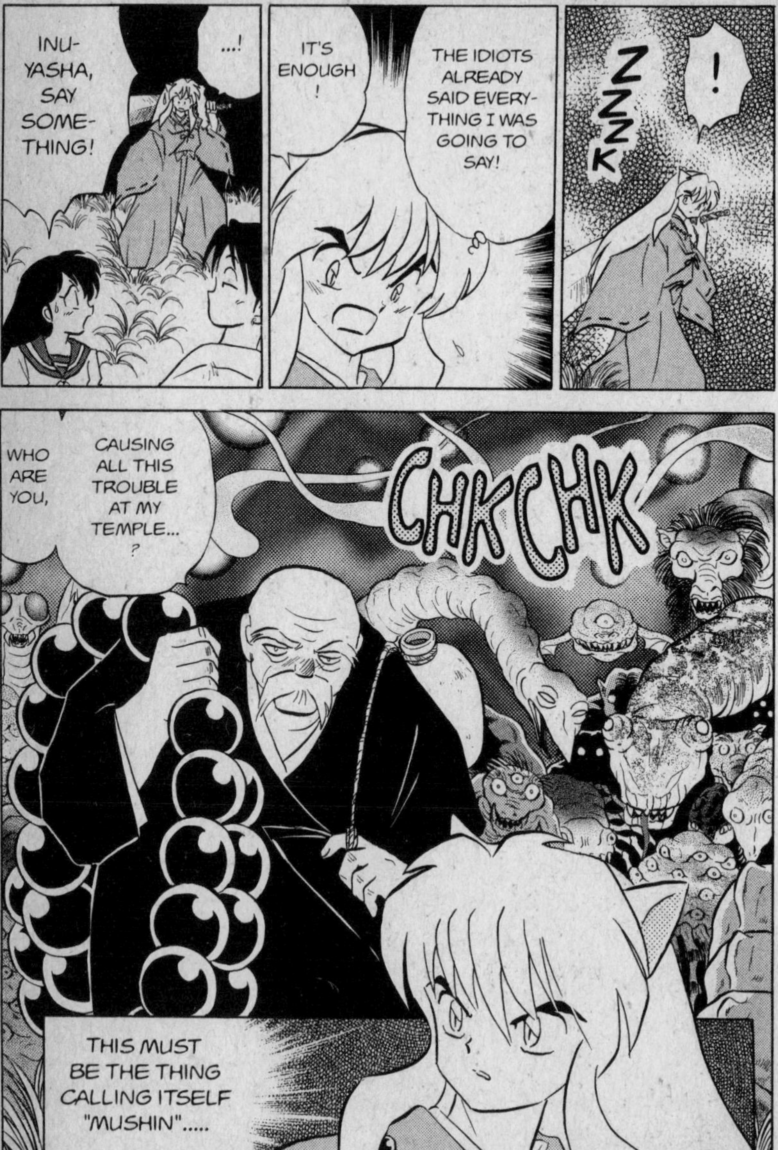
INU-YASHA, SAY SOME-THING!
...!
IT'S ENOUGH!
THE IDIOTS ALREADY SAID EVERY-THING I WAS GOING TO SAY!
ZZZK
!
WHO ARE YOU,
CAUSING ALL THIS TROUBLE AT MY TEMPLE...?
CHKCHK
THIS MUST BE THE THING CALLING ITSELF "MUSHIN".....

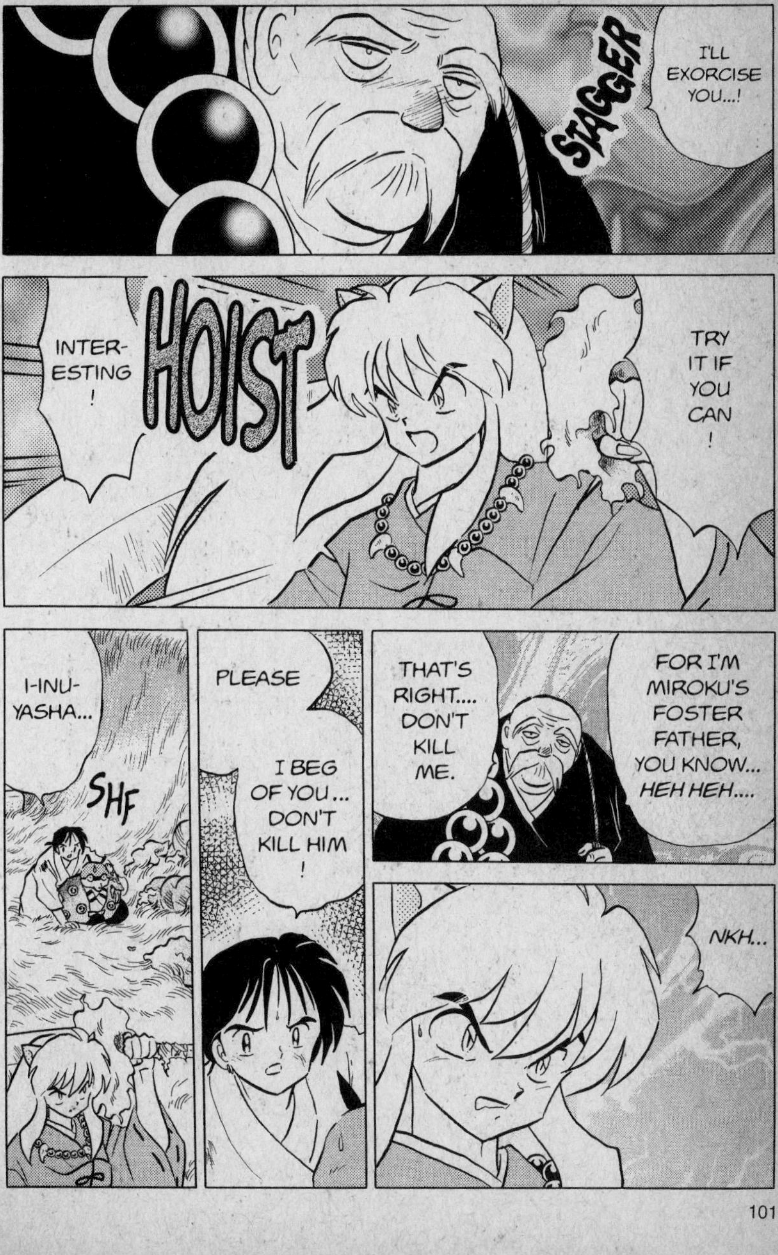
STAGGER
I'LL EXORCISE YOU...!
INTER-ESTING!
HOIST
TRY IT IF YOU CAN!
I-INU-YASHA...
SHF
PLEASE
I BEG OF YOU... DON'T KILL HIM!
THAT'S RIGHT.... DON'T KILL ME.
FOR I'M MIROKU'S FOSTER FATHER, YOU KNOW... HEH HEH....
NKH...

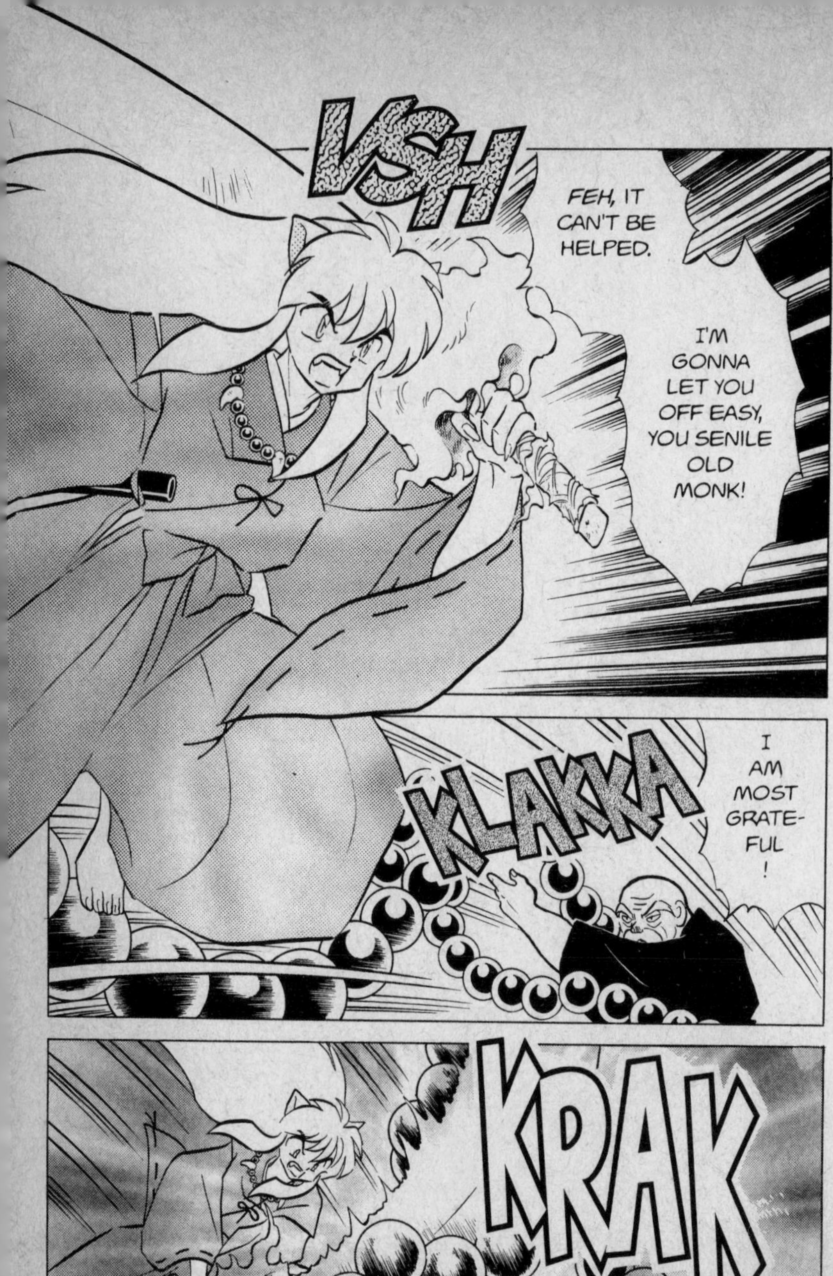
VSH
FEH, IT CAN'T BE HELPED.
I'M GONNA LET YOU OFF EASY, YOU SENILE OLD MONK!
KLAKKA
I AM MOST GRATE-FUL!
KRAK

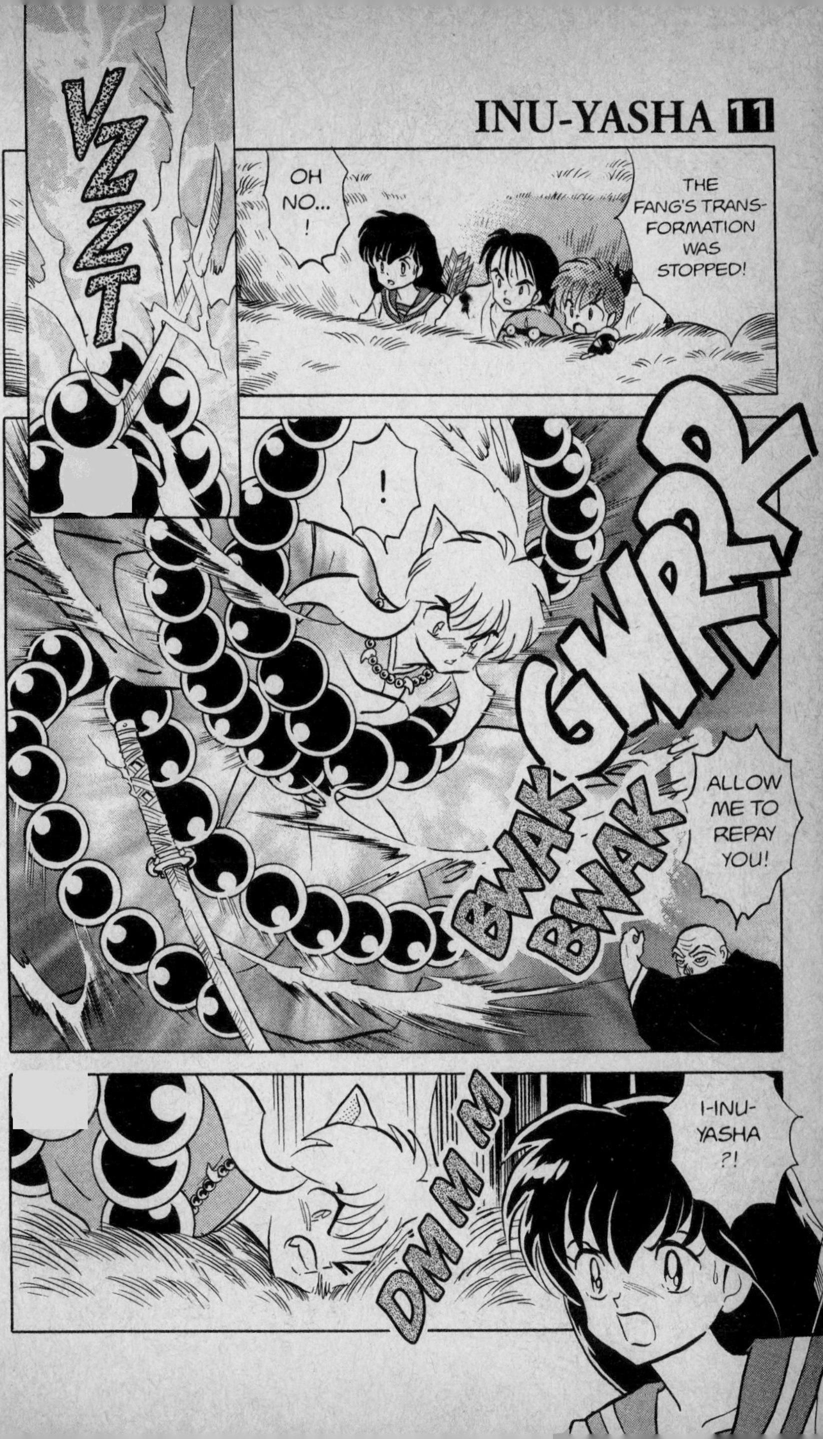
VZZT
OH NO... !
THE FANG'S TRANS-FORMATION WAS STOPPED!
!
GWRR
BWAK BWAK
ALLOW ME TO REPAY YOU!
DMMM
I-INU-YASHA ?!

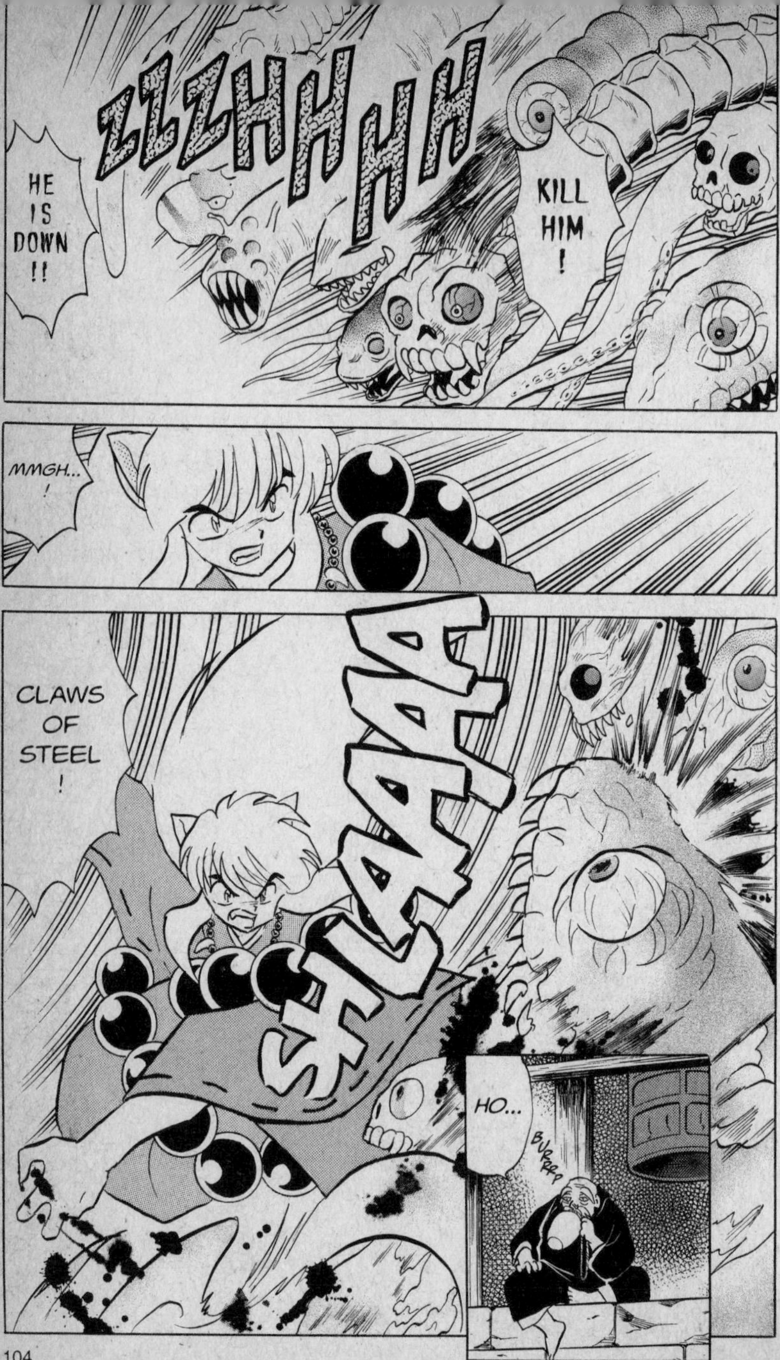
HE IS DOWN !!
ZZZHHHHH
KILL HIM !
MMGH... !
CLAWS OF STEEL !
SHLAAAA
HO...
BURRRP

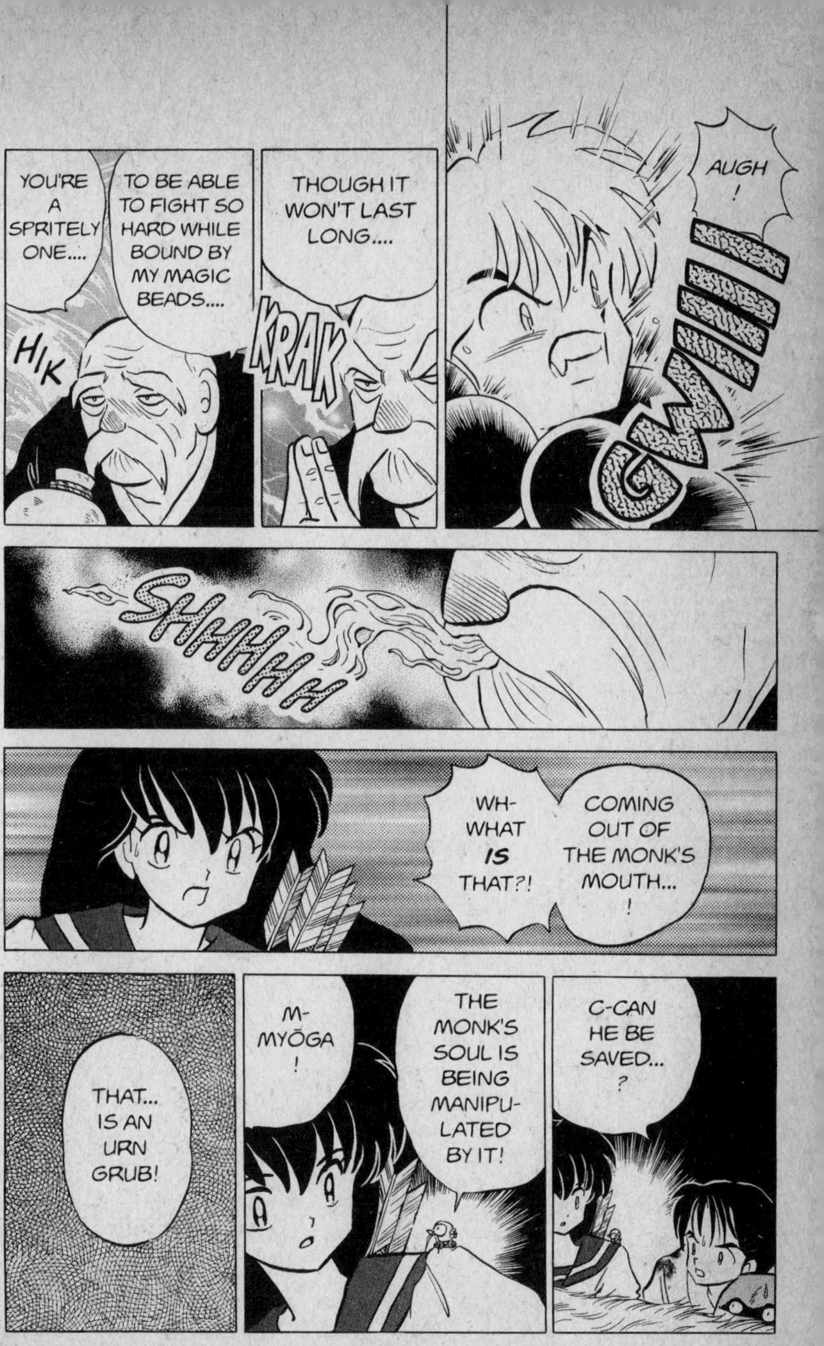
YOU'RE A SPRITELY ONE....
TO BE ABLE TO FIGHT SO HARD WHILE BOUND BY MY MAGIC BEADS....
HIK
THOUGH IT WON'T LAST LONG....
KRAK
AUGH!
GWIIII
SHHHHHH
WH-WHAT *IS* THAT?!
COMING OUT OF THE MONK'S MOUTH...!
THAT... IS AN URN GRUB!
M-MYŌGA!
THE MONK'S SOUL IS BEING MANIPULATED BY IT!
C-CAN HE BE SAVED...?

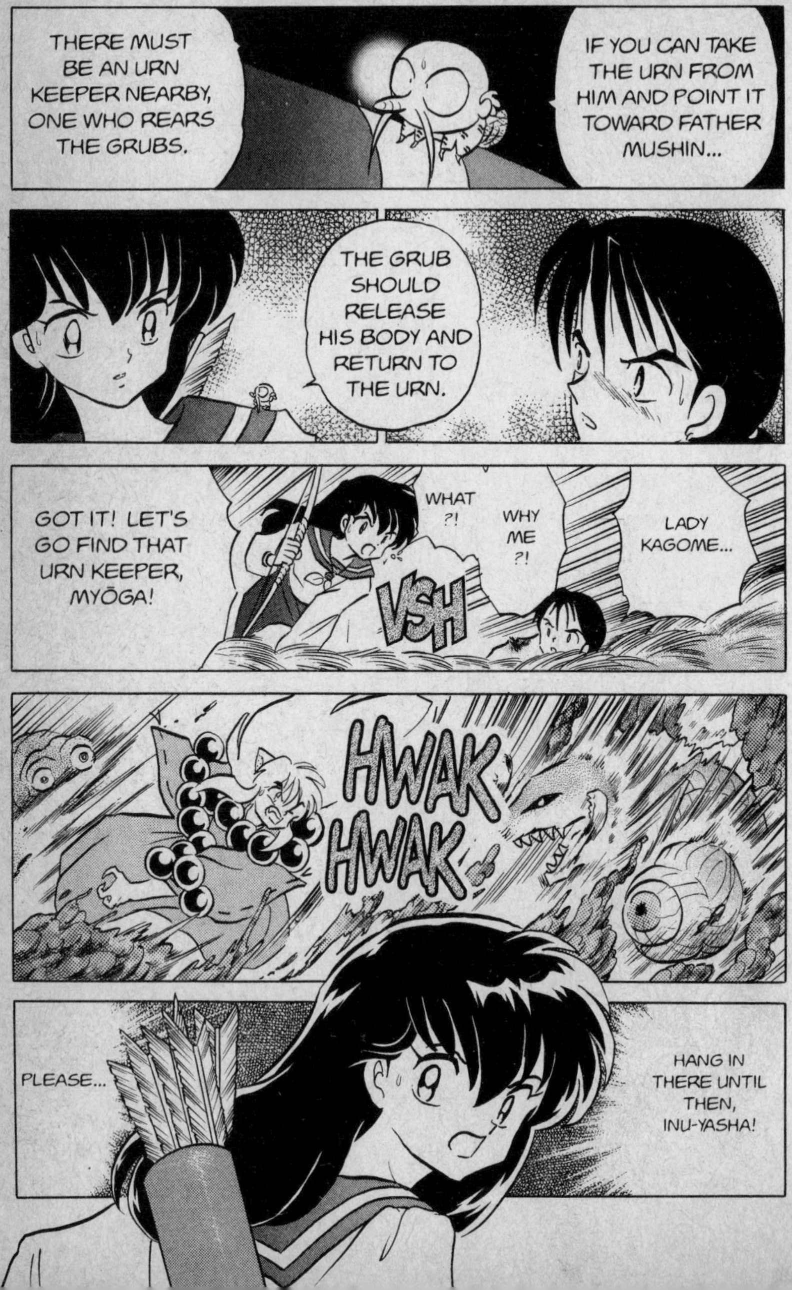
THERE MUST BE AN URN KEEPER NEARBY, ONE WHO REARS THE GRUBS.
IF YOU CAN TAKE THE URN FROM HIM AND POINT IT TOWARD FATHER MUSHIN...
THE GRUB SHOULD RELEASE HIS BODY AND RETURN TO THE URN.
GOT IT! LET'S GO FIND THAT URN KEEPER, MYŌGA!
WHAT ?!
VSH
WHY ME ?!
LADY KAGOME...
HWAK HWAK
PLEASE...
HANG IN THERE UNTIL THEN, INU-YASHA!

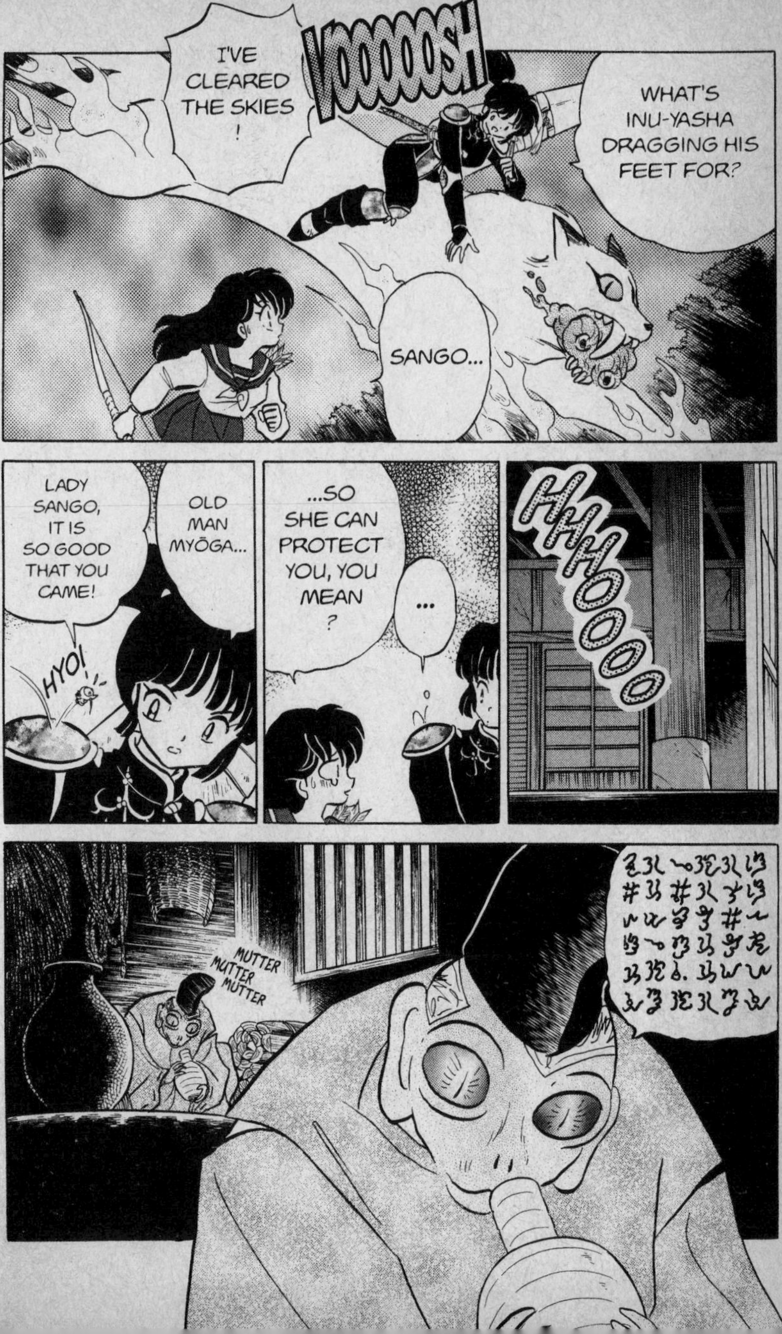
I'VE CLEARED THE SKIES!
VOOOOOSH
WHAT'S INU-YASHA DRAGGING HIS FEET FOR?
SANGO...
LADY SANGO, IT IS SO GOOD THAT YOU CAME!
OLD MAN MYŌGA...
HYO!
...SO SHE CAN PROTECT YOU, YOU MEAN?
...
HHHOOOOO
MUTTER MUTTER MUTTER

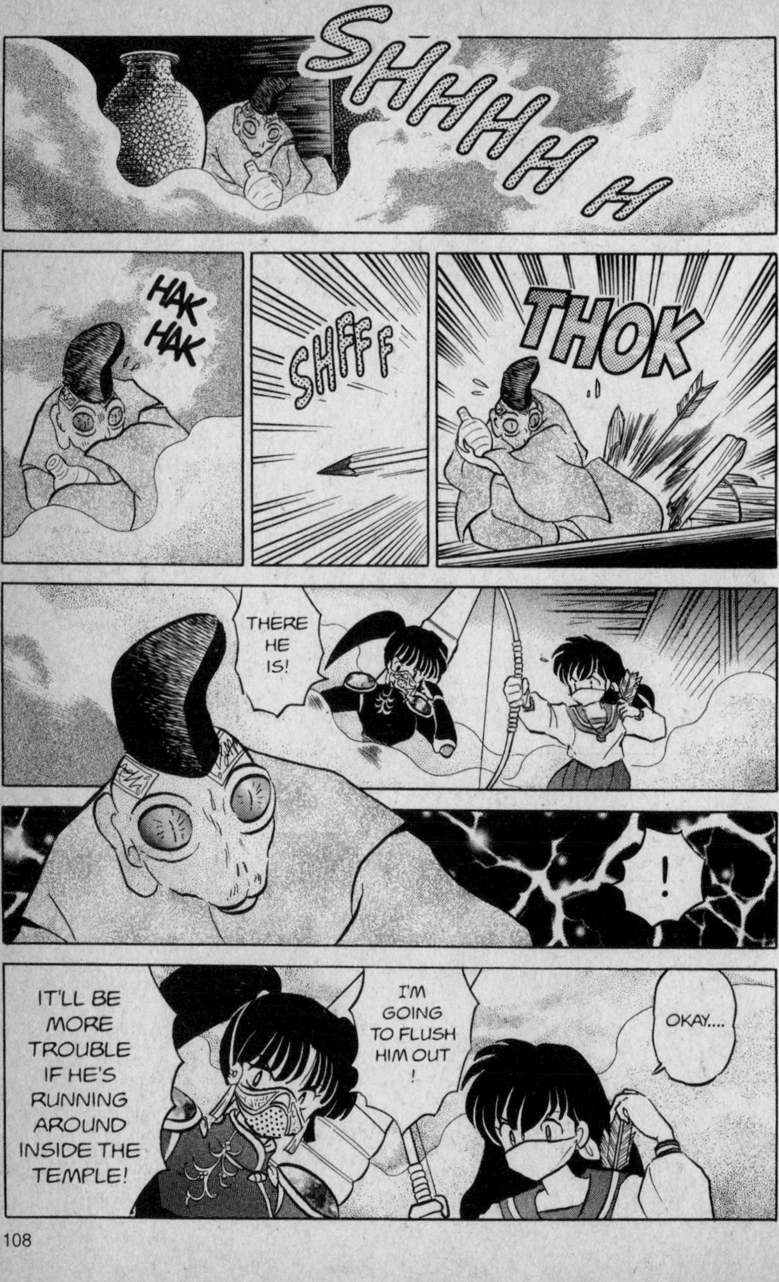
SHHHHH H
HAK HAK
SHFFF F
THOK
THERE HE IS!
!
IT'LL BE MORE TROUBLE IF HE'S RUNNING AROUND INSIDE THE TEMPLE!
I'M GOING TO FLUSH HIM OUT!
OKAY....

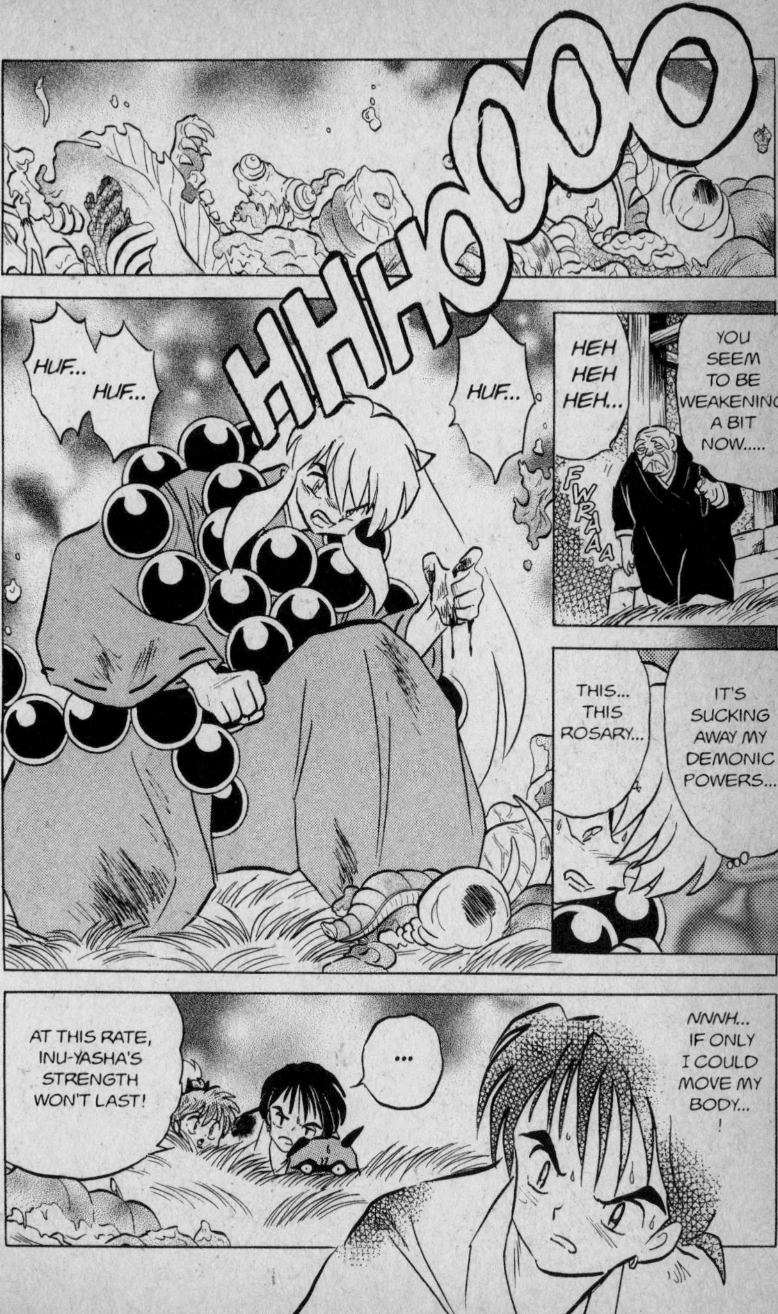
HHHOOOOO
HUF... HUF...
HUF...
HEH HEH HEH...
YOU SEEM TO BE WEAKENING A BIT NOW.....
FWRAAA
THIS... THIS ROSARY...
IT'S SUCKING AWAY MY DEMONIC POWERS...
AT THIS RATE, INU-YASHA'S STRENGTH WON'T LAST!
...
NNNH... IF ONLY I COULD MOVE MY BODY...!

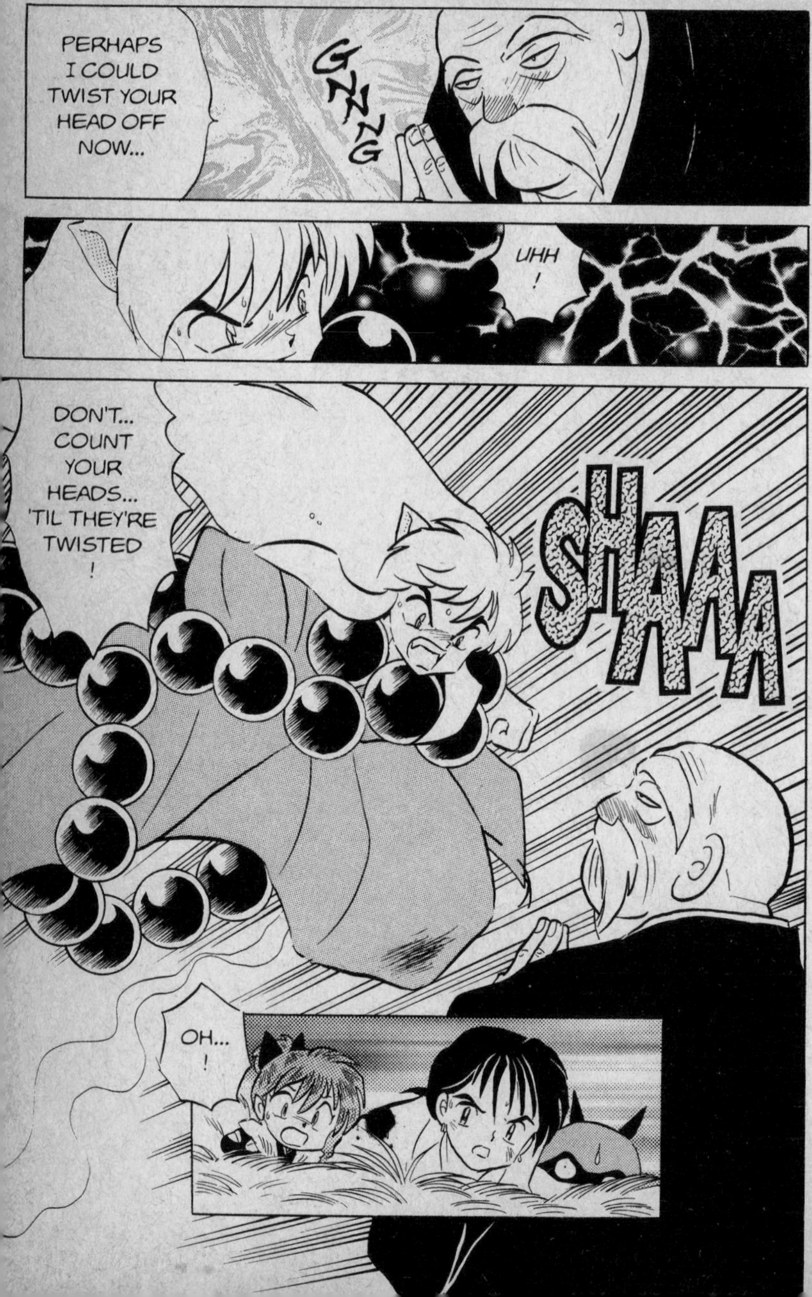
PERHAPS I COULD TWIST YOUR HEAD OFF NOW...
GNNNG
UHH!
DON'T... COUNT YOUR HEADS... 'TIL THEY'RE TWISTED!
SHAAAA
OH...!

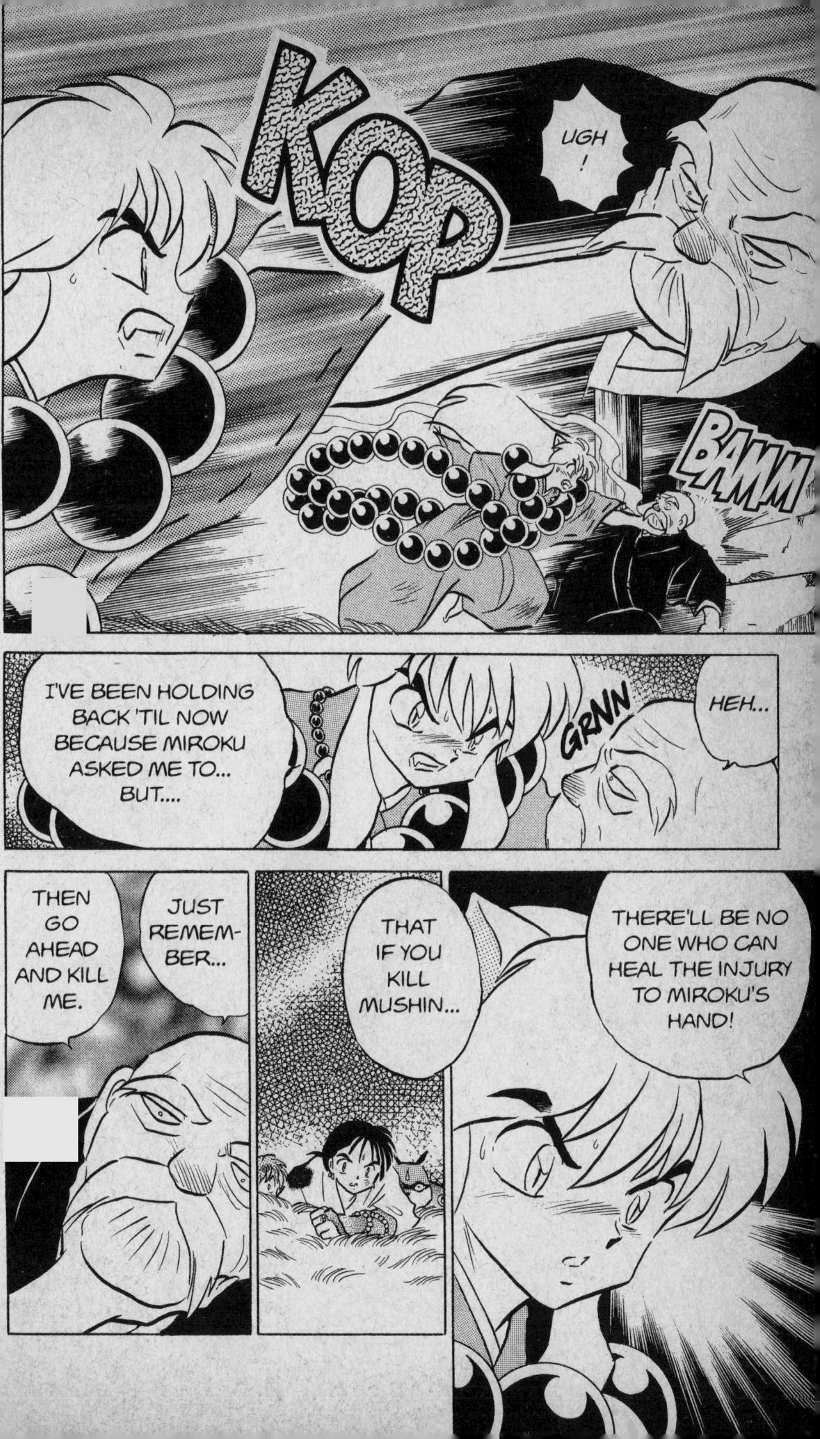
KOP
UGH!
BAMM
I'VE BEEN HOLDING BACK 'TIL NOW BECAUSE MIROKU ASKED ME TO... BUT....
GRNN
HEH...
THEN GO AHEAD AND KILL ME.
JUST REMEMBER...
THAT IF YOU KILL MUSHIN...
THERE'LL BE NO ONE WHO CAN HEAL THE INJURY TO MIROKU'S HAND!

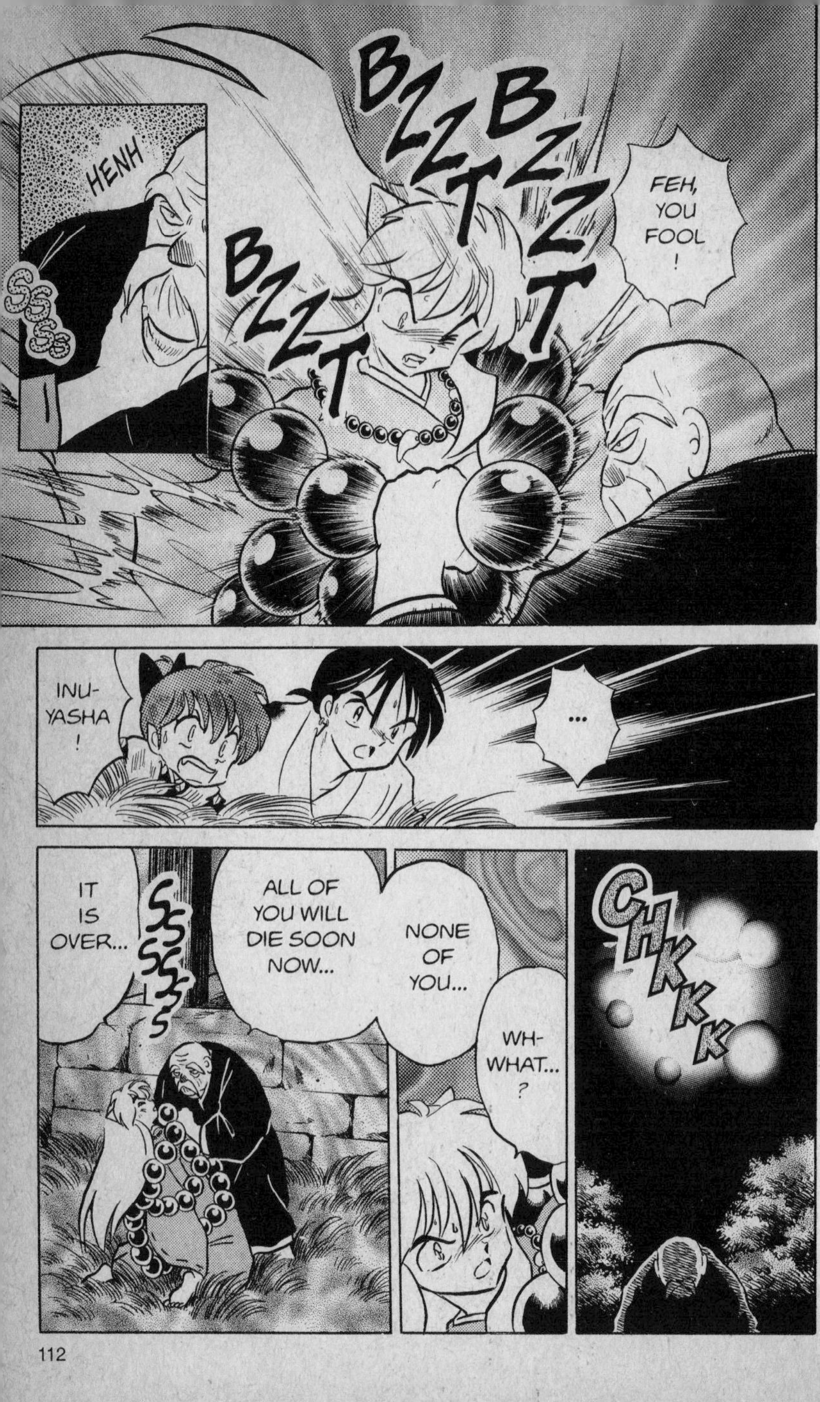
HENH
SSSS
BZZZT
BZZZT
BZZZT
FEH, YOU FOOL!
INU-YASHA!
...
IT IS OVER...
SSSSS
ALL OF YOU WILL DIE SOON NOW...
NONE OF YOU...
WH-WHAT...?
CHKKKK

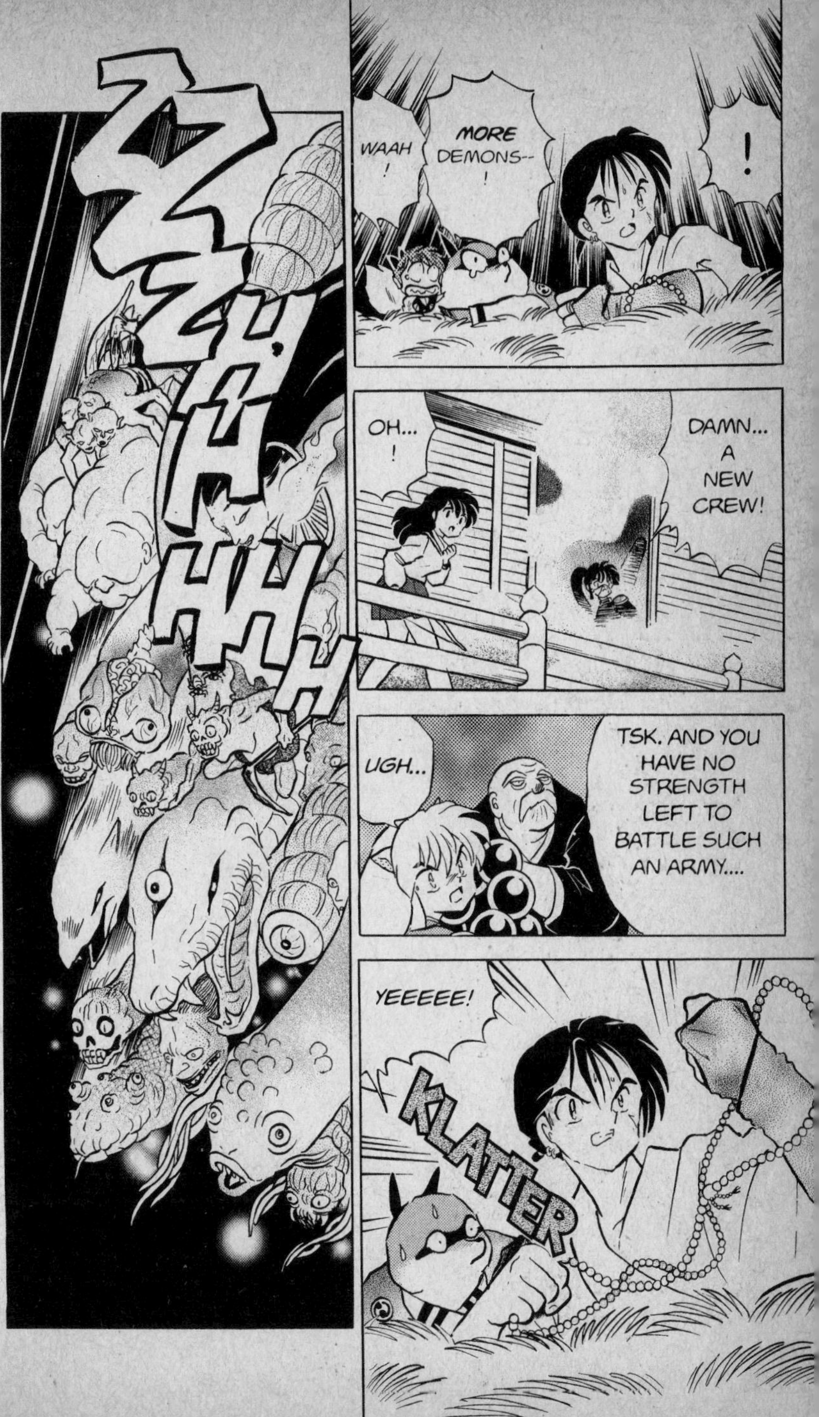
WAAH !
MORE DEMONS-- !
!
OH... !
DAMN... A NEW CREW!
UGH...
TSK. AND YOU HAVE NO STRENGTH LEFT TO BATTLE SUCH AN ARMY....
YEEEEE!
KLATTER

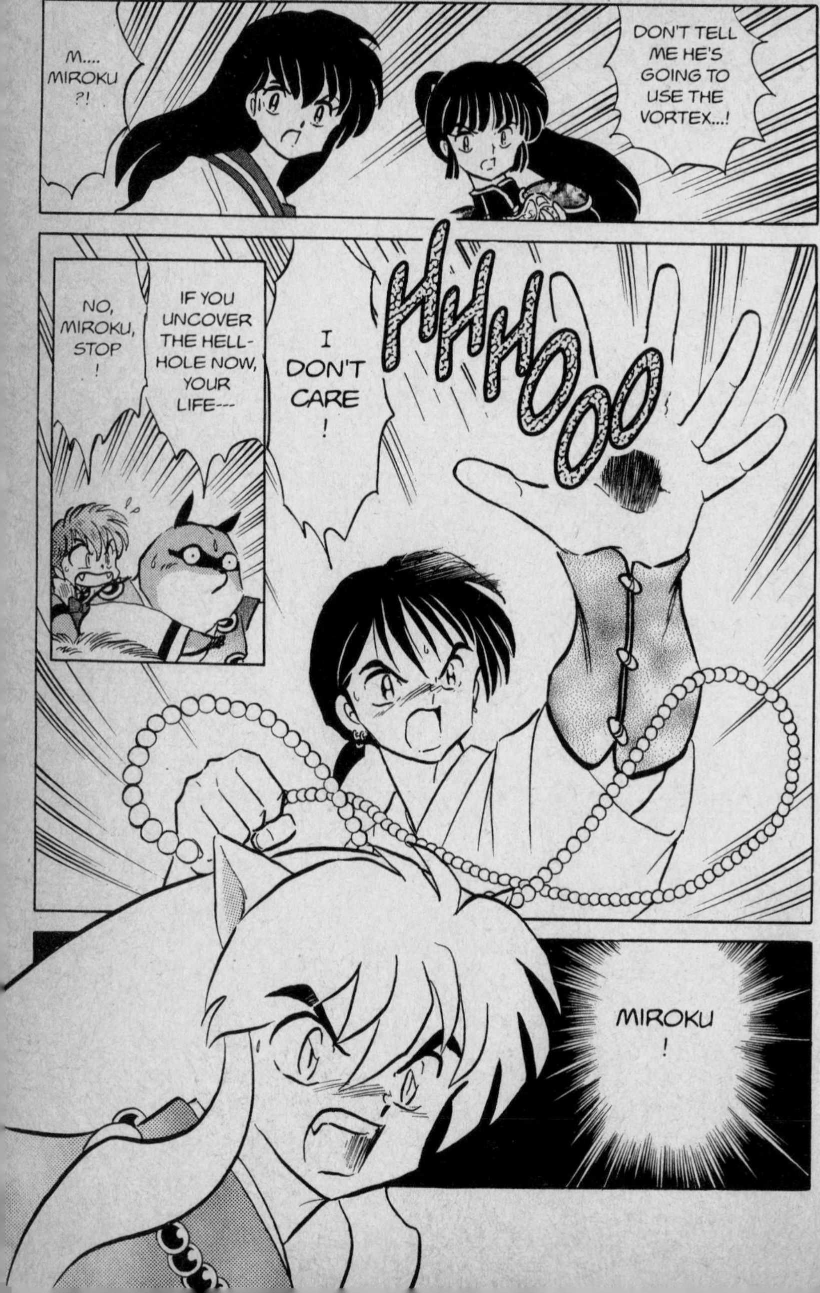

M.... MIROKU ?!
DON'T TELL ME HE'S GOING TO USE THE VORTEX...!
NO, MIROKU, STOP !
IF YOU UNCOVER THE HELL-HOLE NOW, YOUR LIFE---
I DON'T CARE !
HHHOOO
MIROKU !

SCROLL SEVEN

THE SPAN OF A LIFE

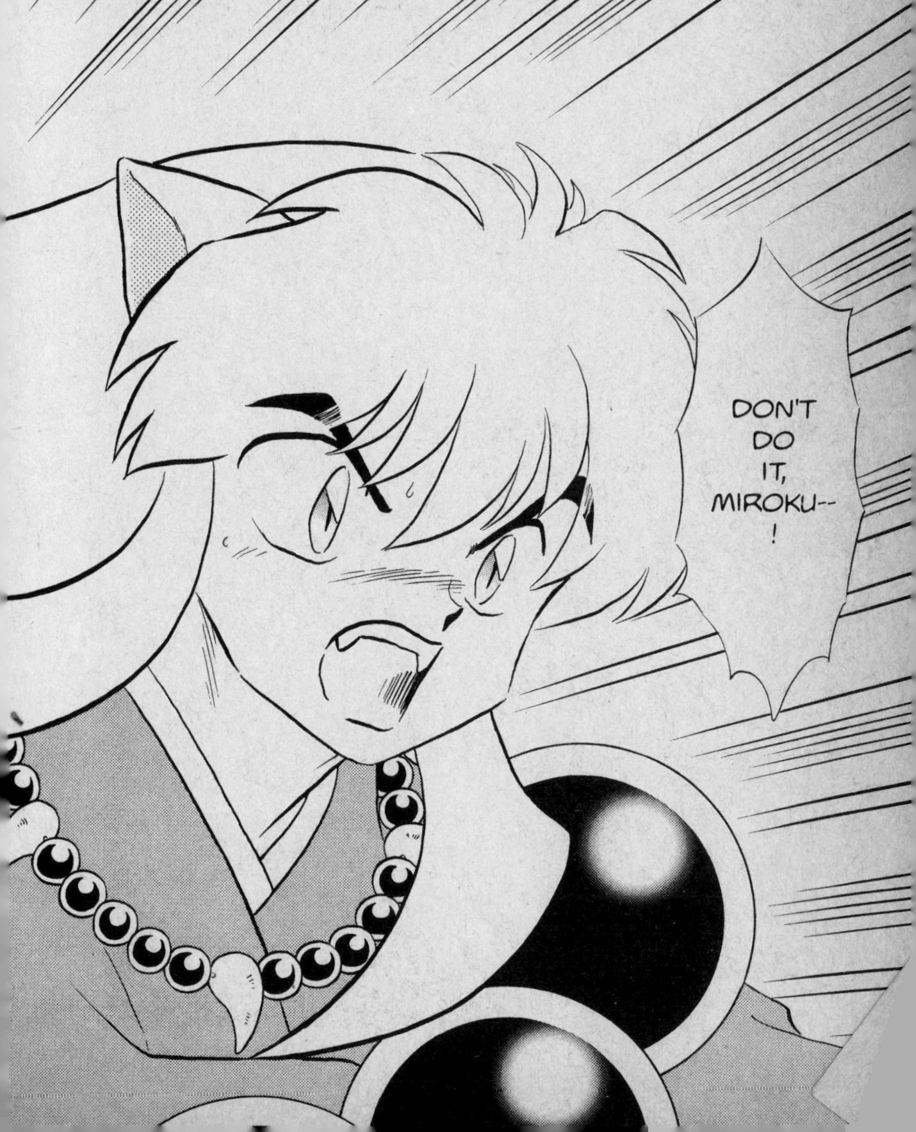
DON'T DO IT, MIROKU--!

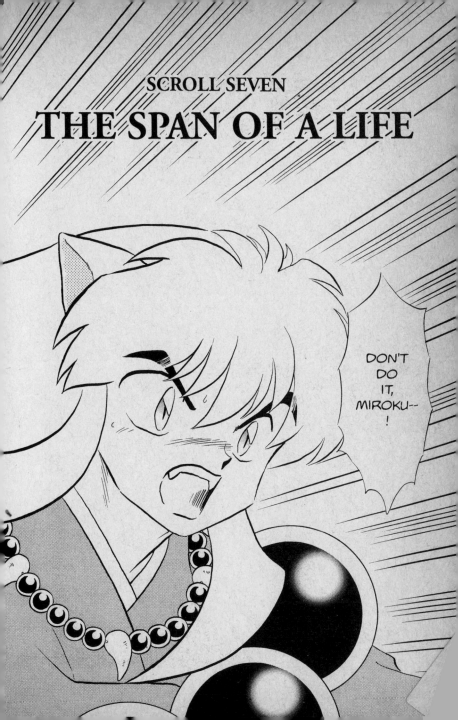

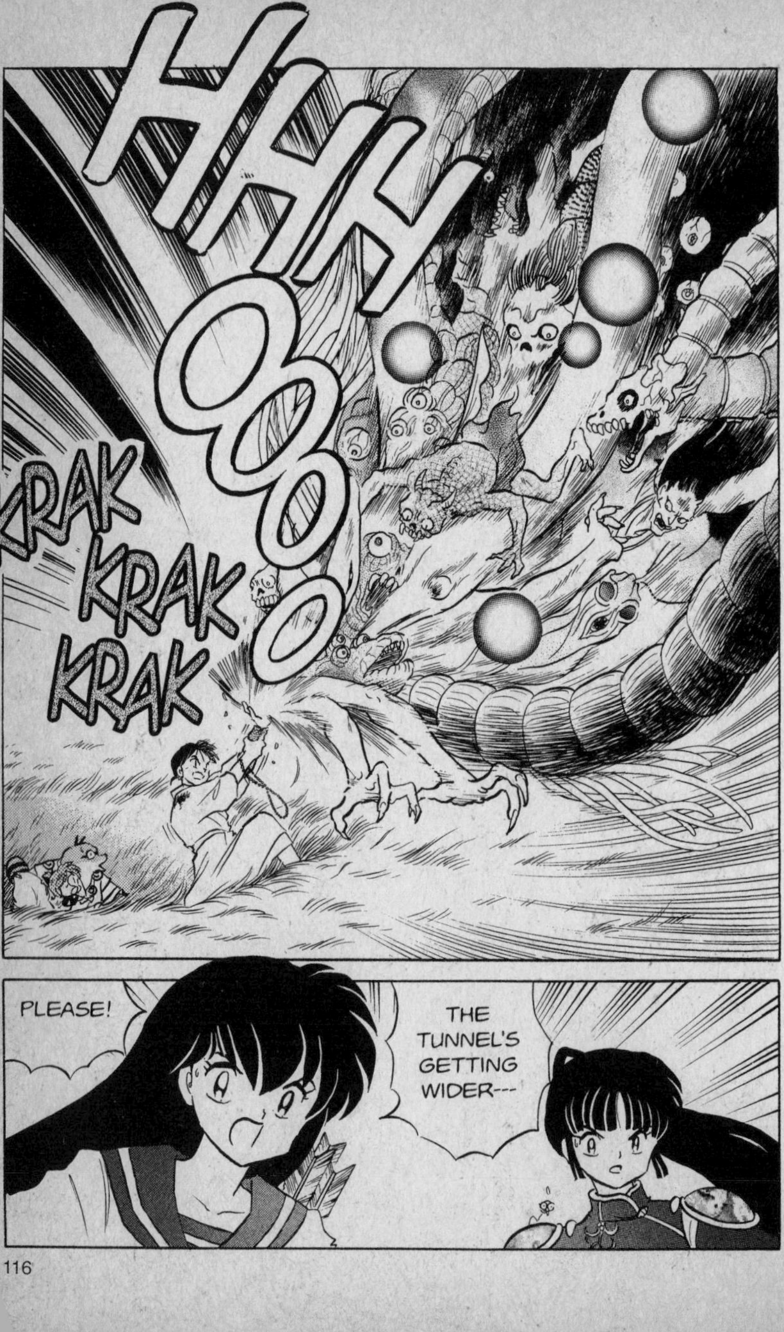
HHHOOOOO
KRAK
KRAK
KRAK
PLEASE!
THE TUNNEL'S GETTING WIDER---

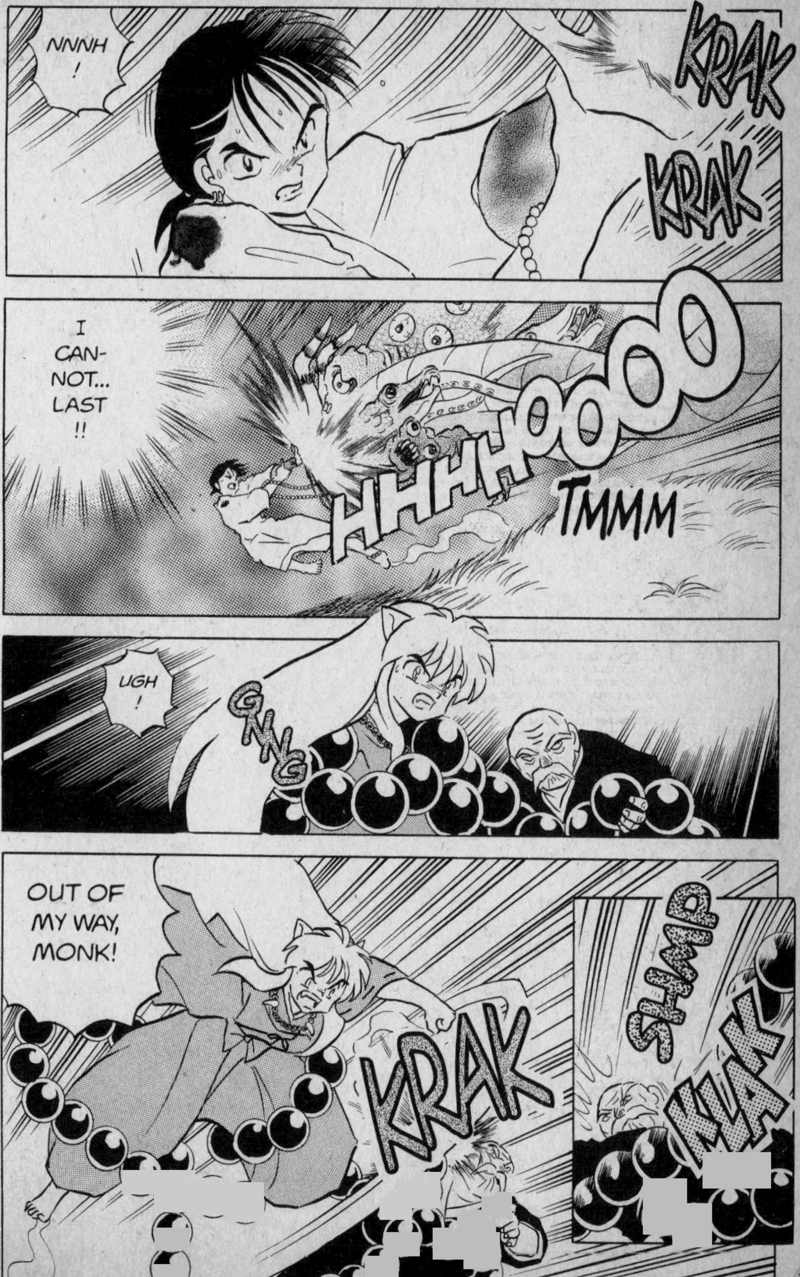
NNNH !
KRAK
KRAK
I CAN-NOT... LAST !!
HHHHOOOO
TMMM
UGH !
GNNG
OUT OF MY WAY, MONK!
KRAK
SHMP
KLAK

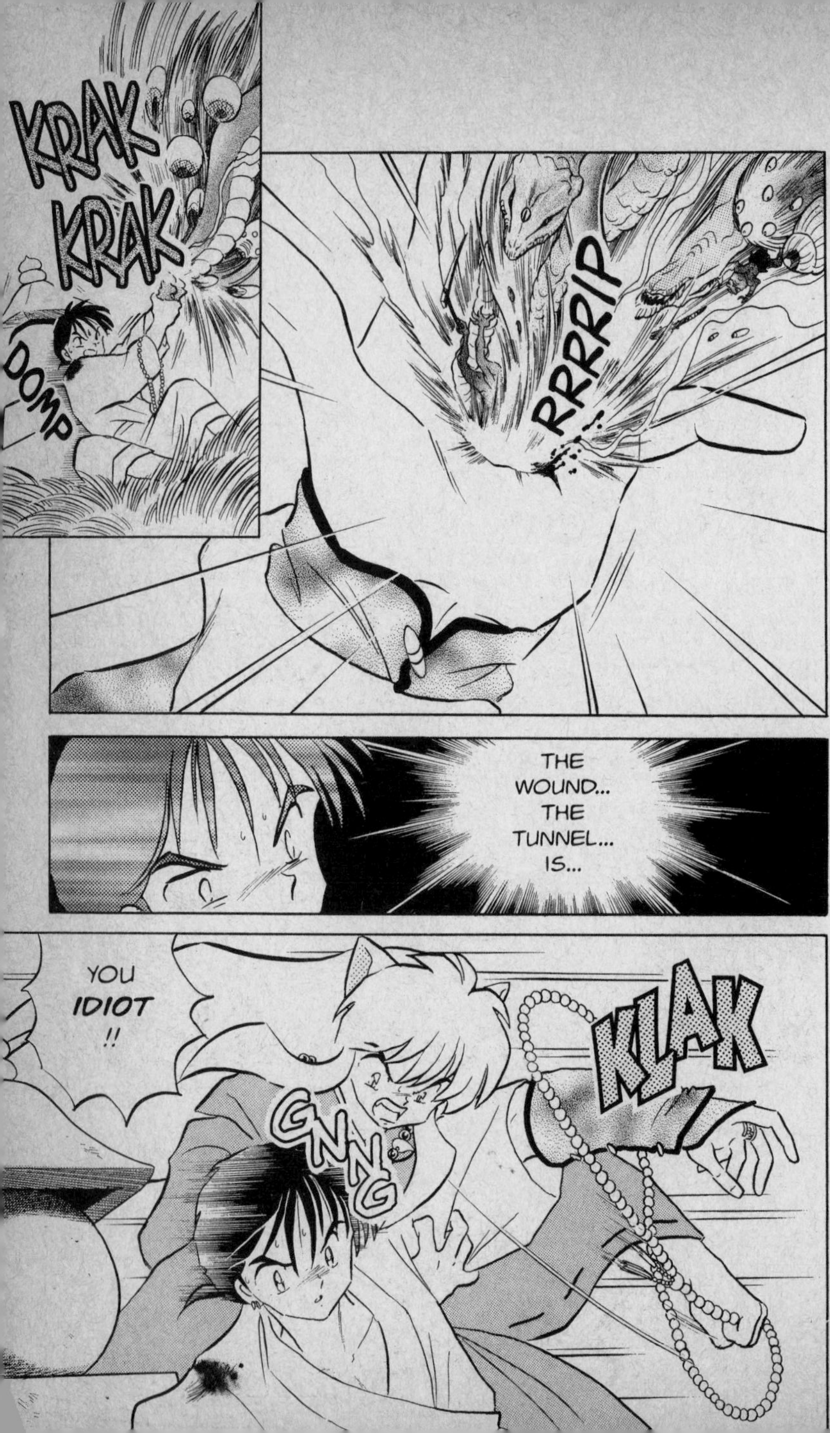
KRAK
KRAK
DOMP
RRRRIP
THE WOUND... THE TUNNEL... IS...
YOU IDIOT !!
GNNG
KLAK

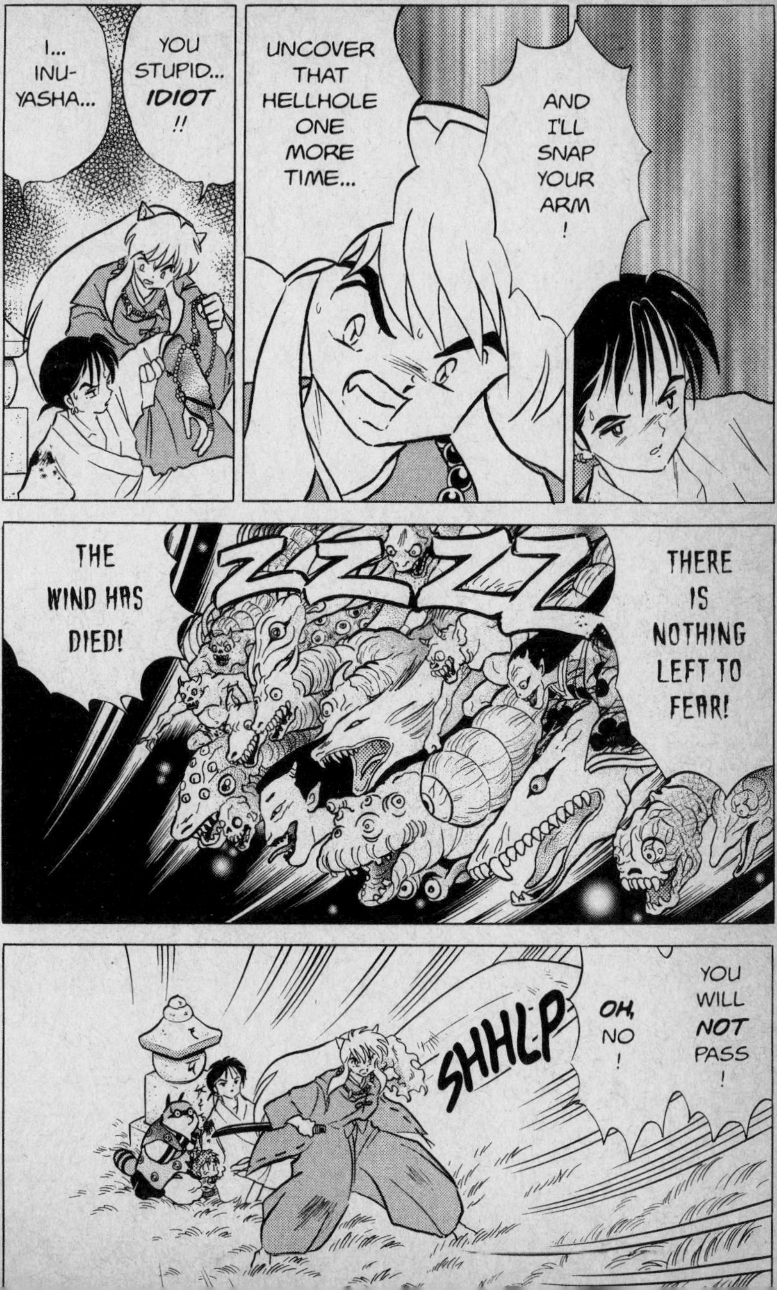
I... INU-YASHA...
YOU STUPID... IDIOT !!
UNCOVER THAT HELLHOLE ONE MORE TIME...
AND I'LL SNAP YOUR ARM !
THE WIND HAS DIED!
ZZZZZ
THERE IS NOTHING LEFT TO FEAR!
SHHLP
OH, NO !
YOU WILL NOT PASS !

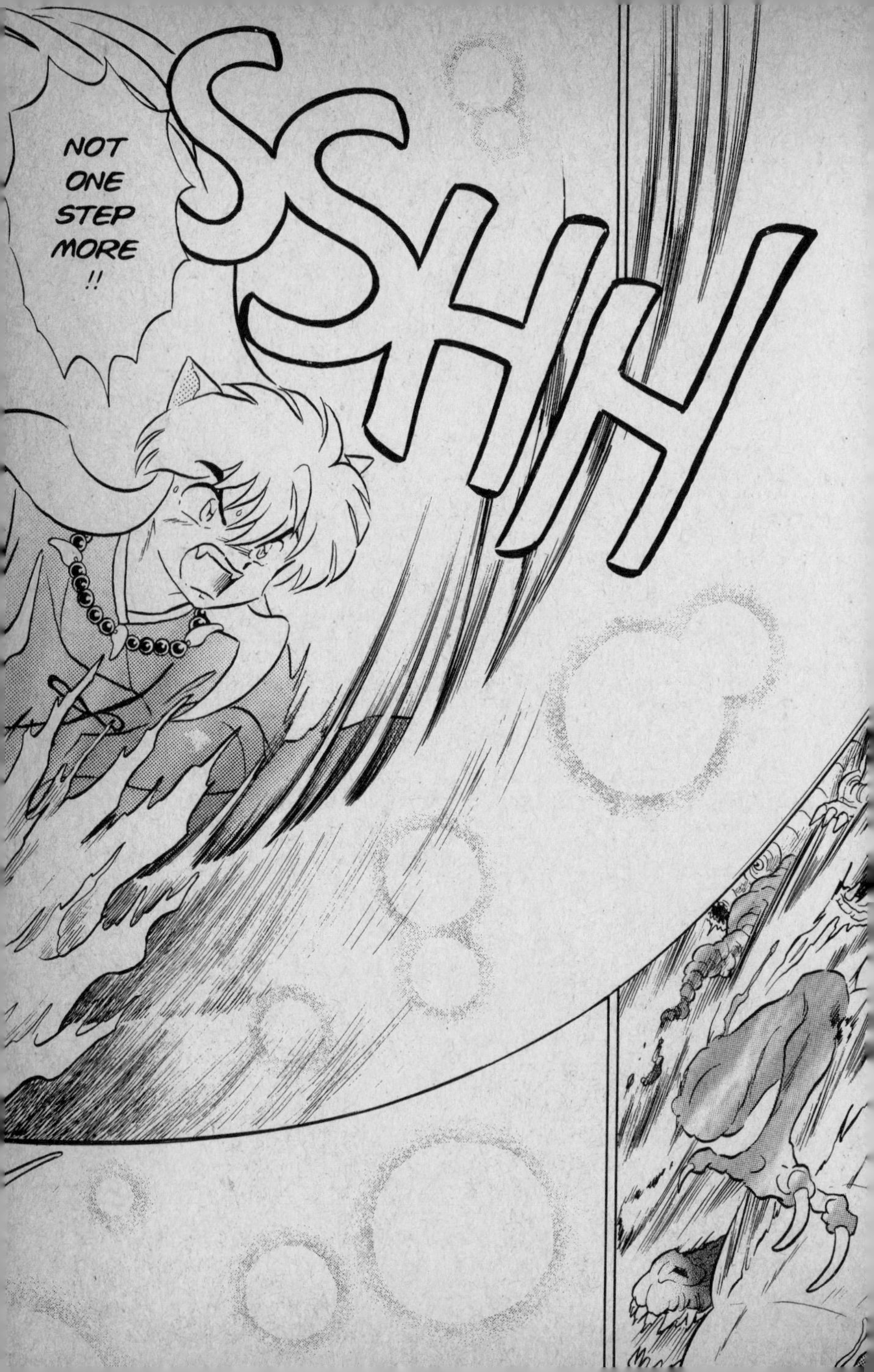
NOT ONE STEP MORE !!
SSHHH

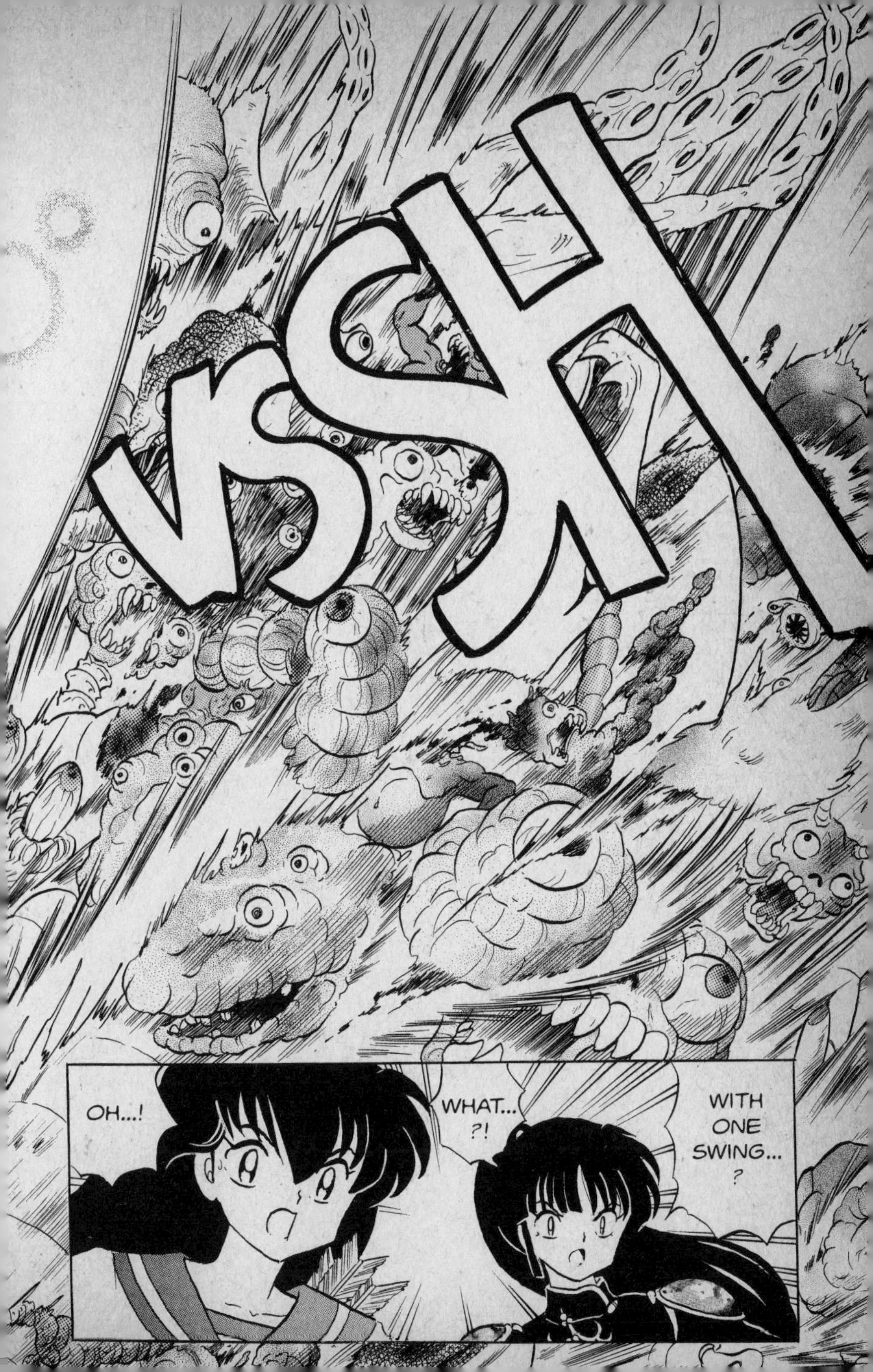
VSSH
OH...!
WHAT... ?!
WITH ONE SWING... ?

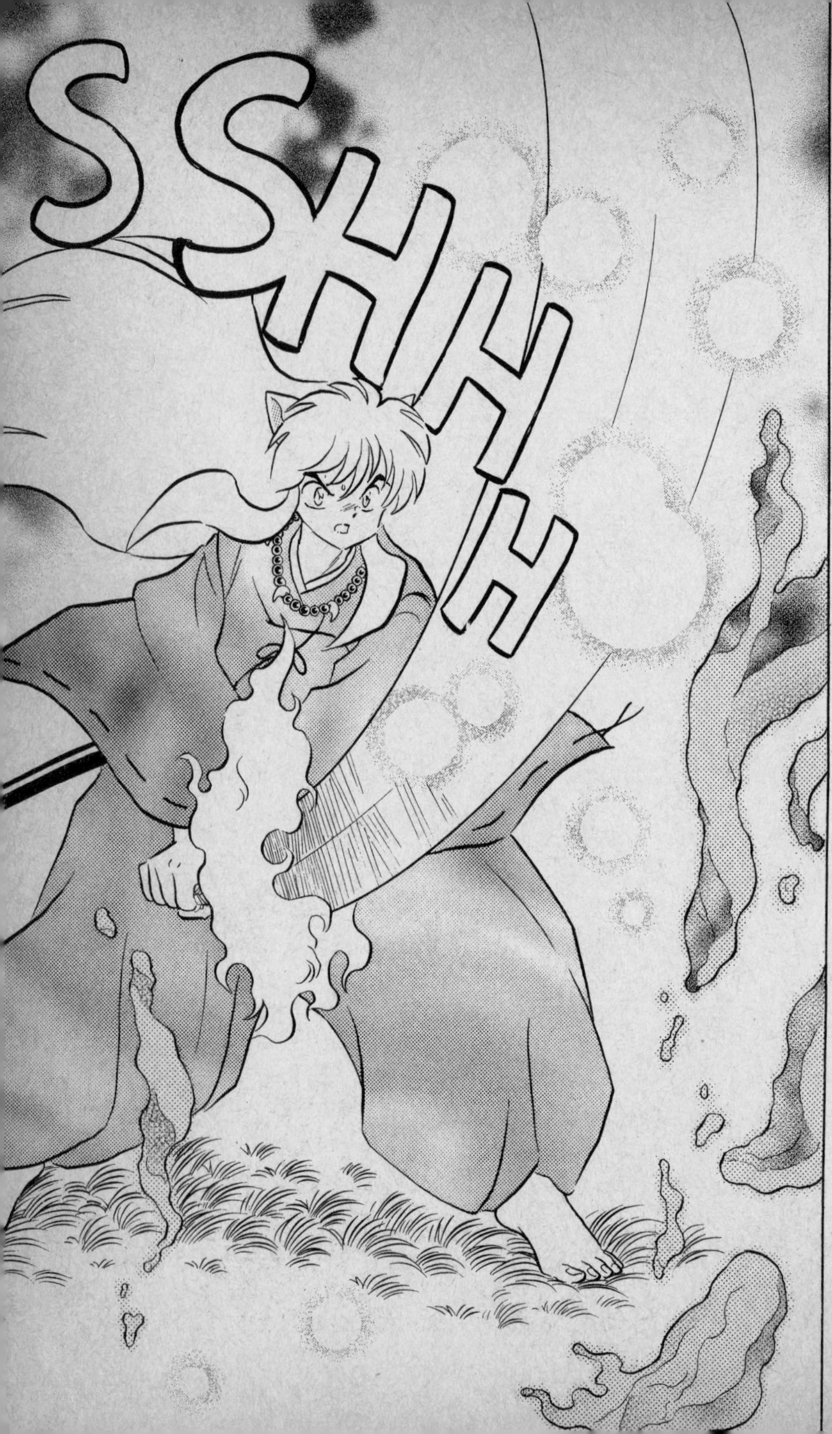
SSHHHH

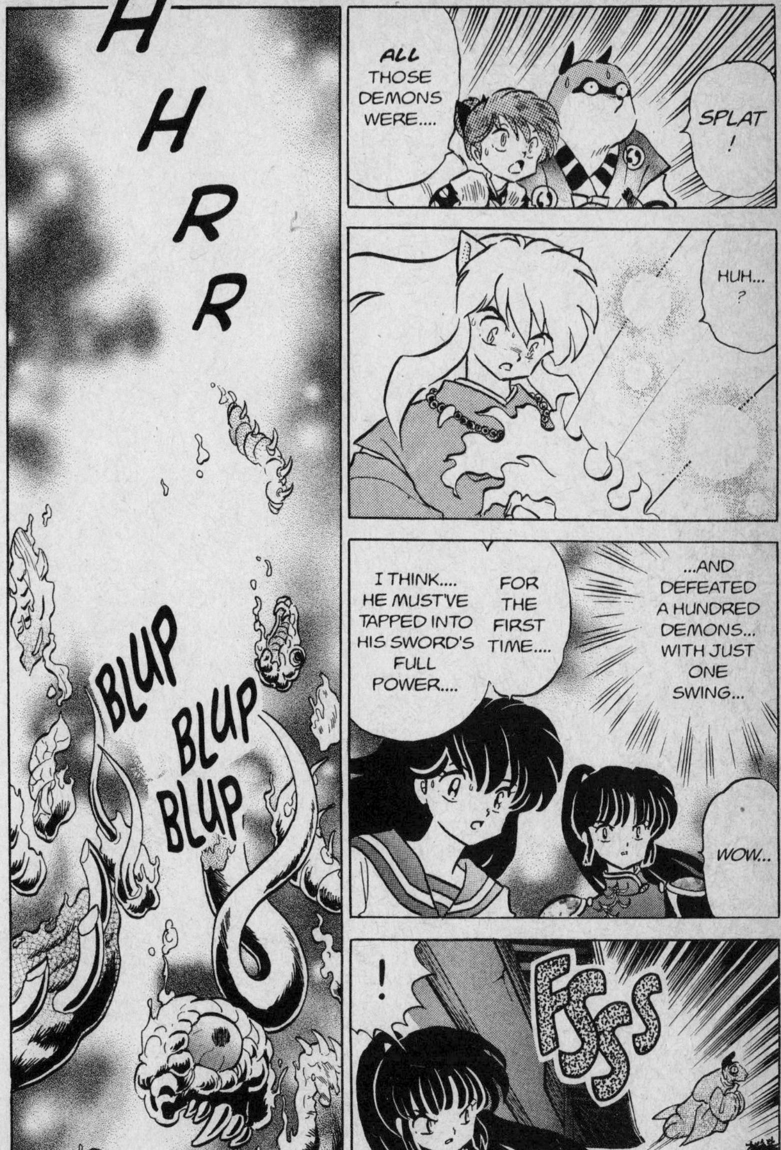
HHRR
BLUP
BLUP
BLUP
ALL THOSE DEMONS WERE....
SPLAT!
HUH...?
I THINK.... HE MUST'VE TAPPED INTO HIS SWORD'S FULL POWER....
FOR THE FIRST TIME....
...AND DEFEATED A HUNDRED DEMONS... WITH JUST ONE SWING...
WOW...
!
FSSS

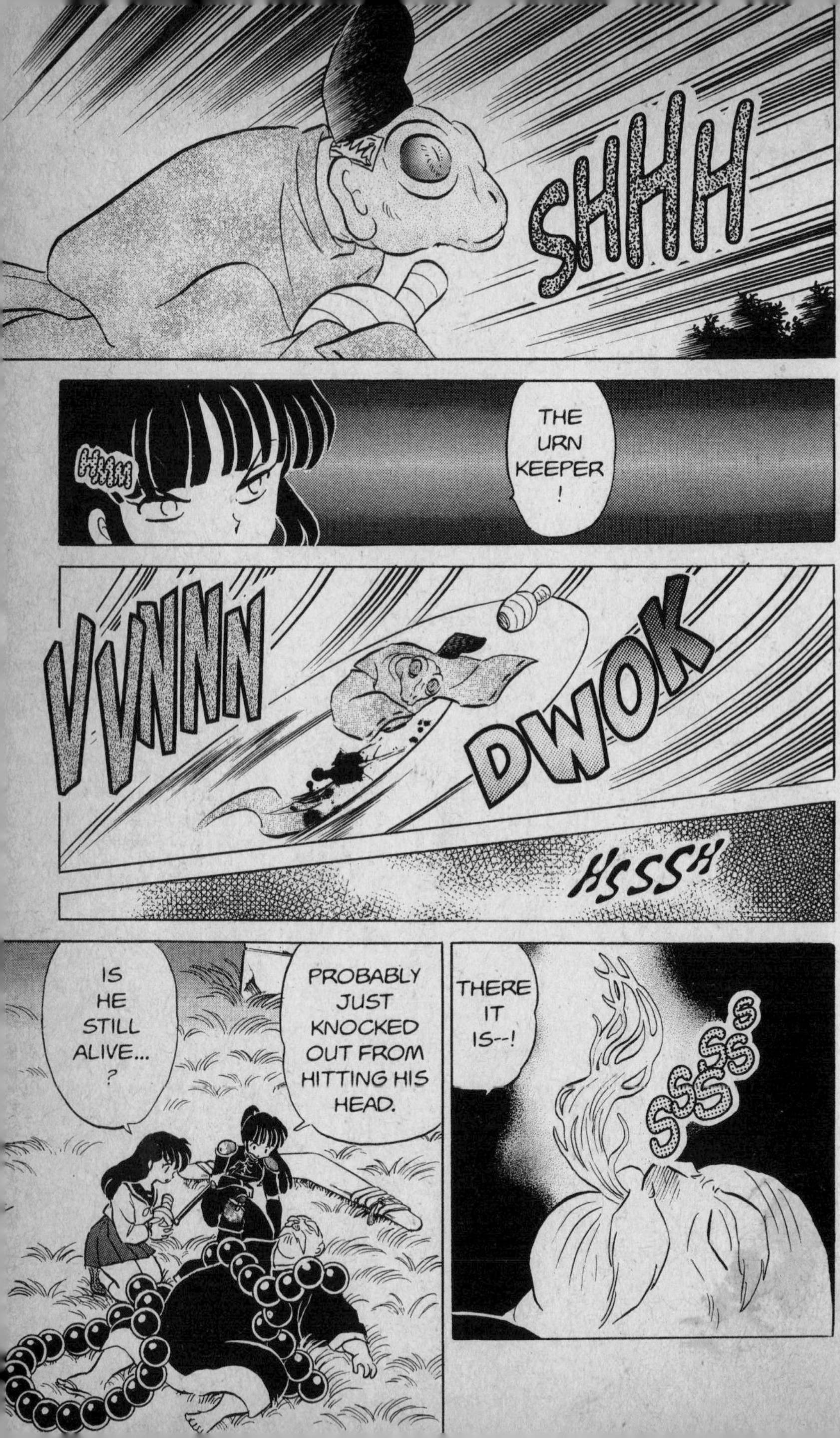
SHHH
THE URN KEEPER!
VVNNN
DWOK
HSSSH
IS HE STILL ALIVE...?
PROBABLY JUST KNOCKED OUT FROM HITTING HIS HEAD.
THERE IT IS--!
SSSSSS

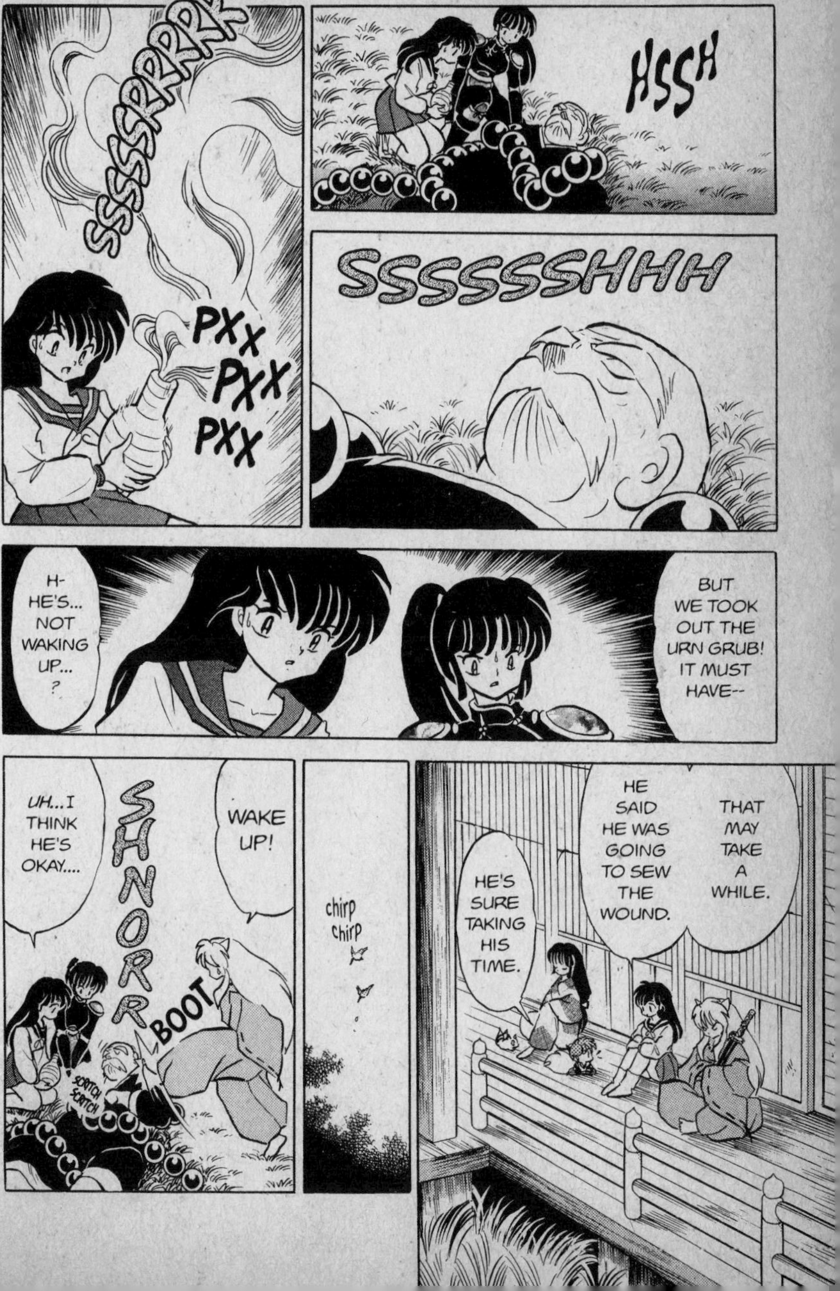
SSSSSRRRRR
PXX PXX PXX
HSSH
SSSSSSHHH
H- HE'S... NOT WAKING UP... ?
BUT WE TOOK OUT THE URN GRUB! IT MUST HAVE--
UH...I THINK HE'S OKAY....
SHNORR
WAKE UP!
BOOT
SCRATCH SCRATCH
chirp chirp
HE'S SURE TAKING HIS TIME.
HE SAID HE WAS GOING TO SEW THE WOUND.
THAT MAY TAKE A WHILE.

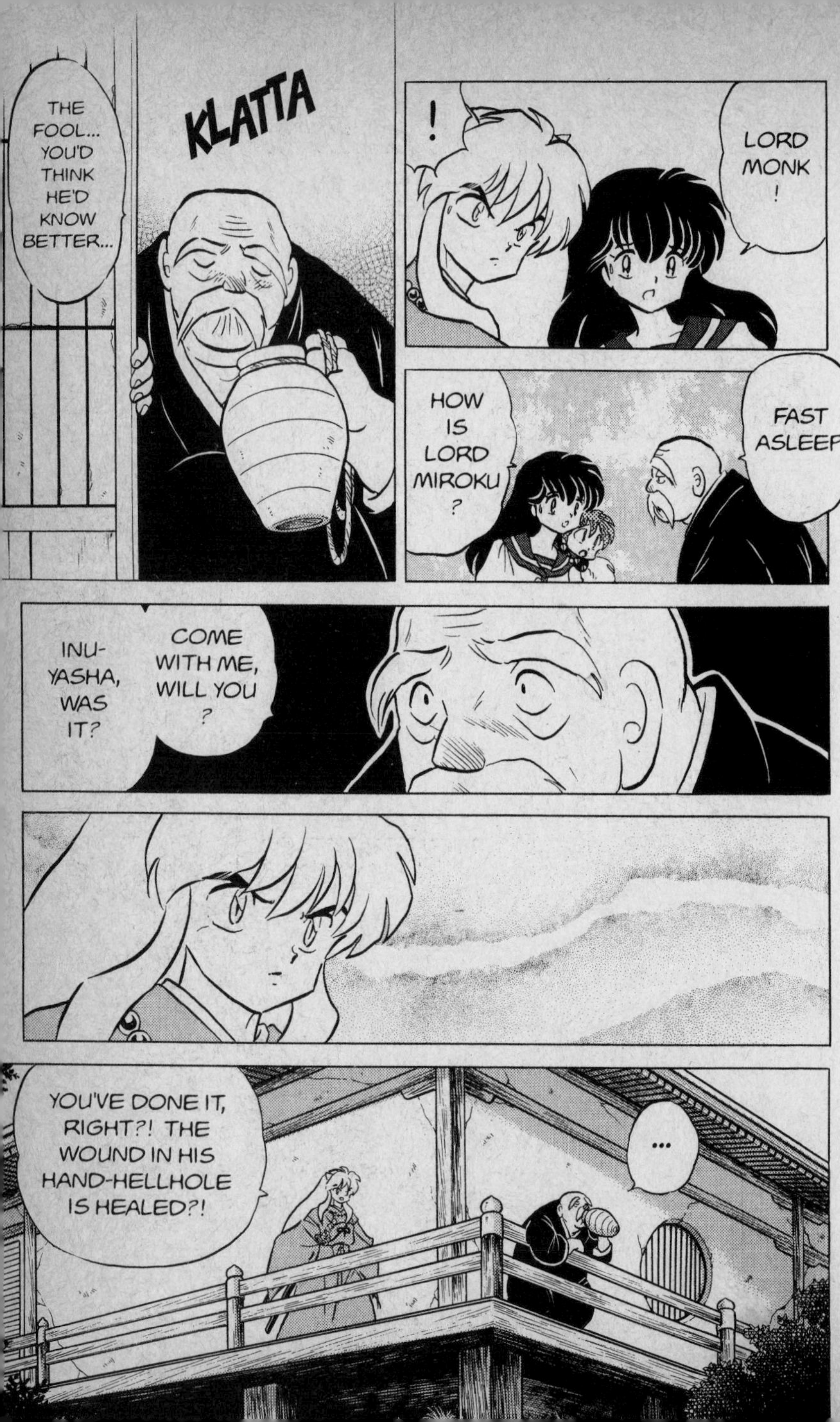
THE FOOL... YOU'D THINK HE'D KNOW BETTER...
KLATTA
!
LORD MONK !
HOW IS LORD MIROKU ?
FAST ASLEEP.
INU-YASHA, WAS IT?
COME WITH ME, WILL YOU ?
YOU'VE DONE IT, RIGHT?! THE WOUND IN HIS HAND-HELLHOLE IS HEALED?!
...

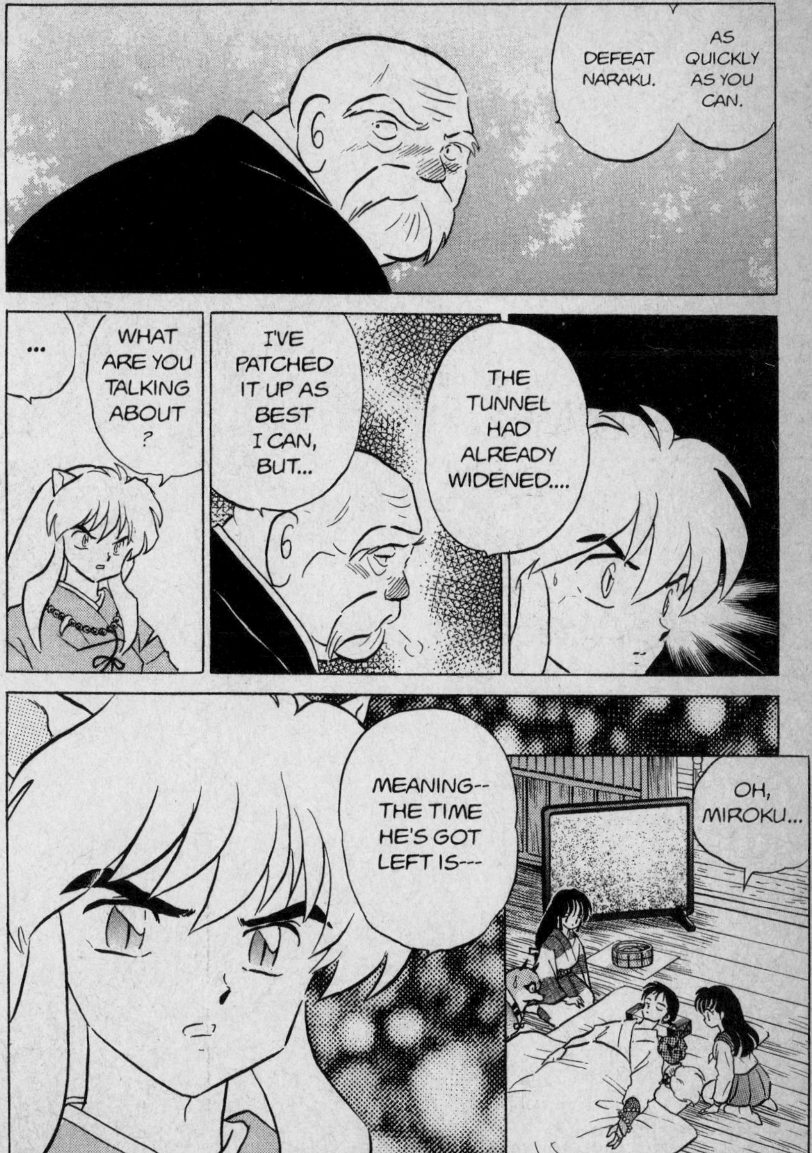
DEFEAT NARAKU.
AS QUICKLY AS YOU CAN.
...
WHAT ARE YOU TALKING ABOUT?
I'VE PATCHED IT UP AS BEST I CAN, BUT...
THE TUNNEL HAD ALREADY WIDENED....
MEANING-- THE TIME HE'S GOT LEFT IS---
OH, MIROKU...

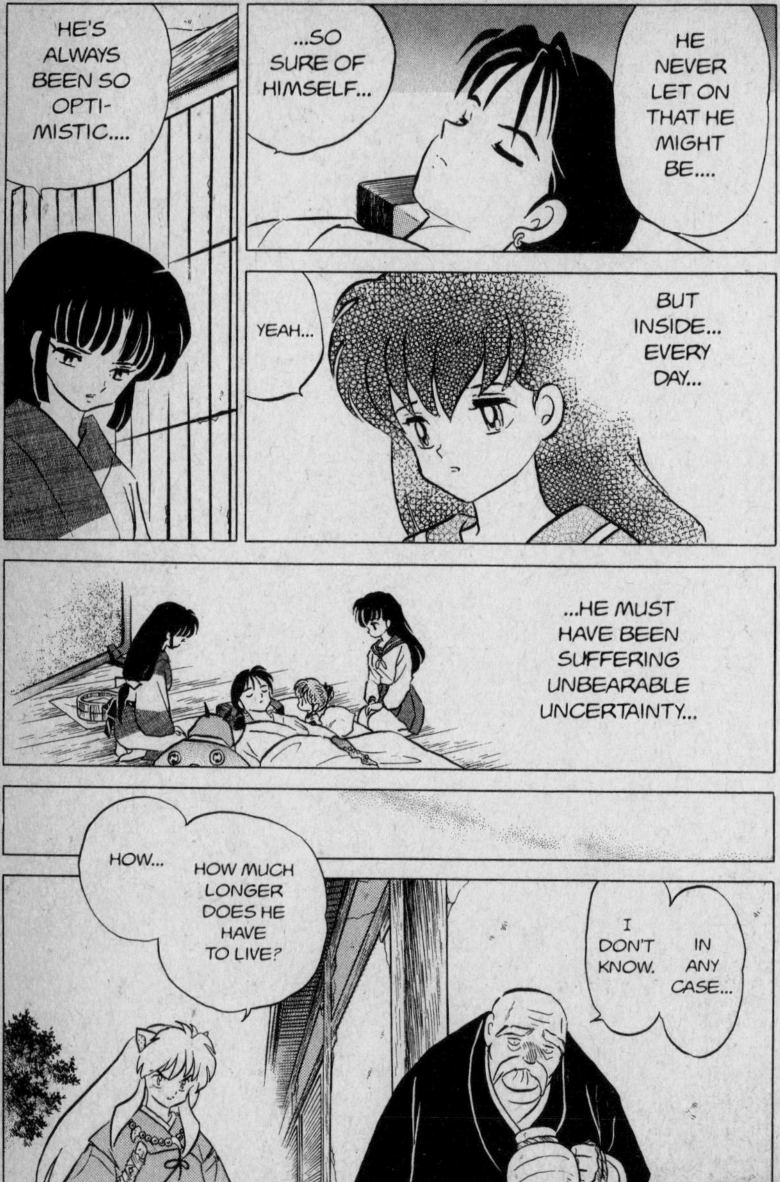
HE'S ALWAYS BEEN SO OPTI-MISTIC....
...SO SURE OF HIMSELF...
HE NEVER LET ON THAT HE MIGHT BE....
YEAH...
BUT INSIDE... EVERY DAY...
...HE MUST HAVE BEEN SUFFERING UNBEARABLE UNCERTAINTY...
HOW...
HOW MUCH LONGER DOES HE HAVE TO LIVE?
I DON'T KNOW.
IN ANY CASE...

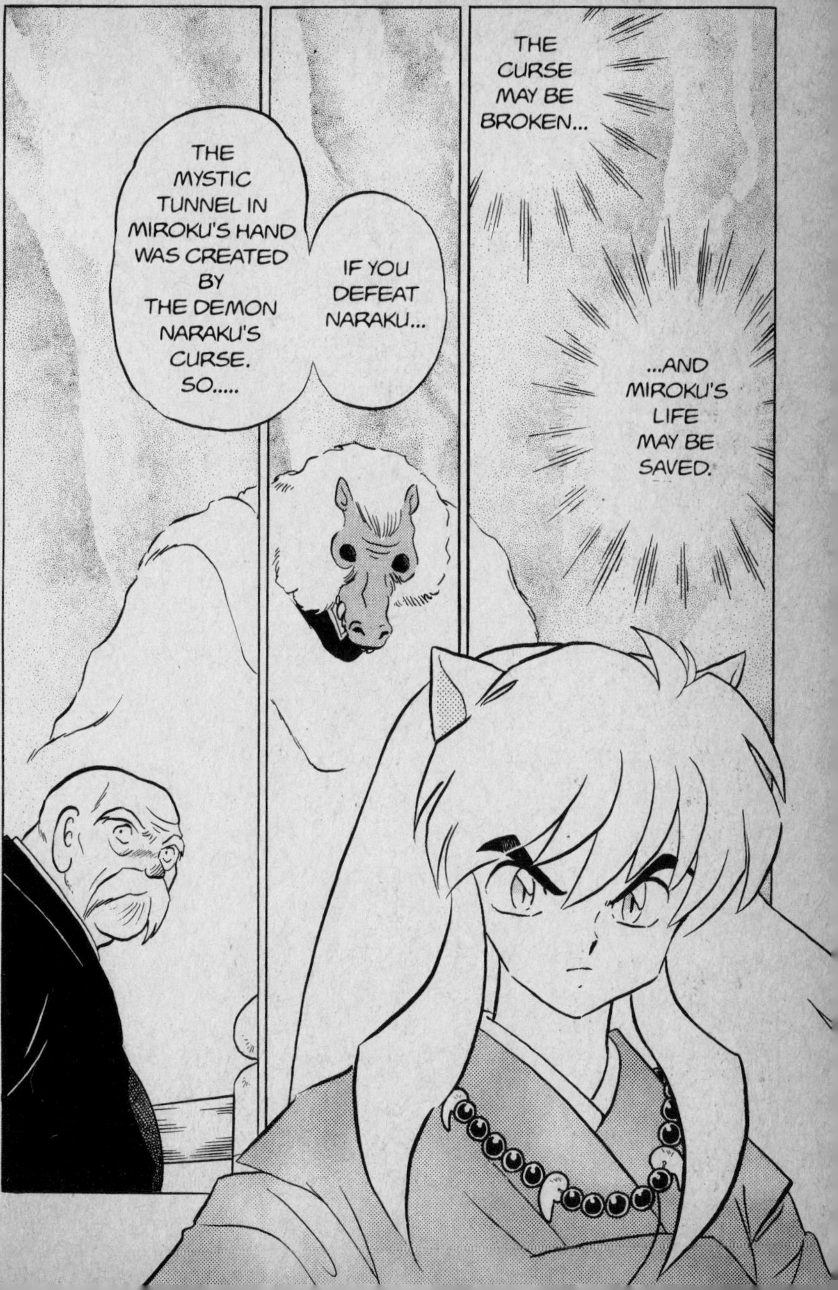
THE MYSTIC TUNNEL IN MIROKU'S HAND WAS CREATED BY THE DEMON NARAKU'S CURSE. SO.....
IF YOU DEFEAT NARAKU...
THE CURSE MAY BE BROKEN...
...AND MIROKU'S LIFE MAY BE SAVED.

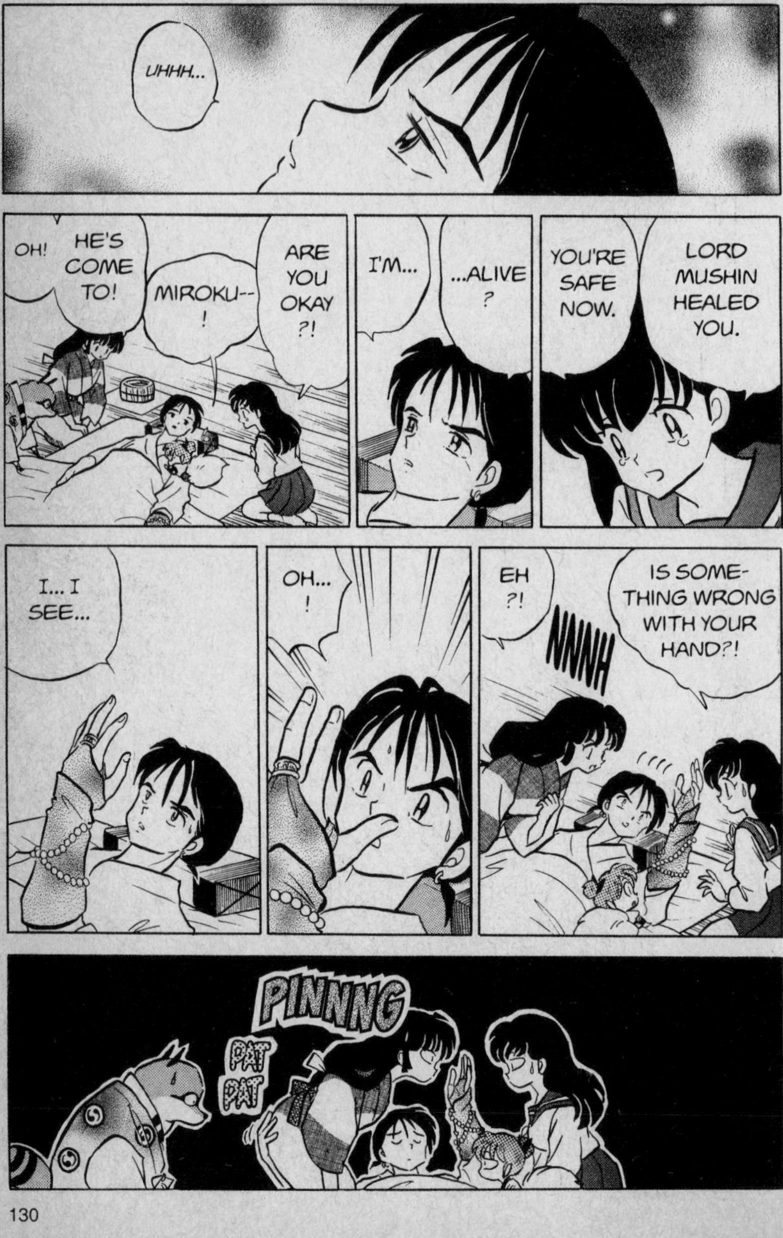
UHHH...
OH!
HE'S COME TO!
MIROKU--!
ARE YOU OKAY?!
I'M...
...ALIVE?
YOU'RE SAFE NOW.
LORD MUSHIN HEALED YOU.
I... I SEE...
OH...!
EH?!
NNNH
IS SOME-THING WRONG WITH YOUR HAND?!
PINNNG
PAT PAT

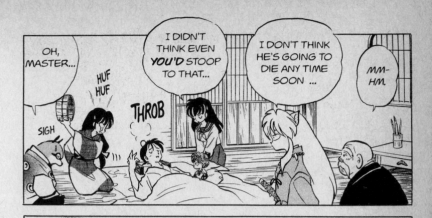

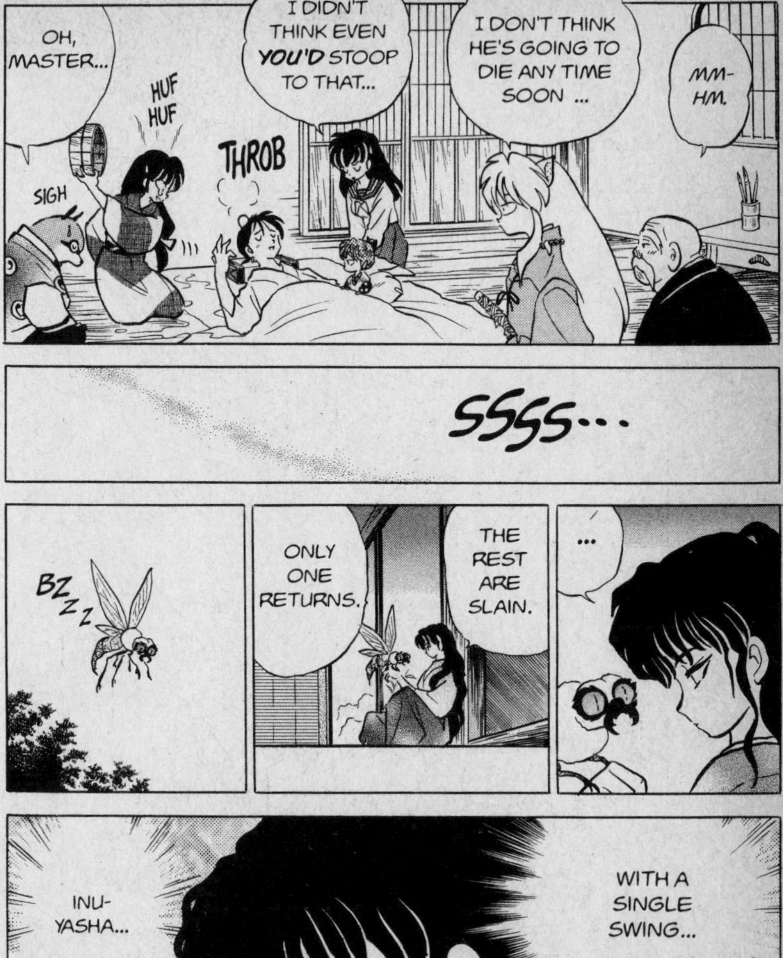
OH, MASTER...
I DIDN'T THINK EVEN *YOU'D* STOOP TO THAT...
I DON'T THINK HE'S GOING TO DIE ANY TIME SOON ...
MM-HM.
HUF HUF
THROB
SIGH
SSSS...
BZZZ
ONLY ONE RETURNS.
THE REST ARE SLAIN.
...
INU-YASHA...
WITH A SINGLE SWING...

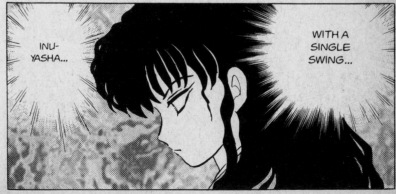

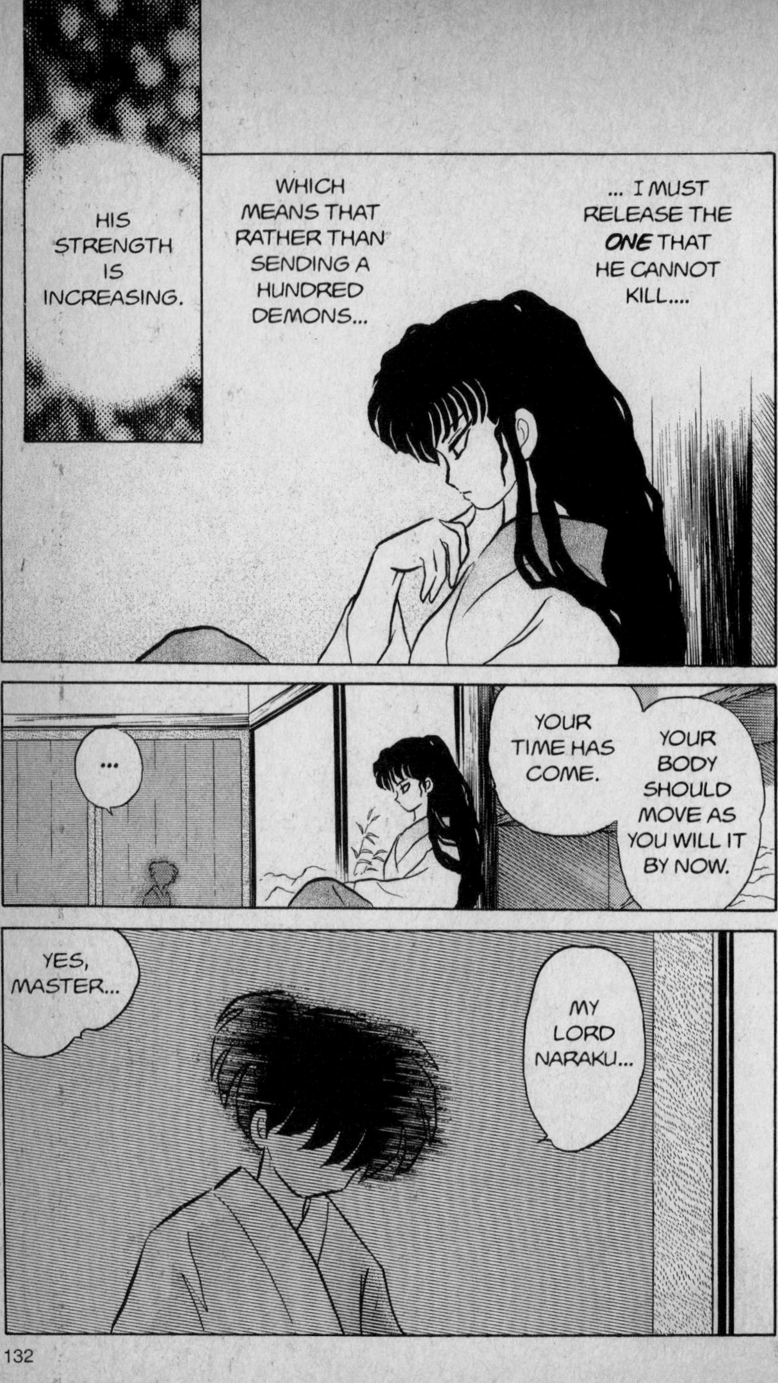
HIS STRENGTH IS INCREASING.
WHICH MEANS THAT RATHER THAN SENDING A HUNDRED DEMONS...
... I MUST RELEASE THE ONE THAT HE CANNOT KILL....
...
YOUR TIME HAS COME.
YOUR BODY SHOULD MOVE AS YOU WILL IT BY NOW.
YES, MASTER...
MY LORD NARAKU...

SCROLL EIGHT

KOHAKU

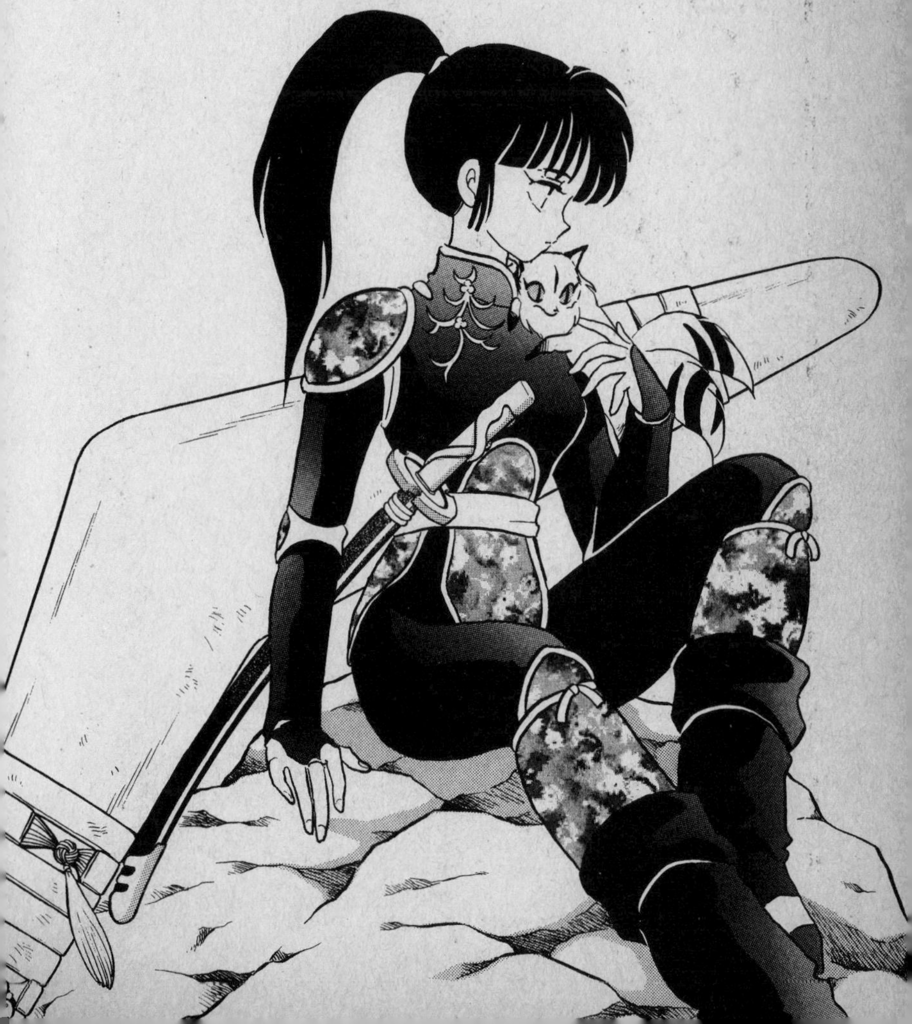

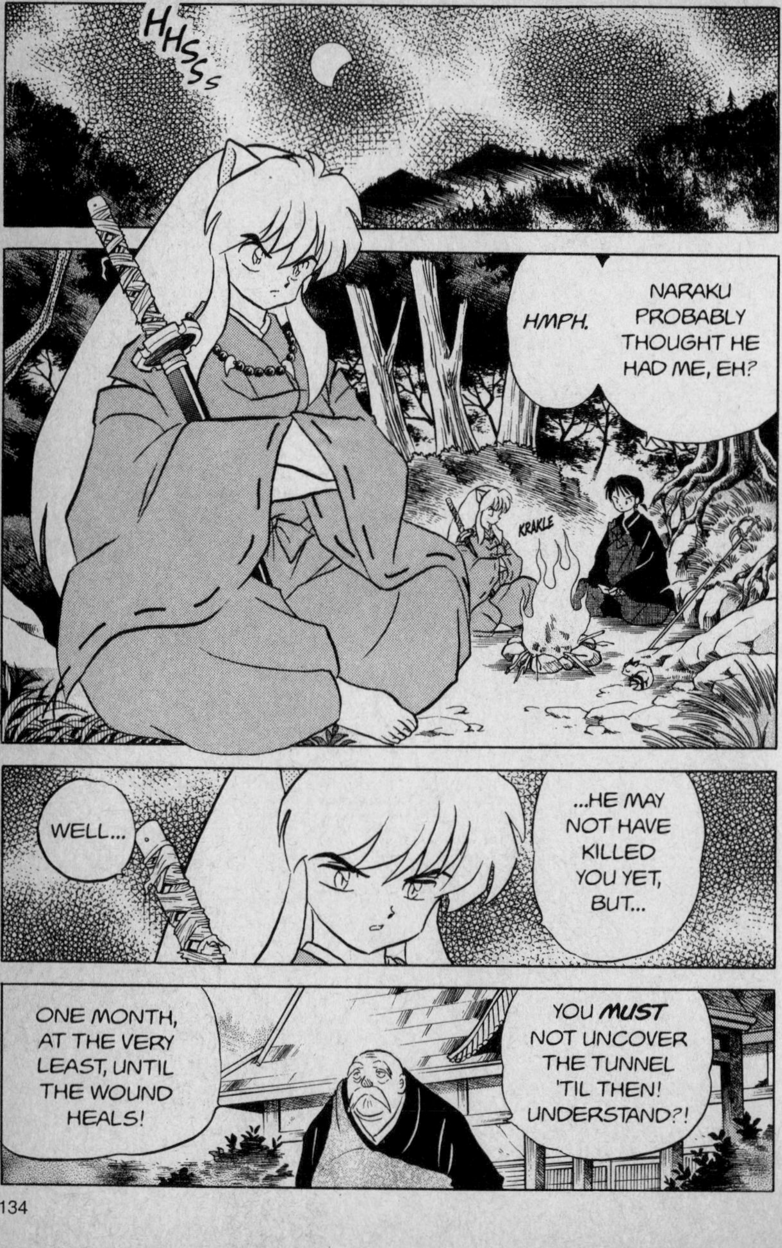
HHSSS
HMPH.
NARAKU PROBABLY THOUGHT HE HAD ME, EH?
KRAKLE
WELL...
...HE MAY NOT HAVE KILLED YOU YET, BUT...
ONE MONTH, AT THE VERY LEAST, UNTIL THE WOUND HEALS!
YOU **MUST** NOT UNCOVER THE TUNNEL 'TIL THEN! UNDERSTAND?!

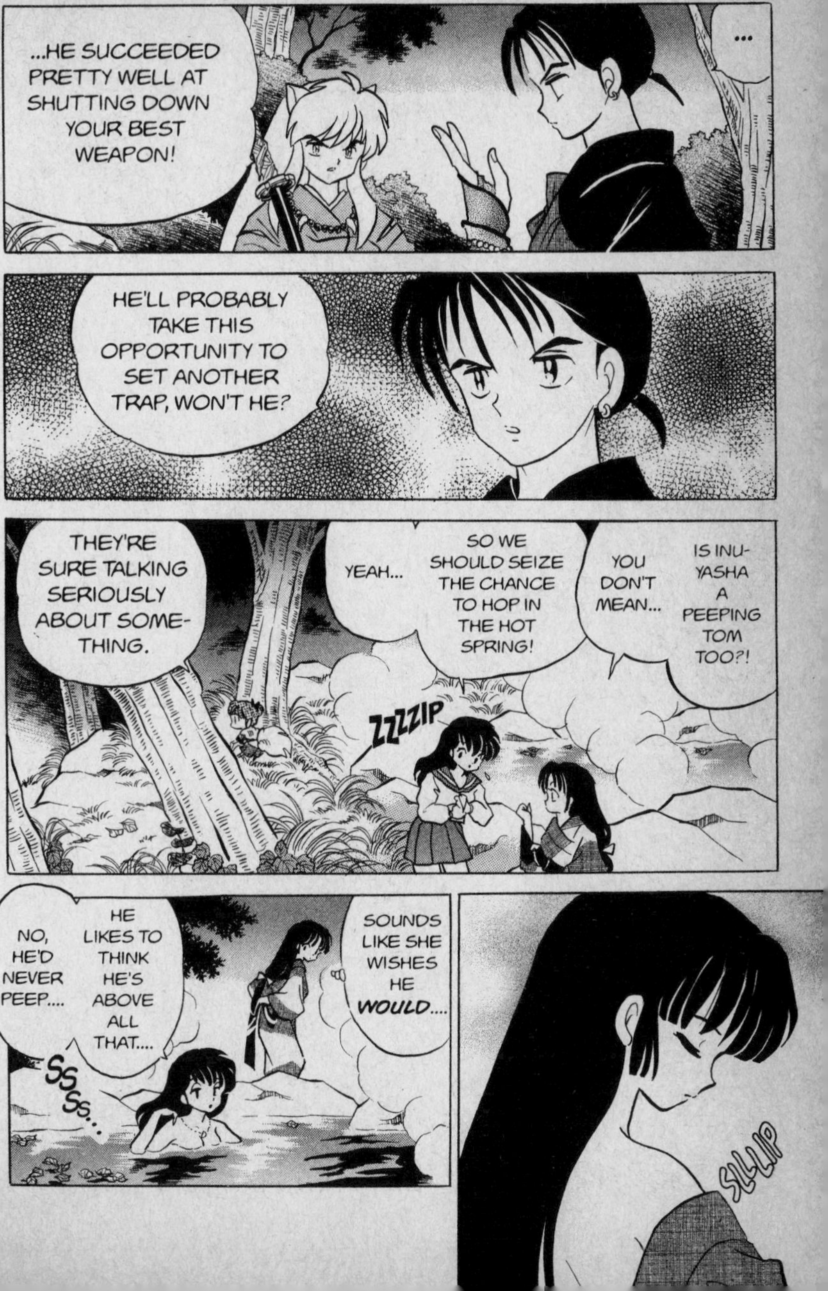
...HE SUCCEEDED PRETTY WELL AT SHUTTING DOWN YOUR BEST WEAPON!
...
HE'LL PROBABLY TAKE THIS OPPORTUNITY TO SET ANOTHER TRAP, WON'T HE?
THEY'RE SURE TALKING SERIOUSLY ABOUT SOME-THING.
YEAH...
SO WE SHOULD SEIZE THE CHANCE TO HOP IN THE HOT SPRING!
YOU DON'T MEAN...
IS INU-YASHA A PEEPING TOM TOO?!
ZZZZIP
NO, HE'D NEVER PEEP....
HE LIKES TO THINK HE'S ABOVE ALL THAT....
SOUNDS LIKE SHE WISHES HE *WOULD*....
SSSS...
SLLLIP

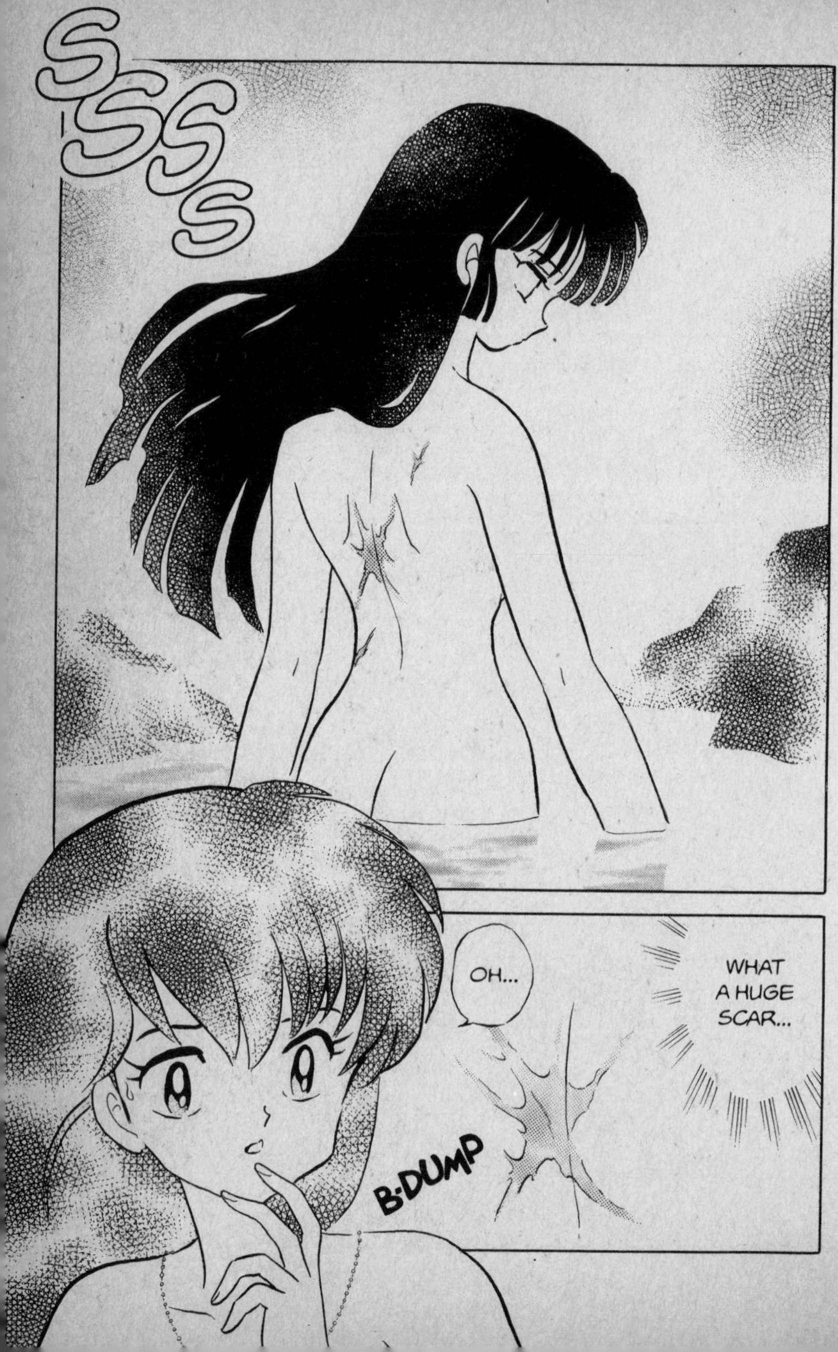
SSSS
OH...
WHAT A HUGE SCAR...
B-DUMP

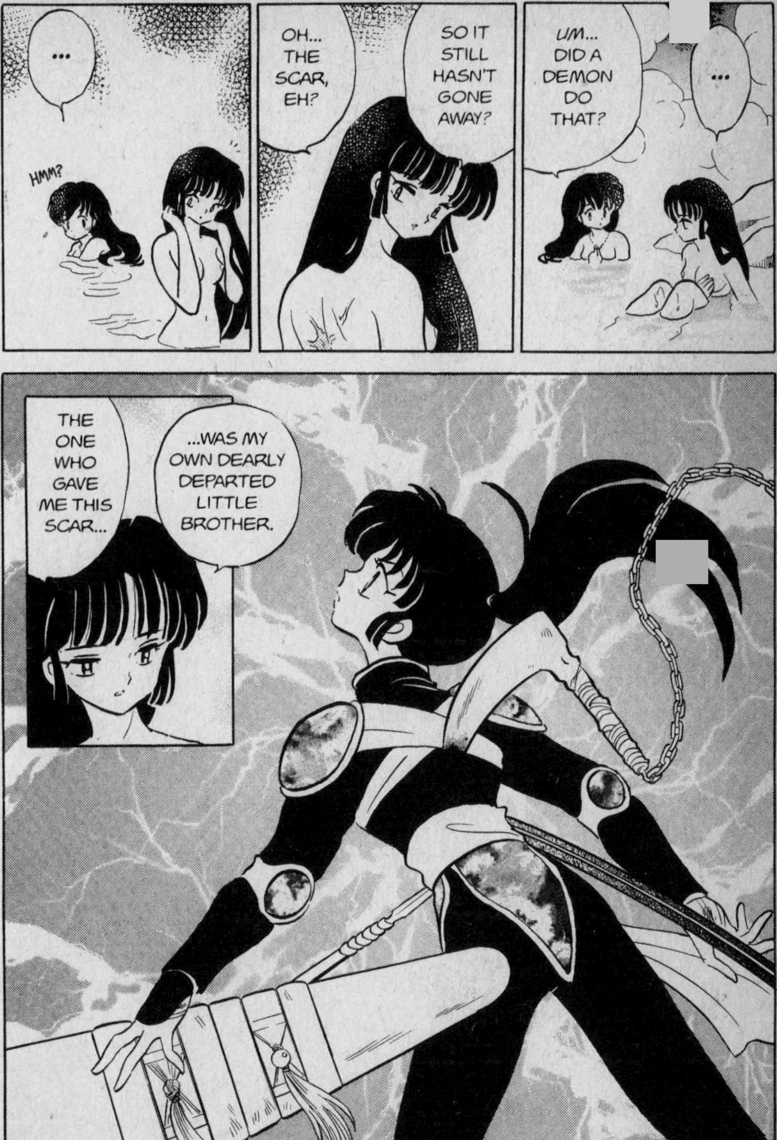
...
HMM?
OH... THE SCAR, EH?
SO IT STILL HASN'T GONE AWAY?
UM... DID A DEMON DO THAT?
...
THE ONE WHO GAVE ME THIS SCAR...
...WAS MY OWN DEARLY DEPARTED LITTLE BROTHER.

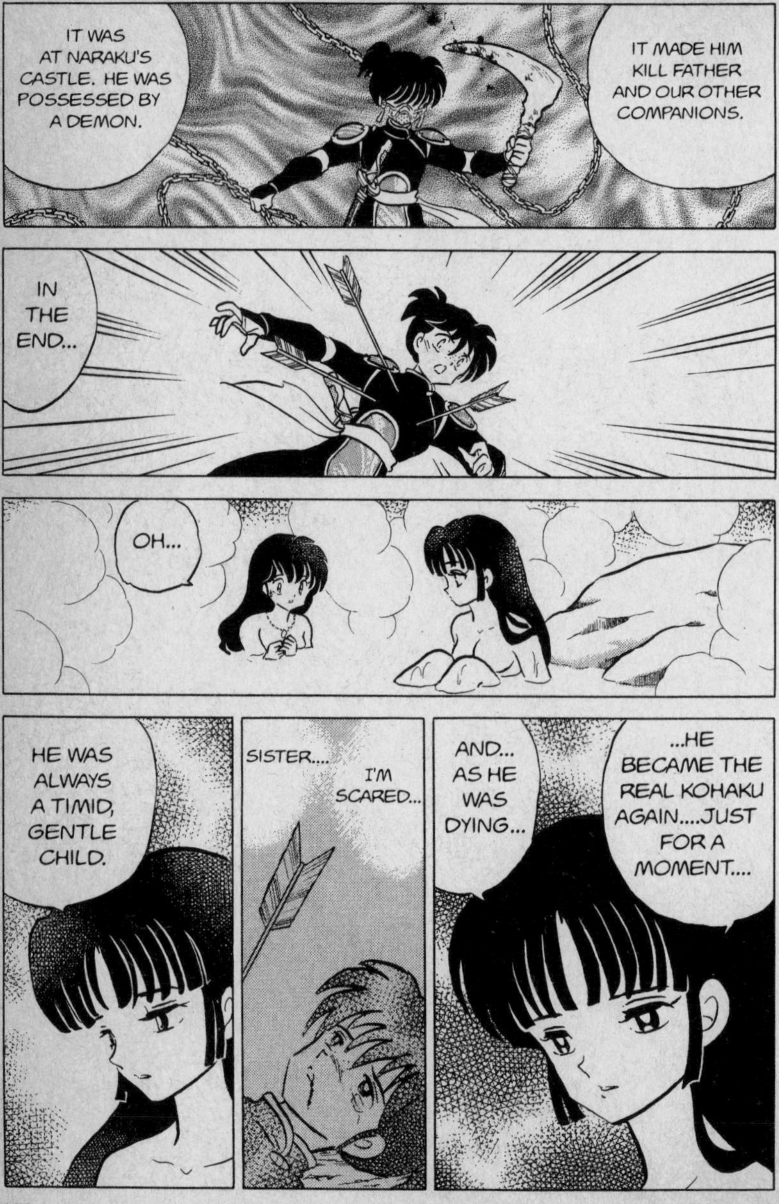

IT WAS AT NARAKU'S CASTLE. HE WAS POSSESSED BY A DEMON.
IT MADE HIM KILL FATHER AND OUR OTHER COMPANIONS.
IN THE END...
OH...
HE WAS ALWAYS A TIMID, GENTLE CHILD.
SISTER....
I'M SCARED...
AND... AS HE WAS DYING...
...HE BECAME THE REAL KOHAKU AGAIN....JUST FOR A MOMENT....

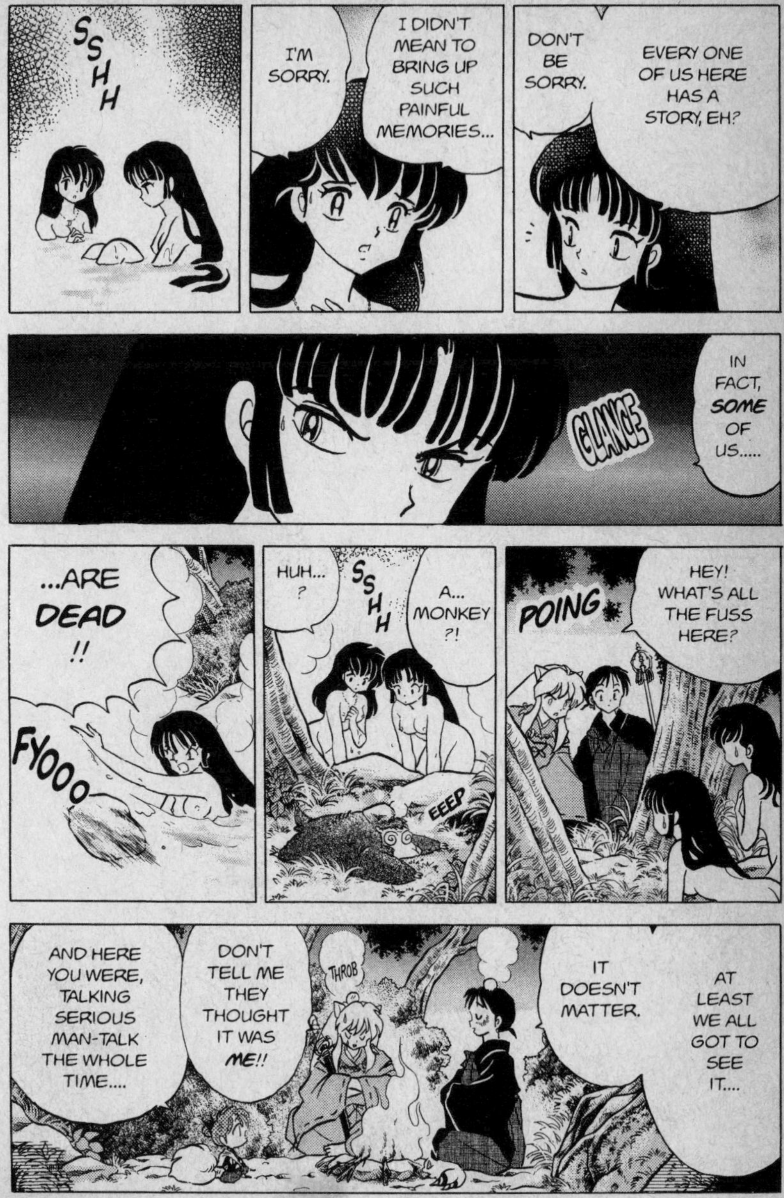
SSHH
I'M SORRY.
I DIDN'T MEAN TO BRING UP SUCH PAINFUL MEMORIES...
DON'T BE SORRY.
EVERY ONE OF US HERE HAS A STORY, EH?
GLANCE
IN FACT, SOME OF US.....
...ARE DEAD !!
FYOOO—
HUH... ?
SSHH
A... MONKEY ?!
EEEP
POING
HEY! WHAT'S ALL THE FUSS HERE?
AND HERE YOU WERE, TALKING SERIOUS MAN-TALK THE WHOLE TIME....
DON'T TELL ME THEY THOUGHT IT WAS ME!!
THROB
IT DOESN'T MATTER.
AT LEAST WE ALL GOT TO SEE IT....

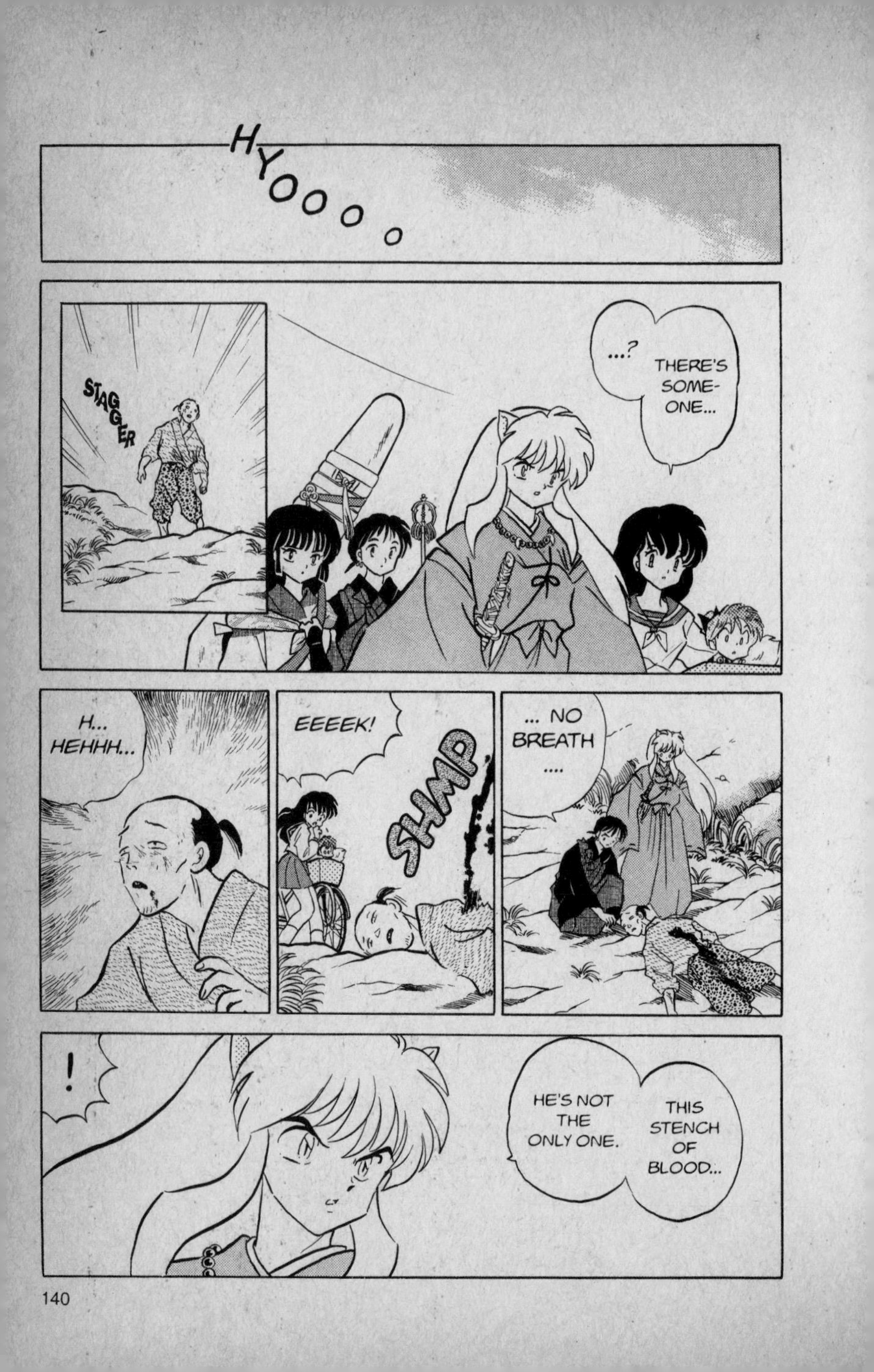
HYOOOO
STAGGER
...? THERE'S SOME-ONE...
H... HEHHH...
EEEEK!
SHMP
... NO BREATH ....
!
HE'S NOT THE ONLY ONE.
THIS STENCH OF BLOOD...

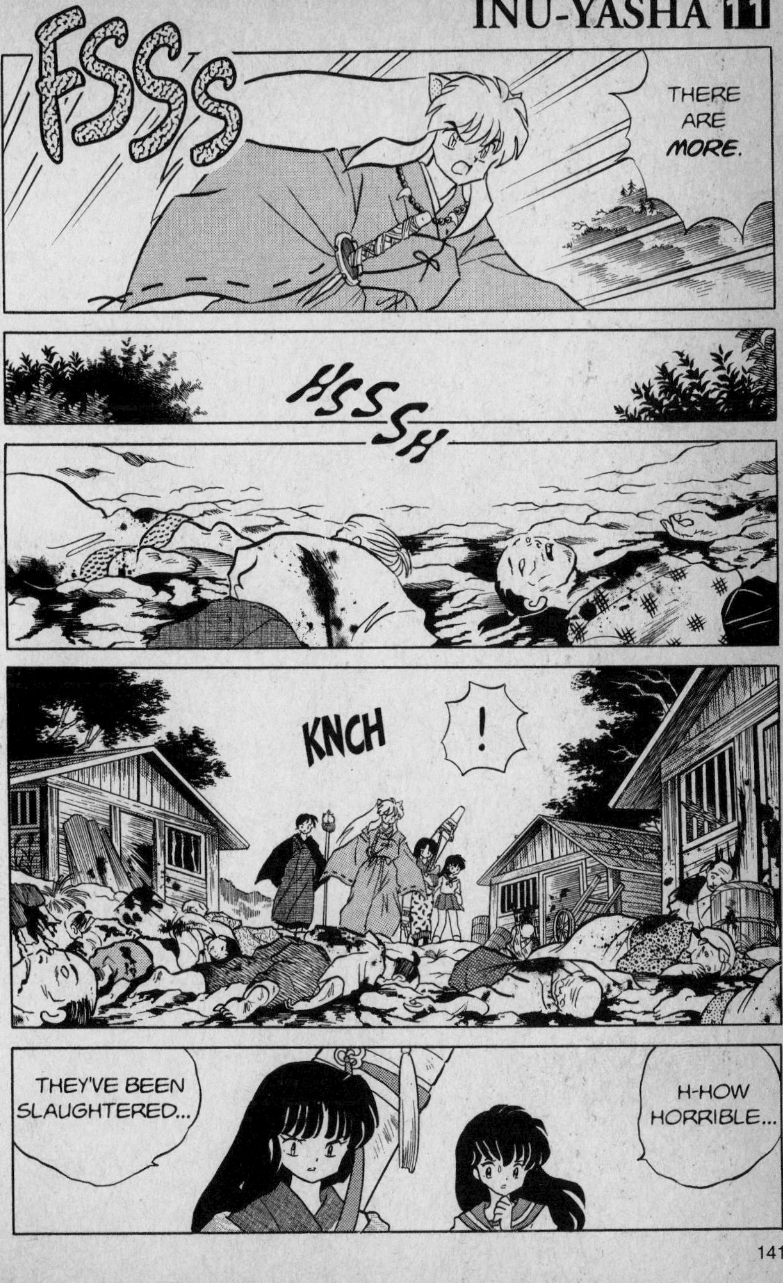
FSSS
THERE ARE MORE.
HSSSH
KNCH
!
THEY'VE BEEN SLAUGHTERED...
H-HOW HORRIBLE...

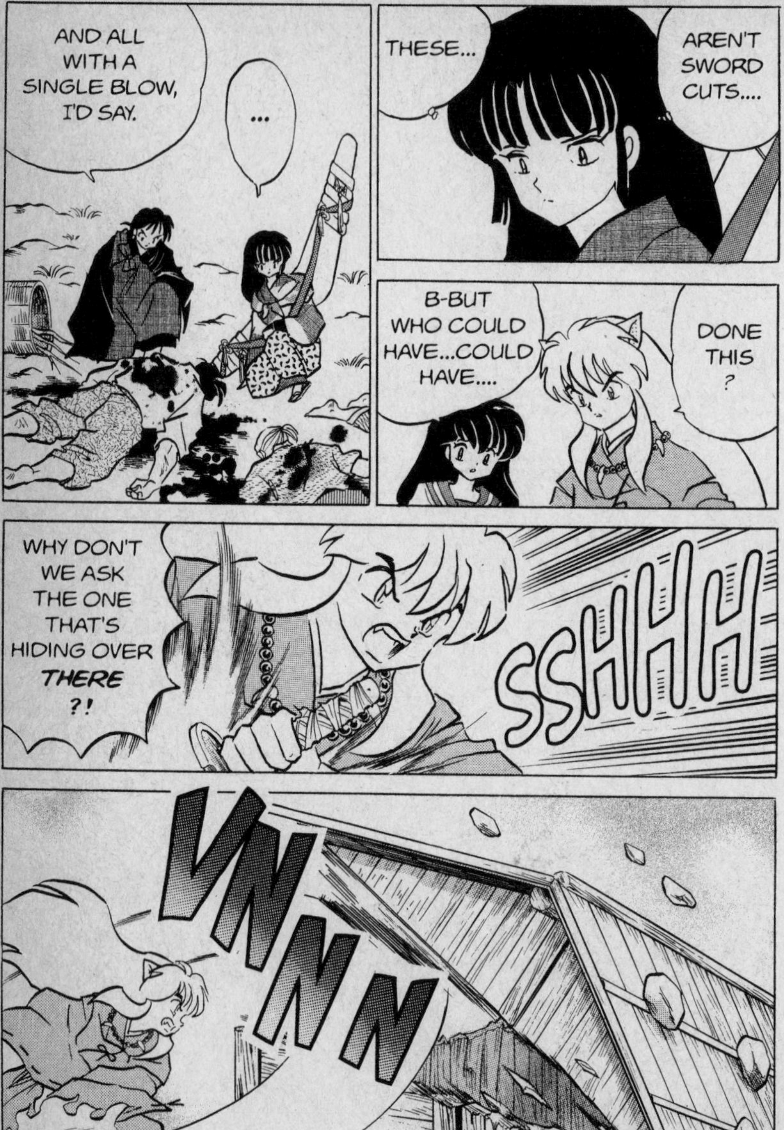
AND ALL WITH A SINGLE BLOW, I'D SAY.
...
THESE...
AREN'T SWORD CUTS....
B-BUT WHO COULD HAVE...COULD HAVE....
DONE THIS ?
WHY DON'T WE ASK THE ONE THAT'S HIDING OVER *THERE* ?!
SSHHH
VNNN

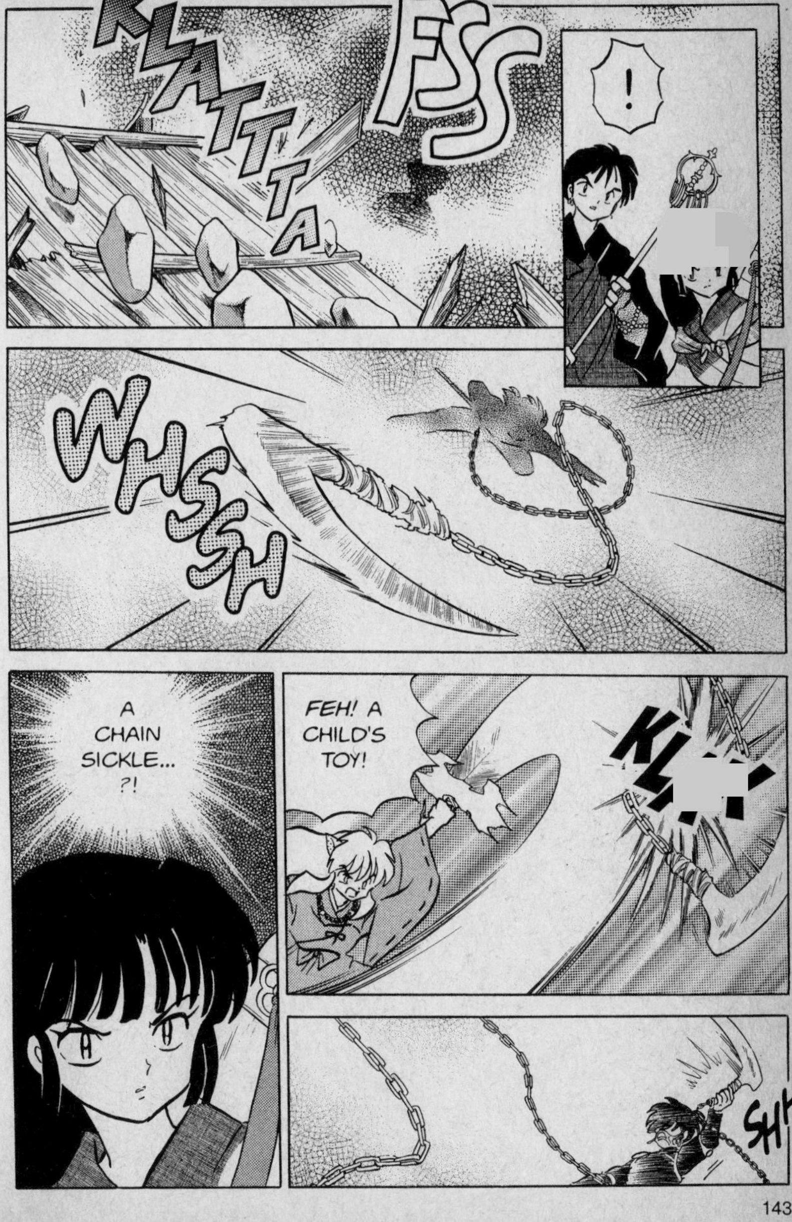
KLATTTTA
FSS
!
WHSSSH
A CHAIN SICKLE... ?!
FEH! A CHILD'S TOY!
SHHP

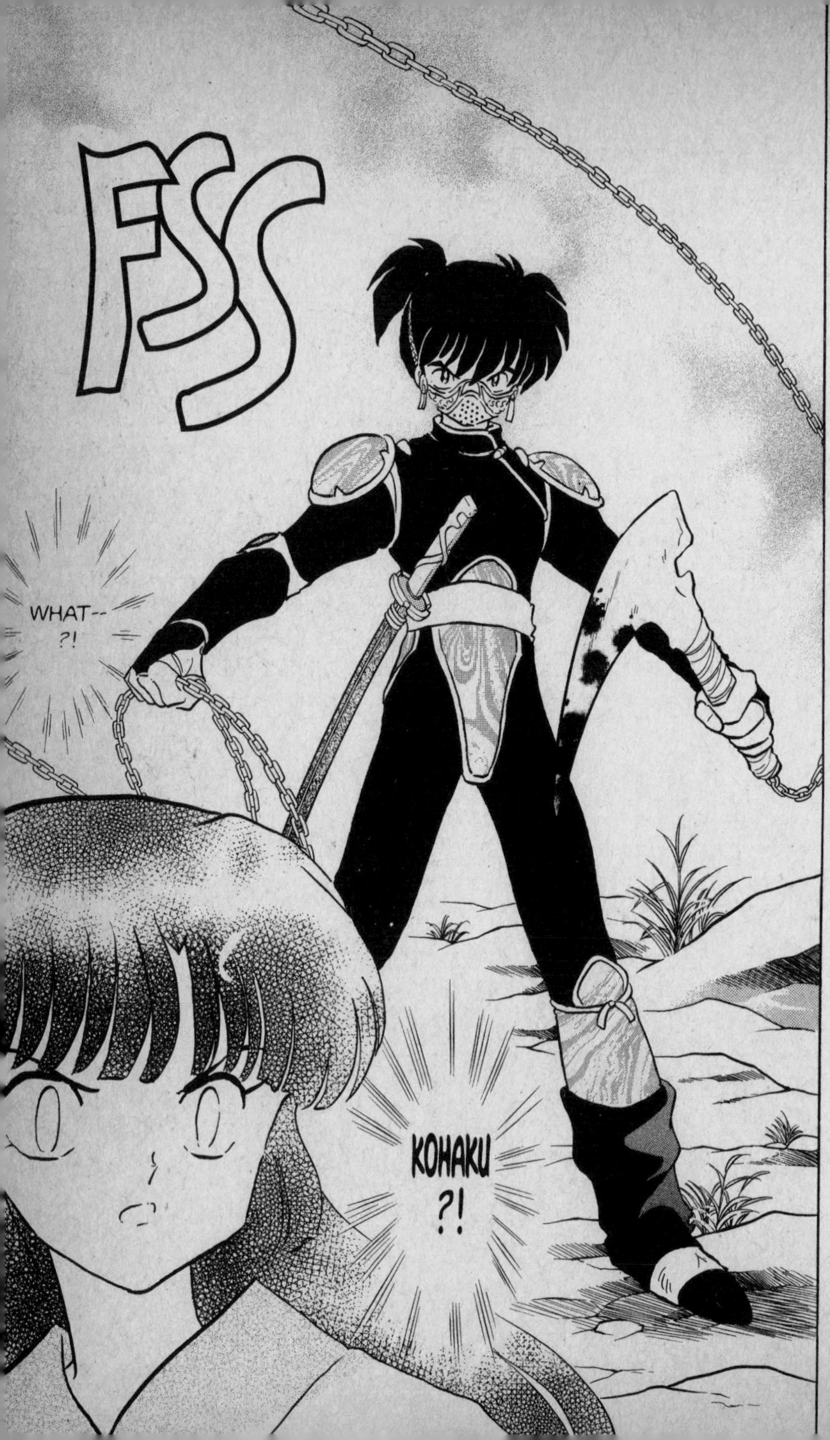
FSS
WHAT-- ?!
KOHAKU ?!

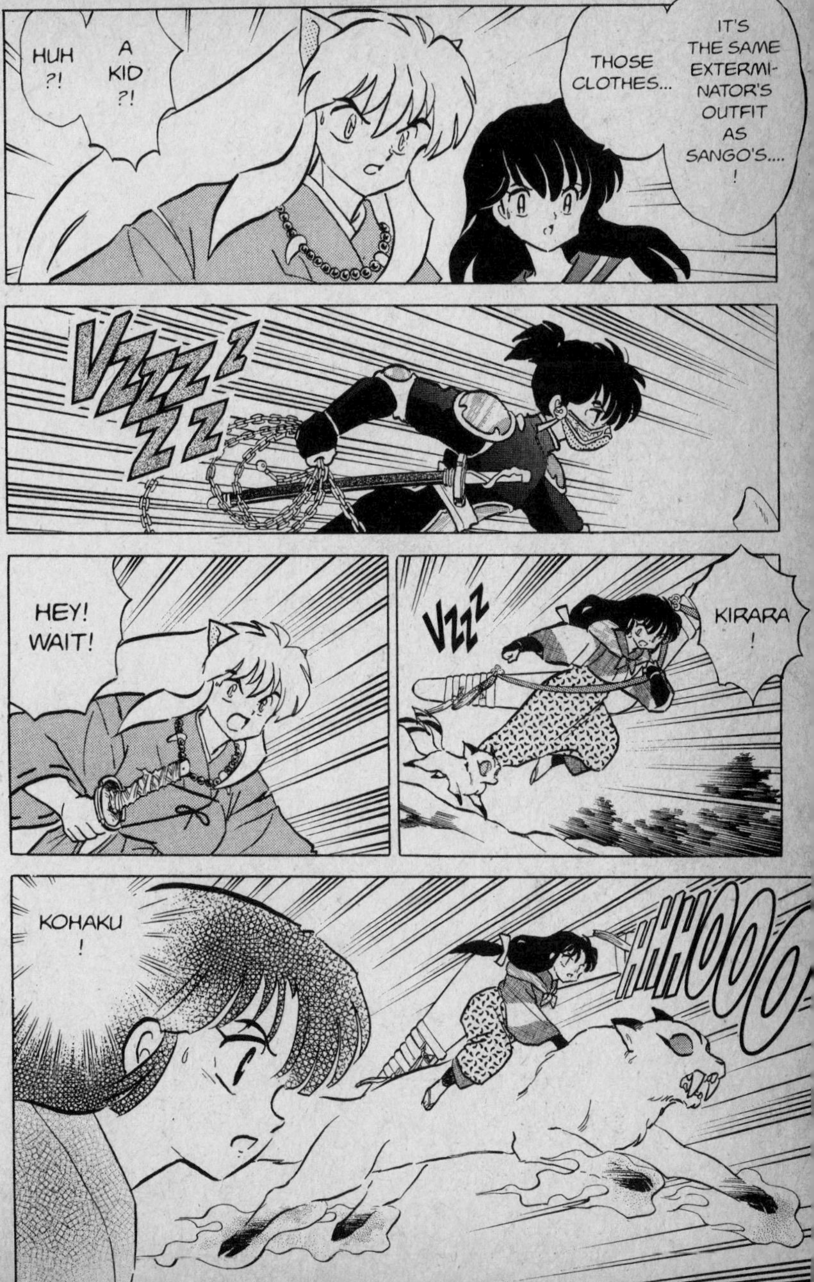
HUH ?!
A KID ?!
THOSE CLOTHES...
IT'S THE SAME EXTERMINATOR'S OUTFIT AS SANGO'S.... !
VZZZZZZZ
HEY! WAIT!
VZZZ
KIRARA !
KOHAKU !
HHHOOOO

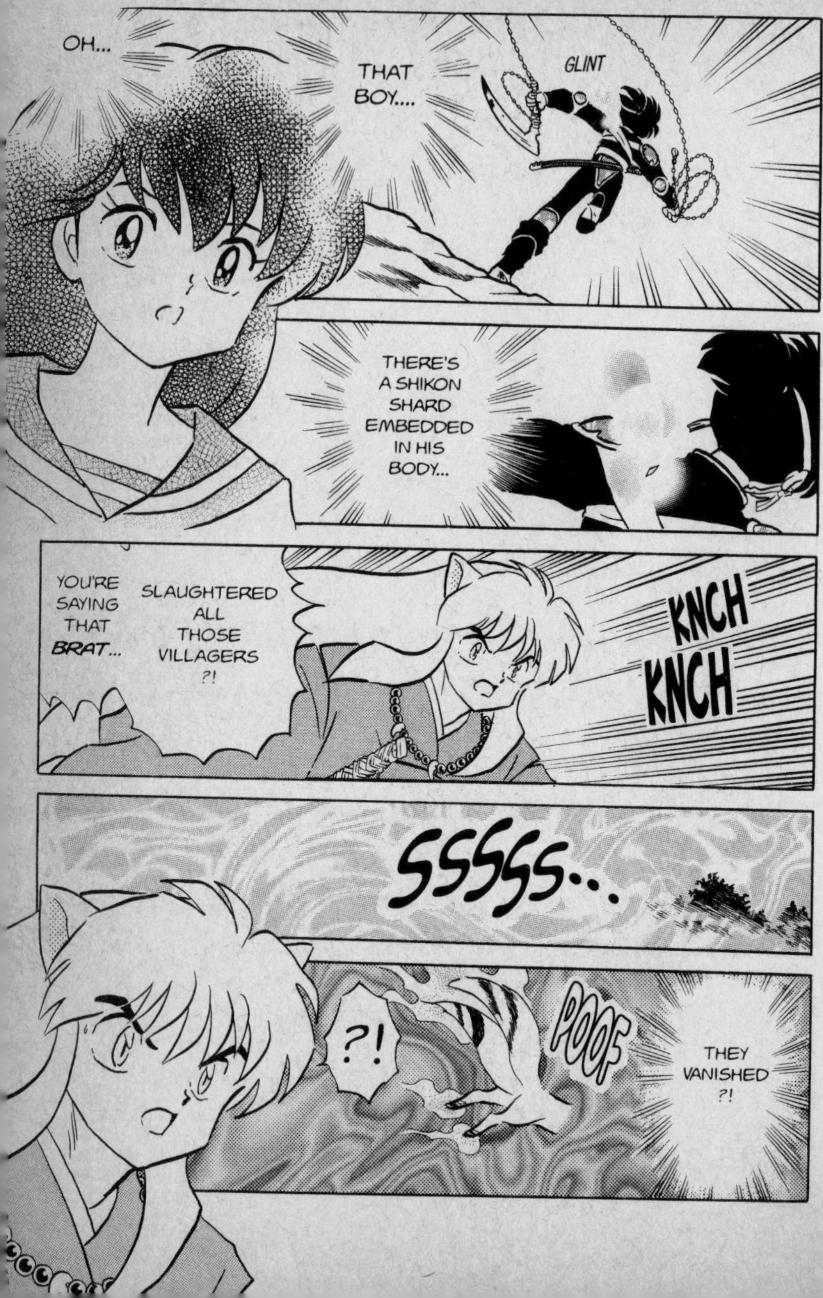
OH...
THAT BOY....
GLINT
THERE'S A SHIKON SHARD EMBEDDED IN HIS BODY...
YOU'RE SAYING THAT *BRAT*...
SLAUGHTERED ALL THOSE VILLAGERS ?!
KNCH KNCH
SSSSS...
?!
POOF
THEY VANISHED ?!

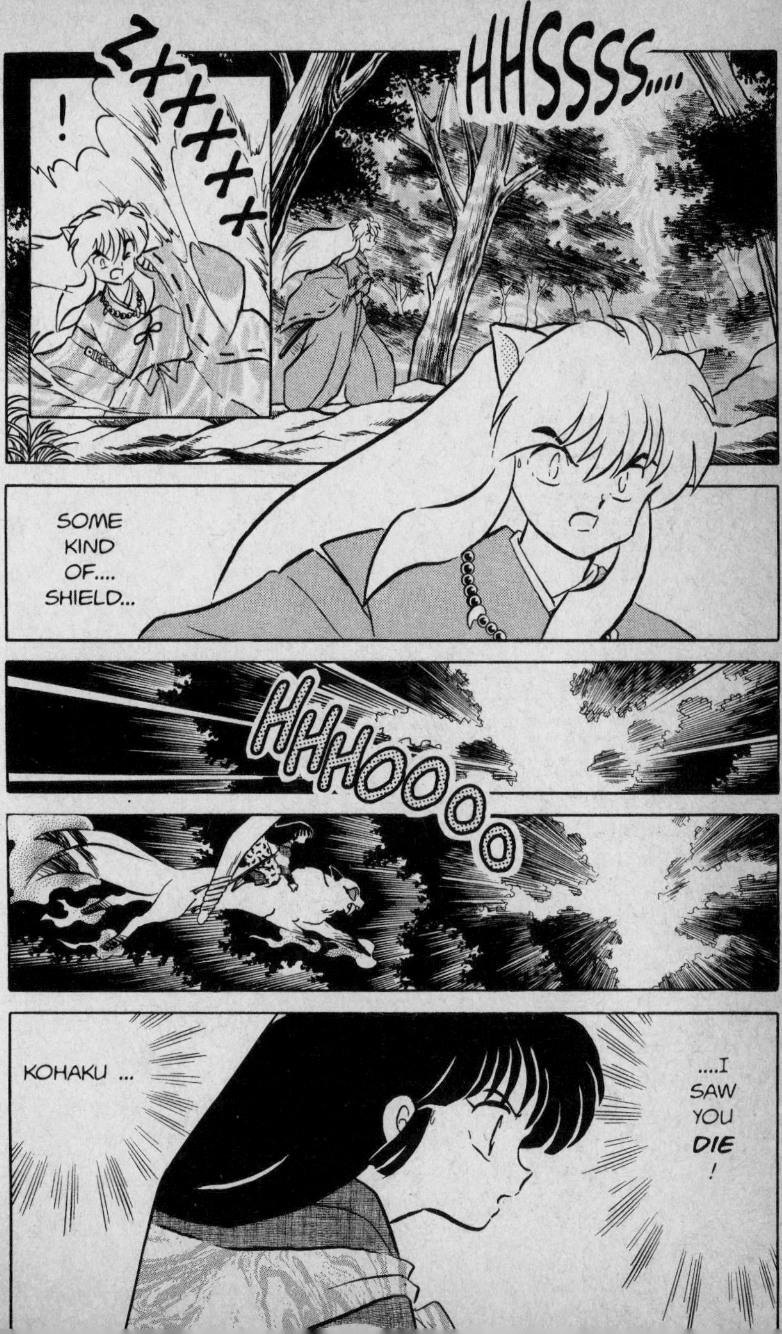
ZZZZZZ
!
HHSSSSS....
SOME KIND OF.... SHIELD...
HHHOOOO
KOHAKU ...
....I SAW YOU DIE !

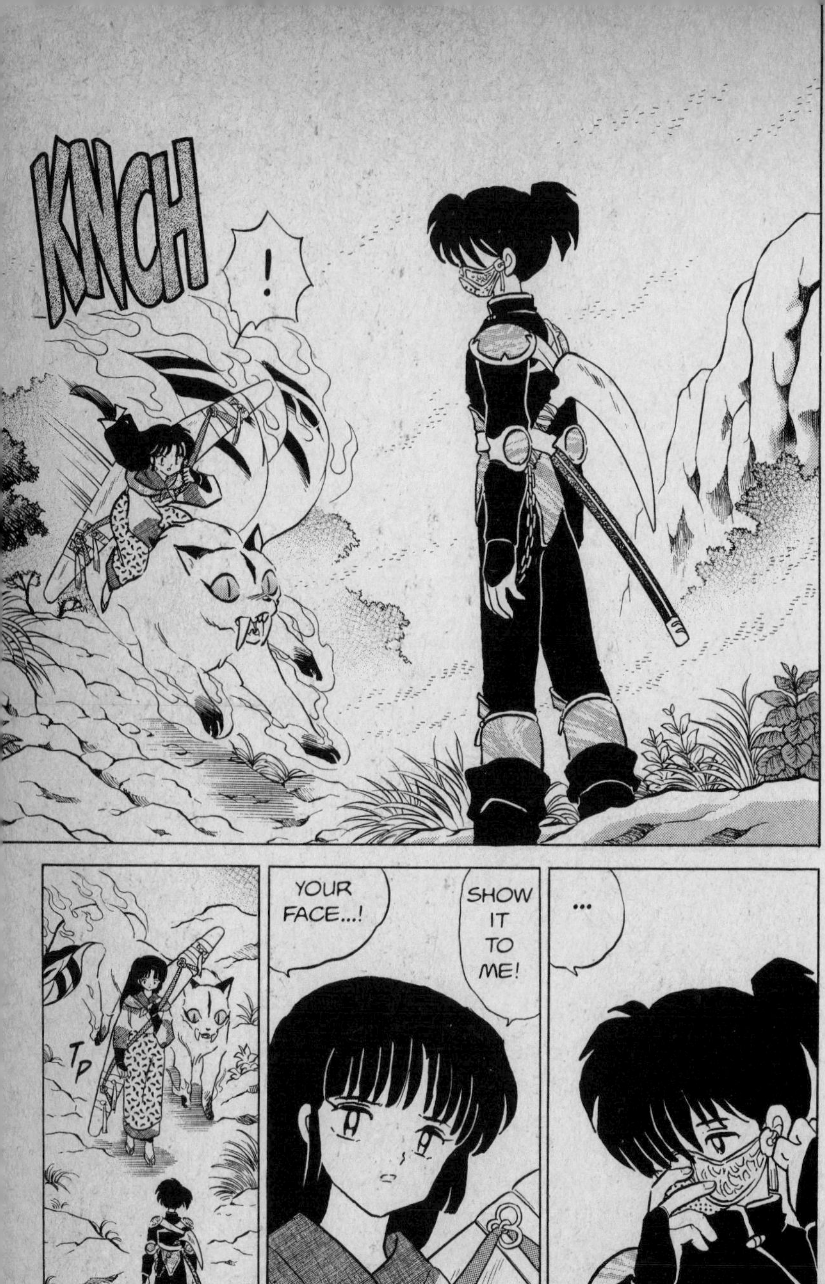
KNCH
!
TP
YOUR FACE...!
SHOW IT TO ME!
...

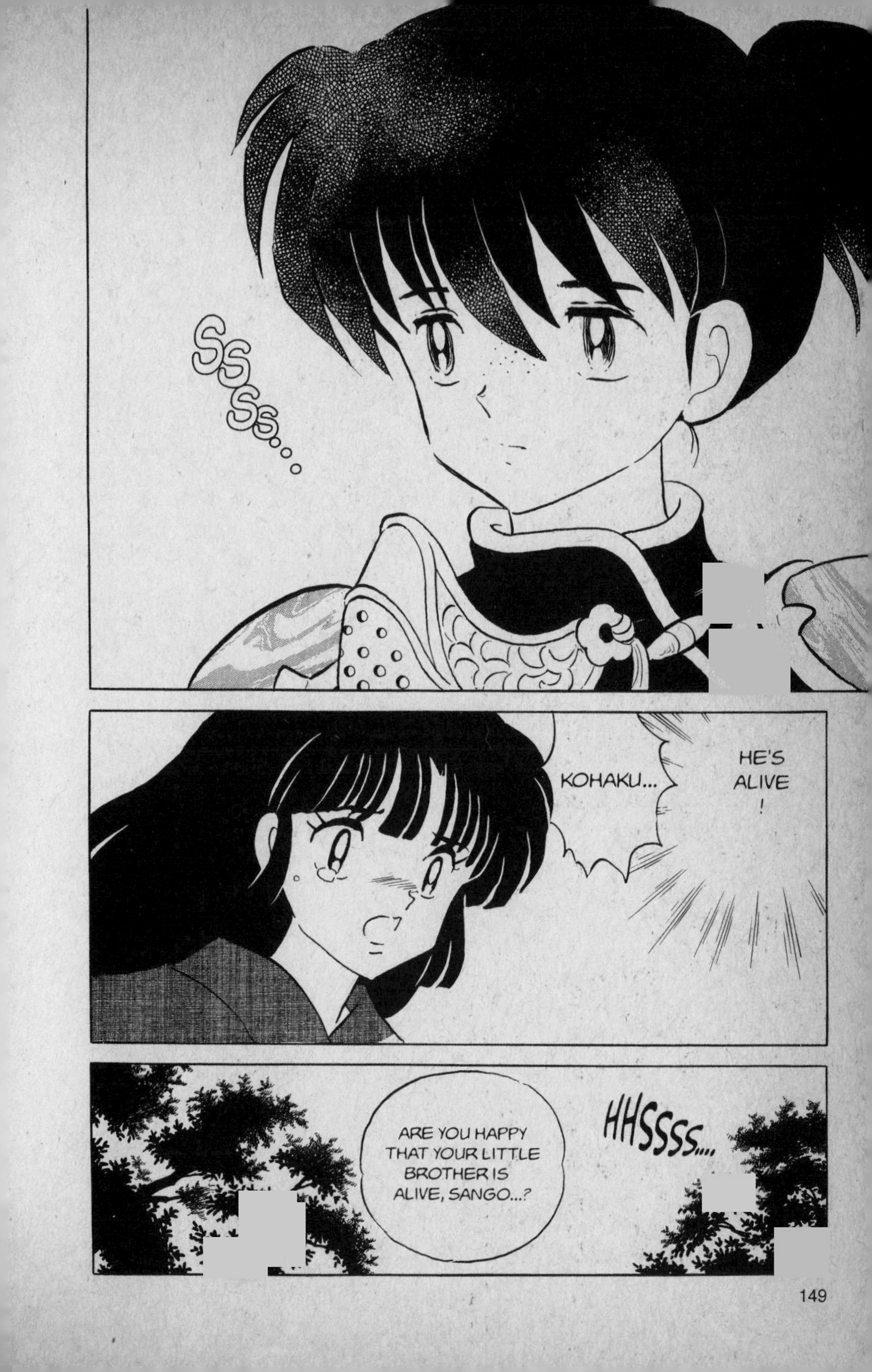
SSSs...
KOHAKU...
HE'S ALIVE!
ARE YOU HAPPY THAT YOUR LITTLE BROTHER IS ALIVE, SANGO...?
HHSSSS....

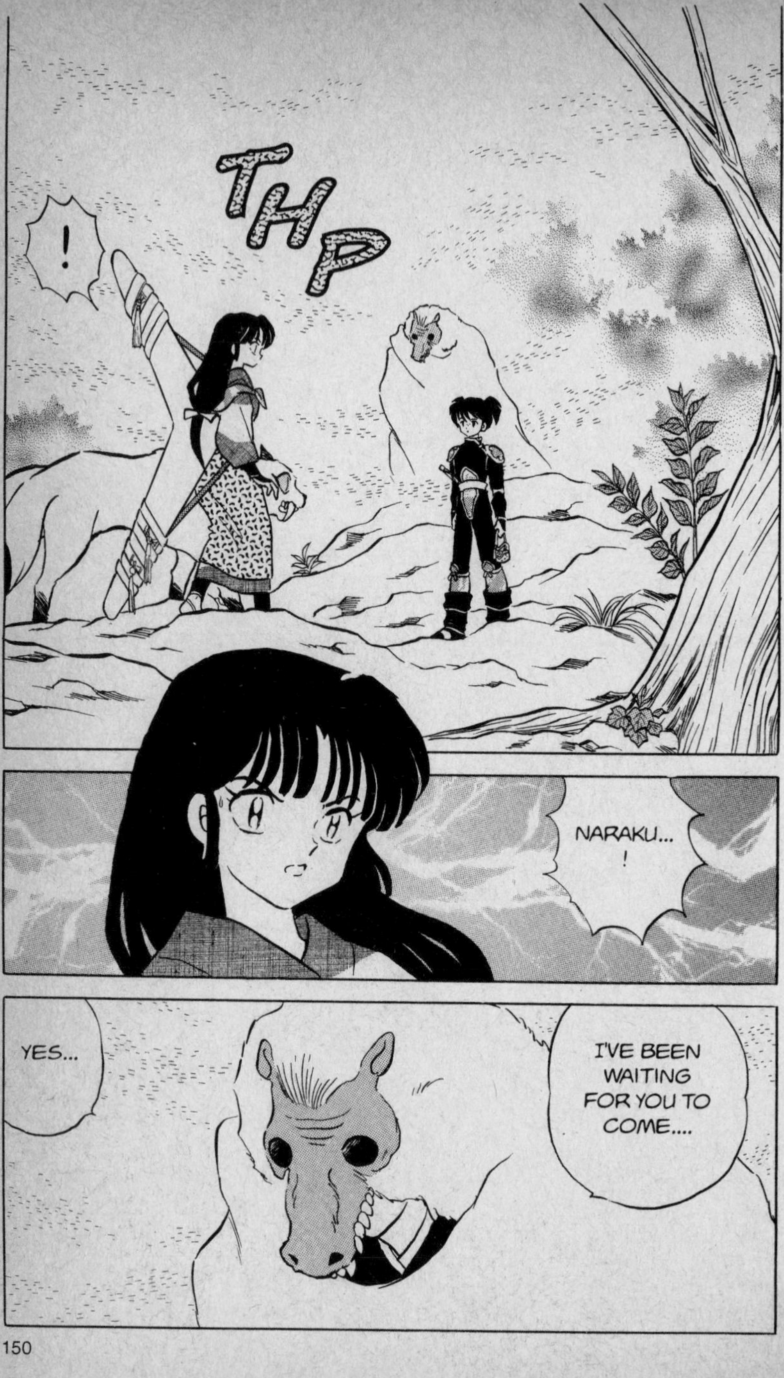
!
THP
NARAKU... !
YES...
I'VE BEEN WAITING FOR YOU TO COME....

SCROLL NINE
NEW LIFE

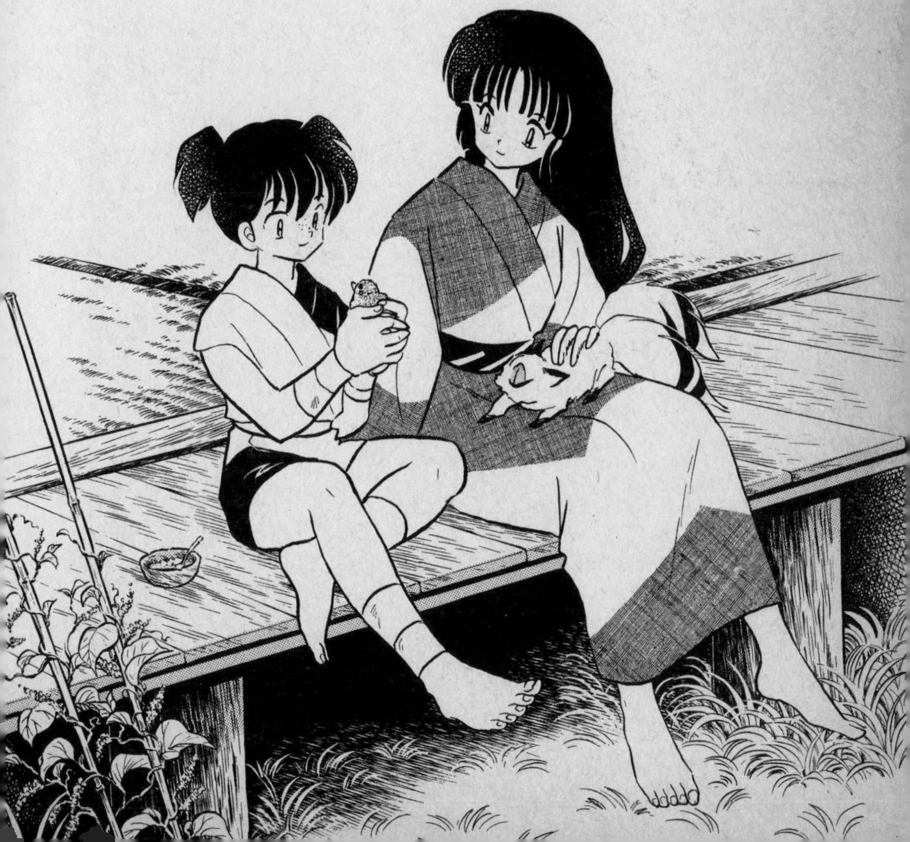

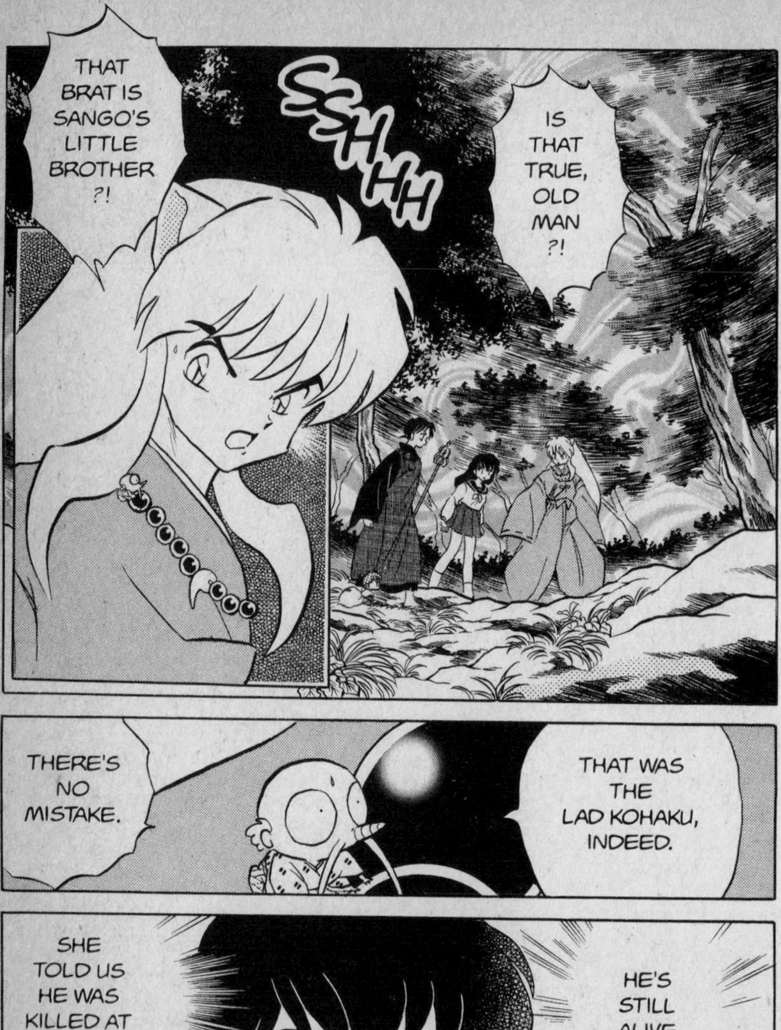
THAT BRAT IS SANGO'S LITTLE BROTHER ?!
SSHHH
IS THAT TRUE, OLD MAN ?!
THERE'S NO MISTAKE.
THAT WAS THE LAD KOHAKU, INDEED.
SHE TOLD US HE WAS KILLED AT NARAKU'S CASTLE, BUT...
HE'S STILL ALIVE ?!

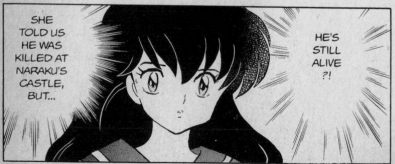

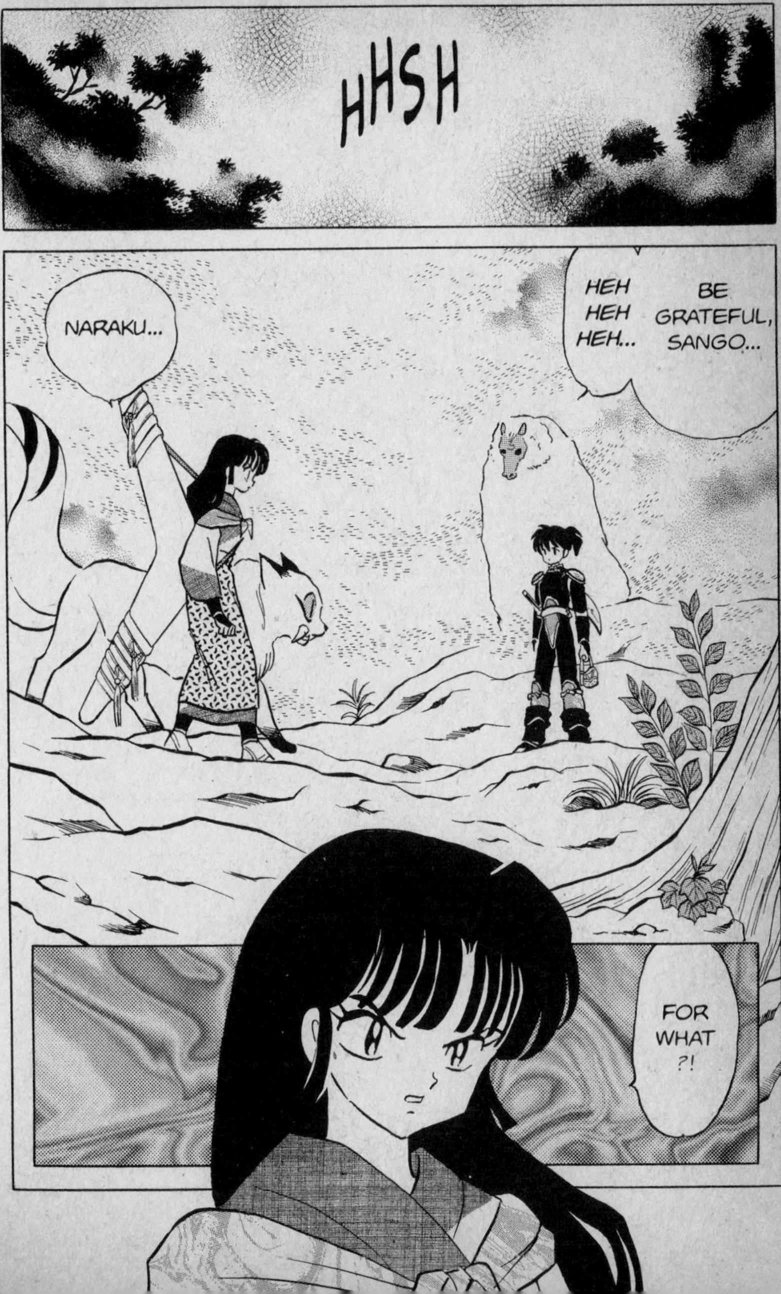
HHSH
NARAKU...
HEH HEH HEH...
BE GRATEFUL, SANGO...
FOR WHAT ?!

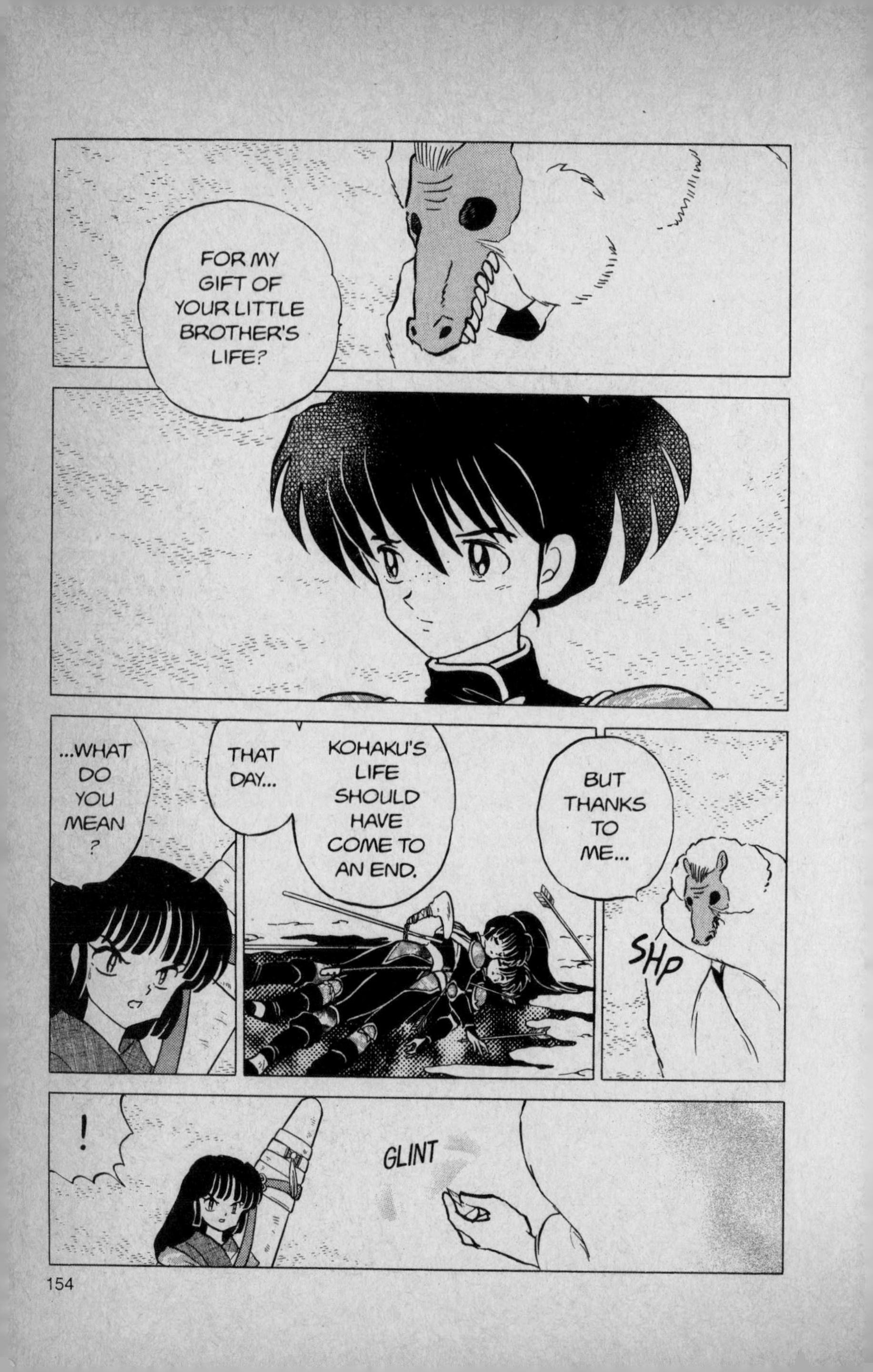
FOR MY GIFT OF YOUR LITTLE BROTHER'S LIFE?
...WHAT DO YOU MEAN?
THAT DAY...
KOHAKU'S LIFE SHOULD HAVE COME TO AN END.
BUT THANKS TO ME...
SHP
!
GLINT

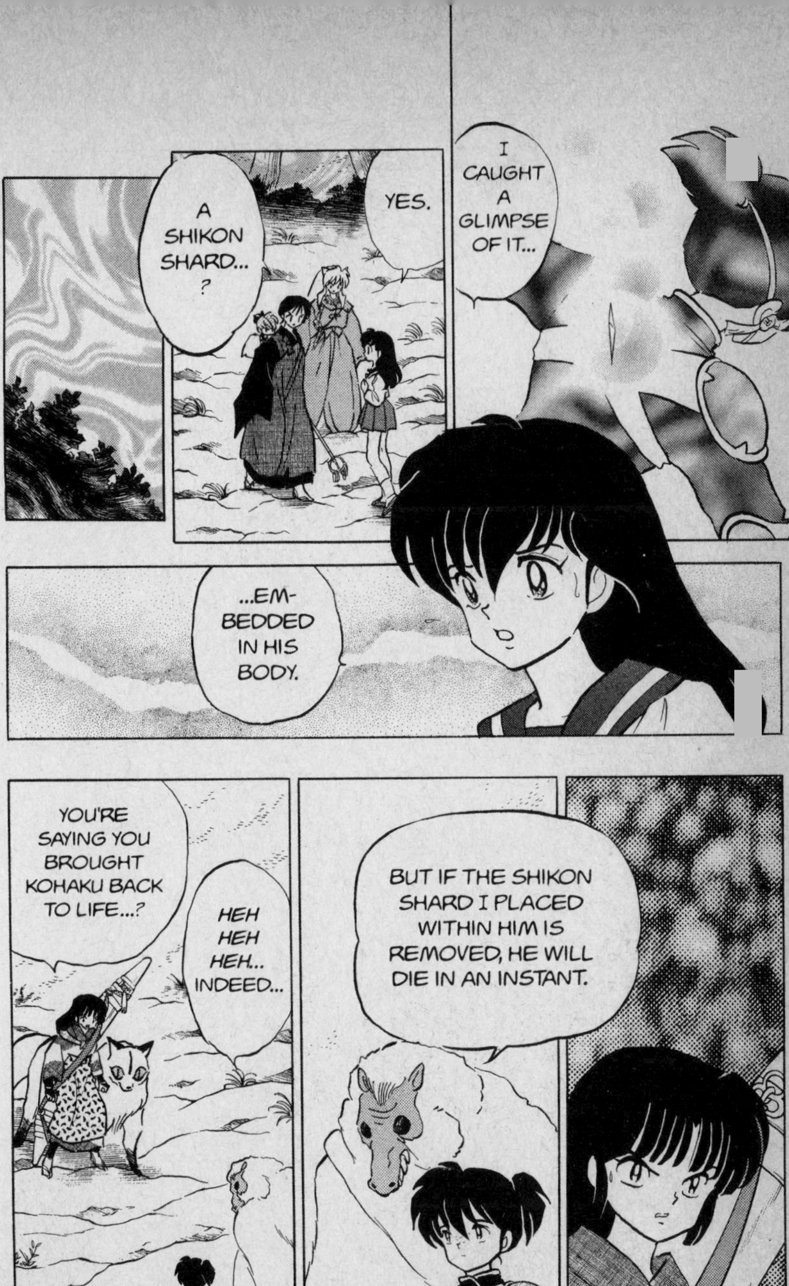
A SHIKON SHARD...?
YES.
I CAUGHT A GLIMPSE OF IT...
...EM-BEDDED IN HIS BODY.
YOU'RE SAYING YOU BROUGHT KOHAKU BACK TO LIFE...?
HEH HEH HEH... INDEED...
BUT IF THE SHIKON SHARD I PLACED WITHIN HIM IS REMOVED, HE WILL DIE IN AN INSTANT.

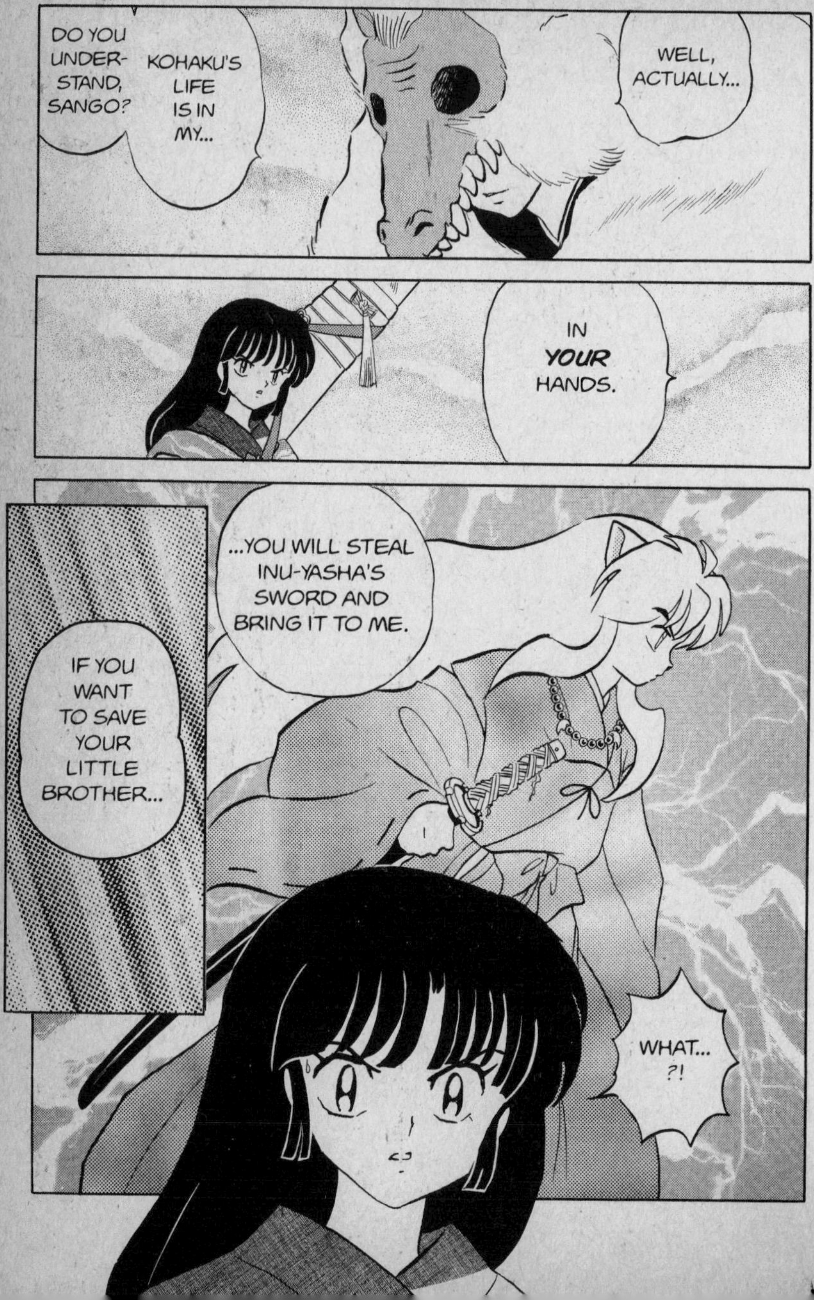
DO YOU UNDER-STAND, SANGO?
KOHAKU'S LIFE IS IN MY...
WELL, ACTUALLY...
IN *YOUR* HANDS.
IF YOU WANT TO SAVE YOUR LITTLE BROTHER...
...YOU WILL STEAL INU-YASHA'S SWORD AND BRING IT TO ME.
WHAT... ?!

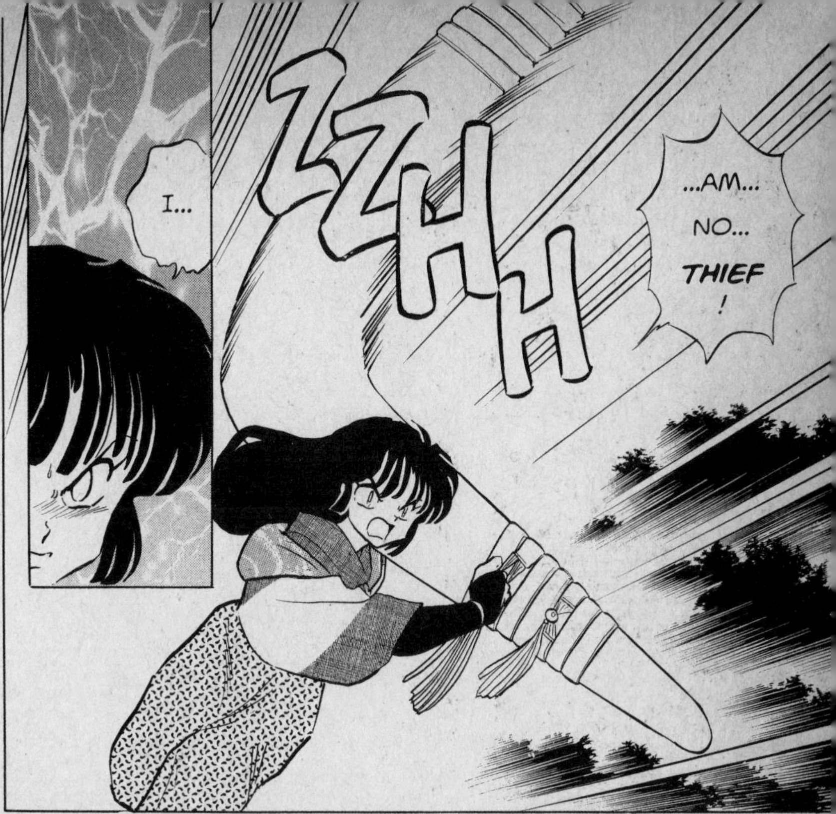
I...
ZZHHH
...AM... NO... THIEF!

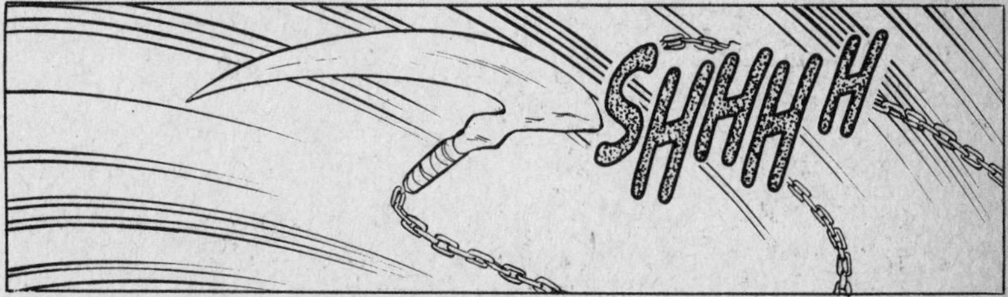
SHHHH

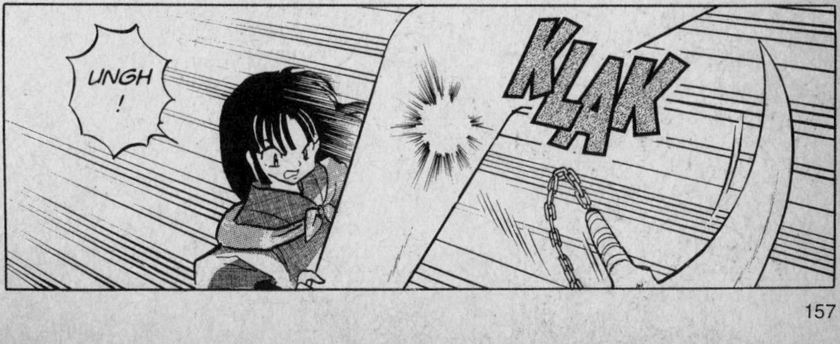
UNGH!
KLAK

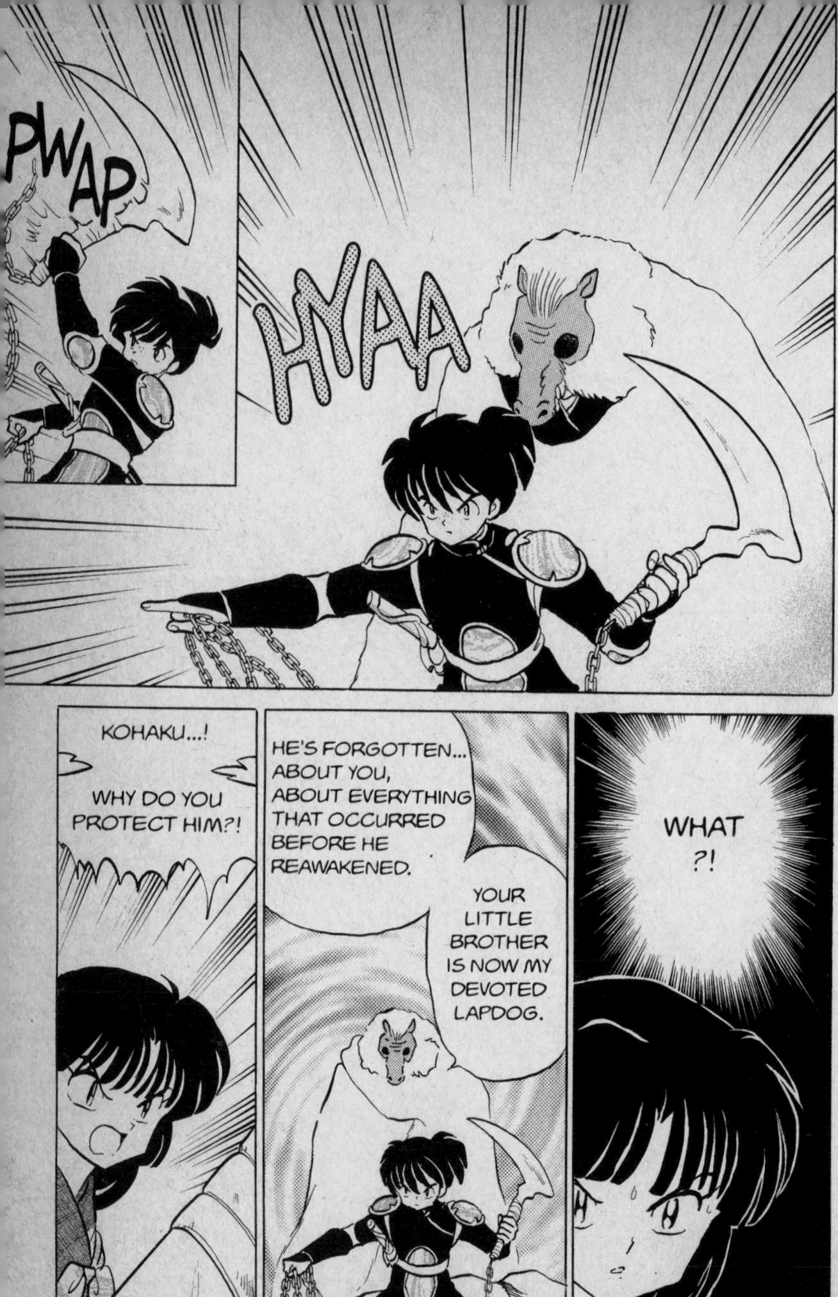
PWAP
HYAA
KOHAKU...!
WHY DO YOU PROTECT HIM?!
HE'S FORGOTTEN... ABOUT YOU, ABOUT EVERYTHING THAT OCCURRED BEFORE HE REAWAKENED.
YOUR LITTLE BROTHER IS NOW MY DEVOTED LAPDOG.
WHAT ?!

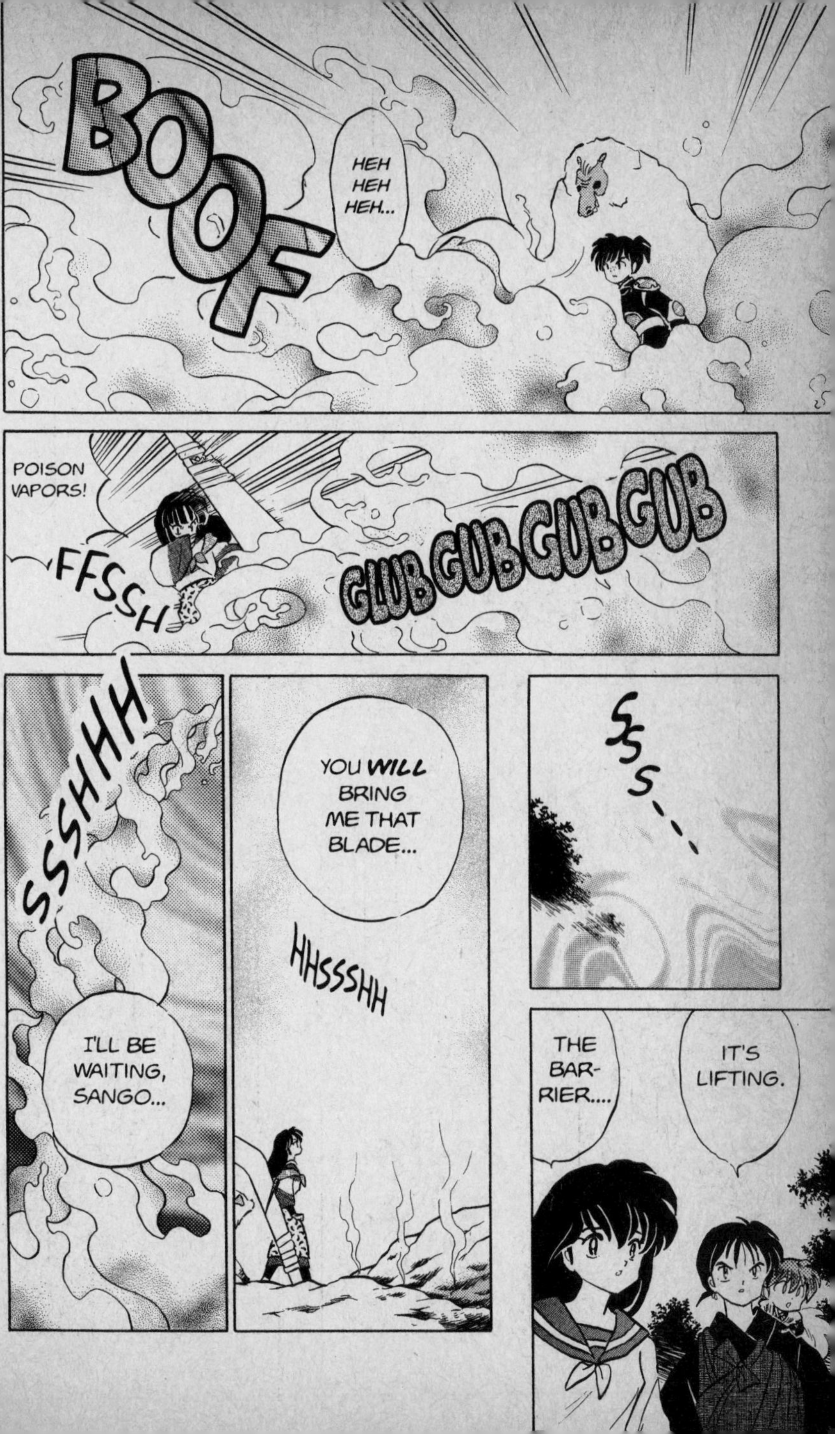
BOOF
HEH HEH HEH...
POISON VAPORS!
FFSSH
GLUB GUB GUB GUB
SSSHHH
I'LL BE WAITING, SANGO...
YOU **WILL** BRING ME THAT BLADE...
HHSSSHH
SSS...
THE BAR-RIER....
IT'S LIFTING.

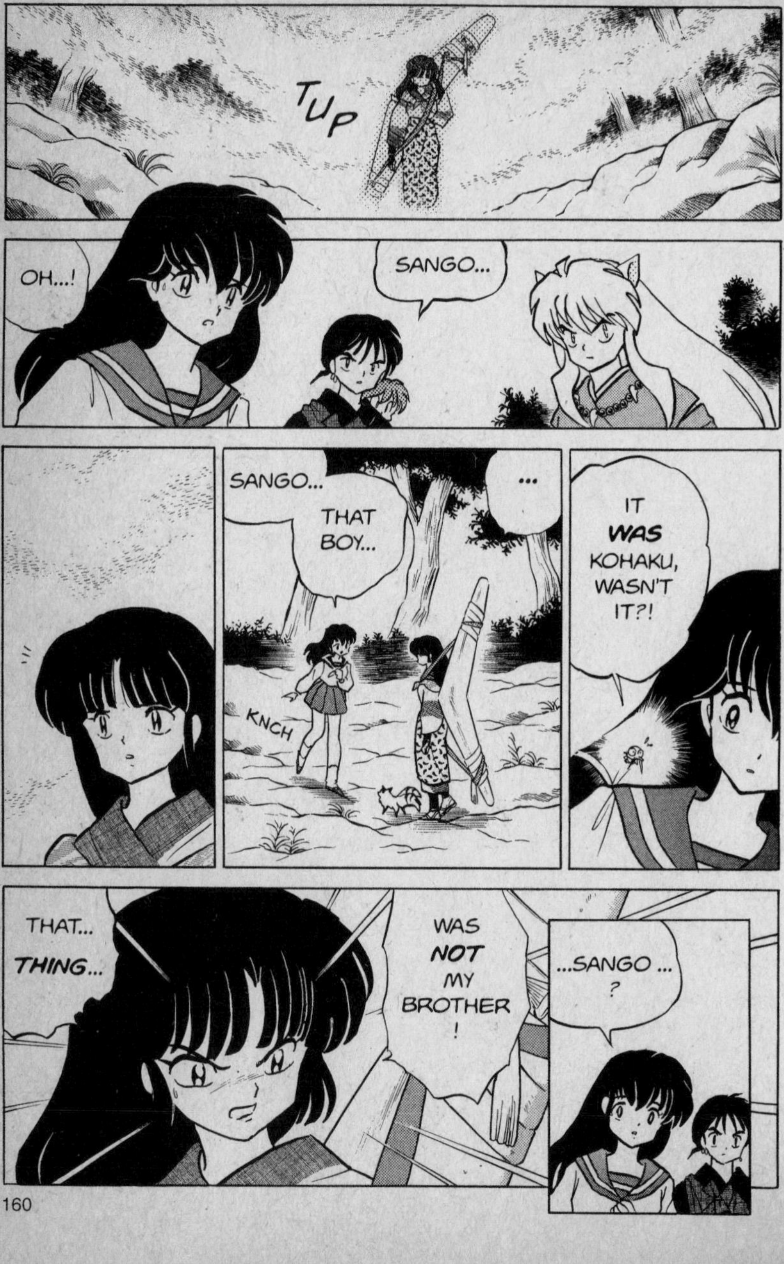
TUP
OH...!
SANGO...
SANGO...
THAT BOY...
...
KNCH
IT WAS KOHAKU, WASN'T IT?!
THAT... THING...
WAS NOT MY BROTHER!
...SANGO ...?

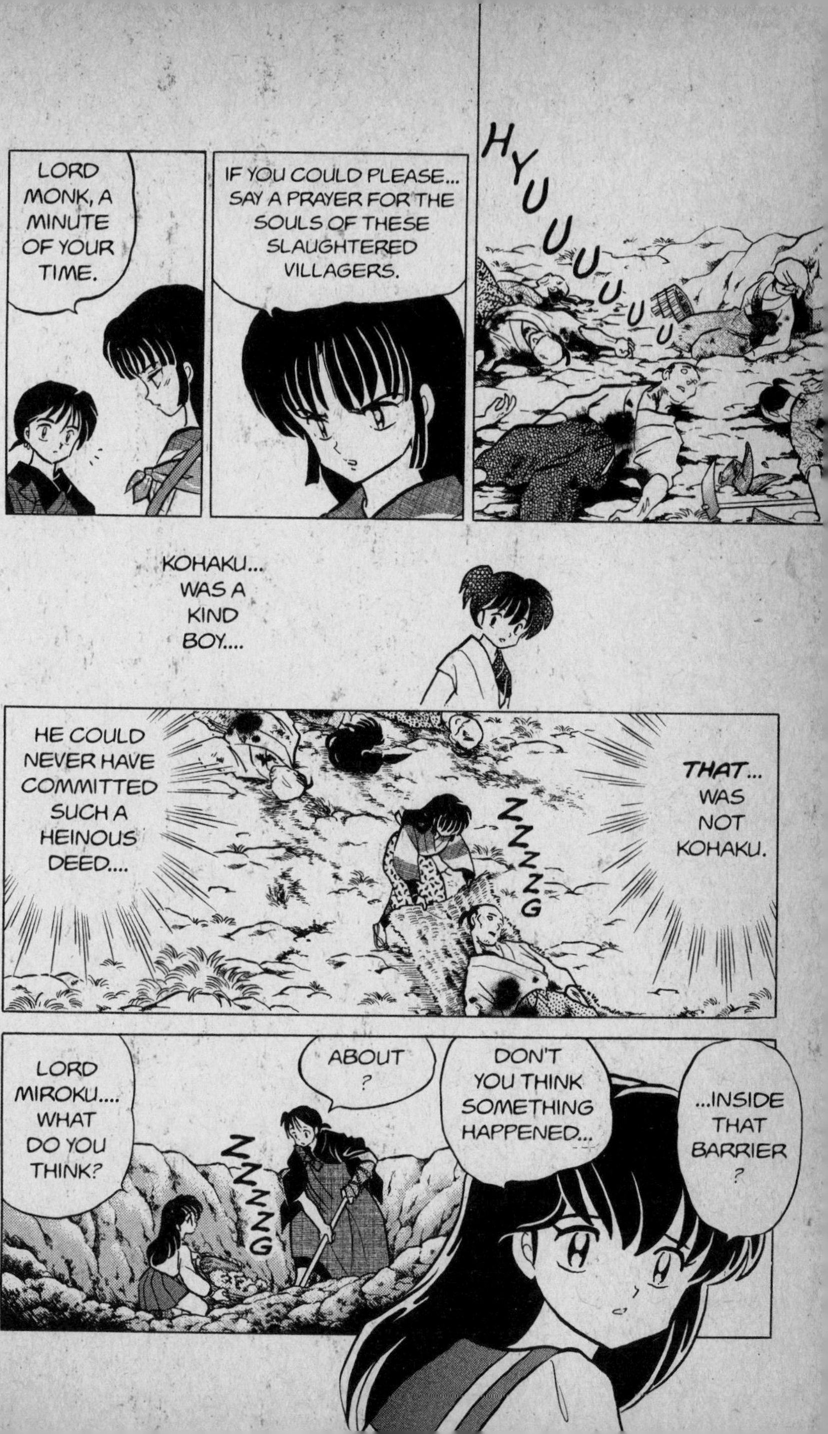
LORD MONK, A MINUTE OF YOUR TIME.
IF YOU COULD PLEASE... SAY A PRAYER FOR THE SOULS OF THESE SLAUGHTERED VILLAGERS.
HYUUUUUUU
KOHAKU... WAS A KIND BOY....
HE COULD NEVER HAVE COMMITTED SUCH A HEINOUS DEED....
ZZZZG
THAT... WAS NOT KOHAKU.
LORD MIROKU.... WHAT DO YOU THINK?
ABOUT?
ZZZZG
DON'T YOU THINK SOMETHING HAPPENED...
...INSIDE THAT BARRIER?

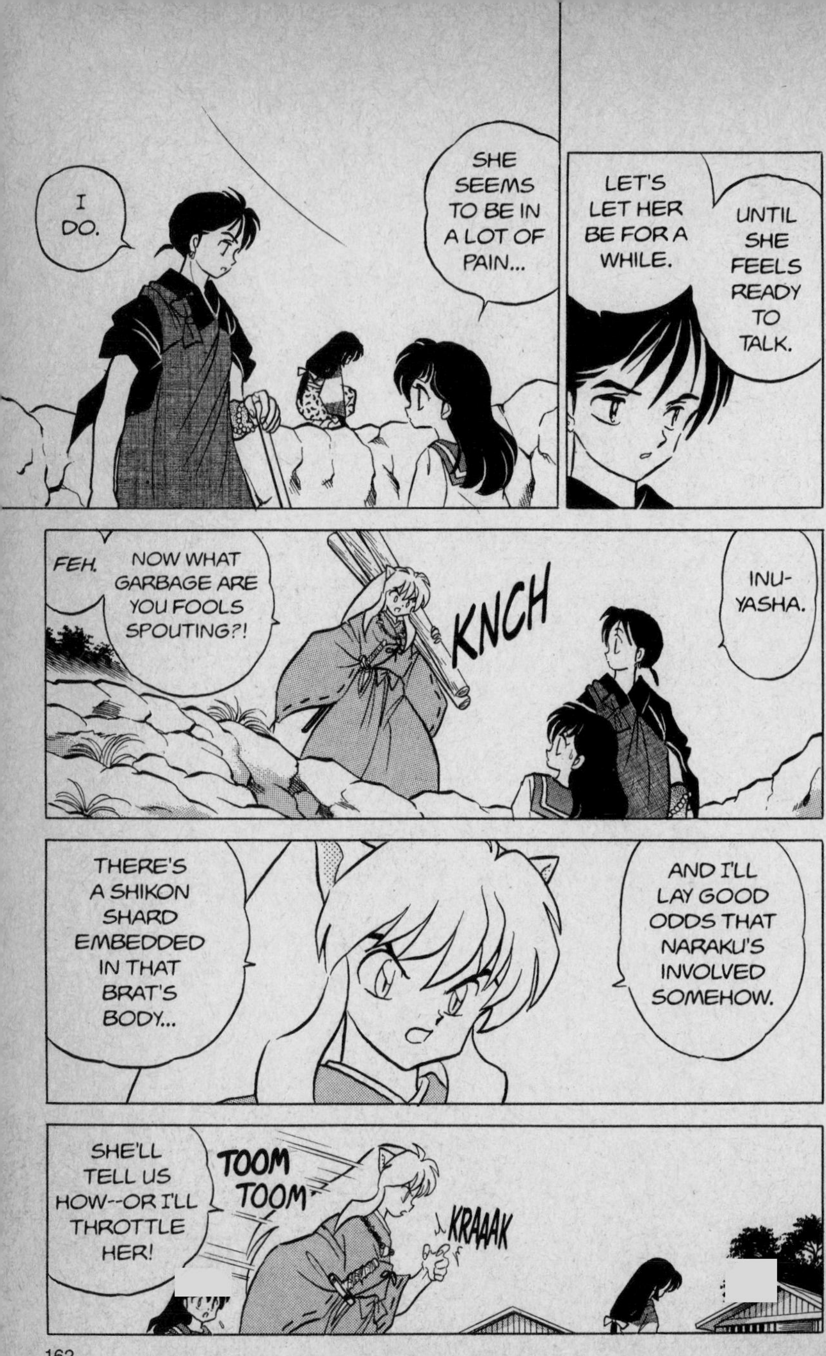
I DO.
SHE SEEMS TO BE IN A LOT OF PAIN...
LET'S LET HER BE FOR A WHILE.
UNTIL SHE FEELS READY TO TALK.
FEH.
NOW WHAT GARBAGE ARE YOU FOOLS SPOUTING?!
KNCH
INU-YASHA.
THERE'S A SHIKON SHARD EMBEDDED IN THAT BRAT'S BODY...
AND I'LL LAY GOOD ODDS THAT NARAKU'S INVOLVED SOMEHOW.
SHE'LL TELL US HOW--OR I'LL THROTTLE HER!
TOOM TOOM
KRAAAK

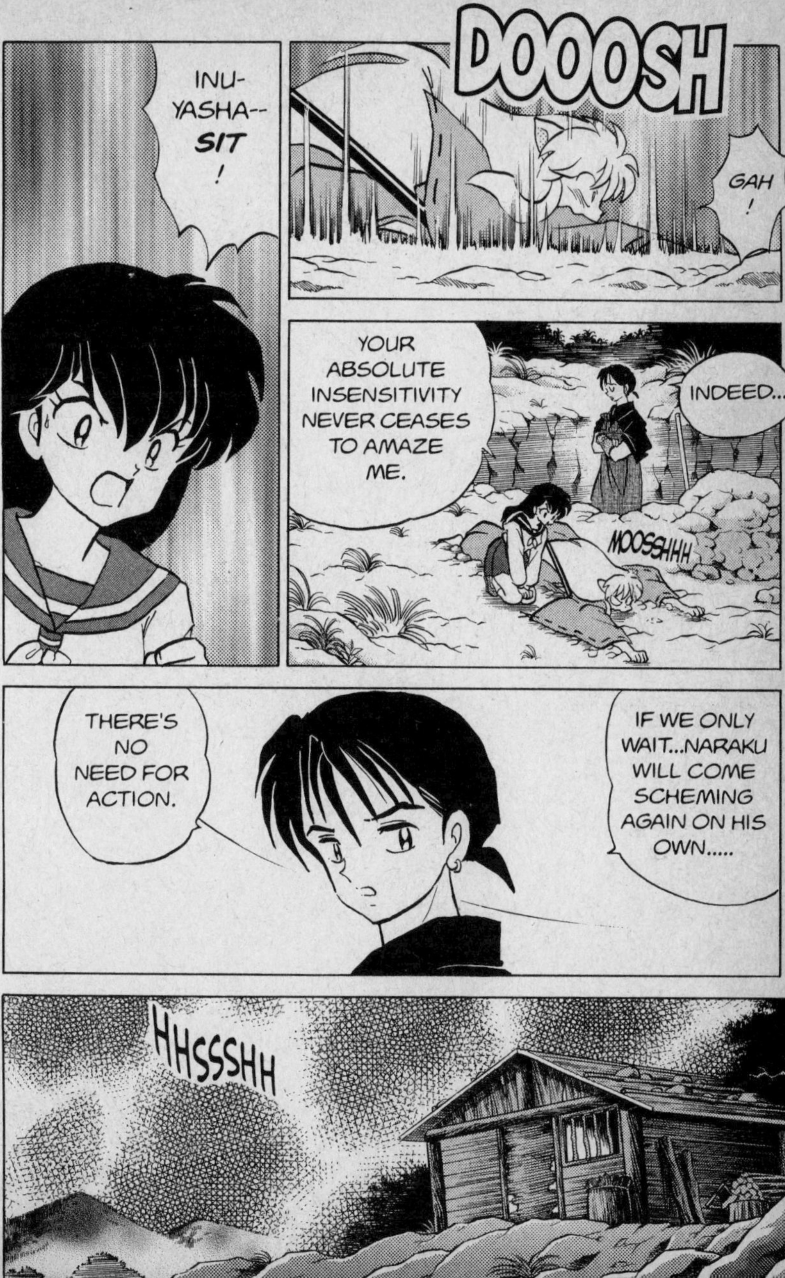
INU-YASHA-- SIT !
DOOOSH
GAH !
YOUR ABSOLUTE INSENSITIVITY NEVER CEASES TO AMAZE ME.
INDEED...
MOOSSHHH
THERE'S NO NEED FOR ACTION.
IF WE ONLY WAIT...NARAKU WILL COME SCHEMING AGAIN ON HIS OWN.....
HHSSSHH

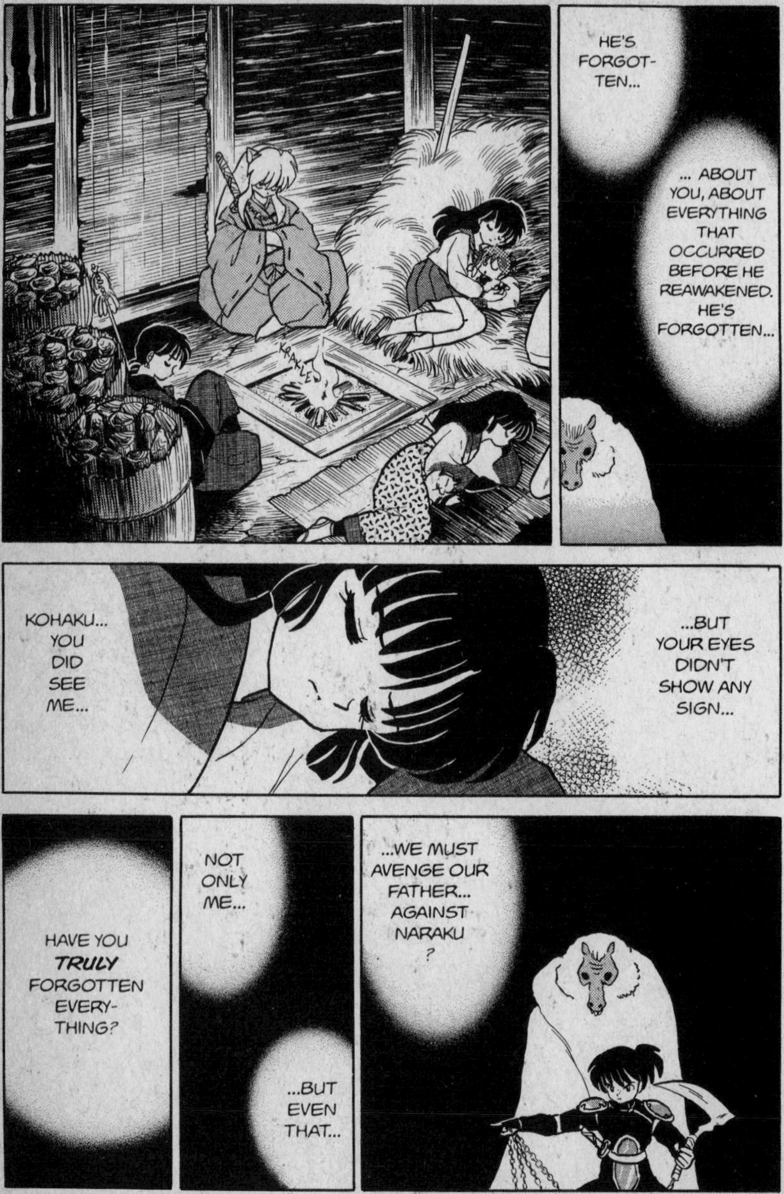
KRAKLE
HE'S FORGOTTEN...
... ABOUT YOU, ABOUT EVERYTHING THAT OCCURRED BEFORE HE REAWAKENED. HE'S FORGOTTEN...
KOHAKU... YOU DID SEE ME...
...BUT YOUR EYES DIDN'T SHOW ANY SIGN...
HAVE YOU ***TRULY*** FORGOTTEN EVERYTHING?
NOT ONLY ME...
...BUT EVEN THAT...
...WE MUST AVENGE OUR FATHER... AGAINST NARAKU?

I MUST WIN KOHAKU BACK...

...FROM NARAKU'S CLUTCHES!

...TO SAVE HIM...

...YOU WILL STEAL INU-YASHA'S SWORD AND BRING IT TO ME.

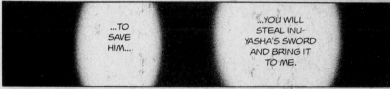

...

FWIP

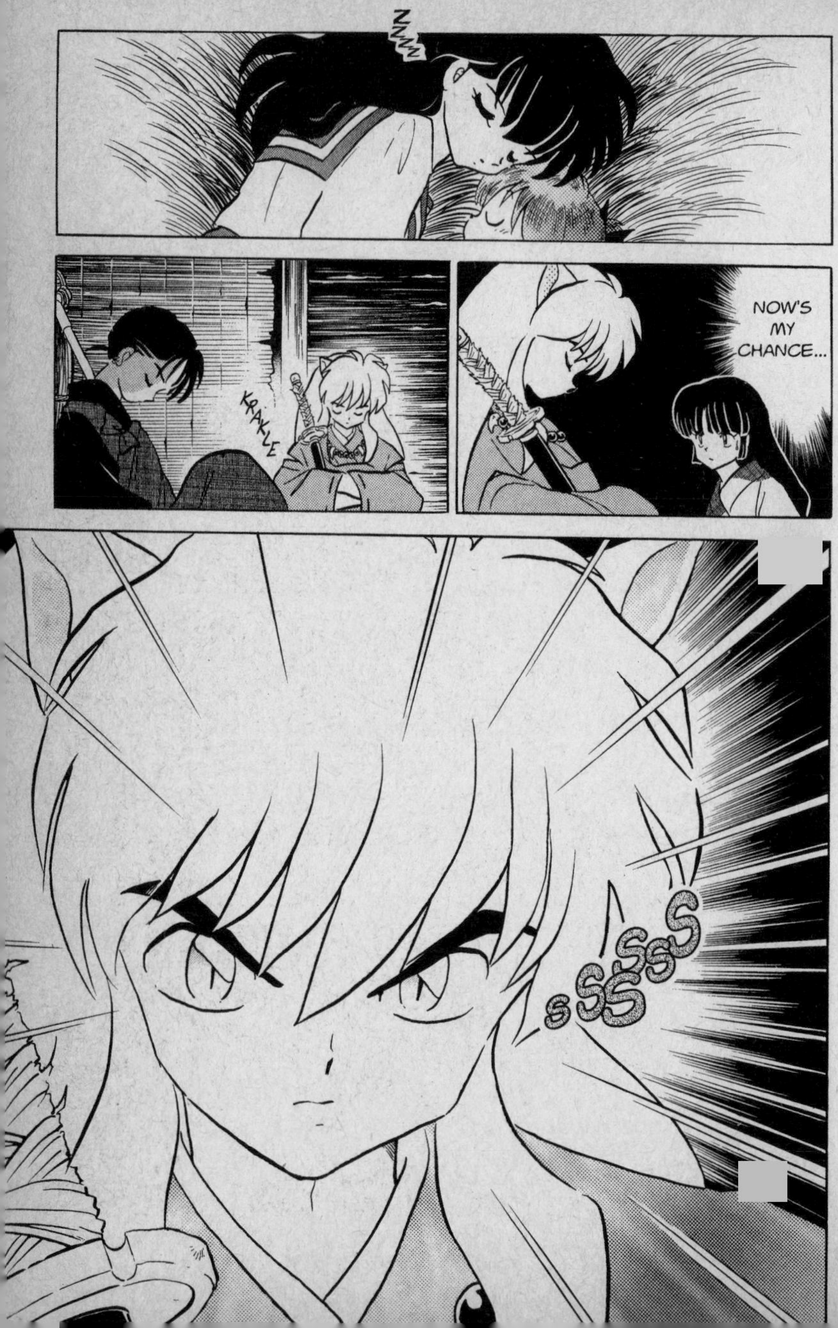
ZZZZ
KRAKLE
NOW'S MY CHANCE...
SSSSSSS

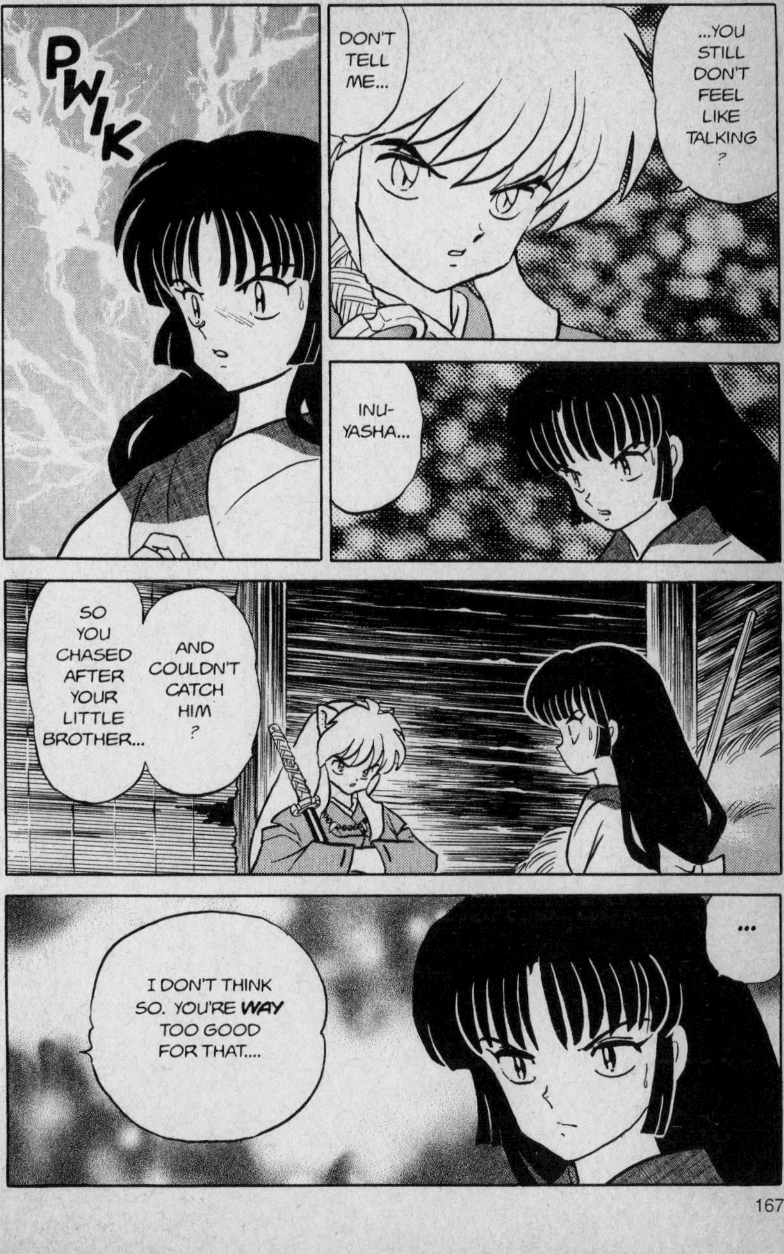
PWIK
DON'T TELL ME...
...YOU STILL DON'T FEEL LIKE TALKING?
INU-YASHA...
SO YOU CHASED AFTER YOUR LITTLE BROTHER...
AND COULDN'T CATCH HIM?
I DON'T THINK SO. YOU'RE ***WAY*** TOO GOOD FOR THAT....
...

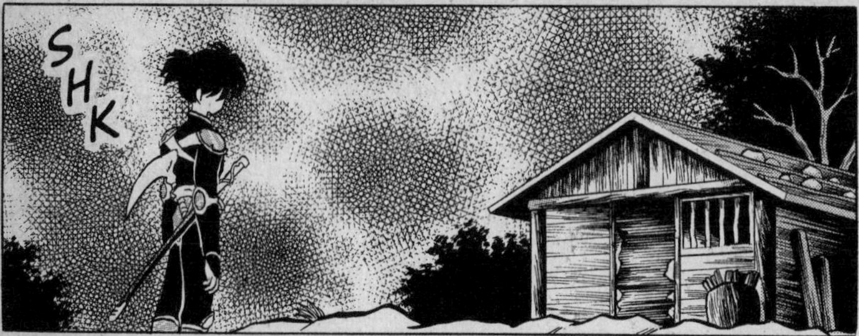
SHK
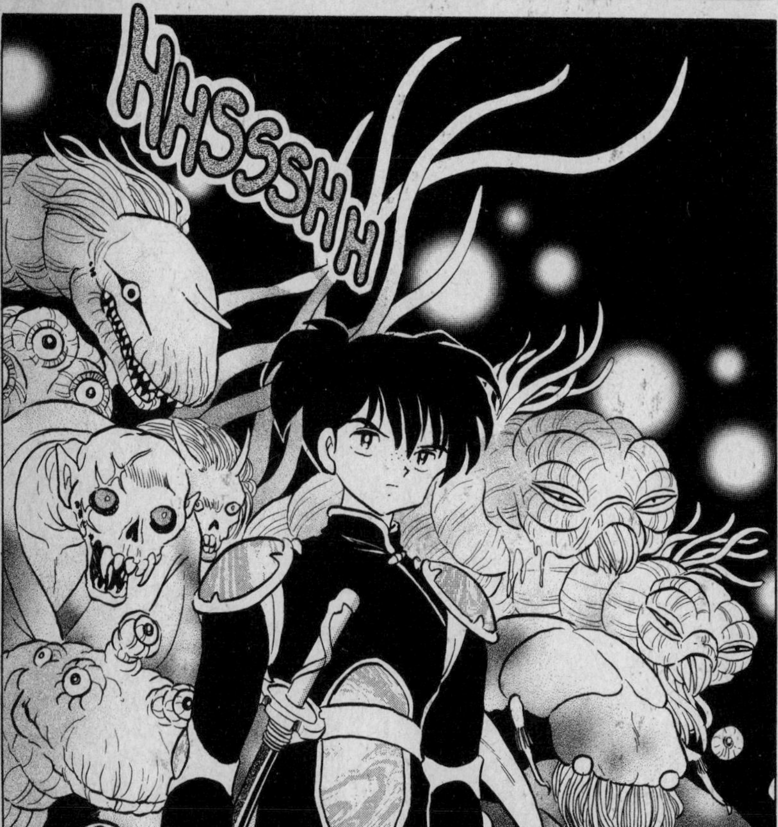
HHSSSHH

SCROLL TEN

SANGO'S BETRAYAL

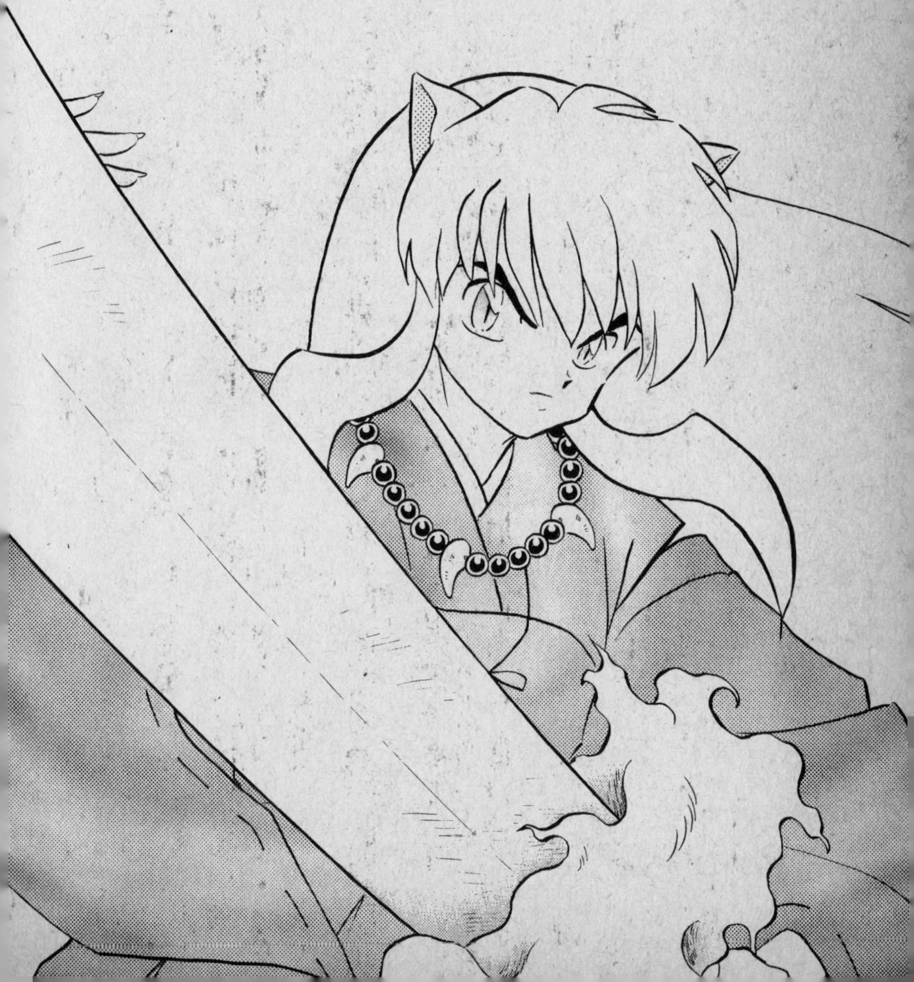

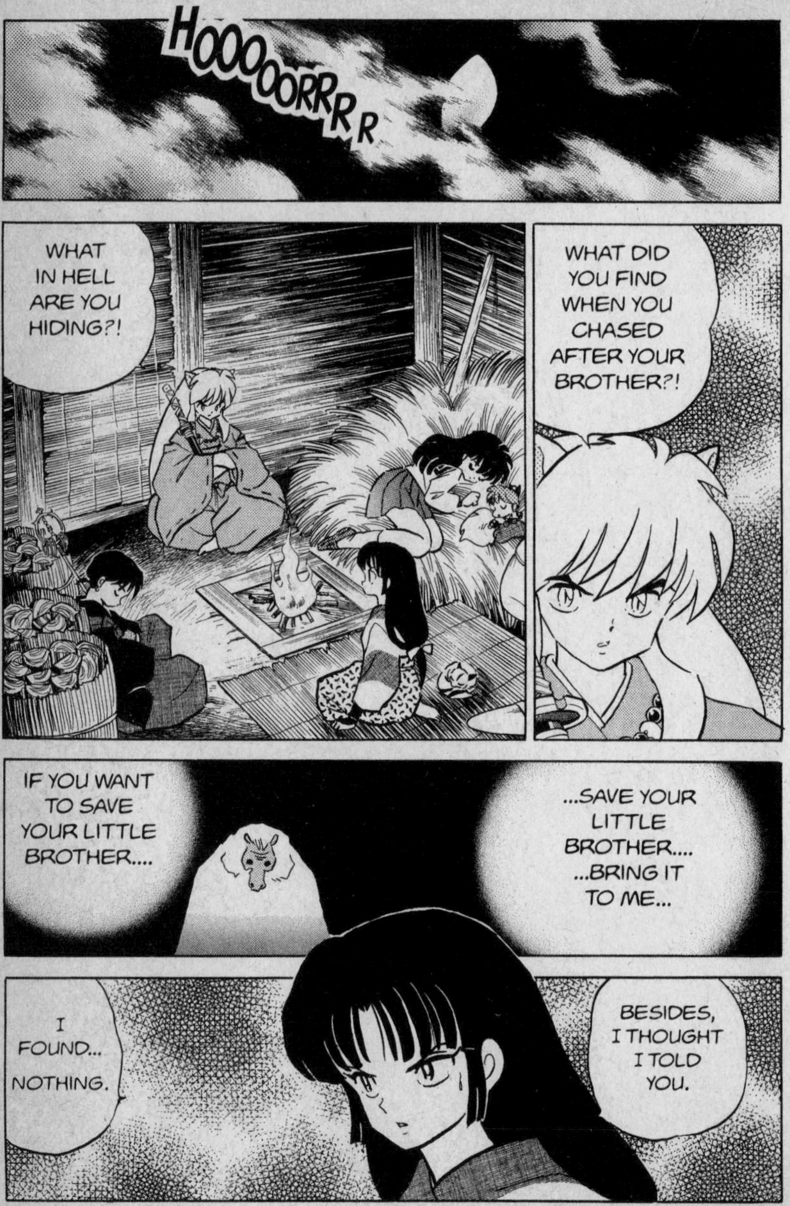
HOOOOORRRR R
WHAT IN HELL ARE YOU HIDING?!
WHAT DID YOU FIND WHEN YOU CHASED AFTER YOUR BROTHER?!
IF YOU WANT TO SAVE YOUR LITTLE BROTHER....
...SAVE YOUR LITTLE BROTHER.... ...BRING IT TO ME...
I FOUND... NOTHING.
BESIDES, I THOUGHT I TOLD YOU.

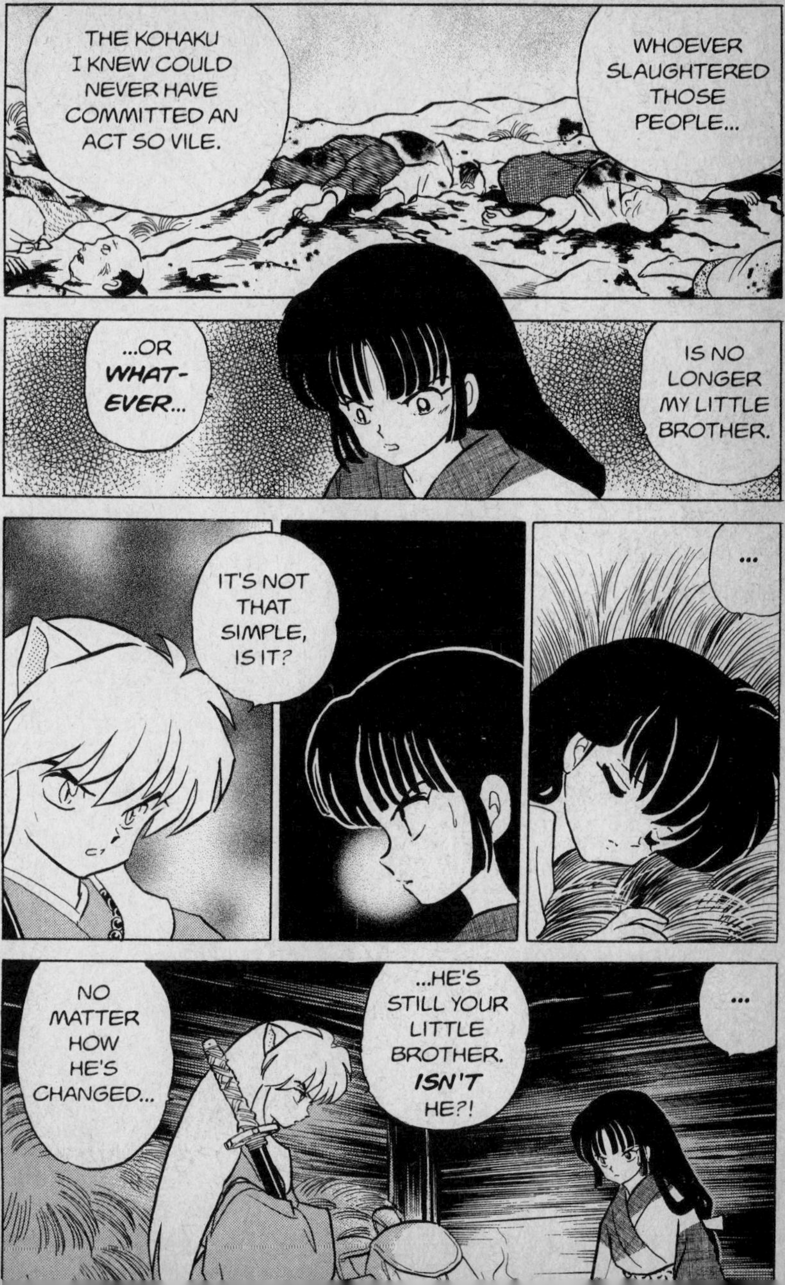
THE KOHAKU I KNEW COULD NEVER HAVE COMMITTED AN ACT SO VILE.
WHOEVER SLAUGHTERED THOSE PEOPLE...
...OR *WHAT-EVER*...
IS NO LONGER MY LITTLE BROTHER.
IT'S NOT THAT SIMPLE, IS IT?
...
NO MATTER HOW HE'S CHANGED...
...HE'S STILL YOUR LITTLE BROTHER. *ISN'T* HE?!
...

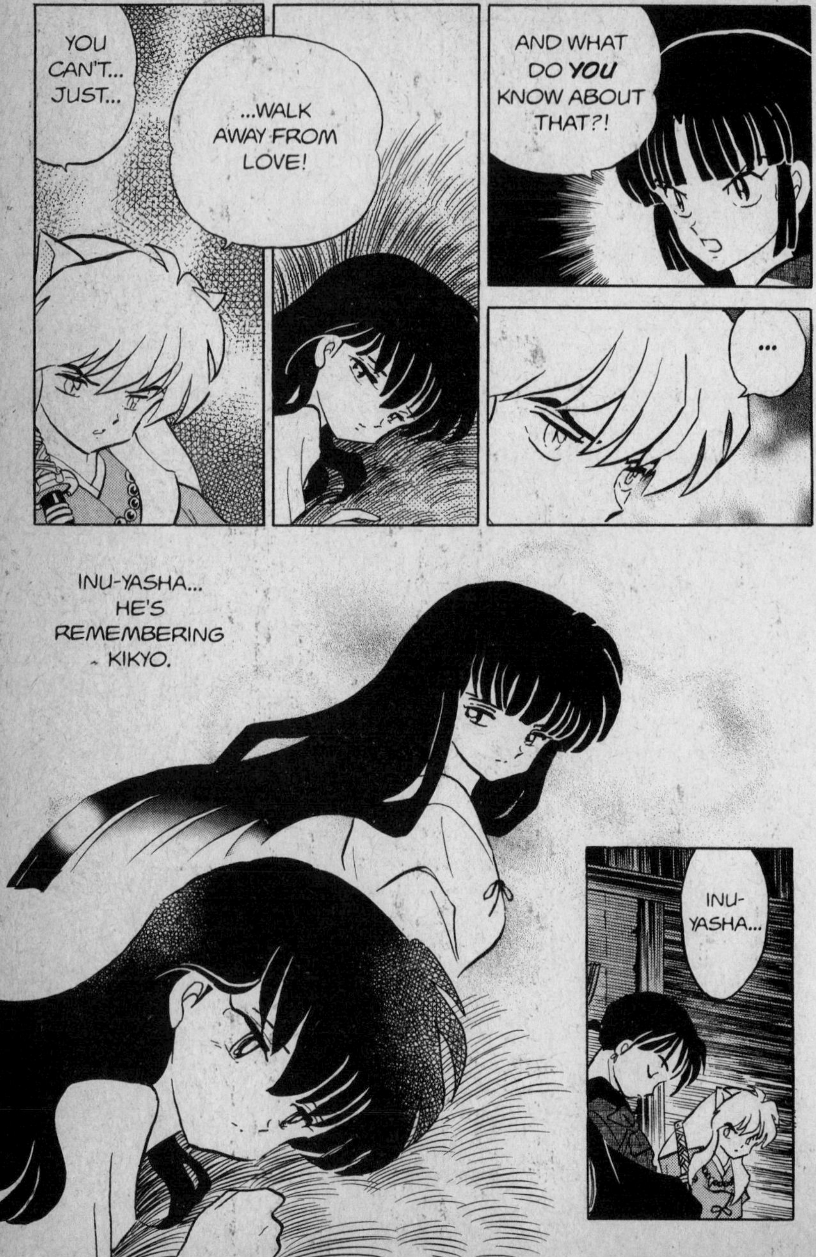
YOU CAN'T... JUST...
...WALK AWAY FROM LOVE!
AND WHAT DO *YOU* KNOW ABOUT THAT?!
...
INU-YASHA... HE'S REMEMBERING KIKYO.
INU-YASHA...

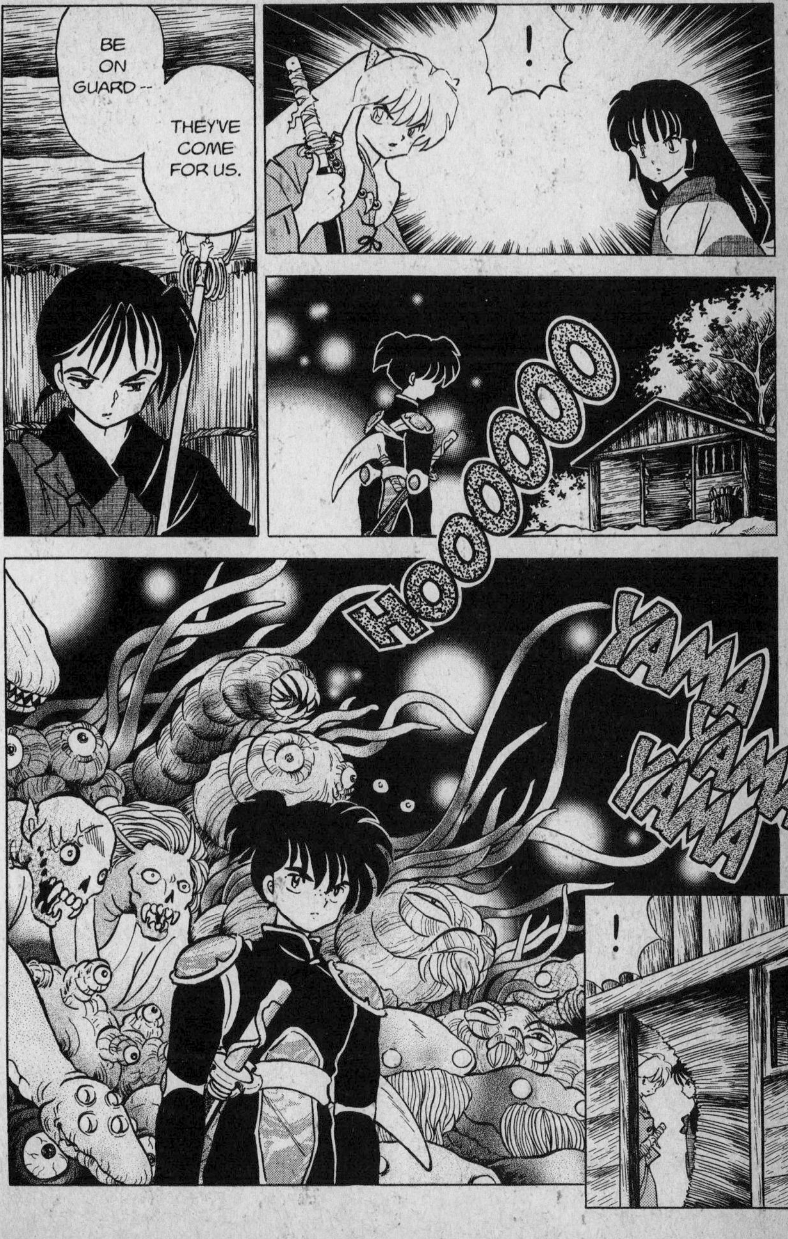
BE ON GUARD --
THEY'VE COME FOR US.
!
HOOOOOOOO
YAMA YAMA YAMA YAMA
!

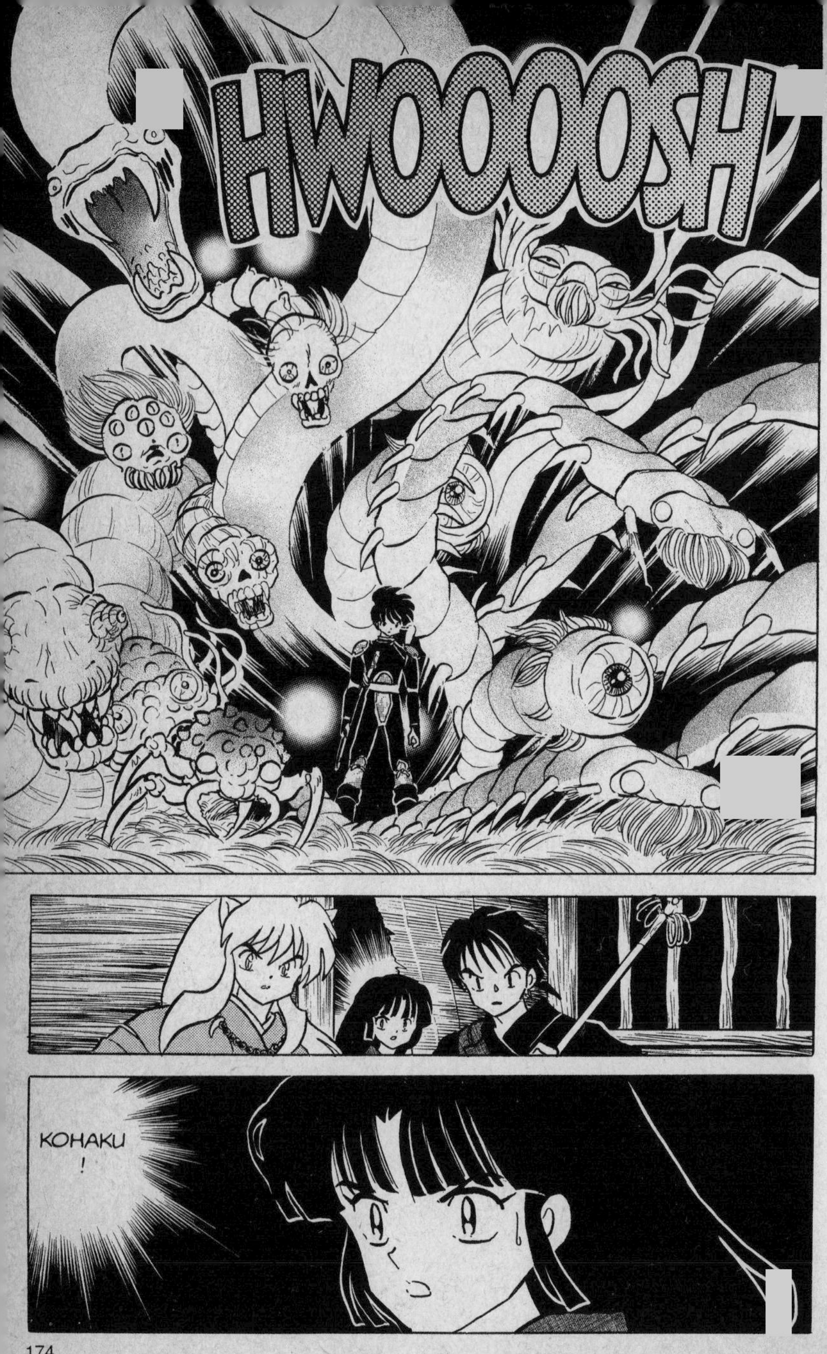
HWOOOOSH
KOHAKU !

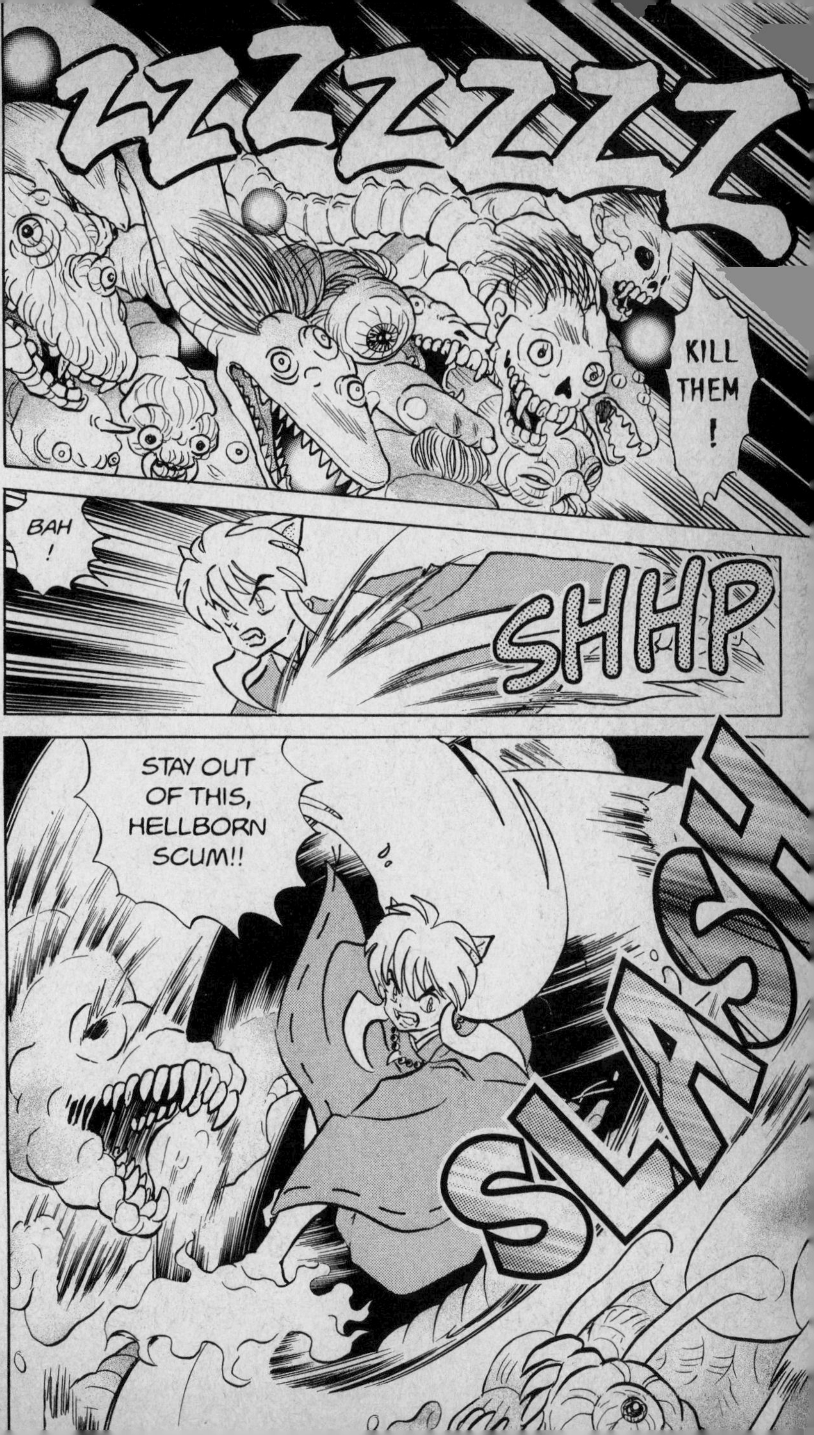
ZZZZZZZ
KILL THEM !
BAH !
SHHP
STAY OUT OF THIS, HELLBORN SCUM!!
SLASH

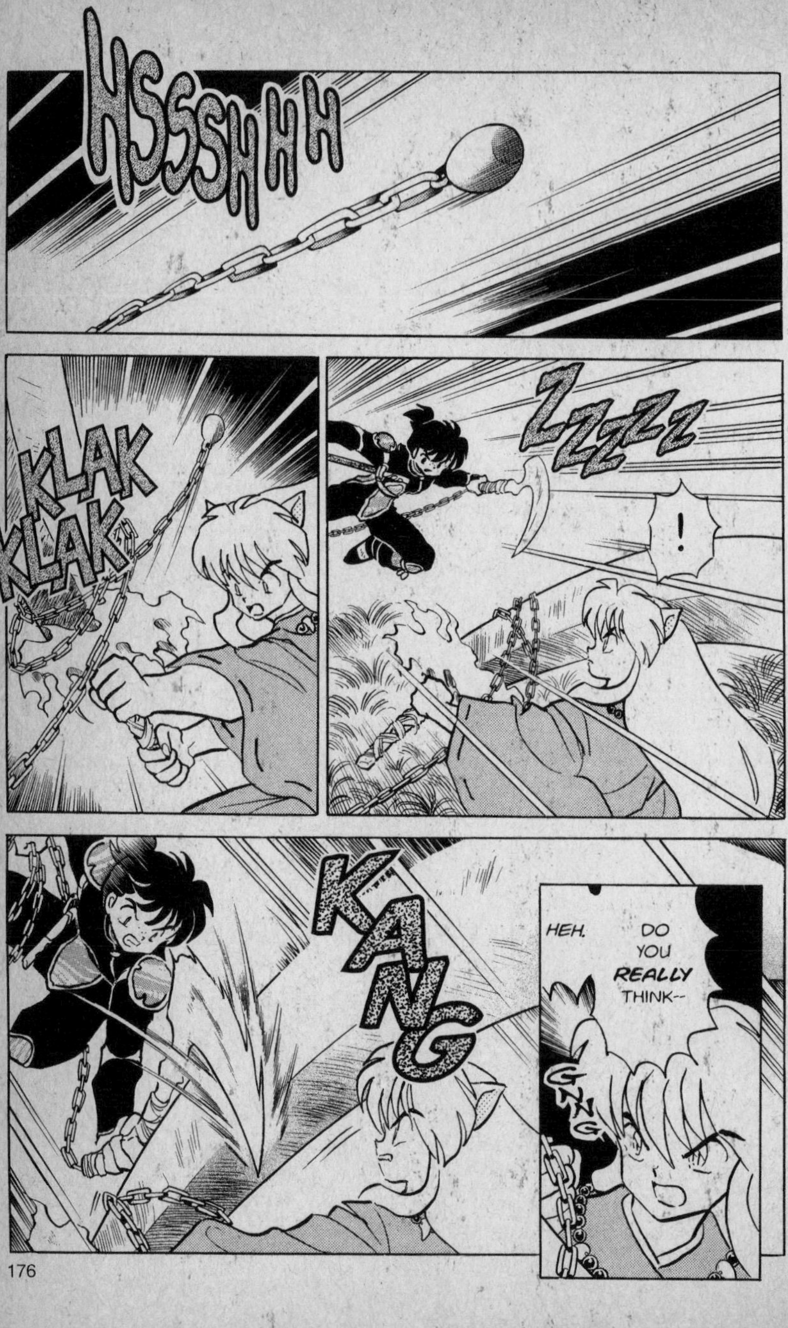
HSSSHHH
KLAK
KLAK
ZZZZZ
!
KANG
HEH.
DO YOU **REALLY** THINK--
GNG

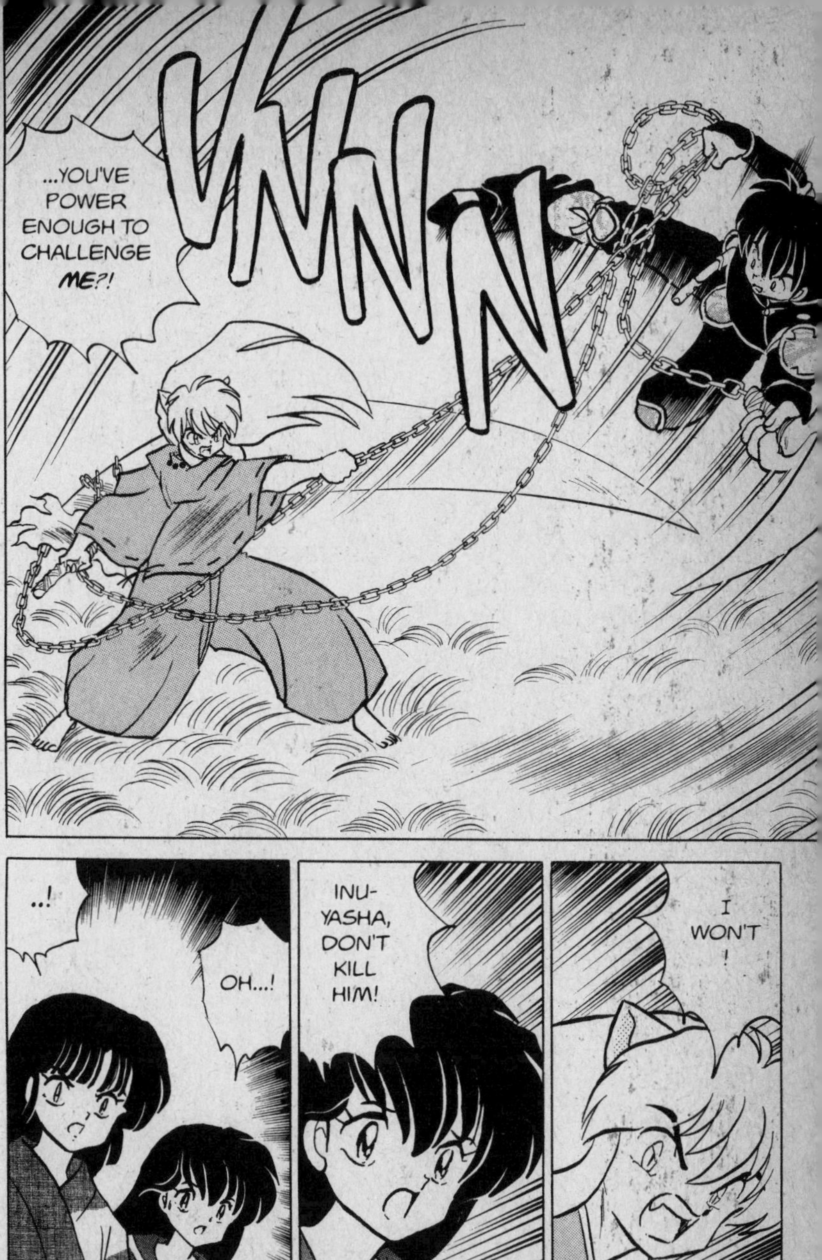

...YOU'VE POWER ENOUGH TO CHALLENGE *ME?!*
VNNN
..!
OH...!
INU-YASHA, DON'T KILL HIM!
I WON'T!

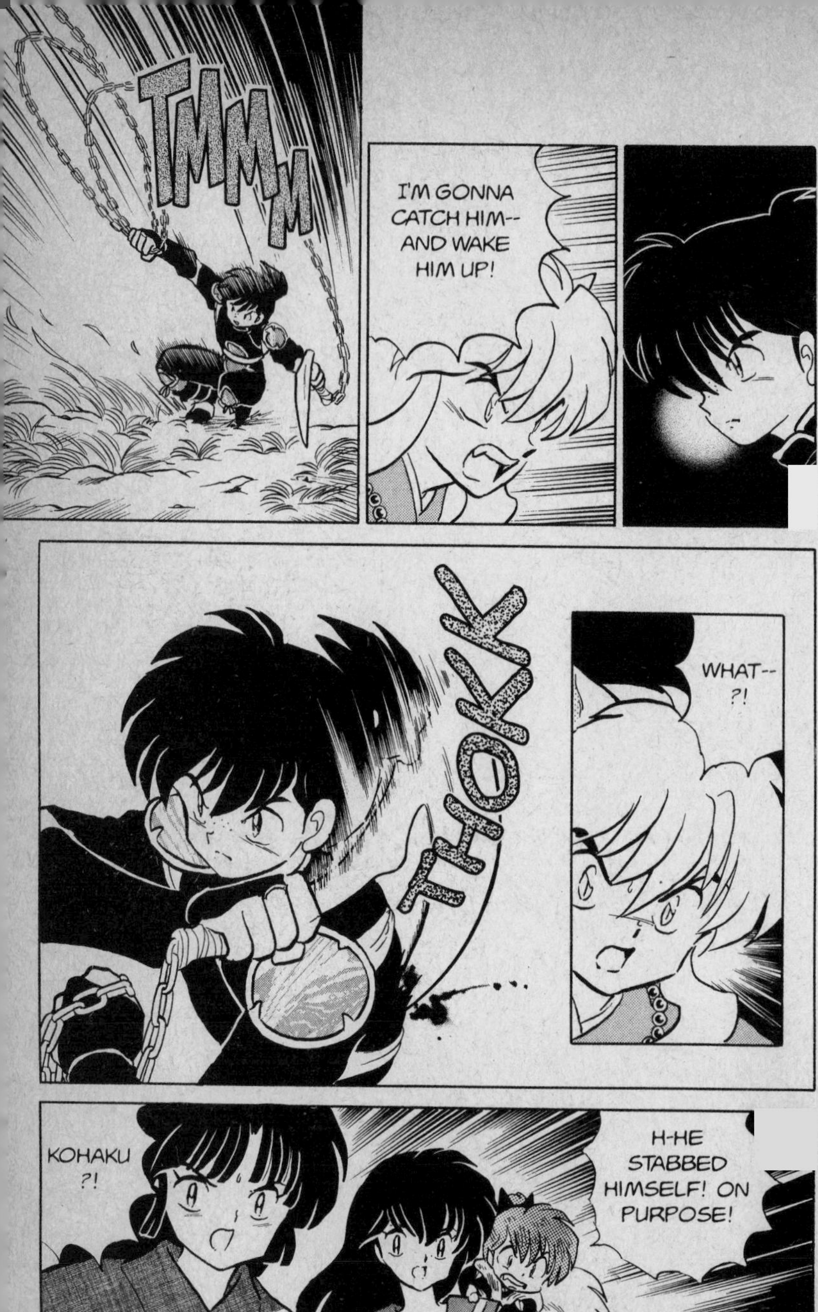
TMMMM
I'M GONNA CATCH HIM-- AND WAKE HIM UP!
THOKK
WHAT-- ?!
KOHAKU ?!
H-HE STABBED HIMSELF! ON PURPOSE!

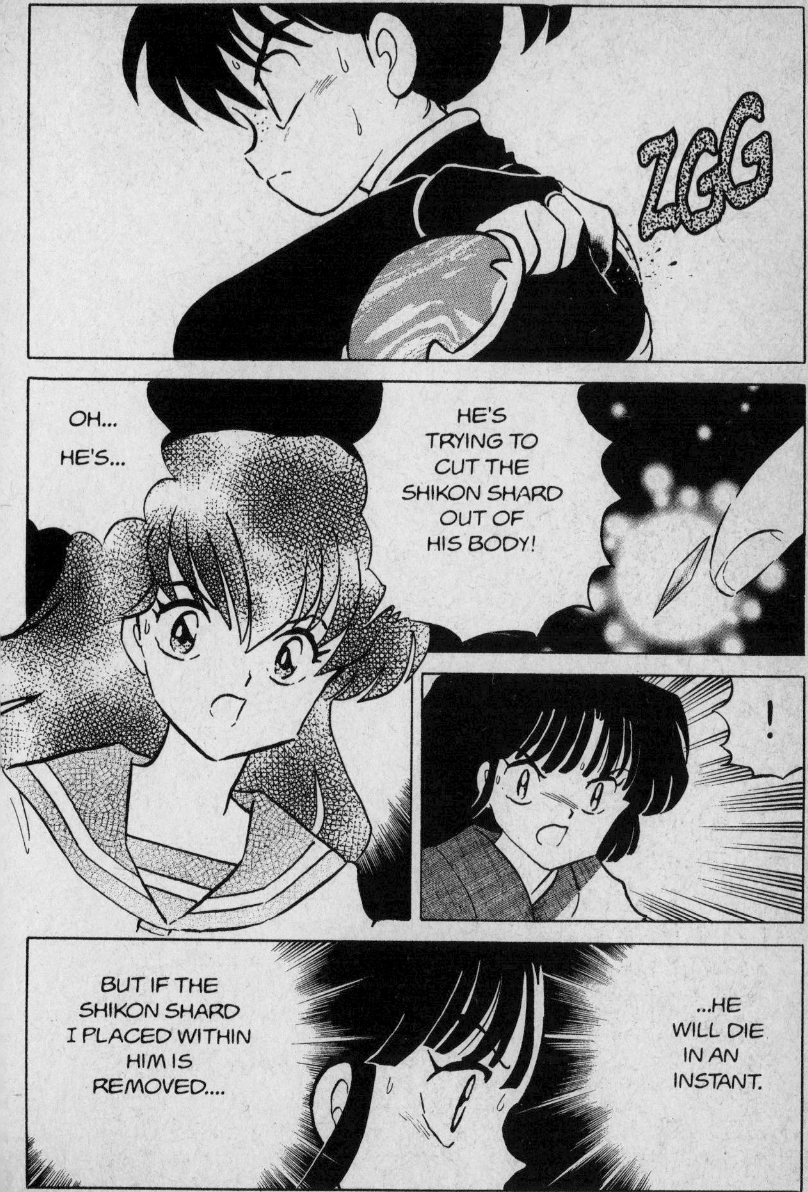
ZGG
OH... HE'S...
HE'S TRYING TO CUT THE SHIKON SHARD OUT OF HIS BODY!
!
BUT IF THE SHIKON SHARD I PLACED WITHIN HIM IS REMOVED....
...HE WILL DIE IN AN INSTANT.

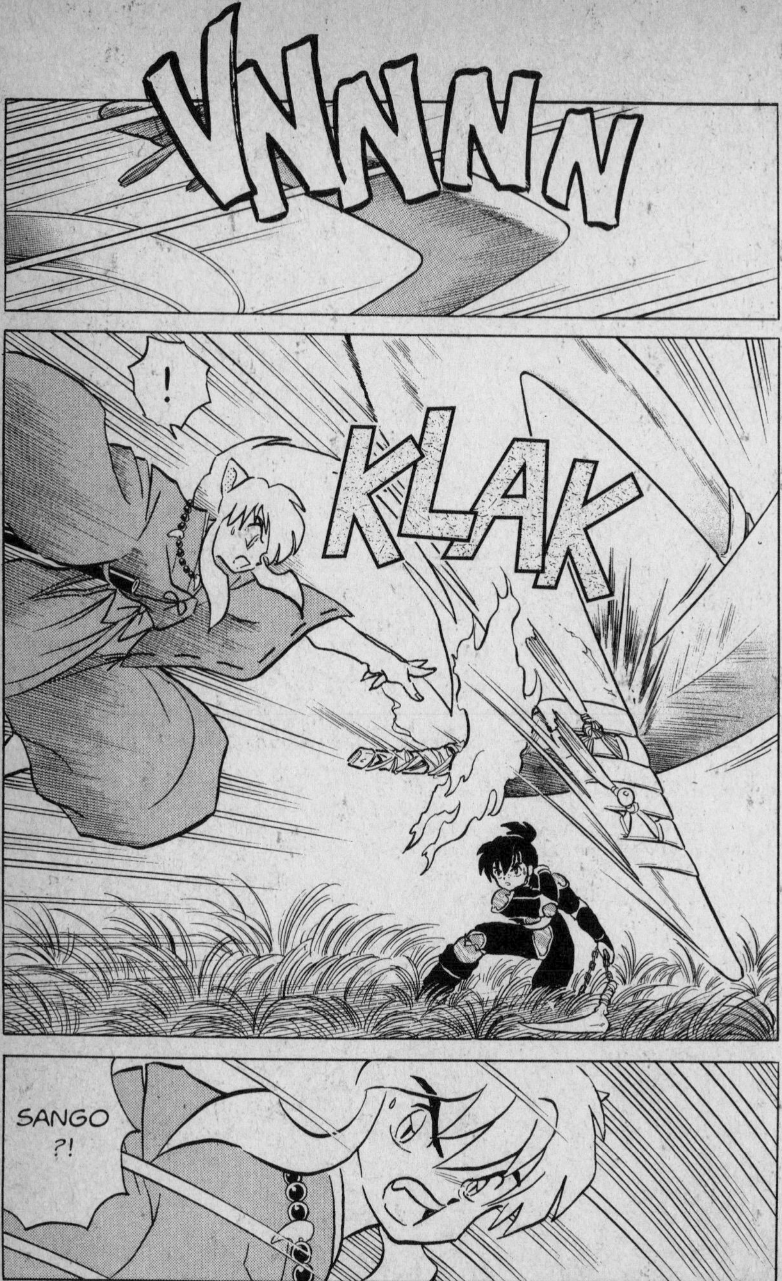
VNNNN
!
KLAK
SANGO ?!

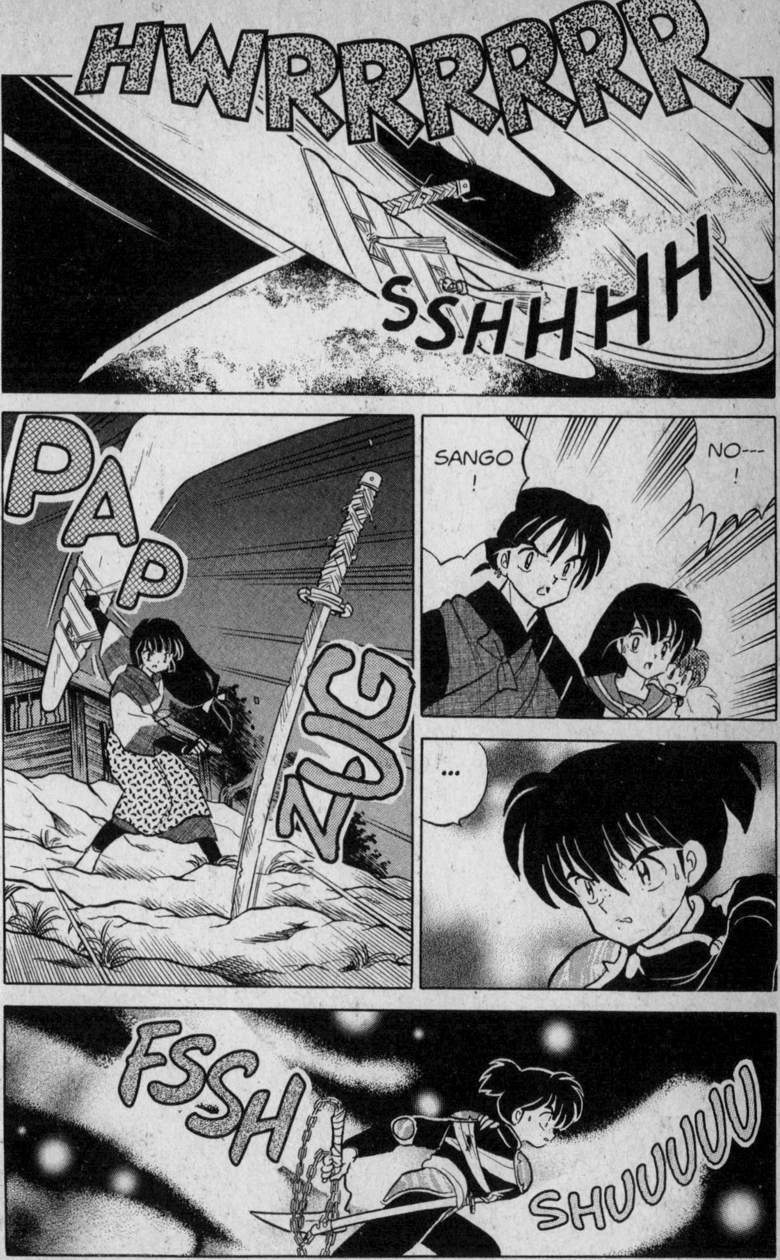
HWRRRRRRR
SSHHHHH
PAP
ZUNG
SANGO!
NO---!
...
FSSH
SHUUUUU

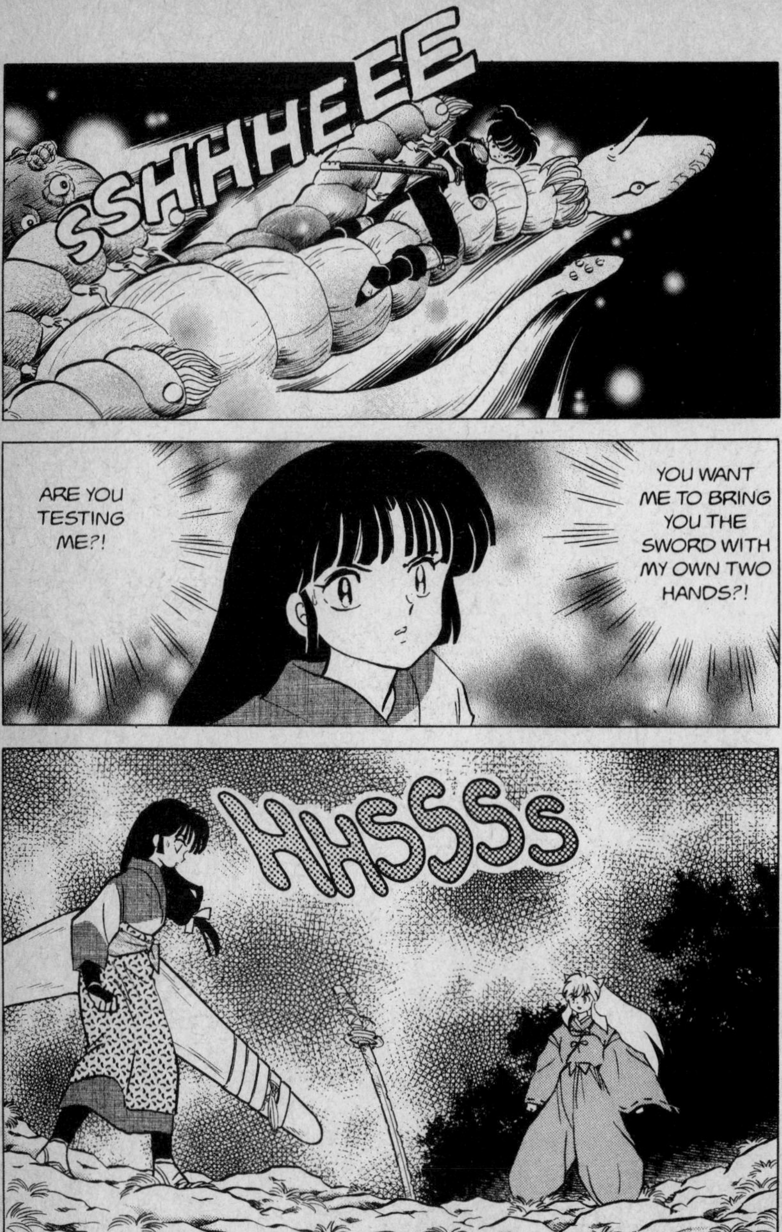
SSHHHEEE
ARE YOU TESTING ME?!
YOU WANT ME TO BRING YOU THE SWORD WITH MY OWN TWO HANDS?!
HHSSSS

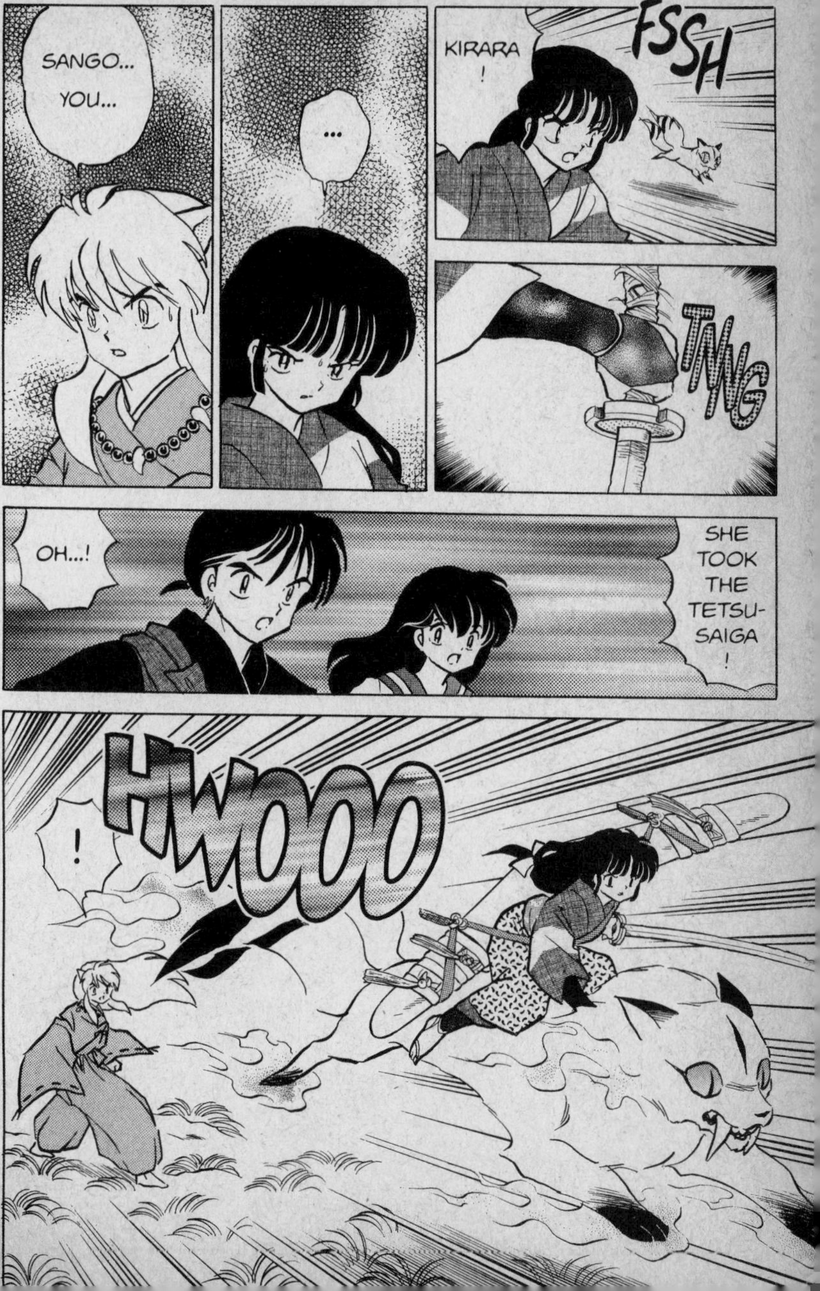
SANGO...
YOU...
...
KIRARA
!
FSSH
TNNG
OH...!
SHE TOOK THE TETSU-SAIGA
!
HWOOO
!

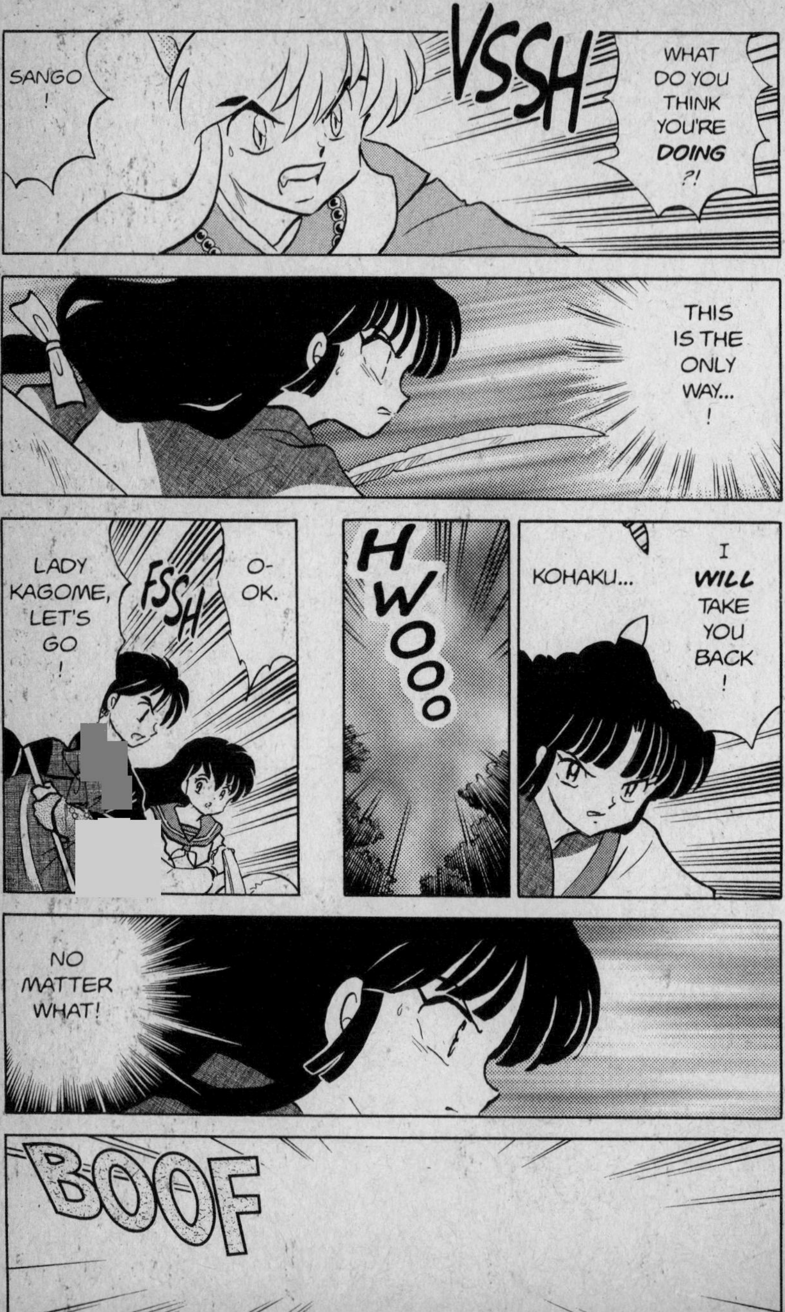
SANGO!
VSSH
WHAT DO YOU THINK YOU'RE **DOING**?!
THIS IS THE ONLY WAY...!
LADY KAGOME, LET'S GO!
FSSH
O-OK.
HWOOOO
KOHAKU...
I **WILL** TAKE YOU BACK!
NO MATTER WHAT!
BOOF

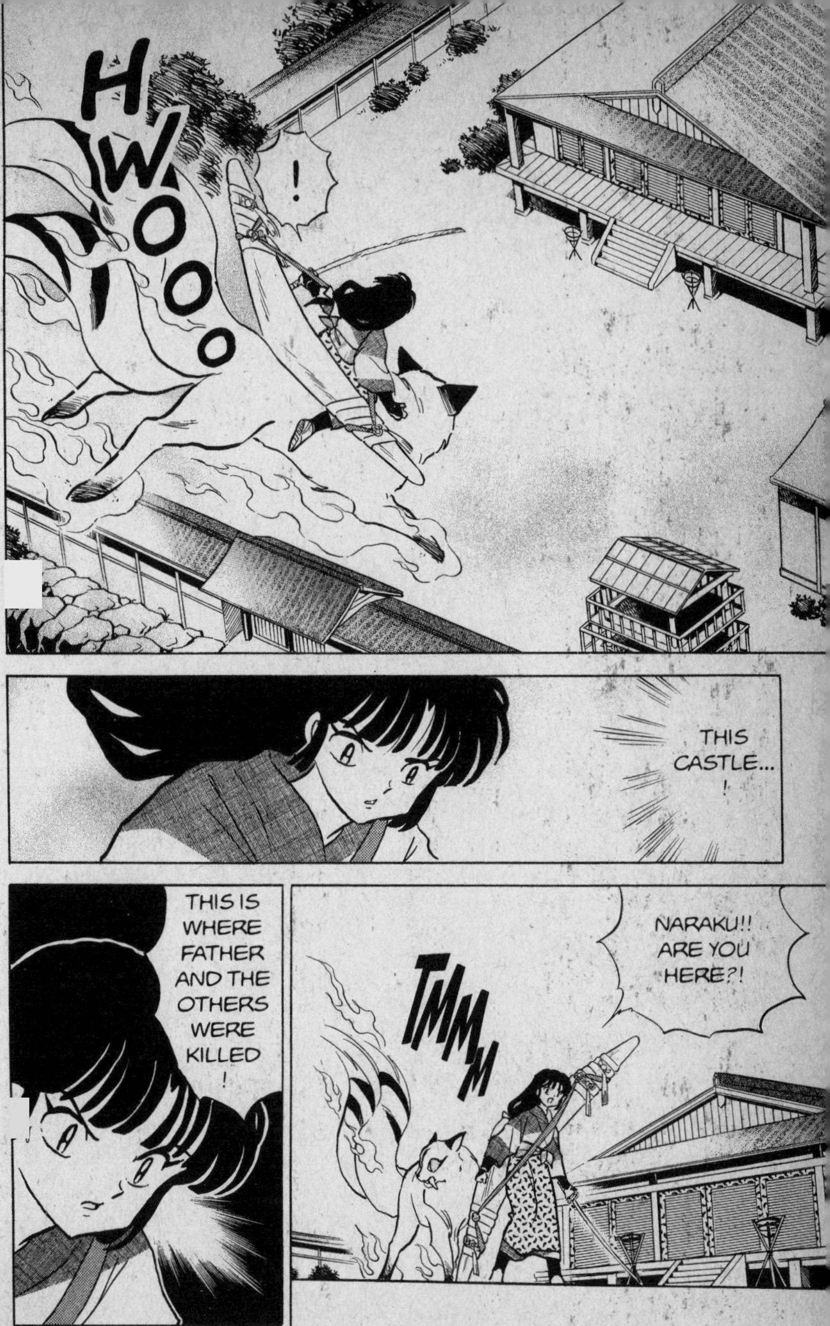
HWOOOO
!
THIS CASTLE... !
THIS IS WHERE FATHER AND THE OTHERS WERE KILLED !
TMMM
NARAKU!! ARE YOU HERE?!

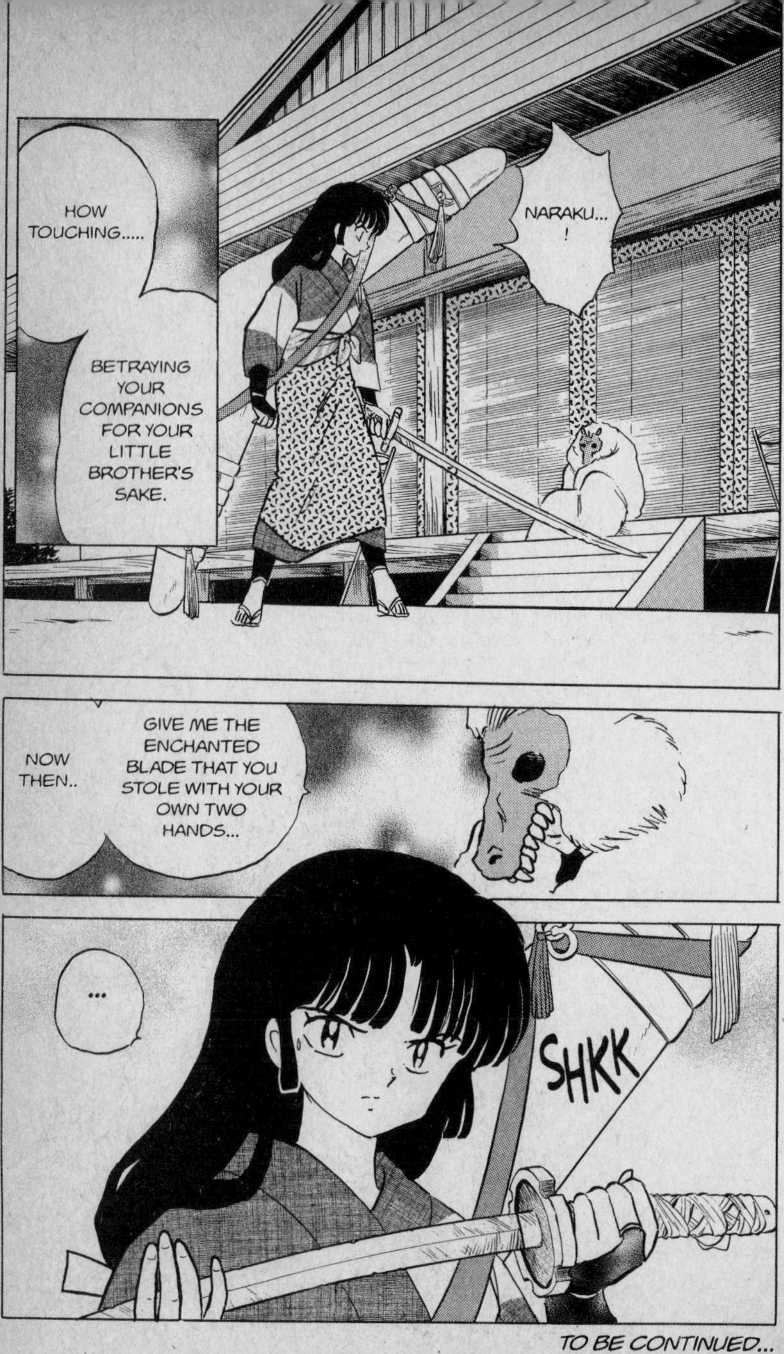
HOW TOUCHING.....
BETRAYING YOUR COMPANIONS FOR YOUR LITTLE BROTHER'S SAKE.
NARAKU... !
NOW THEN..
GIVE ME THE ENCHANTED BLADE THAT YOU STOLE WITH YOUR OWN TWO HANDS...
...
SHKK

TO BE CONTINUED...

About Rumiko Takahashi

Born in 1957 in Niigata, Japan, Rumiko Takahashi attended women's college in Tokyo, where she began studying comics with Kazuo Koike, author of *CRYING FREEMAN*. She later became an assistant to horror-manga artist Kazuo Umezu (*OROCHI*). In 1978, she won a prize in Shogakukan's annual "New Comic Artist Contest," and in that same year her boy-meets-alien comedy series *URUSEI YATSURA* began appearing in the weekly manga magazine *SHÔNEN SUNDAY*. This phenomenally successful series ran for nine years and sold over 22 million copies. Takahashi's later *RANMA 1/2* series enjoyed even greater popularity.

Takahashi is considered by many to be one of the world's most popular manga artists. With the publication of Volume 34 of her *RANMA 1/2* series in Japan, Takahashi's total sales passed *one hundred million* copies of her compiled works.

Takahashi's serial titles include *URUSEI YATSURA, RANMA 1/2, ONE-POUND GOSPEL, MAISON IKKOKU* and *INUYASHA*. Additionally, Takahashi has drawn many short stories which have been published in America under the title "Rumic Theater," and several installments of a saga known as her "Mermaid" series. Most of Takahashi's major stories have also been animated, and are widely available in translation worldwide. *INUYASHA* is her most recent serial story, first published in *SHÔNEN SUNDAY* in 1996.

EDITOR'S RECOMMENDATIONS

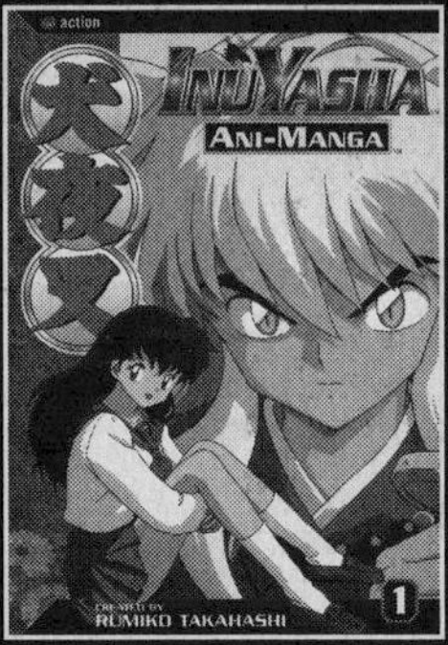
action
InuYasha
Ani-Manga
Created by
Rumiko Takahashi
1

Did you like InuYasha?
Here's what we recommend you try next:

InuYasha Ani-Manga

Here's the story you've come to love using actual frames of film in full color from the TV and video series *Inuyasha!*

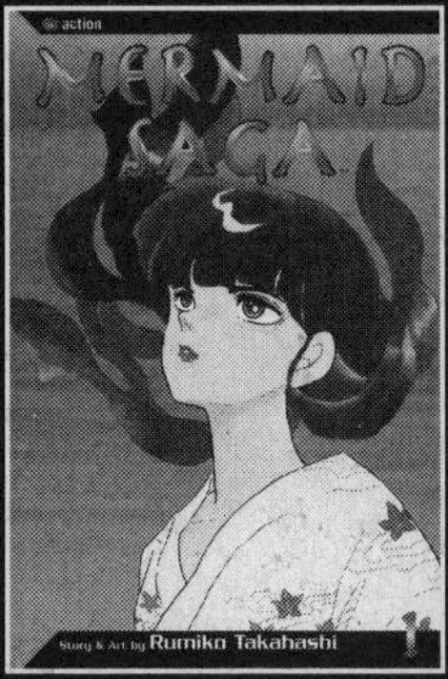
action
Mermaid Saga
Story & Art by Rumiko Takahashi

Mermaid Saga

This is the series Rumiko Takahashi created as her "hobby." Unpressured by editors and deadlines, she lets her creativity flow in this romantic-horror epic. Eating the flesh of a mermaid grants eternal life. But living forever can be a blessing or a curse. Immortal lovers Yuta and Mana are relatively lucky...others who partake of the mermaid's flesh are transformed into savage lost souls!

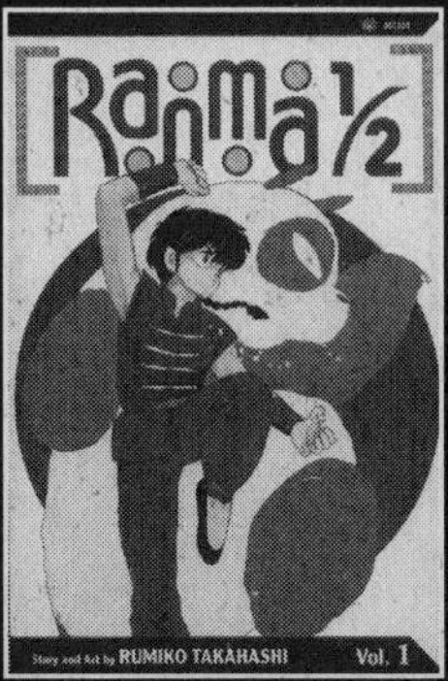
Ranma 1/2
Story and Art by RUMIKO TAKAHASHI
Vol. 1

Ranma 1/2

Rumiko Takahashi's gender-bending martial arts comedy made her famous! Due to an unfortunate accident at a cursed Chinese training ground, when Ranma and his father get splashed with cold water, dad transforms into a giant panda and male Ranma becomes a buxom young girl! Hot water reverses the effect...but only until the next time. Ranma is constantly challenged by battle-crazed martial artists for offenses both real and imagined, and pursued by lovesick suitors of both genders. What's a half-boy, half-girl to do?

COMPLETE OUR SURVEY AND LET US KNOW WHAT YOU THINK!

☐ Please do NOT send me information about VIZ products, news and events, special offers, or other information.

☐ Please do NOT send me information from VIZ's trusted business partners.

Name: _____

Address: _____

City: _____ **State:** _____ **Zip:** _____

E-mail: _____

☐ **Male** ☐ **Female**   **Date of Birth** (mm/dd/yyyy): ___ / ___ / ___   (Under 13? Parental consent required)

What race/ethnicity do you consider yourself? (please check one)

☐ Asian/Pacific Islander ☐ Black/African American ☐ Hispanic/Latino

☐ Native American/Alaskan Native ☐ White/Caucasian ☐ Other: _____

What VIZ product did you purchase? (check all that apply and indicate title purchased)

☐ DVD/VHS _____

☐ Graphic Novel _____

☐ Magazines _____

☐ Merchandise _____

Reason for purchase: (check all that apply)

☐ Special offer ☐ Favorite title ☐ Gift

☐ Recommendation ☐ Other _____

Where did you make your purchase? (please check one)

☐ Comic store ☐ Bookstore ☐ Mass/Grocery Store

☐ Newsstand ☐ Video/Video Game Store ☐ Other: _____

☐ Online (site: _____)

What other VIZ properties have you purchased/own? _____

_____

How many anime and/or manga titles have you purchased in the last year? How many were VIZ titles? **(please check one from each column)**

ANIME	MANGA	VIZ
☐ None	☐ None	☐ None
☐ 1-4	☐ 1-4	☐ 1-4
☐ 5-10	☐ 5-10	☐ 5-10
☐ 11+	☐ 11+	☐ 11+

I find the pricing of VIZ products to be: **(please check one)**

☐ Cheap ☐ Reasonable ☐ Expensive

What genre of manga and anime would you like to see from VIZ? **(please check two)**

☐ Adventure ☐ Comic Strip ☐ Science Fiction ☐ Fighting

☐ Horror ☐ Romance ☐ Fantasy ☐ Sports

What do you think of VIZ's new look?

☐ Love It ☐ It's OK ☐ Hate It ☐ Didn't Notice ☐ No Opinion

Which do you prefer? **(please check one)**

☐ Reading right-to-left

☐ Reading left-to-right

Which do you prefer? **(please check one)**

☐ Sound effects in English

☐ Sound effects in Japanese with English captions

☐ Sound effects in Japanese only with a glossary at the back

THANK YOU! Please send the completed form to:

NJW Research
42 Catharine St.
Poughkeepsie, NY 12601

All information provided will be used for internal purposes only. We promise not to sell or otherwise divulge your information.